AMERICAN AMMO
SELECTION, USE, BALLISTICS

AMERICAN AMMO

SELECTION, USE, BALLISTICS

Edward A. Matunas

GROLIER BOOK CLUBS INC.
Danbury, Connecticut

Copyright © 1989 by Edward A. Matunas

Published by
  Outdoor Life Books
  Grolier Book Clubs Inc.
  Sherman Turnpike
  Danbury, CT 06816

Brief quotations may be used in critical articles and reviews. For any other reproduction of the book, however, including electronic, mechanical, photocopying, recording or other means, written permission must be obtained from the publisher.

Library of Congress Cataloging-in-Publication Data

Matunas, Edward.
    American ammo : selection, use, ballistics / Edward A. Matunas.
        p.   cm.
    ISBN 1-55654-060-4
    1. Cartridges—United States.   2. Ballistics—Tables.   I. Title.
TS538.M329   1989
683.4'06'029673—dc20   89-27484
                                                                  CIP

Manufactured in the United States of America

This work is dedicated to all shooters questing for knowledge, and to all those persons who, throughout the past 40 years, have assisted me in my own search.

Contents

INTRODUCTION — IX

PART I
RIFLE AMMO

1. Practical Considerations — 3
2. Rimfire Ammo — 15
3. Exterior Rimfire Ballistics — 36
4. Recoil — 51
5. Centerfire Rifle Cartridges — 63
6. Exterior Centerfire Rifle-Cartridge Ballistics — 115
7. Selecting Centerfire Rifle Cartridges — 147
8. Rifle-Cartridge Reloading — 159

PART II
HANDGUN AMMO

9. Centerfire Handgun Cartridges — 171
10. Exterior Centerfire Handgun-Cartridge Ballistics — 187
11. Selecting Centerfire Handgun Cartridges — 196
12. Handgun-Cartridge Reloading — 202

PART III
SHOTSHELLS

13. The Confusing Dram Equivalent Rating System	211
14. What You Should About Lead Shot	218
15. Exterior Shotshell Ballistics for Lead Pellets, Slugs, and Buckshot	226
16. Selecting the Right Gauge and Loads	238
17. Steel-Pellet Shotshells	245
18. Shotshell Reloading	255

PART IV
AMMO MANAGEMENT AND SAFETY

19. Ammo Interchangeability	265
20. Ammo Storage and Handling	270
21. Shooting and Ammunition Safety	274

APPENDIX

Historical Exterior Ballistic Tables	277
Glossary	288
Index	299

Introduction

The nomenclature of cartridges can be very confusing. Many cartridge names are no more revealing than the given names of people. That is, ammunition nomenclature sometimes has no more meaning than the name Tom Smith or Bob Jones. A designation doesn't necessarily indicate size or shape, much less performance capability.

Some of the confusion began when someone decided that cartridge names, at least those in the English system, should be prefixed by a decimal point, as in .218 or .300 or .404, indicating fractions of an inch. But the numbers weren't always precise, and different numerical designations were often given to different cartridges employing bullets of the same diameter. Thus, the decimal points lost their meaning, and in fact were misleading. While the catalogs of Remington, Winchester, and Federal usually no longer include such decimals, many who have control over printed material still insist on including them, even though ".270 Winchester" makes no more sense than ".Ed Matunas."

Unfortunately, the elimination of the decimal has not been a panacea for confusion. For example, not many hunters are likely to realize that the 30 Carbine, 30-30 Winchester, 300 Savage, 307 Winchester, 308 Winchester, 30-06 Springfield, and 300 Weatherby Magnum all use bullets of exactly the same diameter (.308"). And how many shooters assume that "magnum" means powerful? Actually, the 224 Weatherby Magnum cartridge is less potent than the 220 Swift, both of which use a .224"-diameter bullet. Even the size of a cartridge often has little bearing on power. The big 45-70 has nowhere near the capability of the much smaller 308 Winchester.

All the confusion does not stem solely from nomenclature. Some misunderstandings are caused by cartridges that simply do not live up to the claimed, or advertised, ballistics. Other misunderstandings may be caused by the fact that cartridges of very different shapes and sizes can turn in very similar, if not identical, ballistic performance.

The countless months that went into the preparation of this work were all motivated by the single-minded obsession of providing—and clarifying—the facts about ammunition and its performance. For example, those who are enamored of novelty-type or unusual cartridges may be surprised to find that the 35 Whelen has no greater potential field performance than the 30-06 Springfield; or that the comparatively huge 375 Holland & Holland Magnum is a tad less effective at long ranges than the smaller 338 Winchester Magnum. Others may find it of great interest to learn that the shape of a bullet (such as round nose versus spitzer) can often be more important than the selection of a specific cartridge.

As each metallic cartridge or shotshell is discussed, clarification will be provided with regard to any confusing nomenclature, and a constant effort will be made to remove the veil of old wives' tales that has surrounded ammunition. It is hoped that each interested reader will complete this book with a new-found "expert" status. And a quick reference to these pages from time to time will enable the reader to remain expert in areas of specific interest.

Discussion of American ammunition includes many cartridges of foreign origin. The final test for inclusion in this book was that the cartridge must be in production by one of the ammunition companies in the U.S. at the time of this writing, or must be generally available throughout the country. Thus, you will find the 22 Short here as well as the giant 500 A-Square, the little 410 and the mighty 10-gauge, and handgun rounds ranging in size from the 25 Automatic to the 44 Remington Magnum.

A glossary is provided to explain any unfamiliar terms, although efforts have been made to explain possibly unfamiliar jargon in the main text.

ACKNOWLEDGMENTS

Special thanks to Arthur Alphin of A-Square, who made invaluable contributions that enabled me to expand the data for many large-bore cartridges. Thanks also to Dick Dietz of Remington, whose assistance helped me to learn a great deal about the performance of today's ammo in current-model firearms, and to Winchester and Federal Cartridge Company for supplying photos for this book.

PART I

RIFLE AMMO

1

Practical Considerations

With more than 130 different cartridges and hundreds of variations available, it's no wonder the American shooter faces difficulties in keeping abreast of what's what. The dilemma was clearly driven home for me during a recent campfire discussion at a hunting camp.

As hunting-camp discussions often do, this conversation turned rather suddenly into a session of cartridge praise and damnation. One gent was expounding on the virtues of his 30-06 Springfield:

"This 180-grain round-nose load I use gives surefire results. It's got a punch no deer can stand up to, at any range you can hit 'em. With such a fine load available, I wonder why anyone would choose a mediocre round!"

Another member of the party had a 300 Savage, and he was not oblivious to the intended slur. "My buck was every bit as dead as yours," he retorted. "He moved not one inch after being hit. Come to think of it, didn't your buck run 30 yards or so? Seems to me that my spitzer 180-grain bullet is every bit as good as your load."

Whereupon Mr. 30-06 dragged me into the conversation: "Ed, will you please tell this guy how superior my 30-06 is compared to his 300 Savage, even if he does use the same-weight bullet?"

I allowed that while his 30-06 cartridge did, indeed, have greater potential, the choice of a round-nose bullet had greatly handicapped that potential. The selection of a spitzer bullet for the 300 Savage, on the other hand, permitted that cartridge to reach its maximum down-range performance.

I added that the nature of ballistics is such that at 250 yards a 180-grain 30-06 round-nose bullet is no better or worse than a 300 Savage

180-grain spitzer. Kinetic energy, momentum, velocity, and Optimum Game Weight ratings are identical for both loads at the range. And at longer range (which is somewhat impractical) the 300 Savage, with a sharp-pointed bullet could actually exceed the performance of a round-nose bullet of identical weight driven at the increased muzzle velocity of the 30-06.

This, I tried to explain, was caused by the rapid velocity loss of a round-nose bullet as compared to one with a sharper profile. Both of my friends seemed skeptical. I got out the camp's tattered ammunition catalog and pointed out that its ballistics tables upheld my statement. Not even that entirely convinced them. They must have thought the data in the catalog table was a misprint.

On another occasion I heard a shooter boast to a friend of his about the 280 Remington cartridge he'd been using for a number of years. His friend then told of his own newer and better choice, the 7mm Express Remington. I did not make the observation that both rounds were identical—really identical—but I have always wondered how those two gents reacted when they ultimately discovered they were both using the same cartridge.

Cartridge or shotshell performance cannot be determined by case size, bullet diameter, or shell gauge.

If there is a lesson to be gained from such encounters, it must be that there are practical considerations to the evaluation and applications of cartridges. For example, a shooter who never fires at a deer past 50 yards may, in effect, be better served by a 308 Winchester than the shooter who insists on taking 400-yard shots with a 300 Winchester Magnum.

At first, there may appear to be a seemingly endless variety of cartridge ballistics, especially among centerfire rifle rounds. But in reality many cartridges produce strikingly similar ballistic levels. This is because a difference of 100 feet per second or 100 foot/pounds of kinetic energy will cause no detectable change in trajectory or animal-taking capability.

Indeed, the field experience of countless hunters suggests that it takes an increase or decrease of 300 foot/pounds of kinetic energy at typical bullet-impact ranges to effect a noticeable difference in the game-taking capability of a specific bullet. Also, the velocity of a specific bullet must be altered by at least 200 feet per second for the shooter to perceive any change in the trajectory of his bullet, and, a 400 fps velocity change will not noticeably change a bullet's drift in a wind.

Examine Table 1.1 and you will be better able to visualize these factors. If you have a 150-grain 30-caliber (.308″) bullet of a specific ballistic coefficient (the bullet's shape as it pertains to velocity reten-

TABLE 1.1

150-GRAIN .308″ SPITZER-BULLET PERFORMANCE

Muzzle	velocity (fps)	2600	2700	2800	2900	3000
100-yd.	velocity (fps)	2360	2453	2547	2642	2737
200-yd.	velocity (fps)	2135	2222	2310	2399	2488
300-yd.	velocity (fps)	1926	2007	2089	2172	2252
muzzle	energy (ft/lbs)	2252	2429	2612	2802	2998
100-yd.	energy (ft/lbs)	1856	2005	2161	2325	2496
200-yd.	energy (ft/lbs)	1519	1645	1778	1917	2062
300-yd.	energy (ft/lbs)	1236	1342	1454	1572	1690
100-yd.	trajectory	+2.5″	+2.5″	+2.5″	+2.5″	+2.5″
200-yd.	trajectory	+0.2″	+0.8″	+1.2″	+1.6″	+1.8″
300-yd.	trajectory	−9.7″	−8.0″	−6.6″	−5.4″	−4.5″
100-yd.	wind drift[1]	1.0″	1.0″	0.9″	0.9″	0.8″
200-yd.	wind drift[1]	4.2″	4.0″	3.8″	3.6″	3.5″
300-yd.	wind drift[1]	10.0″	9.5″	9.0″	8.6″	8.2″

[1]Based on 10 mph wind at 90° angle to bullet's flight

tion) traveling at 2,800 feet per second, a reduction of 200 feet per second in muzzle velocity causes a 300-yard velocity difference of only 163 feet per second. Or, if 200 feet were added to the original muzzle velocity, a 300-yard increase of 163 feet per second would be realized.

Energy differences of approximately 375 foot/pounds will exist at the muzzle with the 200 fps velocity change. But game is seldom shot while it is leaning against a muzzle. At 200 yards, the energy difference is approximately 265 foot/pounds—less than needed to bring about a noticeably different performance level.

Trajectory over a full 300 yards will vary by 3.1 inches to 2.1 inches with a velocity loss or increase of 200 feet per second. Few of us can see a difference of 2 or 3 inches at 300 yards, even when looking through a 4x scope. And wind deflection at 300 yards will change but a scant inch with the same velocity variations. Changes for a velocity of 300 or 400 feet per second can be quickly examined, using the same table. Some differences start to be noticeable with 300 fps variations.

What is to be learned from this table is not exactly how many feet per second are actually gained at a specific range or how many foot/pounds are lost. Indeed, the actual changes will vary with the bullet's shape. What should be noted is that a change in velocity of 200 feet per second at the muzzle simply won't make a great deal of difference in the field performance of a bullet. For example, a 150-grain bullet

TABLE 1.2

BULLET PERFORMANCE, ROUND-NOSE VS. SPITZER

(180-grain .308″)

Muzzle	Velocity (fps)	Round Nose 2700	Spitzer 2700
100-yd.	velocity (fps)	2348	2498
200-yd.	velocity (fps)	2023	2308
300-yd.	velocity (fps)	1727	2127
muzzle	energy (ft/lbs)	2914	2914
100-yd.	energy (ft/lbs)	2203	2495
200-yd.	energy (ft/lbs)	1635	2130
300-yd.	energy (ft/lbs)	1192	1805
100-yd.	trajectory	+2.5″	+2.5″
200-yd.	trajectory	+0.4″	+1.0″
300-yd.	trajectory	−10.7″	−7.0″
100-yd.	wind drift[1]	1.1″	0.8″
200-yd.	wind drift[1]	4.8″	3.2″
300-yd.	wind drift[1]	11.4″	7.5″

[1]Based on 10 mph wind at 90° angle to bullet's flight

fired from a 30-06 at a muzzle velocity of 2,900 feet per second is not going to perform much differently than the same bullet fired from a 308 Winchester with a muzzle velocity of 2,800 feet per second. No animal or hunter can detect a difference in the field performance of these two cartridges when they are loaded to their normal muzzle velocities using the identical bullet. However, the style of bullet chosen can cause a substantial change in external ballistics.

An appreciation for the effect of bullet shape can be gained by reviewing Table 1.2. Two bullets of the same weight, diameter, and muzzle velocity are shown, the difference being only in the nose profile. Compared are a rather blunt round-nose bullet and a comparatively sharp-pointed spitzer. At the muzzle the two bullets have equal ballistics, but at 100 yards the round-nose bullet has almost 300 foot/pounds less kinetic energy than the spitzer. At 200 yards there is a difference of almost 500 foot/pounds, and at 300 yards there is more than a 600 foot/pound advantage for the spitzer bullet. In short, the spitzer will provide an easily detectable advantage at all ranges greater than 100 yards.

Trajectory is also notably flatter over a 300-yard range. The round-nose bullet will drop almost 4 inches farther below the line of sight—when sighted at 100 yards for an identical point of impact—than the

Seemingly identical ammunition will perform differently depending on bullet shape. The hollow point (*left*) will have lower down-range ballistics than the spitzer (*center*). But the round-nose bullet (*right*) will prove notably inferior to either.

Sometimes, despite physical differences in caliber or case size, cartridges will perform surprisingly alike in the field. *From left*: 270 Winchester, 280 Remington, 308 Winchester, and 30-06 Springfield. All perform similarly in the hunting field.

---

spitzer bullet will drop. Wind deflection is also 4 inches greater at the same 300-yard range.

Obviously, while no major differences can be noted in the field between a 30-06 Springfield and a 308 Winchester when identical bullets are used, a change in bullet profile could cause one 30-06 cartridge to perform vastly better than another. Still, we must view everything from a practical viewpoint. For example, if shots are *never* taken past 50 yards, bullet shape will be of little consequence.

Ammunition manufacturers' catalogs tend to suggest a dissimilarity between cartridges that does not actually exist. This is caused partly by the listing of velocities in terms of exactly so many feet per second. Statistically showing velocity increments of one foot per second might suggest to some that the velocity variation between fired shots of identical ammo should be less than one foot pound per second. This certainly is not true.

Typically, using the finest possible ammo, the velocity of each shot fired will vary notably around the published *average* velocity for that load. Indeed, a good box of 30-06 ammunition might well show a velocity variation of 60 feet per second between the fastest and slow-

TABLE 1.3

VELOCITY TEST, 150-GRAIN 30–06 SPRINGFIELD

(advertised velocity 2,910 fps)

Round No.	Bullet A Velocity at 15' (fps)	Bullet B Velocity at 15' (fps)
1	2844	2729
2	2860	2848
3	2818	2812
4	2844	2851
5	2818	2795
6	2853	2711 (lowest)
7	2869 (highest)	2810
8	2828	2721
9	2856	2721
10	2822	2818
11	2845	2738
12	2850	2838
13	2838	2820
14	2808 (lowest)	2776
15	2820	2781
16	2833	2747
17	2825	2829
18	2830	2859 (highest)
19	2854	2747
20	2848	2762
Average	2838	2786

est round. And it is possible to measure an extreme velocity variation as great a 150 fps from a box of factory 30-06 ammunition. Shot-to-shot variations are often far greater than might be assumed by a reading of a ballistics table.

Table 1.3 shows the exact velocity obtained with each round from two different boxes of ammo, both 30-06 Springfield, and both of the same make and bullet weight. The bullet-nose types did vary but this was not responsible for the difference in *muzzle* velocity. The difference is attributable primarily to the uniformity of the powder charge in each case. Note that one box of ammo provided an extreme velocity spread (difference between fastest and slowest shot) of 61 feet per second and the other showed a difference of 148 feet per second. Even with identical powder charges, velocity would vary somewhat from shot to shot.

Common sense must be applied when making comparisons between the average ballistics of different cartridges. If one load has a

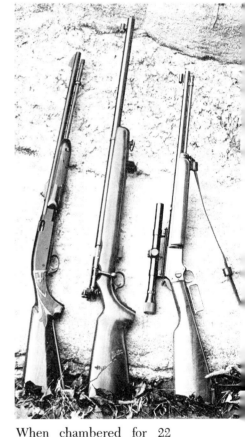

When chambered for 22 rimfire ammunition, rifles with barrels over 23 inches will deliver lower velocity. The 28-inch target 22 Long Rifle (*center*) delivered less velocity than either of the short-barreled rifles.

50 fps advantage over another, the performance of individual shots with the two loads may well overlap. Practically speaking, cartridges with a full 100 fps difference in velocity could be grouped and analyzed as identical performers. Velocity should be reported and considered in 100 fps increments. Anything less is not meaningful and may be deceptive.

Table 1.3 sheds even more light on the need for a practical approach to ballistics. Both loads used 150-grain 30-06 bullets produced by a single manufacturer, and both loads have an advertised velocity of 2,910 feet per second (fired from a 24-inch test barrel). The actual velocities obtained with a sporter rifle having a standard 22-inch barrel averaged 2,838 and 2,786 feet per second. Not only did each shot result in a velocity variation, but none of the shots fired from either box of ammo duplicated the average advertised velocity. In no instance did a single round come closer than 41 feet per second to the advertised level.

Yet the performance of the ammo in both cases was as expected. Barrel lengths do affect velocity. Because the sporter barrel was 2 inches shorter than the barrel used to establish the average reported ballistics, a velocity loss of about 50 feet per second was expected. Indeed, averages were 72 feet per second and 124 feet per second below the published level. Therefore, the lot that averaged 72 feet per second below the listed specifications was, indeed, as advertised. Lot B (124 fps below listed velocity) was admittedly about as slow as we are accustomed to seeing, though certainly acceptable.

But other cartridges are notorious for not delivering advertised velocities. The 270 Winchester stands out as an example among popular cartridges. The generally advertised velocity for a 270 Winchester with a 130-grain bullet is 3,060 fps, based on a 24-inch barrel. Adjusting this for a 22-inch barrel, an average velocity of 3,000 feet per second could be expected. A recent test of a wide range of brands and loadings produced average velocities of: 2,868 fps, 2,667 fps, 2,860 fps, 2,785 fps, 2,618 fps, 2,718 fps, 2,831 fps, and 2,698 fps. At best, of the eight lots tested, only one came within 132 feet per second of "expected" specifications. At worst, one lot of ammo missed the mark by more than 380 fps!

Obviously relying on published specifications in these instances would cause disappointment, with results ranging from somewhat less than hoped-for performance to notably inferior performance. The lesson is that only a shooter equipped with a good chronograph can be certain of the actual ballistic performance of his loads.

Not all ballistic variations can be blamed on the ammunition used. Two different barrels of the same length, model, and manufacture can produce different levels of ballistics. I have detected differences as much as 150 feet per second with the same lot of ammo in two barrels that might have been assumed identical. And I'm sure that larger variations occur.

About the only aspect of published ballistics you can be certain of is that a given lot of ammo is not likely to deliver any notable increase in

Ballistics can be confusing. The 338 Winchester Magnum (*left*) delivers less energy at 100 yards than the 375 H&H Magnum (*right*). However, when ranges exceed 250 yards, the 338 will actually have more punch than the 375 H&H because its bullet retains velocity due to better ballistic shape.

A good chronograph will allow the serious shooter to measure the actual muzzle (or down-range) velocity of his ammunition.

performance level compared to advertised performance. A lower performance level is more often encountered than an "as-expected" level. Rare exceptions do occur.

This does not indicate cheating on the part of those who compile ballistics tables. Safety demands that their test barrels produce the highest possible pressures so that the factories will be able to anticipate a "worst case" scenario for the user. This highest pressure is accomplished by using barrels with the smallest acceptable internal dimensions, and such barrels can produce higher velocities. Sure, the manufacturers could also test in standard sporter barrels, but then they would be faced with the cost of additional testing and the not easy task of deciding what is a standard barrel for a given cartridge. Many sporter models, chambered for a variety of cartridges, are available in several barrel lengths.

All in all, with a few exceptions like the earlier 270 examples, published ballistics are fairly representative of actual ammo performance *if* the shooter remembers that published numbers represent the best to be hoped for. Some variation is inevitable.

Of all the variables that can cause velocity variations with a single load, the one that causes the greatest change is barrel length. But while there may be a 200 fps loss with an abbreviated barrel length, the reduction is reasonably predictable. Table 1.4 shows expected average velocity change with barrel-length variations.

Cartridge nomenclature, as it appears on case heads, gives no real indication of potential performance.

TABLE 1.4

Muzzle Velocity Range in fps	Approximate Change in Velocity (fps) for each 1" change in Barrel Length from Advertised Specifications
1751 to 2000	5
2001 to 2250	10
2251 to 2500	15
2501 to 2750	20
2751 to 3000	25
3001 to 3250	30
3251 to 3500	35
3501 to 3750	40
3751 to 4000	45

Of course, barrel length isn't the single determinant of velocity, and a long barrel will not always increase a bullet's speed. For example, the 22 Long Rifle cartridge has consumed all of its powder in a barrel length of approximately 16 to 19 inches, depending on the propellant used and specific barrel dimensions. Once its bullet has traveled down 17 to 20 inches of the bore, the expanding gases can no longer cause any notable increase in velocity. In fact, velocity with a 22 rimfire begins to *decrease* when a barrel length of 23 inches or so has been exceeded. The largest cartridge cases, which hold the greatest amounts of powder, will benefit the most from extra inches of barrel. Depending upon case size, some minor adjustment of the figures in Table 1.4 might be indicated, but such adjustments would be far smaller than those required for individual barrel or ammunition-lot variations.

Practical considerations also include sidestepping the hype of advertising. For example, the word "magnum" has been greatly abused. Originally, magnum referred to a cartridge that had a belted case and a larger than normal powder capacity for its caliber. Thus, the name 300 H&H Magnum is appropriate, as that cartridge has a belt and it affords a considerable powder-charge increase over the standard 30-caliber cartridge—a 30-06 Springfield. But naming the 224 Weatherby Magnum was based solely on the fact that the case had a belt. This cartridge has less powder capacity than several other 22-caliber cartridges, such as the 22-250 Remington and the 220 Swift.

To cite another example, the 7mm Remington Magnum offers only about a 200 fps muzzle-velocity gain over the standard-size 280 Remington, surely not enough to make a noticeable difference in field performance. This being true, was it fair to name the cartridge a magnum? It's a fine round, indeed, and perhaps our third most popular centerfire big-game cartridge (behind the 30-06 and 270). But whether it's a true magnum could be legitimately questioned, es-

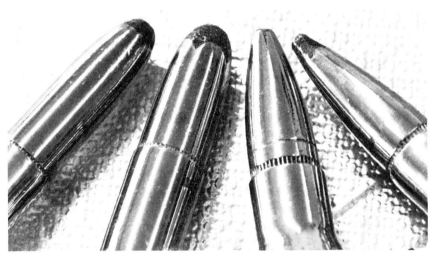

Bullet-nose shape plays an important part in down-range ballistics. The two blunt-nosed bullets at left will lose velocity much faster than the two sharp-pointed bullets at right. When possible, always select spitzer-shaped bullets for retained velocity and energy at longer ranges.

pecially in light of the fact that its originator, the late Les Bowman, intended the cartridge to be capable of killing all North American big game without the abusive recoil of the bigger magnum rounds.

Is it fair to think of the 264 Winchester Magnum as something uniquely potent compared to the standard 270 Winchester? I think not, as the two perform similarly on game. And if the giant 45-70 is not a magnum, then why is the tiny 44 Remington Magnum so called? Sure, this 44 is one of the most potent handgun cartridges manufactured. But a magnum? I think not.

Cartridge size can also be an area of misunderstanding. The 30-40 Krag is notably larger than the 300 Savage, but ballistics are practically identical when like bullet weights and shapes are compared.

Shotshell nomenclature is equally misleading. A 20-gauge 3-inch Magnum shell moves 1¼ ounces of shot out of the muzzle at 1,185 feet per second. Yet the standard 12-gauge 2¾-inch shell can push the same 1¼ ounces of shot from the muzzle at 1,330 feet per second, a gain of 12 percent in velocity. Is the 3-inch 20 a "magnum" performer? It is not when judged by 12-gauge standards or compared to a 20-gauge 2¾-inch shell that can push 1 ounce of shot 1,220 feet per second or 1⅛ ounce of shot at 1,175 feet per second. The longer 20-gauge shell has only a shot-weight advantage.

Indeed, the word "magnum" should be recognized as indicative of increased ballistics performance, but we must know what basis of comparison is being used. The 222 Remington Magnum does offer increased velocity over the standard 222 Remington, but it is not nearly up to the 22-250 Remington's ballistics. The 44 Remington

Cartridge size can be deceiving. Despite its bulk, the 45-70 Government (*right*) is a ballistic midget compared to the 308 Winchesters (*left*).

Magnum is vastly superior to the 38 Special handgun cartridge, but vastly inferior to the otherwise humble 30-30 Winchester rifle cartridge. And the 20-gauge Magnum 3-inch shell may offer a bit more shot capacity than shorter 20-gauge shells but it is no magnum by 12- or even 16-gauge standards. And surely a 22 Winchester Rimfire Magnum is no magnum by any standard except when compared to the 22 Long Rifle cartridge.

Perhaps the most needed piece of information about rifle ammunition is exactly what each cartridge is useful for in the hunting field. How does one determine if a specific load fired from a 30-06 is sufficient for big elk, small bears at moderate range, or caribou at 440 yards? The ammo companies sometimes offer general rules of thumb. But these suggestions, which place a 30-06 load on equal footing with a 338 Winchester Magnum, are bound to cause a thinking person to pause.

The factory folks tend to suggest that the kinetic-energy figures in their ballistics tables give us insight to cartridge application. When someone demands to know what a listing of 3,000 foot/pounds tells him about a bullet's performance, he might get a reply like: "It takes 1,000 foot/pounds to kill a deer, 1,500 foot/pounds to kill an elk, and 2,500 foot/pounds to kill a grizzly bear."

One might get confused, however, when considering that in some parts of the country a deer may weigh only 90 pounds, while in other places it could weigh 300 pounds. Most elk killed probably weigh about 550 pounds, but some go over 1,000 pounds. And grizzly come in 500-pound sizes and in 1,000-pound and heavier sizes. In truth, the ammo companies simply have not provided an answer to how much cartridge for how much game.

Some well-experienced hunters have noted that it takes more than what is suggested by kinetic-energy figures to kill game, especially when the game is large and potentially belligerent. Indeed, some feel there is need for minimum levels of bullet frontal area (caliber) and bullet sectional density (weight) as well as velocity. But still no simple answer has been forthcoming.

Earlier, reference was made to Optimum Game Weight (OGW). This system is discussed in the chapter dealing with rifle ballistics. OGW should end any dilemmas the reader may have about judging a cartridge's potential for application on game of a specific weight.

The Optimum Game Weight formula will help to reduce a lot of exterior-ballistics puffery to simple comparison of a cartridge's Optimum Game Weight rating to the weight of the animal to be hunted. After this, the hunter need be concerned only with trajectory and wind drift. Nothing could be simpler or more practical. The serious shooter can verify velocity by chronographing his ammo. This will then allow him to verify potential OGW. More about this later.

2

Rimfire Ammo

Americans shoot a lot, and mostly they shoot 22 rimfire ammunition. We consume more than 2 billion rounds of 22 rimfire ammo each year. This comes to 5,479,452 rounds per day, or more than 3,800 rounds per second. That's a heap of shooting. Undoubtedly, most of those rounds are fired at such targets as old tin cans and paper bullseyes. But squirrels and rabbits are eagerly sought during hunting season by rimfire rifle and handgun enthusiasts.

Today, rimfire ammunition is synonymous with 22 caliber. There are 22 Shorts, 22 Longs, and 22 Magnums, but mostly it's the ubiquitous 22 Long Rifle that gets our attention. This was not always so. Rimfire cartridges had their beginnings with the Folbert BB Cap during the mid-1840s.

Treasured by Union troops during the Civil War was a then new lever-action repeating rifle called the Spencer. It was chambered for the 56-56 Spencer rimfire cartridge, which used a 350-grain lead bullet driven by 45 grains of black powder. This cartridge continued to be listed in one ammo manufacturer's catalog until 1920, having survived almost 60 years of use. Later, Spencer rifles and carbines were chambered for such rimfire rounds as the 56-50, 56-52, and 56-46.

At one time, the U.S. Navy issued a Remington single-shot rolling-block pistol chambered for a rimfire cartridge. However, it lasted only a year (1865) before being replaced by a similar centerfire round. The 50 Remington Navy was a mighty potent handgun cartridge by the standards of those times. It used a 290-grain bullet with a 24-grain charge of black powder.

The early predecessor of the Winchester rifle, the Henry, was also chambered for a rimfire cartridge—the 44 Henry. With a 200-grain lead bullet and 27 grains of black powder, the 44 Henry was anything

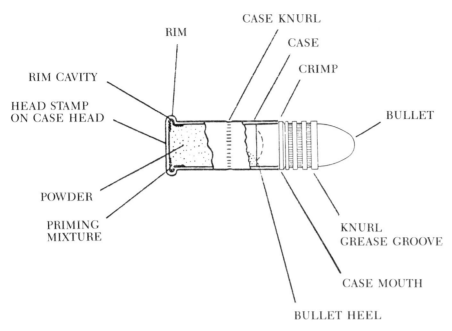

Rimfire cartridge construction and terminology.

but a powerful rifle round. However, it was in near continuous production from 1860 to 1932.

The rimfire cartridge uses a brass case with a folded head, or rim. In manufacture, the priming compound is spun into the rim area. In use, the firing pin collapses the rim, causing the back and forward edges to crush the priming compound between them. This crushing ignites the priming compound, which in turn ignites the main propellant charge.

While the methods of forming the case and inserting the primer material into the rim cavity have varied during the past 140 years, the actual cartridge remains basically the same. Of course, today's cartridges are considerably stronger than their earlier counterparts. Still, the rimfire cartridge's potential is severely restricted by the case construction. Pressures safely handled by a rimfire case are quite modest compared to a centerfire cartridge. But none of this is to suggest that rimfire cartridges have been restricted to small physical dimensions or, for that matter, to simple straight-walled construction.

Most notable among the oversized rimfire cartridges was the 10.4×38R Swiss Vetterli adopted in the late 1860s for the Swiss military bolt-action service rifle. This cartridge and rifle saw service for 20 years. It has been commonly referred to as the 41 Swiss Rimfire. It employed a large, bottlenecked case using a 310- to 335-grain lead bullet at a muzzle velocity of 1,300 to 1,400 feet per second. Interest in this round was sufficient to support its manufacture in the U.S. until about 1940. With a muzzle energy in excess of 1,240 foot/pounds,

The T.B Davies Arms Company catalog (circa 1898) featured an extensive array of rimfire cartridges.

depending on the loading, this rimfire round was actually suitable for the taking of deer-sized game at very short ranges.

At the turn of the century, the catalog of T. B. Davies Arms Company (Portland, Maine) listed a rather extensive line of rimfire cartridges. Included were the tiny 22 Short, 25 Stevens, 30 Long, 32 Extra Long, 38 Extra Long, 41 Short (the famous derringer round), 44 Henry Flat, 46 Pistol Short, 46 Rifle Long, and 56-56 Spencer—all loaded with black powder. Smokeless-powder rimfire cartridges were available in 22 Short, 22 Long, and 32 Extra Short.

Rimfire ammo was loaded with charges of small shot very early on. Indeed, a catalog from the year 1900 shows shot cartridges as small as the BB cap and as large as the 56-56 Spencer. For a shot load, the BB cap designation was a misnomer because BB stood for "ball bullet" or "bullet breech," depending on which historian you agree with.

An interesting development, parallel with the development of early

Shot (Rim Fire) Cartridges.	Per Box of 50	List Per 1000
B. B. Cap	$0 30	$ 8 00
22-50 Long	35	11 00
32 Long	70	22 00
38 Short	1 00	30 00
38 Long	1 15	34 00
44 Long	1 35	40 00
44 Henry	1 35	40 00
44 Short	1 35	40 00
56-50 Per Box of 25	70	42 00
56-52 Per Box of 25	70	42 00
56-56 Per Box of 25	70	42 00

Early rimfire ammo (circa 1900) came in a wide variety of shot cartridges.

rimfire cartridges, was a unique cartridge design called pinfire. Pinfire cartridges used a tubular case with a pin or nail-like protrusion extending from its side. They were available in a wide range of metric calibers. Firearms chambered for pinfire cartridges had a groove cut into the rear of the chamber to allow the pin to protrude from the barrel. Ignition was accomplished when the firearm's hammer struck the pin, driving it into the case. The pin moved downward, crushing the internal priming charge against the far side of the case to cause ignition.

Pinfire ammunition quickly faded from use for several reasons, one being that the protruding pin represented a potential hazard—unintentional ignition should the pin be inadvertently driven into the case. Another major disadvantage was that the protruding pin eliminated the possibility of use in any type of practical repeating firearm except a revolver.

More than three dozen different rimfire cartridges gained some degree of popularity in the United States. However, only the 22 Short, 22 Long, 22 Long Rifle, and 22 Winchester Magnum Rimfire have survived the test of time.

The most recent rimfire cartridge to be dropped from manufacture was the Remington 5mm (20 caliber). This cartridge became available in 1970. Remington had hoped its bottlenecked shape and high velocity of 2,100 feet per second would catch the imagination of shooters. Indeed, its field performance outpaced the 22 Magnum rimfire round. However, before nine years had passed, Remington discontinued production of all 5mm rifles, and shortly thereafter dropped

Early pinfire cartridges. Ignition occurred when the hammer struck the pin, driving it into the case.

the manufacture of the ammunition. The 22-caliber rimfire reputation had simply closed the door to newcomers.

Today, the 22 Short, Long, Long Rifle, and Magnum rimfire cartridges are available in a wide range of bullet weights and even shot-loaded rounds. Each cartridge has specific levels of performance and application, as well as shortcomings.

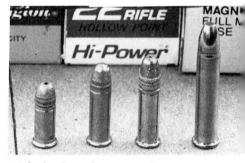

Today's four basic rimfire cartridges, *from left*: 22 Short, 22 Long, 22 Long Rifle, 22 Winchester Mag.

22 SHORT

The 22 Short was the original rimfire in this caliber and has been with us for well over 130 years, making it the oldest cartridge in continuous production. It was originally developed for the 1857 Smith & Wesson revolver. Today, a number of 22 Short variations are available. These include:

22 CB[1], low velocity
22 Short, standard velocity
22 Short, high velocity
22 Short, high-velocity hollow-point

([1] CB stands for conical bullet.)

Generally, the various Short loads now use a 29-grain lead round-nose bullet or a 27-grain lead hollow-point bullet. Complete ballistics on the various loads will be found in a subsequent chapter.

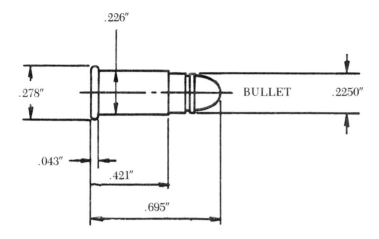

Maximum dimensions of 22 Short cartridge.

The use of a Short is, naturally, demanded in any rifle or handgun specifically chambered for this tiny 22. A great many of the early "gallery" rifles were chambered exclusively for it. In addition, a recent Browning semiauto rifle and older Winchester pump rifles were chambered solely for the Short. However, at this writing no generally available firearms are being chambered for the exclusive use of the 22 Short except for a few high-grade target pistols and some inexpensive semiauto pistols.

Short ammunition can be used in many firearms chambered for Long or Long Rifle ammunition. Such use is always safe, but not without drawbacks. Shorts will not usually function in the action of a semiautomatic chambered for the Long Rifle cartridge, but they will often function smoothly in lever-action rifles and in many bolt-action repeating rifles chambered for the longer cartridges. Of course, they work well in all revolvers and single-shot rifles.

A drawback to using Short ammunition in longer chambers is that extensive use of the Short will result in a certain amount of chamber erosion at the point where the Short case ends. When this erosion becomes sufficiently deep, Long or Long Rifle ammunition can jam in the firearm.

What happens is that the Long or Long Rifle case extends past the eroded area. Upon firing, the longer case expands into the enlarged, eroded part of the chamber, creating a fired case that is bigger in diameter at the front end than at the rear. This naturally prevents easy extraction of the fired case, as it must be squeezed—or "sized down"—if the large front end is to pass through the smaller-diameter rear section of the chamber. If the erosion is minor, the shooter will experience difficult extraction of the cartridge. If the erosion is extensive, it may be impossible to pull the fired cartridge free of the chamber in a normal fashion. Sometimes the gun will need to be disassembled and the case driven out with a close-fitting rod placed into the muzzle of the firearm.

Once a chamber suffers from heavy erosion of this type, it will be suitable for further use only with Short ammunition. Such damage greatly lessens the value of the firearm, as Shorts are both noticeably less accurate than Long Rifles in a conventional hunting and plinking arm, and considerably less potent. (Match-grade 22 Short ammunition in a top-quality target pistol chambered and rifled exclusively for the Short is, of course, very accurate at the ranges for which it is intended.)

Depending on the quality of the barrel, and perhaps to some extent on the type of propellant used in the Short, troublesome chamber erosion can occur after as few as 1,000 rounds or perhaps not until 5,000 rounds have been fired. This same erosion occurs with Long and Long Rifle cartridges, but because no case normally extends into the area where the erosion occurs, no difficulties are encountered.

Short rounds are most often used for tin-can shooting—plinking. Shorts are popular for this because of their low noise level. For use on small-game animals, the Short is adequate up to about 25 yards if high-velocity hollow-points are used. And if the sporting hunter will restrict himself to targets no larger than rabbits and will pay careful attention to range.

22 LONG

The Long generally uses the same bullet as the Short in a 22 Long Rifle case. However, the Long does pre-date the Long Rifle round. Some firearms were specifically chambered for the Long cartridge.

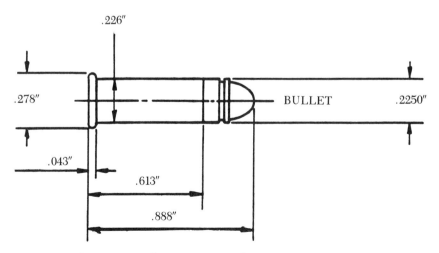

Maximum dimensions of 22 Long cartridge.

Early pump-action Winchester rifles are the most common. The Long has been available in the following popular variations:

- 22 CB Long, low velocity
- 22 Long, standard velocity
- 22 Long, high velocity
- 22 Long, high-velocity hollow-point

The Long is the least used and least accurate of the 22 rimfires. For these reasons it has, from time to time, been dropped from the manufacturers' catalogs, but usually has been reinstated. Undoubtedly, at some point the Long will be discontinued finally, never again to return. The continuing modest popularity of the Long is probably due to shooters simply requesting "Longs" when purchasing ammunition, instead of asking for the more potent and more accurate Long Rifle. The Long has the same applications as the Short—plinking and small-game hunting at short ranges. Its use in a Long Rifle chamber is safe and will not damage the gun.

22 LONG RIFLE

This is by far the most popular rimfire cartridge, and for good reasons. It can be extremely accurate and quite potent compared to the Short or Long. Indeed, it is often notably more accurate than the bigger Magnum. The Long Rifle comes in a wide range of loadings:

- 22 Long Rifle, standard-velocity
- 22 Long Rifle, standard-velocity hollow-point
- 22 Long Rifle, high velocity
- 22 Long Rifle, high-velocity hollow-point
- 22 Long Rifle, hyper velocity
- 22 Long Rifle, hyper-velocity hollow-point
- 22 Long Rifle, match (varying styles)
- 22 Long Rifle, shot

Usually, Long Rifle ammunition is loaded with a 39/40-grain round-nose or 36- to 38-grain hollow-point lead bullet. Variations include the Winchester Super Silhouette match-grade ammunition, loaded with a 42-grain bullet, and the hyper-velocity loads which use a 32 to 36-grain solid or hollow-point lead bullet.

Because of the very high degree of accuracy available with standard and high-velocity Long Rifle ammunition, the hunter most often selects his ammo from this category. For use on smaller animals, standard-velocity loads are adequate and often the most accurate. For difficult squirrel hunting—when the only shot might be a tiny head—match-grade ammunition is often selected despite its greater cost. For tougher and heavier animals, such as woodchuck, the high-speed Long Rifle hollow-points are best.

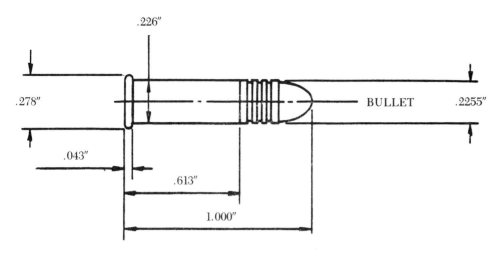

Maximum dimensions of 22 Long Rifle cartridge.

The Long Rifle will supply enough punch to kill an 18-pound woodchuck at 50 yards with a carefully placed shot. But at longer ranges, more than one "killed" chuck has managed to get into his burrow. Squirrels and rabbits can be taken cleanly at ranges to 75 yards, perhaps a bit farther, with a very accurate rifle and good ammo. But 100-yard shots demand a careful hold-over of 5 to 7 inches, so it becomes difficult to make a clean kill at such range.

The hyper-velocity loadings had their beginning, I believe, with a marketing department that felt higher muzzle velocities would create greater consumer interest and purchases. But the somewhat lighter bullets used in the hyper-velocity loads lose their high velocity quickly. At 50 yards, most hyper-velocity rounds will deliver somewhat more energy than a high-velocity round. But out past 50 yards, the lighter bullet has lost enough velocity so that it becomes no more effective than a high-speed round. More importantly, the hyper-velocity rounds, on a consistent basis, have proven to be not as accurate as the high-velocity loadings. Thus, the appropriate application of hyper-velocity loads would seem to be when accuracy is not paramount and when violent expansion at modest ranges is desired. Calling in foxes and shooting them at 50 yards or less is one example of a suitable application for hyper-velocity ammo.

The shot-loaded Long Rifle rounds are, for the most part, a novelty. However, if ridding the barn of starlings or getting rid of small pests such as mice is on your list of activities, the shot loads will get the job done when used at ranges not exceeding 20 feet. The spin imparted by the rifling causes the pellets to disperse rapidly, and it becomes impossible to hit small targets when ranges approach 10 yards. In specially made smoothbore 22 "shotguns," such as the discontinued Remington pump rifle, the effective range of shot cartridges might well be 30 feet, depending on the quarry's size.

When hunting with the 22 Long Rifle cartridge, great care should be taken to ensure proper bullet placement. Head shots are a must on tough critters like woodchuck and fox to make sure that the quarry doesn't become a lost cripple. Besides, when hunting for the cooking pot, head shots will ensure a great deal more edible meat for that squirrel or rabbit stew.

Generally, the rimfire user should learn to become a hunter, stalking as close to his quarry as practical before shooting. Most competent folks can use a 22 very effectively to 50 or 60 yards. But a small animal at 75 or 80 yards may be very hard to hit properly. Handgunners can often be effective at ranges of 25 to 30 yards without incurring lost cripples.

The use of hollow-points will help anchor game, but will result in a bit greater loss in edible meat. Animals larger than woodchuck or fox should not be hunted with the 22 Long Rifle, but there are a lot of squirrels, rabbits, opossum, raccoons, and the like that are ideally hunted with the Long Rifle cartridge.

22 WINCHESTER MAGNUM RIMFIRE

This round's lengthy official title is often subject to abbreviation by shooters and is simply called the 22 Mag. The Mag offers notably greater velocity and energy compared to any of the Long Rifle loadings. Its extra punch, however, is somewhat handicapped by a less than Long Rifle level of accuracy. Indeed, the 22 Mag's accuracy is quite similar to the accuracy often obtained with the hyper-velocity Long Rifle loads. Currently, 22 Mag loadings include:

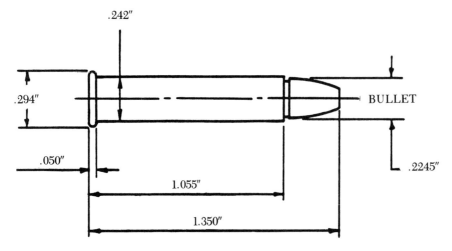

Maximum dimensions of 22 Winchester Magnum Rimfire cartridge.

22 Magnum 40-grain jacketed hollow-point
22 Magnum 40-grain full metal jacket
22 Magnum 50-grain jacketed hollow-point (Federal brand only)
22 Magnum shot cartridge (CCI brand only)

Appropriate applications for this Magnum rimfire cartridge are large varmints (such as woodchuck) or furbearers (with the full metal jacket). The Magnum will destroy too much edible meat to be an ideal choice for smaller game hunting.

It is never safe to use the smaller-diameter 22 Short, Long, or Long Rifle ammunition in a Magnum chamber. The only other cartridge that may be fired in a Magnum is the now discontinued 22 WRF (Winchester Rim Fire).

OBSOLETE RIMFIRE CARTRIDGES

From time to time, certain ammunition factories will manufacture a quantity of a discontinued rimfire cartridge. For example, the 22 WRF (Winchester Rim Fire) round saw a limited production run in 1986 by Winchester. At other times, certain importers have marketed newly manufactured cartridges of calibers long ago discontinued in the U.S. An example of this is the 41 Short Remington derringer ammo imported not too long ago by Navy Arms Company. Generally speaking, however, an old rifle suitable for use with such ammo will have greater value as a collector's item rather than a shooter's. Such

Some firearms, such as this Butler derringer, are chambered for the exclusive use of 22 Shorts.

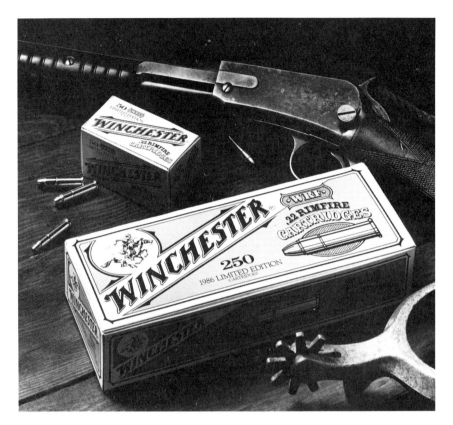

Obsolete rimfire cartridges are sometimes made in small quantities. In 1986 Winchester produced 22 WRF rimfire cartridges, ideally suited to many of their old pump-action exposed-hammer rifles.

guns can often be traded for a first-class modern rifle chambered for the 22 Long Rifle cartridge.

RIMFIRE ACCURACY

That rimfire ammunition is accurate has long been established. Some small-bore rifle shooters, using firearms costing $1,000 or more, are quite capable of firing 10 Long Rifle bullets into a 1-inch circle at 100 yards. To do so, they carefully select only the finest match ammunition, and they may test a half-dozen different brands and types of ammunition to determine which lot will provide the best accuracy in a specific rifle.

Even inexpensive 22 rifles and handguns can benefit from similar accuracy testing. If a certain brand and type of ammo does not perform well in a specific firearm, it does not mean that a different brand or type might not prove outstanding in the same rifle or handgun. Accuracy testing also can show that specific types of 22 rimfire ammunition will generally outperform other types. For example, the low-velocity match-grade Long Rifle rounds almost always shoot more accurately than the higher-velocity hollow-point loads. And hyper-

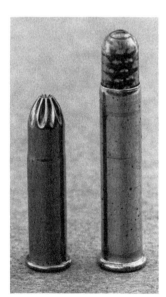

Shot cartridges suitable for very small pests at distances to 20 feet are available in Long Rifle (*left*) and Mag.

velocity ammo is often the least accurate of the various types of Long Rifle loadings.

Just how much accuracy is sufficient will depend on the application. If hitting a tin can at 25 yards is all that is needed, almost any 22 Long Rifle ammunition will do. However, a few Short or Long loadings may not be up to even such informal accuracy. With a rimfire rifle, the best way to determine any ammunition's capability is to fire on paper targets at a 50-yard range. Fire several 10-shot groups before forming an opinion. Keep in mind that the same ammunition may do well in one rifle and not in another. The spread in group sizes using the same ammo might vary from ½ inch at 50 yards to perhaps 2½ inches, depending on the firearm used. Generally, bolt-action rifles will provide more accuracy than semiautomatic rifles. And the semiautos most often shoot more accurately than the lever- and pump-actions. A rimfire revolver will generally be about as accurate as a semiauto pistol.

Table 2.1, Accuracy Results, is based on findings with a specific rifle. Accuracy in another rifle might well vary. However, the table is informative in that it clearly shows how accuracy differs with ammunition types in a specific firearm. Note that the top three loads, the only

Testing various brands and types of Long Rifle ammo from a benchrest is the best way to find the one that delivers the best accuracy. This Kimber rifle was tested with more than 40 types of ammo. Five 10-shot 50-yard groups were fired with each, ranging from just under 1 inch to well over 6 inches.

TABLE 2.1

ACCURACY RESULTS

22 SHORT

Type	Brand	Bullet Weight (gr) and Style	10-Shot Group Size (inches) at 50 yards Smallest	Largest	Average[1]	Overall Ranking
Mini Mag	CCI	27–HP	1.195	2.348	1.871	25
Mini Mag	CCI	29–S	2.110	2.193	2.163	28
CB	Win	29–S	2.173	2.455	2.312	29
Super-X	Win	29–HP	1.229	3.117	2.447	31
R25	RWS	28–S	2.534	3.275	2.969	34
Target	Rem	29–S	2.781	3.225	3.003	35
Mini Group	CCI	29–S	2.438	3.673	3.085	36
High Velocity	Rem	27–HP	3.137	3.984	3.621	37
High Velocity	Rem	29–S	2.408	5.228	3.927	38
Super-X	Win	29–S	3.835	5.016	4.262	40
Mini Cap	CCI	29–S	3.809	4.727	4.268	41
Hi-Power	Fed	29–S	4.424	5.976	5.334	42
Hi-Power	Fed	29–HP	4.918	7.042	5.712	43

22 LONG

Type	Brand	Bullet Weight (gr) and Style	Smallest	Largest	Average[1]	Overall Ranking
Super-X	Win	29–S	1.995	2.720	2.423	30
Hi-Power	Fed	29–S	1.647	3.814	2.510	32
Mini Mag	CCI	29–S	2.338	3.690	2.919	33
High Velocity	Rem	29–S	3.681	4.132	3.945	39
Mini Cap	CCI	29–S	3.609	7.733	6.357	44

22 LONG RIFLE

Type	Brand	Bullet Weight (gr) and Style	Smallest	Largest	Average[1]	Overall Ranking
R50	RWS	39–S	0.761	1.200	0.944	1
Biathlon	RWS	39–S	0.910	1.143	0.994	2
Green Tag	CCI	40–S	0.756	1.078	0.999	3
T22	Win	40–S	0.790	1.214	1.056	4
Silhouette	Fed	40–S	0.929	1.198	1.060	5
Champion	Fed	40–S	0.919	1.490	1.111	6
Super Silhouette	Win	42–S	0.956	1.348	1.125	7
Pistol Match	Fed	40–S	0.899	1.426	1.175	8
Super-X	Win	40–S	1.020	1.270	1.182	9
Mini Mag	CCI	37–HP	0.984	1.424	1.208	10
Pistol Match	Win	40–S	0.915	1.428	1.209	11
High Velocity	Rem	36–HP	1.193	1.329	1.217	12
Lightning	Fed	40–S	1.067	1.444	1.246	13
Hi-Power	Fed	38–HP	1.131	1.442	1.248	14
Target	Rem	40–S	1.132	1.495	1.269	15
Standard	RWS	39–S	1.076	1.449	1.279	16
Pistol Match	RWS	39–S	1.268	1.455	1.330	17
Super-X	Win	37–HP	1.256	1.585	1.428	18
Mini Group	CCI	40–S	0.957	1.770	1.477	19
Yellow Jacket	Rem	33–HP	1.337	1.586	1.501	20

Type	Brand	Bullet Weight (gr) and Style	10-Shot Group Size (inches) at 50 yards		Average[1]	Overall Ranking
			Smallest	Largest		
Hi-Power	Fed	40–S	1.475	1.630	1.569	21
High Velocity	Rem	40–S	1.434	1.821	1.650	22
Rifle Match	RWS	39–S	1.348	2.330	1.724	23
Stinger	CCI	32–HP	1.506	1.905	1.726	24
Mini Mag	CCI	40–S	1.559	2.345	1.880	26
Viper	Rem	36–S	2.452	2.929	1.900	27
22 WINCHESTER MAGNUM						
Super-X	Win	40–HP	1.277	2.201	1.603	1
Maxi Mag	CCI	40–FMC	1.789	2.133	1.915	2
Super-X	Win	40–FMC	1.378	2.574	1.935	3
Maxi Mag	CCI	40–HP	1.108	2.735	2.091	4

HP = hollow point
S = solid lead bullet
FMC = full metal case
[1]average of 5 groups

ones providing average (for five 10-shot groups at 50 yards) group sizes of less than 1 inch were all match-grade Long Rifle loadings. Also note that if a 1½ inch group size were used as a criterion for acceptable ammunition, there would be 20 different acceptable loads for the test rifle—all Long Rifle variations. Only six Long Rifle rounds proved less than satisfactory in the test rifle. Also note that none of the Short or Long loadings proved acceptable based on the arbitrary acceptance standard of 1½-inch average group size.

A Kimber rifle was used to test the Short, Long, and Long Rifle rounds. Accuracy figures for the listed 22 Magnum rimfire ammunition were obtained using a popular Mossberg rifle. All accuracy tests were conducted using a 1½-5x Leupold scope set at the 5x magnification. All test firing was done from a bench using sandbag rests.

Generally, the ammunition manufacturers all try to maintain a minimum level of accuracy. This level of performance is most often exceeded in actual ammunition-lot tests. However, Table 2.2 will suggest the manufacturer's general criteria for 22 rimfire cartridges. The results shown are based on the use of a match-grade rifle, except for the pistol-match category which is based on the use of a high-grade target handgun. Note that only Long Rifle and Magnum cartridges have their accuracy requirement usually geared to a 100-yard range. Short and Long specifications are based on 25-yard testing.

TABLE 2.2
EXPECTED AMMUNITION PERFORMANCE[1]

Cartridge	Range (yards)	Average Group (inches)[2]
22 Short CB	10	2.00
22 Short, all velocities	25	2.00
22 Long, all velocities	25	2.00
22 Long Rifle, standard velocity	100	2.00
22 Long Rifle, high velocity	100	3.00
22 Long Rifle, hyper velocity	50	2.00
22 Long Rifle, match grade	100	1.25
22 Long Rifle, pistol match[3]	50	2.50
22 Winchester Magnum Rimfire	100	3.00

NOTES: [1]Based on use of match-grade rifle.
[2]Based on average of five 10-shot groups.
[3]Based on use of match-grade handgun.

Handgun accuracy is highly variable. The dimensions and fit of parts in each handgun will play a large role in determining accuracy. However, based on the use of varying styles of firearms, tests conducted at 25 yards indicate a generally high level of accuracy with guns of good quality. Table 2.3 shows results obtained with eight different handguns, both revolvers and semiautomatics, with barrel lengths varying from 2 inches to 8⅜ inches. The results were based on the average group size of five 5-shot groups fired from a bench using a two-hand hold with wrists supported by a sandbag rest.

TABLE 2.3
HANDGUN ACCURACY TEST RESULTS[1]

Firearm	Barrel Length (inches)	Cartridge	Average Group (inches)
S&W Model 34	2	22 LR	3.00
S&W Model 17	6	22 LR	1.75
S&W Model 17	8⅜	22 LR	1.50
S&W Model 17	8⅜	22 Short	4.50
Ruger Mark I	5½	22 LR	1.50
Ruger Single Six	4⅝	22 LR	2.50
Ruger Single Six	4⅝	22 Magnum	2.75
S&W Model 41	5½	22 LR Match	1.00
S&W Model 41	7	22 LR Match	1.25

[1]Group sizes rounded to nearest ¼", fired at 25 yards

RIMFIRE DIFFICULTIES

Rimfire ammunition is extremely reliable. With several billion rounds manufactured each year, the number of rounds that are truly defective is meaningless. Yet rimfire shooters do experience problems such as cartridge misfire or cases pierced by the firing pin. The most frequent causes of such difficulties lie with the firearm rather than the ammunition.

The accompanying drawing shows firing-pin patterns on the cartridge rim. A firing-pin indent occurring too far from the central portion of the rim can cause misfires by failing to crush the priming compound. A firing pin that is too pointed also can result in failure of the priming compound to ignite. Excessively deep case indents or very sharp corners on the firing pin could cause the cartridge to be

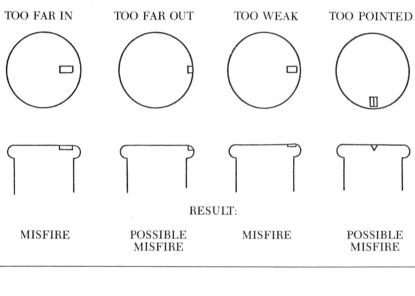

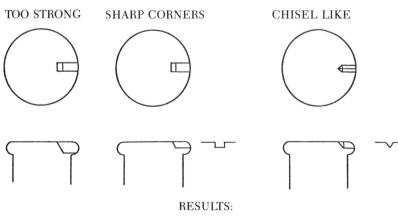

Firing-pin indents on 22 cartridge rims which can cause misfires or pierced shell cases.

pierced. This can be dangerous as the shell may burst at the weakened area.

Fired cartridge cases may show signs of abnormalities due to dangerous gun conditions. For example, an excessively enlarged chamber can cause shell cases to expand to the point where they may split. It is remotely possible for a cartridge case to split as a result of a factory defect. Should a case ever split, first assume the gun to be at fault, discontinue any further use of it, and have a competent gunsmith carefully inspect the firearm.

A ruptured case indicates a serious problem. Sometimes it may be that a less than qualified person has drilled the barrel for a scope mount and inadvertently drilled through the chamber, or left so little

CARTRIDGE FLAWS

Fired 22 caliber cartridge cases can give indications of dangerous firearm conditions. Examine a sampling of your fired cases occasionally to be sure no warning signs are present.

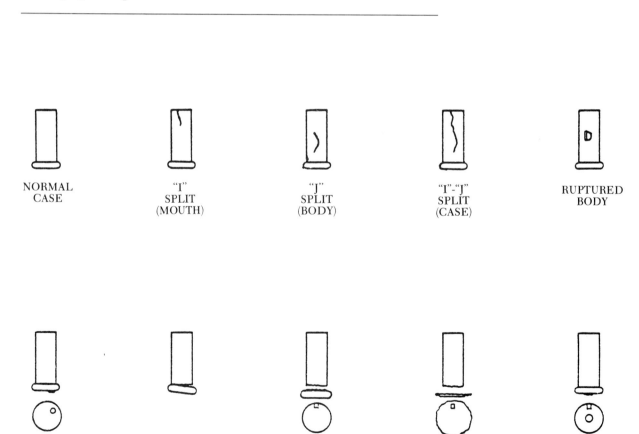

material as to cause the chamber to expand in the area under the screw hole. A firearm in this condition is unsafe to use.

A shell rim that bursts at the firing-pin hole may be caused by a number of firing-pin problems or an enlarged firing-pin cut in the firearm's bolt face. When a rim partially or completely separates from a case it may indicate that the headspace (distance from the back of a seated cartridge head to the bolt face) is dangerously excessive. Discontinue use of the firearm immediately.

Anything that can raise chamber pressure, such as a partially obstructed bore, oil or cleaning fluid in the bore, or a cleaning patch left in the bore, can also cause a shell case to burst at the rim. Such a condition may also cause the case head to rupture at a point corre-

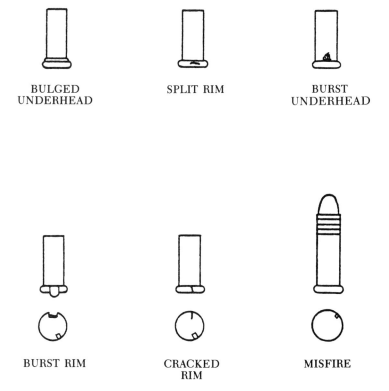

sponding with the bolt's ejector cut or the extractor cut in the barrel. Note the drawing of a rupture at a typical ejector-hole location. Another rupture, shown as a burst underhead, is typical of one occurring at an extractor cut.

Bulged underheads and split rims are typical of excessive headspace or enlarged chambers. Any abnormal condition should be viewed very seriously. The gun should be repaired before firing even a single additional shot.

The shooter should examine each cartridge before loading it into his firearm. Rimfire ammunition has reached a stage of near perfection with some manufacturers. However, when any product is manufactured in such huge quantities, some errors will occasionally slip by. Another illustration shows the basic cartridge abnormalities that the shooter might encounter. When these or any other abnormalities are found, the cartridge should not be used and it should be disposed of in a safe manner.

CARTRIDGE FLAWS

Abnormalities in 22 rimfire cartridges. Any shells with these or other defects should not be fired and should be disposed of in a safe manner.

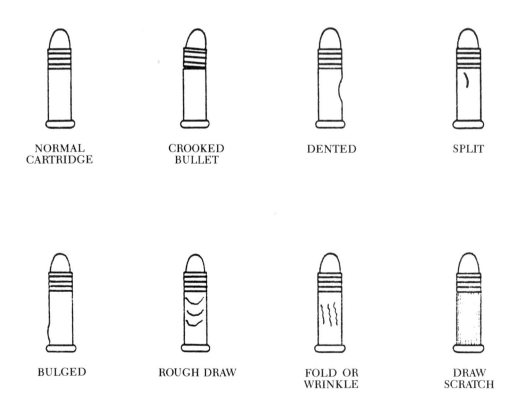

RIMFIRES ARE USEFUL CARTRIDGES

Because rimfire ammunition is inexpensive, has a low noise level, and produces no noticeable recoil, it is ideal for beginners to learn with, and, in the best Long Rifle loadings, it's also accurate enough to satisfy the most demanding shooter. Smallbore match shooting and metallic-silhouette shooting are demanding sports that will challenge the most serious athlete. Rimfire shooting is, therefore, entertaining, fun, and a demanding sport. It is a pastime in which almost all shooters can participate extensively. The most fortunate among us started out shooting the 22 rimfire, and the most knowledgeable continue a lifelong affair with rimfire shooting.

No shooter should be without a 22 rimfire firearm. It's one of the best tools for marksmanship training, Saturday afternoon fun, or highly competitive shooting. Wherever a safe backstop can be found and where a low level of noise is not objectionable—that's 22 country.

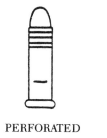

PERFORATED

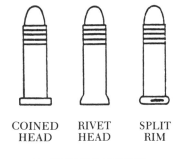

COINED HEAD   RIVET HEAD   SPLIT RIM

DEFORMED HEADS

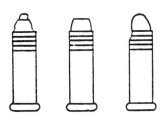

ABNORMAL BULLETS

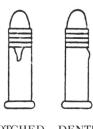

NOTCHED MOUTH   DENTED MOUTH

3

Exterior Rimfire Ballistics

Being satisfied with a rimfire cartridge's performance begins with proper application, which requires knowledge of its ballistics in order to determine the size of the game that can be hunted, the range over which shots can be made, and, of course, the effect of wind on the bullet's flight.

When using the various tables contained in this chapter, keep in mind that ballistics data alone will not serve as a guide to cartridge application. For example, while velocity and energy figures are shown for the 22 Short at 100 yards, such a distance is far too great to attempt serious use of a Short cartridge. Moreover, listed ballistics show merely an average velocity. As mentioned earlier, an average muzzle velocity of 1,150 feet per second may be shown for a standard-velocity Long Rifle cartridge, yet the actual velocity may well vary by plus or minus 50 feet per second, or perhaps more.

This same variability applies to all information contained in exterior ballistics tables. Values for velocity, trajectory, energy, wind drift, and maximum range are *average* evaluations or *nominal* specifications. The actual values obtained by the shooter will vary with the individual lot of ammunition and with the firearm used. Listed values are never absolutes, but merely indications of approximately what the shooter may realize with his ammunition and firearms.

To establish nominal specifications, Table 3.1 will show the average advertised performance of rimfire ammunition. A specific manufacturer's load might have a slightly different value, but such variations are less real than the published specifications might suggest. For each current rimfire cartridge, and several obsolete loadings, the various tables will list velocity, energy, trajectory, wind drift, maximum ranges, and other useful information. The abbreviations used in the tables are as follows:

CB	Conical Bullet
LV	Low Velocity
SV	Standard Velocity
HV	High Velocity
RF	Rimfire
Dis	Disintegrating Bullet
HP	Hollow-Point
LR	Long Rifle
FMC	Full Metal Case
JHP	Jacketed Hollow-Point
Ball	Round-Nose Lead Bullet
Rem	Remington
Win	Winchester
Auto	Automatic
Mag	Magnum

The conditions that apply to the listed average factory ballistics are:

Temperature:	59°F
Barometer:	29.53" of mercury
Elevation:	0.0 feet (sea level)
Trajectory:	assumed sight height over bore 0.9"

Table 3.1 is for advertised rifle ballistics, based on a 24-inch test barrel, while Table 3.2 is for advertised handgun ballistics based on a 6-inch barrel. Table 3.3 provides additional exterior ballistics, including wind drift, up- or downhill hold-over or -under, time of flight, maximum cartridge range, velocity at maximum range, and the angle of departure required to achieve maximum range—all based on the use of a 24-inch barrel.

The values listed in Table 3.3 deserve some brief discussion. All data are based on the specified muzzle velocity and a standard bullet profile. However, individual shots will vary around the listed velocity. Hence, the values shown in each column could be somewhat greater or lesser, depending on the exact velocity achieved by the individual cartridge.

The wind-drift figures are for a wind crossing the bullet's flight path at a right angle. Winds at different angles will naturally produce less bullet drift.

When a bullet is fired at an up- or downhill angle, the effect of gravity is, of course, constant. However, while the distance from muzzle to target may be, for example, 100 yards, the bullet is affected by gravity for a shorter distance. This is shown in the diagram on page 40.

Table 3.3 lists hold-under data for a 45° hill with the target at 100

TABLE 3.1
AVERAGE ADVERTISED RIMFIRE RIFLE BALLISTICS (24" BARREL)

Cartridge	Type	BULLET WEIGHT in grains	VELOCITY[1] (FPS) AT:			ENERGY (FT/LBS) AT:			TRAJECTORY (INCHES) AT:	
			Muzzle	50 yds	100 yds	Muzzle	50 yds	100 yds	50 yds	100 yds
22 Short	CB LV	29	720	650	600	33	27	23	0.0	−18.8
22 Short	SV	29	1045	940	870	72	57	49	0.0	− 8.7
22 Short	HV	29	1095	985	900	77	62	52	0.0	− 8.0
22 Short	HVHP	27	1120	1000	905	75	60	49	0.0	− 7.9
22 Long	CB LV	29	720	650	600	33	27	23	0.0	−18.8
22 Long	SV	29	1180	1035	945	90	69	58	0.0	− 8.0
22 Long	HV	29	1240	1085	960	99	76	59	0.0	− 6.8
22 LR	Match	40	1080	990	900	104	87	72	0.0	− 8.5
22 LR	SV	40	1150	1055	975	117	99	84	0.0	− 7.0
22 LR	HV	40	1255	1150	1015	140	117	92	0.0	− 6.2
22 LR	HVHP	36	1280	1165	1010	131	109	82	0.0	− 6.2
22 LR	Hyper Vel.	36	1410	1200	1055	159	115	89	0.0	− 6.2
22 LR	Hyper VelHP	33	1500	1240	1075	165	113	85	0.0	− 5.6
22 WinAuto*	SV	45	1035	—	915	107	—	84	0.0	− 8.3
22 WinRF*	HV	45	1320	—	1055	174	—	111	0.0	− 5.6
22 WinMag	JHP	40	1910	1565	1325	324	218	156	0.0	− 2.6
22 WinMag	JHP	50	1650	1420	1280	302	224	182	0.0	− 3.3
5mm RemRF*	JHP	38	2105	—	1610	374	—	219	0.0	− 1.7
25 Stevens Short*	SV	65	935	—	845	126	—	103	0.0	−10.1
25 Stevens Long*	SV	65	1115	—	980	179	—	139	0.0	− 7.2
32 Short*	SV	80	935	—	830	155	—	122	0.0	−10.3
32 Long*	SV	80	1030	—	910	189	—	147	0.0	− 8.4
22 LR	Shot	#12 pellets	1050	—	—	—	—	—	—	—
22 WinMag	Shot	#11 pellets	1125	—	—	—	—	—	—	—
41 Swiss*	SV	310	1350	—	1000	1255	—	689	0.0	− 9.0

NOTES: [1]All velocities rounded to nearest 5 feet per second
       0.0 Indicates range at which gun is sighted in
      (*) Obsolete Loading

TABLE 3.2

AVERAGE ADVERTISED RIMFIRE HANDGUN BALLISTICS (6″ BARREL)

Cartridge	Type	Bullet Weight (gr)	Muzzle Velocity[1] (fps)	Muzzle Energy (ft/lbs)
22 Short	SV	29	865	48
22 Short	HV	29	1010	66
22 Long	HV	29	1095	77
22 LR	Pistol Match	40	1060	100
22 LR	SV	40	960	82
22 LR	HV	40	1060	100
22 LR	Silhouette	42	1025	98
22 WinMag	JHP	40	1480	195
41 Short*	SV	129	430	53

NOTES: [1] All velocities rounded to nearest 5 fps

(*) Obsolete loading for Remington derringer

TABLE 3.3

EXTERIOR BALLISTICS OF RIMFIRE CARTRIDGES

Cartridge	Type	Bullet Weight (gr)	Muzzle Vel. (fps)	100-yard Wind Drift 10 mph wind	100 yard 45° Angle Up- or Downhill hold under target	100-yard Time of Flight (seconds)	Maximum Bullet Range (yards)	Velocity at Max. Range (fps)	Muzzle Angle Required to Achieve Max. Range
22 Short	SV	29	1045	5.0″	5.3″	0.316	1210	206	31°16′
22 Short	HV	29	1095	5.3″	4.9″	0.301	1232	207	30°95′
22 Short	HVHP	27	1120	5.9″	4.8″	0.304	1175	200	30°58′
22 Long	HV	29	1240	6.9″	4.1″	0.281	1271	208	30°57′
22 LR	SV	40	1150	4.4″	4.4″	0.286	1589	240	32°10′
22 LR	HV	40	1255	5.5″	3.9″	0.270	1623	241	31°86′
22 LR	HVHP	36	1280	6.2″	3.8″	0.270	1506	230	31°37′
22 WinMag	JHP	40	1910	5.7″	1.8″	0.190	1715	237	30°37′
22 WinAuto*	SV	45	1035	3.3″	5.2″	0.307	1632	249	32°93′
22 WinRF*	HV	45	1320	5.5″	3.5″	0.259	1757	253	32°13′
5mm RemRF*	JHP	38	2105	3.6″	1.4″	0.163	2176	275	31°48′
25 Stevens Short*	SV	65	935	3.0″	6.2″	0.338	1659	258	33°99′
25 Stevens Long*	SV	65	1115	3.4″	4.5″	0.288	1819	263	33°06′
32 Short*	SV	80	935	3.5″	6.3″	0.341	1486	241	32°32′
32 Long*	SV	80	1030	3.5″	5.2″	0.311	1569	243	32°74′

NOTES: *Discontinued load

See text for explanation of values listed.

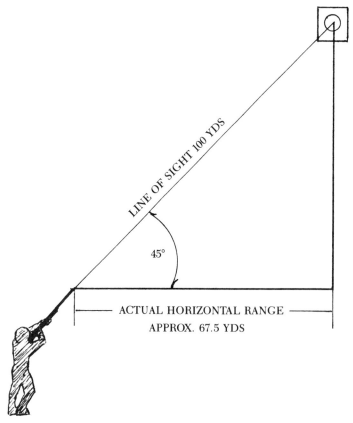

When firing uphill, distance from muzzle to target is greater than actual horizontal distance so gravity affects bullet drop over a shorter range.

---

yards. The data may be computed to any other angle by using the formula:

$$h \left(\frac{N}{45}\right)^2 = \text{hold-under for new angle in which:}$$

h = hold-under for a 45° angle
  (obtained from ballistics tables for the load you are using).
N = new angle for which you wish to calculate hold-under.

Granted, you won't be taking time out during a hunt to calculate precise hold-under, but it's nonetheless useful to understand the ballistics of your ammunition. So let's assume that, as an inquisitive shooter, you'd like to know the hold-under for the 22 Long Rifle hollow-point with 1,280 fps muzzle velocity at 100 yards for an angle of 30°. Referring to the appropriate ballistics table, we find that the hold-under at 100 yards and a 45 angle is 3.8 inches. Therefore:

$$h \left(\frac{N}{45}\right)^2 = \text{hold-under}$$

$$h \left(\frac{30}{45}\right)^2 = \text{hold-under}$$

$$3.8 \left(\frac{30}{45}\right)^2 = \text{hold-under}$$

$$3.8\ (.6666)^2 = \text{hold-under}$$
$$3.8 \times .4444 = \text{hold-under}$$
$$1.68'' = \text{hold-under for new angle of 30°}$$

Keep in mind that the hold-under figure you arrive at, either from the ballistics tables or your calculations, does not mean you would aim that distance below your target. Rather, it means you would subtract that distance from the required normal hold-over.

In the instance described above, the normal hold-over for a rifle sighted-in at 50 yards would be 6.2 inches. We therefore subtract the hold-under of 1.68 inches from the normal hold-over (on flat land) of 6.2 inches. Our new hold-over for a 30 angle is then reduced to 4.52 inches.

You may also calculate the height of trajectory when your sight height differs from the table's assumed sight height of 0.9 inch above bore line. To do so, use the following formula:

$$\left[\left(\frac{R_t}{R_s}\right) - 1\right](h - 0.9) = \text{new height of trajectory to be added to original height of trajectory where:}$$

R_t = target range in yards
R_s = sight-in range in yards
h = new height of sight above bore line in inches

What would the new height of trajectory be for a 22 Long Rifle hollow-point (36 grains) at a muzzle velocity of 1,280 feet per second when the sights are 2 inches above bore line, the distance is 100 yards, and the zero was at 50 yards?

Referring to the proper ballistics table you will find that the original trajectory was −6.2 inches. We then have:

$$\left[\left(\frac{R_t}{R_s}\right) - 1\right](h - 0.9) = \text{new height of trajectory to be added to original } -6.2 \text{ inches}$$

$$\left[\left(\frac{100}{50}\right) - 1\right](2.0 - 0.9) = \text{new height of trajectory to be added to original } -6.2 \text{ inches}$$

$$[(2) - 1]\,(1.1) = \text{new height of trajectory to be added to original } -6.2 \text{ inches}$$

$1 \times 1.1 =$ new height of trajectory to be added to original -6.2 inches

$1.1 + (-6.2$ inches$) = -5.1$ inches (new trajectory)

It has been stressed that advertised ballistics will not always correspond to actual ballistics obtained by the shooter, since individual barrel lengths, interior chamber and barrel dimensions, as well as the individual lot of ammunition can all cause variations, and a particular company may list product specifications that differ from the average advertised ballistics shown in Tables 3.1 and 3.2. Moreover, 22 rimfire cartridges usually reach maximum velocity in a barrel of about 22½ inches. All or most of the propellant charge is burned in approximately 17 to 19 inches of bullet travel in the bore. By the time the bullet has traveled 23 or 24 inches through the bore, the propellant gases can no longer expand rapidly enough to cause further acceleration. At that point, velocity will begin to fall off. Thus, barrels longer than 24 inches can actually reduce velocity.

To show the variation that can occur compared to advertised values

Shape of 22 rimfire cartridges is not indicative of their ballistics. *From left*: standard-velocity 22 Short; subsonic velocity 22 Long Rifle; and Long Rifle rounds of standard velocity, high velocity, match grade, premium match grade, and high-velocity hollow point.

and from one lot of ammunition to another, more than 50 different 22 rimfire cartridge types and brands were tested in the same rifle under identical conditions. The results of this extensive testing are shown in Table 3.4.

Bear in mind that tests using a different lot of ammunition of the same brand and style shown in the table could deliver different ballistics even if fired in the original test rifle. To show the highest likely velocities, the barrel length of the test rifle used for Short, Long, and Long Rifle ammunition was 22½ inches. Velocity tests for the 22 Magnum rimfire were conducted with a 24-inch barrel to take advantage of this cartridge's increased powder capacity and its resultant ability to use a longer barrel to increase velocity.

It is interesting to note that the highest velocity obtained with 22 Long Rifle high-speed ammunition, using 40-grain bullets, was 1,212 feet per second. This is only 43 feet per second less than the average advertised velocity. In the case of high-speed hollow-point ammunition, the highest obtained velocity was only 38 feet per second less than advertised. Hyper-velocity Long Rifle ammunition, in one case, missed reaching the advertised velocity by 85 feet per second and in another case by 78 feet per second. Thus, the tested hyper-velocity long-range performance is almost identical to high-velocity Long Rifle ammunition performance. The Magnum cartridge's best performance was some 143 feet per second below advertised values. All this means it would be prudent to expect somewhat less in field performance than suggested by advertised ballistics, albeit the difference is of no great consequence.

The same test was repeated with a 6-inch revolver, firing ammunition from the same lots used in the rifle test. These results are shown in Table 3.5.

Note that the velocities listed in Tables 3.4 and 3.5 are values obtained 10 feet from the muzzle. Actual velocity at the muzzle would be only slightly higher—*very* slightly.

The standard deviation given for the velocity data is a statistical value that can be used to interpret the velocity uniformity of the ammo used in our test. In brief, the smaller the standard deviation, the more uniform is the actual velocity.

In evaluating ammunition lots, a good chronograph such as the Oehler Research Model 33 is an invaluable tool. Such a chronograph will not only measure the velocity of each shot fired through its "screens" but will store the information, count the shots fired, and then, with the press of a button, give you a read-out on the highest velocity, lowest velocity, and the velocity standard deviation. Other chronograph brands and models, some without as many features, can of course be purchased.

Keep in mind that a good chronograph will last over a lifetime of heavy use, requiring only a new set of batteries after every 40 or 50 hours of use. The models that calculate only velocity are often deemed inadequate by the shooter who becomes interested in ammunition performance. Because a misdirected shot can cause havoc, I

Cutaway of a typical 22 rimfire cartridge.

Remington Yellow Jacket Long Rifle, a typical 22 rimfire hyper-velocity cartridge.

TABLE 3.4

ACTUAL BALLISTICS IN 22½" RIFLE BARREL

Cartridge	Trade Name	Brand	Bullet Weight (gr) and Style	Actual Velocity (fps) at 10 feet					Energy (ft/lbs) at 10 feet
				Lowest	Highest	Extreme Var	Average	Standard Dev	
22 CB Short	Mini Cap	CCI	29–S	666	742	76	708	23	32
22 CB Short	Low Velocity	Win	29–S	652	724	72	696	24	31
22 CB Long	Mini Cap	CCI	29–S	536	645	109	605	28	26
22 Short	Mini-Group	CCI	29–S	797	914	117	836	32	45
22 Short	Target	Rem	29–S	968	1065	97	999	35	64
22 Short	Mini Mag	CCI	29–S	1075	1112	37	1091	12	77
22 Short	High Velocity	Rem	29–S	1021	1130	109	1084	34	76
22 Short	Super-X	Win	29–S	1019	1068	49	1045	14	70
22 Short	Hi-Power	Fed	29–S	1031	1165	134	1083	39	76
22 Short	Mini Mag	CCI	27–HP	1026	1089	63	1060	19	67
22 Short	High Velocity	Rem	27–HP	993	1092	99	1037	28	64
22 Short	Super-X	Win	27–HP	1042	1074	32	1056	12	67
22 Short	Hi-Power	Fed	29–HP	1025	1063	38	1044	13	70
22 Long	Mini Mag	CCI	29–S	1118	1152	34	1128	10	82
22 Long	High Velocity	Rem	29–S	1186	1257	71	1227	20	97
22 Long	Super-X	Win	29–S	1181	1232	51	1210	16	94
22 Long	Hi-Power	Fed	29–S	1167	1239	72	1204	21	93
22 LR	Pistol Match	Win	40–S	1111	1139	28	1124	9	112
22 LR	Pistol Match	Fed	40–S	1157	1216	59	1192	19	126
22 LR	Silhouette	Fed	40–S	1066	1130	64	1102	22	109
22 LR	Green Tag	CCI	40–S	1039	1097	58	1076	16	103
22 LR	Mini Group	CCI	40–S	1011	1069	57	1043	20	97
22 LR	Target	Rem	40–S	1128	1183	55	1156	17	118
22 LR	T22	Win	40–S	1116	1133	17	1126	5	113
22 LR	Champion	Fed	40–S	1102	1153	51	1128	14	113
22 LR	Mini Mag	CCI	40–S	1100	1207	107	1154	35	119
22 LR	High Velocity	Rem	40–S	1185	1249	64	1212	16	131
22 LR	Super-X	Win	40–S	1175	1212	37	1201	10	128
22 LR	Lightning	Fed	40–S	1183	1275	92	1208	27	130
22 LR	Hi-Power	Fed	40–S	1128	1252	124	1199	34	128
22 LR	Mini Mag	CCI	37–HP	1132	1401	269	1226	69	124
22 LR	High Velocity	Rem	36–HP	1187	1258	71	1223	23	120
22 LR	Super-X	Win	37–HP	1178	1284	106	1233	29	125
22 LR	Hi-Power	Fed	38–HP	1226	1289	63	1242	18	130
22 LR	Viper	Rem	36–S	1292	1352	60	1324	19	140
22 LR	Yellow Jacket	Rem	33–HP	1400	1456	56	1422	17	148
22 LR	Spitfire	Fed	33–HP	no test			no test		no test
22 LR	Stinger	CCI	32–HP	1440	1515	75	1472	21	154

Cartridge	Trade Name	Brand	Bullet Weight (gr) and Style	Actual Velocity (fps) at 10 feet					Energy (ft/lbs) at 10 feet
				Lowest	Highest	Extreme Var	Average	Standard Dev	
22 LR	Super-X	Win	#12 Shot	780	1100	320	974	128	
22 LR	Hi-Power	Fed	#12 Shot	698	1336	638	1041	255	
22 LR	Mini Mag	CCI	#12 Shot	802	954	152	980	51	
22 Mag RF*	Super-X	Win	40–FMC	1601	1679	78	1646	25	240
22 Mag RF*	Super-X	Win	40–JHP	1731	1777	46	1750	18	272
22 Mag RF*	Maxi Mag	CCI	40–FMC	1700	1855	155	1760	55	275
22 Mag RF*	Maxi Mag	CCI	40–JHP	1699	1860	161	1767	46	277
22 Mag RF*	Maxi Mag	CCI	#11 Shot	721	922	201	826	71	—
22 Short	R25	RWS	28–S	819	875	56	845	18	44
22 LR	Standard	RWS	39–S	1086	1159	73	1113	21	107
22 LR	Pistol Match	RWS	39–S	973	1034	61	1012	16	89
22 LR	Rifle Match	RWS	39–S	971	1036	65	1005	19	87
22 LR	Biathlon	RWS	39–S	951	1033	82	1009	23	88
22 LR	R50	RWS	39–S	1068	1088	20	1078	6	101

Extreme Var = Extreme Variation
S = Solid Lead Bullet
JHP = Jacketed Hollow-Point
HP = Hollow-Point
LR = Long Rifle
Standard Dev = Standard Deviation
FMC = Full Metal Case
(*) = Velocity in 24″ barrel

TABLE 3.5
ACTUAL BALLISTICS IN 6″ REVOLVER BARREL

Cartridge	Trade Name	Brand	Bullet Weight (gr) and Style	Actual Velocity (fps) at 10 feet					Energy (ft/lbs) at 10 feet
				Lowest	Highest	Extreme Var	Average	Standard Dev	
22 CB Short	Mini Cap	CCI	29–S	587	697	110	650	29	27
22 CB Short	Low Velocity	Win	29–S	622	660	38	645	11	27
22 CB Long	Mini Cap	CCI	29–S	444	587	143	516	47	17
22 Short	Mini-Group	CCI	29–S	732	798	66	767	23	37
22 Short	Target	Rem	29–S	874	1004	130	953	39	56
22 Short	Mini Mag	CCI	29–S	1008	1051	43	1026	13	67
22 Short	High Velocity	Rem	29–S	967	1093	126	1044	33	70
22 Short	Super-X	Win	29–S	980	1018	38	1002	13	65
22 Short	Hi-Power	Fed	29–S	975	1075	100	1011	30	66
22 Short	Mini Mag	CCI	27–HP	1024	1087	63	1053	21	66
22 Short	High Velocity	Rem	27–HP	958	1028	70	993	24	59
22 Short	Super-X	Win	27–HP	963	1051	88	1014	26	62
22 Short	Hi-Power	Fed	29–HP	939	1020	81	979	24	62

ACTUAL BALLISTICS IN 6" REVOLVER BARREL (continued)

Cartridge	Trade Name	Brand	Bullet Weight (gr) and Style	Actual Velocity (fps) at 10 feet					Energy (ft/lbs) at 10 feet
				Lowest	Highest	Extreme Var	Average	Standard Dev	
22 Long	Mini Mag	CCI	29–S	941	1062	121	1004	39	65
22 Long	High Velocity	Rem	29–S	1090	1141	51	1119	17	81
22 Long	Super-X	Win	29–S	1094	1142	48	1114	16	80
22 Long	Hi-Power	Fed	29–S	1045	1104	59	1071	18	74
22 LR	Pistol Match	Win	40–S	1007	1045	38	1020	11	92
22 LR	Pistol Match	Fed	40–S	990	1092	102	1051	28	98
22 LR	Silhouette	Fed	40–S	923	1024	101	981	28	86
22 LR	Green Tag	CCI	40–S	934	988	54	955	15	81
22 LR	Mini Group	CCI	40–S	884	935	51	915	18	74
22 LR	Target	Rem	40–S	999	1052	53	1022	18	93
22 LR	T22	Win	40–S	973	1022	49	1004	14	90
22 LR	Champion	Fed	40–S	952	1011	59	977	18	85
22 LR	Mini Mag	CCI	40–S	938	1043	105	995	38	88
22 LR	High Velocity	Rem	40–S	1041	1078	37	1060	11	100
22 LR	Super-X	Win	40–S	1008	1054	46	1025	13	93
22 LR	Lightning	Fed	40–S	1036	1085	50	1068	17	101
22 LR	Hi-Power	Fed	40–S	983	1081	98	1038	31	96
22 LR	Mini Mag	CCI	37–HP	1026	1094	68	1065	24	93
22 LR	High Velocity	Rem	36–HP	1038	1101	63	1066	20	91
22 LR	Super-X	Win	37–HP	1027	1095	68	1069	19	94
22 LR	Hi-Power	Fed	38–HP	1045	1121	76	1088	24	100
22 LR	Viper	Rem	36–S	1114	1210	96	1152	28	106
22 LR	Yellow Jacket	Rem	33–HP	1221	1269	48	1249	16	114
22 LR	Spitfire	Fed	33–HP	no test		no test		no test	
22 LR	Stinger	CCI	32–HP	1206	1298	92	1242	25	107
22 LR	Super-X	Win	#12 Shot	763	1088	325	876	130	
22 LR	Hi-Power	Fed	#12 Shot	726	1358	631	948	255	
22 LR	Mini Mag	CCI	#12 Shot	788	934	146	877	53	
22 Mag RF	Super-X	Win	40–FMC	—	—	80	1273	21	144
22 Mag RF	Super-X	Win	40–JHP	—	—	41	1361	22	165
22 Mag RF	Maxi Mag	CCI	40–FMC	—	—	170	1387	52	171
22 Mag RF	Maxi Mag	CCI	40–JHP	—	—	147	1390	48	172
22 Mag RF	Maxi Mag	CCI	#11 Shot	—	—	195	722	78	—
22 Short	R25	RWS	28–S	758	857	99	810	32	41
22 LR	Standard	RWS	39–S	899	1033	134	971	44	82
22 LR	Pistol Match	RWS	39–S	911	958	47	933	13	75
22 LR	Rifle Match	RWS	39–S	704	888	184	848	53	62
22 LR	Biathlon	RWS	39–S	781	897	116	852	36	63
22 LR	R50	RWS	39–S	926	984	58	952	20	79

Extreme Var = Extreme Variation
S = Solid Lead Bullet
JHP = Jacketed Hollow-Point
HP = Hollow-Point
LR = Long Rifle
Standard Dev = Standard Deviation
FMC = Full Metal Case

strongly suggest units that have remote screens to shoot over or through. Those that have the actual chronograph and screen as a single unit can be wrecked with a single misdirected shot.

Serious 22 rimfire shooters often become extremely interested in exact trajectories so as to be able to place shots precisely where wanted. Since actual velocities vary from advertised velocity, actual trajectories also will vary from advertised values. The serious shooter should carefully sight-in at 50 yards, then set up targets at 5- or 10-yard intervals and fire a group at each. The actual point of impact can then be recorded. In an attempt to show actual trajectories, we tested a lot of 22 Long Rifle high-speed hollow-point ammunition that delivered a 10-foot velocity of 1,242 feet per second (versus advertised muzzle velocity of 1,280 feet per second). Our scope reticle was 1.45 inches over the bore. The results were as follows:

22 LONG RIFLE 36-GRAIN HOLLOW-POINT

10-Foot Velocity of 1242 fps

yards	5	10	15	20	25	30	35
point of impact[1]	−1.2″	−0.7″	−0.4″	−0.2″	−0.1″	+0.2″	+0.3″

yards	40	45	50	55	60	65	70
point of impact[1]	+0.2″	+0.1″	0.0″	−0.2″	−0.5″	−0.8″	−1.3″

yards	75	80	85	90
point of impact[1]	−1.6″	−2.7″	−3.9″	−4.4″

[1]Point of impact shown as a minus (−) is for bullet impacts centered below the point of aim. Those shown as a plus (+) are for bullet impacts centered above the point of aim. 0.0″ is range at which the bullet hits the point of aim.

To show the variations caused by barrel length and internal dimensions, a test using a single lot of Remington high-speed 22 Long Rifle hollow-point ammunition was conducted with a number of firearms. A repeat test was conducted, using one lot of standard-velocity Short ammunition in the same rifles. From Tables 3.6 and 3.7, it can be seen that a longer barrel does not always mean more velocity. The 16½-inch-barreled test rifle actually provided greater velocity than the 18½-inch-barreled test rifle. This was due to internal dimensional differences in the two barrels. And as expected, the 27¼-inch barrel provided the lowest velocity of all lengths, from 16½ to 27¼ inches. Note how the Short cartridge, for practical purposes, attained full velocity in a 16½-inch barrel, with velocity fairly constant until 22½ inches.

Similar tests were run, using the same ammunition in a combination of revolvers and semiautomatic pistols. It will be noted from

TABLE 3.6

EFFECT OF RIFLE'S BARREL LENGTH ON VELOCITY FOR 22 LR AMMO

Firearm (type)	Barrel Length	Velocity (fps) at 10 feet			Standard deviation
		lowest	highest	average	
Rossi 62SAC (pump)	16½"	1227	1317	1259	26
Ruger 10/22 (semi)	18½"	1198	1288	1243	28
Marlin 39M (lever)	20½"	1226	1308	1267	27
Kimber 82 (bolt)	22½"	1241	1348	1282	32
Mossberg 144 (bolt)	27¼"	1178	1289	1211	30

TABLE 3.7

EFFECT OF RIFLE'S BARREL LENGTH ON VELOCITY FOR 22 SHORT AMMO

Firearm (type)	Barrel Length	Velocity (fps) at 10 feet			Standard deviation
		lowest	highest	average	
Rossi 62SAC (pump)	16½"	995	1072	1040	21
Ruger 10/22 (semi)	18½"	984	1063	1023	24
Marlin 39M (lever)	20½"	1028	1074	1049	15
Kimber 82 (bolt)	22½"	1019	1057	1040	12
Mossberg 144 (bolt)	27¼"	956	1018	987	17

semi = semiautomatic

Tables 3.8 and 3.9 that maximum velocity in a revolver is reached in about 6 inches of barrel, and that at 8⅜ inches velocities have fallen off. This phenomenon is due to the gap between the cylinder and barrel, which allows the escape of a great portion of the expanding gases. Obviously, a loss of expanding gases also occurs with centerfire revolver cartridges; for the centerfires, an 8⅜-inch barrel seems to deliver maximum velocity, but with only a slight gain over a 6-inch barrel. This is not true in semiautomatics, since they have no barrel-to-cylinder gap.

There is, however, still an advantage to the longer revolvers—an increased sighting radius (greater distance between front and rear sight). This translates to more precise sight alignment and potentially more shooting accuracy if the shooter can handle the increased weight and the change in balance that comes with the longest revolver barrels.

TABLE 3.8

EFFECT OF HANDGUN'S BARREL LENGTH ON VELOCITY FOR 22 LR AMMO

Firearm (type)	Barrel Length	Velocity (fps) at 10 feet			Standard deviation
		lowest	highest	average	
S & W Model 34 (R)	2"	888	943	917	16
Ruger Mark I (S)	5"	1081	1130	1100	18
S & W Model 17 (R)	6"	1094	1146	1124	18
S & W Model 17 (R)	8⅜"	1080	1153	1116	22

TABLE 3.9

EFFECT OF HANDGUN'S BARREL LENGTH ON VELOCITY FOR 22 SHORT AMMO

Firearm (type)	Barrel Length	Velocity (fps) at 10 feet			Standard deviation
		lowest	highest	average	
S & W Model 34 (R)	2"	760	877	847	33
Ruger Mark I (S)	5"	933	988	956	20
S & W Model 17 (R)	6"	947	1015	986	19
S & W Model 17 (R)	8⅜"	950	1009	981	19

(R) = revolver
(S) = semiautomatic

Finally, Table 3.10 shows the effect of various handgun barrels and makes, and a comparison of velocity with a 24-inch rifle barrel, when using the 22 Magnum Rimfire cartridge. It will be noted that when an identical barrel length was used, but on three different revolvers, velocities ranged from 1,122 fps to 1,297 fps—a full 172 fps difference with the same ammunition and the same barrel lengths. Even two barrels of the same make and model resulted in a velocity difference of 150 feet per second. These data were supplied by CCI.

TABLE 3.10

EFFECT OF HANDGUN'S BARREL LENGTH ON VELOCITY FOR 22 MAGNUM RIMFIRE AMMO

Firearm (type)	Barrel Length	VELOCITY (fps) at 11½ feet		Standard Deviation
		average	extreme var	
High Standard Double Nine (R#1)	5½"	1122	124	53
High Standard Double Nine (R#1)	5½"	1272	153	53
Ruger New Model (R)	5½"	1294	110	30
S & W Model 48 (R)	6"	1328	200	62
Colt New Frontier (R)	6"	1273	102	26
Test SAAMI P & V Barrel	24"	1807	114	31

extreme Var. = extreme variation
(R) = revolver
P & V = pressure and velocity

Because of the variations in performance which are invariably encountered, the savvy firearms enthusiast will carefully check field trajectory performance against table-suggested levels and make careful note of deviations. This will enable the shooter to score more hits and, therefore, derive more pleasure from his shooting.

4
Recoil

Firearm recoil should be one of the most important criteria used by shooters in the selection of a rifle or handgun cartridge or a shotgun gauge, yet, there are widespread misconceptions about how much a given cartridge or gauge will recoil. For instance, some loads fired in the average-weight 20-gauge shotgun will have more recoil than some loads fired in the average-weight 12-gauge gun.

Little is gained by being handicapped with excess recoil. A painful experience can cause a shooter to develop a flinch that will adversely affect his marksmanship. Many shooters have had their ability to shoot seriously hampered by the selection of a cartridge or load that simply had too much recoil for them to handle.

Shooters do not always have the opportunity to test a firearm and cartridge combination extensively prior to purchase. Knowing how to calculate the recoil of any cartridge/gun combination can therefore help the shooter make a sensible selection.

A new shooter should carefully note the calculated recoil levels of various combinations and work his or her way up the recoil ladder, staying with each load until there is no noticeable sensation of recoil. Doing so will prevent any gun-shyness or flinching. And an understanding of free recoil energy will help a shooter become more skillful.

Keep in mind, however, that certain other factors are important with respect to the sensation of *perceived* recoil. What you actually feel depends on how the recoil is delivered to, and absorbed by, your body.

A poorly fitting gun will seem to kick much harder than one that fits well (all other factors being equal). The sensation of recoil is greatly

A recoil pad can make a firearm more shootable. It works by cushioning (slowing down) recoil and thus reducing perceived recoil.

influenced by stock design, buttplate design, how the gun is held, and so on. One should always take advantage of the use of a recoil pad on all but the lightest-kicking guns or perhaps on special-purpose guns. As a bonus, the non-slip surface of a recoil pad protects your gun from slipping when you stand it in a corner and, thus, prevents damage. A recoil pad also will help your shooting by preventing the butt from slipping about on your shoulder.

Semiautomatic guns deliver substantially less perceived recoil than fixed-breech guns. This explains, at least in part, the great popularity of semiautomatic guns. Recoil-shy persons should consider the use of a semiautomatic firearm, especially for shotgunning.

In a fixed-breech shotgun system, normal ignition/barrel time for acceptable loads is in the order of 3 milliseconds, 3.5 milliseconds being about maximum. This is the total time in which the originally motionless gun is acted upon by the forces that generate recoil.

In a semiautomatic shotgun, the same ignition/barrel time occurs, but another factor comes into play—the moving parts of the gun mechanism. These include all the various parts of the gas system, bolt, springs, and so forth. Their movement has the effect of storing

Pin-on recoil absorbers, made of modern cushioning material, are extremely effective in reducing perceived recoil.

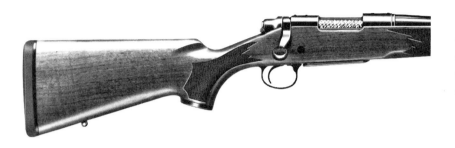

Some rifles are factory fitted with recoil pads. These, all else being equal, are always a wise choice. Comfort always means better accuracy.

For most shooters using a 12-gauge shotgun, a recoil pad can add a great deal of enjoyment. This Remington 870 trap grade is factory equipped with a thick, soft recoil pad.

the recoil energy and spreading out the time of application of recoil to the shooter.

The cycle time of most semiautomatic shotguns is on the order of 10 to 15 milliseconds, depending on gun characteristics, model, and so on. This spreads perceived recoil over a considerably longer period for semiautomatics than for fixed-breech guns. This time spread is enough to cause the sensation of recoil to seem milder. It is much like someone applying a sharp blow to your shoulder in comparison to someone pushing on your shoulder more slowly, though applying the same total force.

When properly instructed in safe gun handling, a new shooter will always find a semiautomatic shotgun more enjoyable and easier to shoot, all other things being equal. The same basics apply to semiautomatic rifles and handguns.

Calculating free recoil energy is not at all difficult. Armed with the appropriate equation, one need only insert the proper values to quickly calculate the recoil of any specific combination. Recoil calculations are related to the law of physics which states that for every action there is an opposite and equal reaction. In a shotgun, rifle, or handgun, the action generated by the burning gases pushing the ejecta from the muzzle is, of course, creating a reaction: recoil.

Recoil calculations are based on the gun weight, the weight of the

Slip-on recoil pads, such as this Uncle Mike's, are an affordable solution to heavy recoil and require no gunsmithing to install.

A semiautomatic 20-gauge shotgun will be comfortable for most beginners or recoil-shy shooters.

---

wad (if any), the weight of the shot charge or bullet, the muzzle velocity of the shot charge or bullet, the weight of the powder, and the velocity of the escaping gases at the muzzle.

Technically speaking, recoil is based on the law of the conservation of momentum. Some readers may remember from physics classes that this law states: If a force and its reaction act between two bodies (with no other forces present), equal and opposite changes in momentum will be given to the two bodies. The first body, of course, is the weight of the ejecta driven from the muzzle. (The weight of the ejecta includes the combined weights of the wad and the shot charge or bullet, as well as the weight of the propellant.) The second body is, of course, your gun.

So, the momentum of a free-recoiling gun is equal and opposite in direction to the momentum of the ejecta. Mathematically expressed, we have:

$$\text{Wt.}_{gun} \times \text{Vel.}_{gun} = \text{Wgt.}_{ejecta} \times \text{Vel.}_{ejecta} + \text{Wgt.}_{powder} \times \text{Vel.}_{powder\ gases}$$

or simply: $W_g V_g = W_e V_e + W_p V_p$

Calculations are with all weights in pounds and all velocities in feet per second.

Turning this about, the velocity of free recoil of a firearm, is, therefore, as follows:

$$\text{Vel.}_{gun} = \frac{\text{Wgt.}_{ejecta} \times \text{Vel.}_{ejecta} + \text{Wgt.}_{powder} \times \text{Vel.}_{powder\ gases}}{\text{Wgt.}_{gun}}$$

or: $V_g = \dfrac{W_e V_e + W_p V_p}{W_g}$

Naturally, all our weights are readily determined with the use of appropriate scales, and by chronograph we determine the velocity of the ejecta.

Even the smallest and youngest shooter will do well with centerfire cartridges if they are carefully selected. This youngster is using a lightweight Remington Model Seven chambered for the 223 Remington cartridge.

The effective velocity of the powder gases has been found, for all practical purposes, to be equal to the velocity of the ejecta multiplied by a factor of 1.5. This relationship has been established by well-documented scientific experiments both in Great Britain and the United States. Hence, our formula for velocity of free recoil of a gun becomes:

$$V_g = \frac{W_e V_e + 1.5 W_p V_e}{W_g}$$

To calculate the energy of free recoil, we have:
Kinetic energy = ½ Mass × Velocity²
or K.E. = ½MV²

$$\text{in which M = Mass} = \frac{\text{weight in pounds}}{32.174 \text{ (gravitational constant)}}$$

and V = Velocity.
Therefore, K.E., or recoil, can be expressed by:

$$\text{Free Recoil Energy} = \frac{W_g V_g^2}{64.348}$$

By substitution of V_g^2 we finally arrive at the standard equation:

$$\text{Free Recoil Energy} = \frac{(W_e V_e + 1.5 W_p V_e)^2}{64.348 W_g}$$

Wherein: W_e = Weight of ejecta (shot and wad or bullet in pounds). To obtain the weight in pounds, divide grain weights by 7,000. To convert ounces to pounds, divide by 16.

V_e = Velocity of ejecta in feet per second. Obtain this speed from ballistics tables in this book (under muzzle velocity).

W_p = Weight of powder in pounds. To obtain weight in pounds, divide grain weight by 7,000.

W_g = Weight of gun in pounds.

The foregoing formula can be rewritten as:

$$\text{Free Recoil Energy} = \frac{[V_e (W_e + 1.5 W_p)]^2}{64.348 W_g}$$

This last formula is easier to use when calculating and writing figures in long-hand or on an inexpensive calculator than the so-called standard formula. It simply is the result of applying the distributive principle of multiplication over addition.

Do not prematurely round values when working through the formula. Early rounding can create substantial errors.

As you can see, calculating the recoil for any specific load and gun combination is quick and easy. Powder-charge weights can be obtained by carefully breaking down a factory load using a collet-type bullet puller—or from a handloading data book.

An example of formula use is as follows: Assume a 7½ pound shotgun, a 1,200 fps muzzle velocity, a shot weight of 1⅛ ounces (492

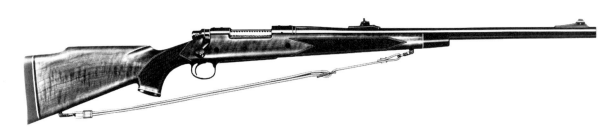

Remington 700 Safari-Grade rifle is available in 375 H&H Magnum, 416 Remington Magnum and 458 Winchester Magnum. Such cartridges produce a heap of recoil and are not for the novice or recoil-shy person.

grains), a powder-charge weight of 20.5 grains, and a wad of 38.0 grains. Solve for Free Recoil Energy.

$$F.R.E. = \frac{[V_e(W_e + 1.5\,W_p)]^2}{64.348 W_g}$$

$$F.R.E. = \frac{\left[1200\left(\left(\frac{492+38}{7000}\right)+1.50\left(\frac{20.5}{7000}\right)\right)\right]^2}{64.348 \times 7.5}$$

$$F.R.E. = \frac{[1200\,((0.0757143) + 1.50\,(0.0029286))]^2}{482.61}$$

$$F.R.E. = \frac{[1200\,(0.0757143 + 0.0043929)]^2}{482.61}$$

$$F.R.E. = \frac{[1200\,(.0801072)]^2}{482.61}$$

$$F.R.E. = \frac{(96.1284)^2}{482.61}$$

$$F.R.E. = \frac{9240.7154}{482.61}$$

F.R.E. = 19.147377
F.R.E. = 19.2 foot pounds

Important: When working with a load that has a muzzle velocity in excess of 2,499 feet per second, the constant 1.5 in the formula should be changed to a constant of 1.75. This allows for the increased velocity of the escaping gases.

Table 4.1 of shotshell/shotgun combinations was developed using the foregoing method. It will prove most useful in selecting suitable loads for new shooters, for advancing shooters through various recoil levels, for selecting loads for shooters who are recoil-shy, and so on. Obviously, the exact recoil of a load can vary slightly from brand to brand due to the variable of powder-charge weight and, in the case of shotshells, the variable wad weight. However, the tables will give a relative value that will be very close to the actual value of your selected load.

Velocities shown are industry nominals. These, of course, can vary and there will be some recoil change with any such variation.

Table 4.2 shows rifle-cartridge recoil based on a single rifle weight for ease of comparison. Velocities are advertised nominals.

Table 4.3 shows handgun-cartridge recoil based on a single gun weight for ease of use. Velocities are advertised nominals.

TABLE 4.1

12-GAUGE 3" CHAMBER, ASSUMED GUN WEIGHT = 8 POUNDS

Shot-Charge Weight (oz)	Dram Equivalent and Velocity		Free Recoil Energy
1⅞	4 D.E., 1210 fps	=	47.7 ft/lbs
1⅝	4 D.E., 1280 fps	=	41.5 ft/lbs
1⅜	3¾ D.E., 1295 fps	=	31.8 ft/lbs

12-GAUGE 2¾" CHAMBER, ASSUMED GUN WEIGHT = 7½ POUNDS

Shot-Charge Weight (oz)	Dram Equivalent and Velocity		Free Recoil Energy
1½	3¾ D.E., 1260 fps	=	36.7 ft/lbs
1¼	3¾ D.E., 1330 fps	=	29.7 ft/lbs
1¼	3¼ D.E., 1220 fps	=	24.0 ft/lbs
1⅛	3½ D.E., 1330 fps	=	24.5 ft/lbs
1⅛	3¼ D.E., 1255 fps	=	21.4 ft/lbs
1⅛	3 D.E., 1200 fps	=	19.2 ft/lbs
1⅛	2¾ D.E., 1145 fps	=	17.4 ft/lbs
1	3¼ D.E., 1290 fps	=	18.2 ft/lbs

16-GAUGE 2¾" CHAMBER, ASSUMED GUN WEIGHT = 7 POUNDS

Shot-Charge Weight (oz)	Dram Equivalent and Velocity		Free Recoil Energy
1¼	3¼ D.E., 1260 fps	=	27.9 ft/lbs
1⅛	3¼ D.E., 1295 fps	=	24.3 ft/lbs
1⅛	2¾ D.E., 1185 fps	=	20.1 ft/lbs
1	2½ D.E., 1165 fps	=	15.0 ft/lbs

20-GAUGE 3" CHAMBER, ASSUMED GUN WEIGHT = 7 POUNDS

Shot-Charge Weight (oz)	Dram Equivalent and Velocity		Free Recoil Energy
1¼	3 D.E., 1185 fps	=	23.7 ft/lbs

20-GAUGE 2¾″ CHAMBER, ASSUMED GUN WEIGHT = 6¾ POUNDS

Shot-Charge Weight (oz)	Dram Equivalent and Velocity		Free Recoil Energy
1⅛	2¾ D.E., 1175 fps	=	19.9 ft/lbs
1	2¾ D.E., 1220 fps	=	17.3 ft/lbs
1	2½ D.E., 1165 fps	=	15.7 ft/lbs
⅞	2½ D.E., 1210 fps	=	13.2 ft/lbs

28-GAUGE 2¾″ CHAMBER, ASSUMED GUN WEIGHT = 6½ POUNDS

Shot-Charge Weight (oz)	Dram Equivalent and Velocity		Free Recoil Energy
¾	2¼ D.E., 1295 fps	=	12.1 ft/lbs

.410 BORE 3″ CHAMBER, ASSUMED GUN WEIGHT = 5½ POUNDS

Shot-Charge Weight (oz)	Dram Equivalent and Velocity		Free Recoil Energy
11⁄16	Maximum, 1135 fps	=	7.6 ft/lbs

.410 BORE 2½″ CHAMBER, ASSUMED GUN WEIGHT = 5½ POUNDS

Shot-Charge Weight (oz)	Dram Equivalent and Velocity		Free Recoil Energy
½	Maximum, 1135 fps	=	4.8 ft/lbs

TABLE 4.2
RIFLE WEIGHT = 8 POUNDS

Caliber	Bullet Weight (gr)	Velocity (fps)		Free Recoil Energy (ft/lbs)
22 Hornet	45	2690	=	1.2
222 Remington	50	3140	=	3.3
22-250 Remington	55	3730	=	8.5
243 Winchester	100	2960	=	10.7
250-3000 Savage	87	3030	=	8.9
250-3000 Savage	100	2820	=	8.3
257 Roberts	117	2650	=	10.4
270 Winchester	100	3480	=	18.2
270 Winchester	130	3110	=	21.3
7mm Mauser	175	2420	=	13.5
7mm Rem. Mag.	175	2860	=	25.4
30 M1 Carbine	110	1990	=	2.8
30-30 Winchester	170	2200	=	9.1
300 Savage	180	2350	=	12.5
308 Winchester	150	2820	=	17.1
30-06 Springfield	180	2700	=	26.9
300 Win. Mag.	180	2950	=	32.0
338 Win. Mag.	250	2660	=	40.2
375 H&H Magnum	270	2530	=	42.2
44 Rem. Mag.	240	1760	=	9.4
444 Marlin	240	2350	=	21.1
45-70 Government	405	1330	=	13.3

TABLE 4.3
GUN WEIGHT = 40 OUNCES

Caliber	Bullet Weight (gr)	Velocity (fps)		Free Recoil Energy (ft/lbs)
9mm Luger	100	1320	=	2.6
38 Special	110 +P	1020	=	1.9
38 Special	158	755	=	2.0
357 Magnum	110	1295	=	3.2
357 Magnum	158	1235	=	6.1
44 Magnum	240	1350	=	13.7
45 ACP	230	810	=	4.7
45 Colt	255	860	=	6.6

In addition to the fact that advertised velocities are not always the velocities you will obtain, it is important to remember that a gun's weight plays a very influential role in determining recoil. Increase the gun weight by a factor of two, and recoil is cut in half; reduce the gun weight by half, and recoil is increased by a factor of two. Many of the rifle calibers listed are available only in guns somewhat lighter or heavier than our arbitrary 8 pounds. You will have to calculate the recoil for your own combination to obtain exact figures. Be sure to include all accessories in the weight of the gun—scope, mounts, etc.

Another consideration in selecting a cartridge is muzzle blast. So-called magnum-type cartridges, owing to their relatively large amounts of powder and high muzzle velocities, tend to create a very loud muzzle blast. Generally, this ear-shattering noise is handled best by experienced shooters. Many a shooter has developed a serious flinch from the muzzle blast of the 357 Magnum cartridge with 110-grain bullets. The recoil is only moderate, but the noise is deafening.

While current trends seem to be toward guns with more recoil and usually more muzzle blast, the average shooter would be wise to go in the other direction. His ability to shoot well and therefore perform satisfactorily on targets or in the field will be greatly enhanced.

The average practiced rifle shooter can usually handle up to about 22 foot/pounds of recoil without noticing the actual recoil. Most beginners can handle 11 to 13 foot/pounds without any problems. There are, of course, exceptions in both directions. An experienced shooter usually will find about 25 to 30 foot/pounds the maximum for comfortable shooting. In shotgun games where gun and body are kept in motion, about 2 or 3 foot/pounds can be added to those numbers.

Those who suffer from various physical handicaps may find that a cartridge/gun combination with recoil of no more than 10 or 11 foot/pounds will enable them to enjoy a sport they might otherwise have to give up.

In handguns, a beginner should choose loads having no more than 2 foot/pounds of recoil, while the more experienced shooter can handle up to 5 foot/pounds. It takes a lot of determination to handle recoil heavier than 7 foot/pounds in a handgun.

For rifle shooters, a natural order of progression with respect to recoil (and noise) would be as follows:

Start with the 22 Long Rifle cartridge and then progress to a 222 Remington or 223 Remington as the first centerfire round. Graduating to the 243 Winchester will provide the first big-game capability. The next jump, after plenty of shooting with the 243, can be a major step, perhaps to a 270 Winchester. This will give the shooter his first exposure to a modest level of recoil. Begin with brief sessions (perhaps 10 rounds) of shooting with the 270. *Slowly* work up until 40 rounds can be fired during a range session without fatigue or any tendency to flinch.

Handgunners can start with the 22 Long Rifle and then step up to a 38 Special using light 148-grain wadcutter bullets at modest target-level velocities. From there, it's easy to go on to 38 Special standard

158-grain loads and then to 38 Special +P high-velocity loads. The next jump, to a 357 Magnum or a 45 Auto cartridge, is a big one and short shooting sessions are a must in the beginning.

Shotgunners would do well to start with a 20-gauge using ⅞-ounce target loads and a medium-weight semiautomatic shotgun, then work up according to the loads shown in the accompanying recoil tables.

Keep in mind that felt, or perceived, recoil is generally much more severe on the target range than in the hunting field. When sighting-in and practicing with my 12-pound A-Square rifle chambered for the 416 Hoffman for an African safari, I did not find its recoil level (due to its substantial weight) unduly harsh, but I was conscious of it and fatigued after 30 or 40 rounds. However, when I used the same rifle in the field in Africa, the recoil went totally unnoticed. Indeed, it could not be remembered after the shot, even when special thought was later given to picturing it in my mind.

Hunters are often oblivious to considerably heavier recoil in the field than on a range. The trick is to ensure that a flinch is not developed at the range and carried into the field. A heavy gun may be a bit tiresome to carry all day, but it can make the range sessions a good deal more comfortable—and this can translate to better marksmanship in the field. Harsh recoil on the practice range, and the shooter's reaction to it, is often unconsciously memorized and carried into the field.

Making the right choice will ensure years of good shooting with your selected cartridges, even if you have not purchased a status symbol with respect to awesome power.

There may well be special situations in which a light rifle is a blessing, but if a shooter cannot carry a 9- to 12-pound rifle all day, how will he drag out a 200-pound deer carcass or handle the 150-pound quarter of an elk?

5

Centerfire Rifle Cartridges

At one time, all rifle shooters were handloaders. Like today's muzzleloading enthusiasts, they measured a quantity of black powder, which they then poured into the muzzle of the barrel, and then started a patched lead ball into the muzzle, pushing it down the bore with a ramrod to seat it tightly on the powder charge. The advent of rimfire cartridges was a quantum step forward for shooters. No longer did each shot have to be handloaded. And with rimfire cartridges came the first real opportunities to develop fast-loading single-shot and repeating firearms. From the rimfire shell, a "central-fire" cartridge was developed. The priming mixture was now moved from the rim of the cartridge into the central portion of the case head. This priming mix was inserted from the mouth end of the cartridge, for there was no primer-pocket opening. From these cartridges, which saw early use in 45-70 caliber, were developed the modern centerfire rounds with their exposed primer pockets at the rear of the case.

By the mid-1880s, centerfire cartridges were firmly established, making possible the first efforts with smokeless powder and higher velocities. By the mid-1890s, cartridges such as the 30-30 Winchester were changing shooters' ideas about bullet weights, case sizes, and velocities.

Attempts have been made to improve upon the centerfire cartridge. During the 1950s, there were the Gyro-Jet cartridges, caseless rounds that were actually tiny rockets. And there was the Daisy caseless cartridge which used a self-consuming case. Other attempts have been made to advance beyond the conventional modern cartridge. However, each has failed to catch on because of a number of factors. Accuracy, cost, convenience, producibility, practicality, and terminal

Typical of early centerfire cartridges, the 45-70-405 Government had a bullet of comparatively large diameter, a straight-walled case, and a rimmed head.

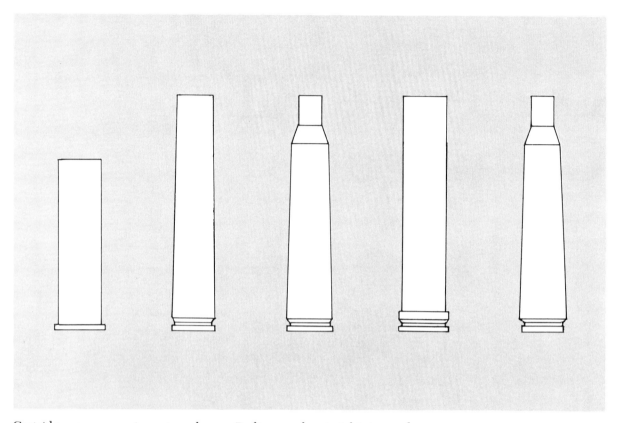

Cartridge cases come in various shapes. Bodies may be straight, tapered, or necked. Case heads may be rimmed, semirimmed, rimless, belted, or rebated. Almost every possible combination can be encountered.

---

ballistics have all been less than well served by such attempts at improving ammunition. It is highly likely that, for sporting purposes, our current state-of-the-art rimfire and centerfire ammunition will maintain a *status quo* for at least another 50 years.

Brass centerfire cartridge cases have taken many forms. The earliest, like the 45-70, were often of large caliber with a straight-walled body and an enlarged rim area. The rim served to give the firearm's extractor a purchase and it was also used to headspace the firearm—that is, to control chamber and cartridge dimensions to assure proper cartridge-to-rifle fit.

Other cases had a tapered body and a sloping shoulder area, but retained the rim of the earliest cartridges. Examples of this configuration are the 30-30 Winchester and the 303 British. Later cartridge development concentrated on bottleneck rimless cases. Some examples of this type are the 222 Remington, 270 Winchester, and 35 Whelen. Bottleneck cases using a belt, an enlarged portion at the head section, are often associated with "magnum" calibers.

The primer used in today's centerfire cartridge is a highly devel-

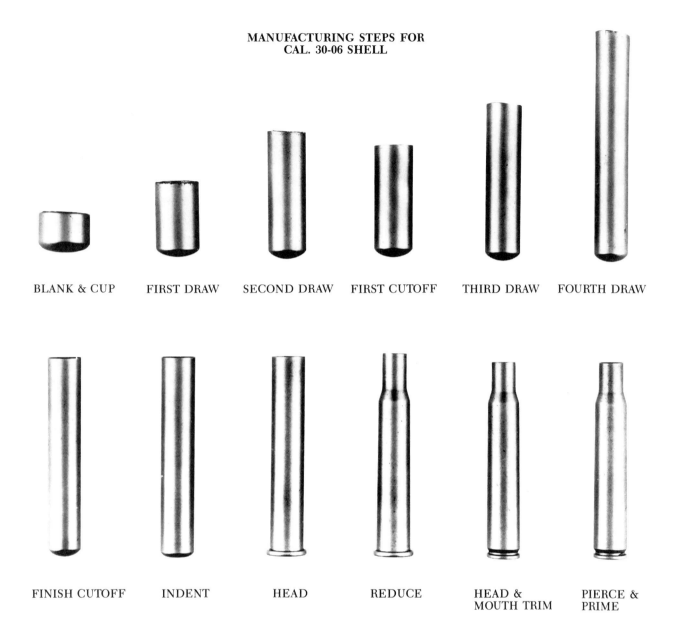

Manufacturing steps in making a cartridge case from a brass "coin," as practiced by Winchester.

oped ignition system. Its sensitivity to firing-pin blows and its ability to provide the necessary heat and fuel to ignite the powder charge have been highly refined. At one time, the chemicals used in the priming mix caused cartridge cases to become brittle (and unusable for repeated reloading) and also caused bores to corrode. Today, all primers are non-mercuric (mercury was ruinous to brass) and non-corrosive. It is, however, still possible to encounter old (pre-1950) ammunition that contains mercuric and corrosive primers. The use of such ammunition makes little sense considering the damage it can inflict on the firearm's bore or the cartridge case.

Bullet development progressed at a much slower rate than case and primer development. With jacketed bullets came problems of bore fouling (smears of jacket being deposited on the bore's surface) and difficulties with expansion. Turn-of-the-century hunting bullets often were crude by today's standards. Expansion, if it occurred at all, was often unreliable. Today, the shooter will find that almost all factory bullets are accurate, leave a minimal amount of bore fouling, and expand quite well. Indeed, we now have the advantage of controlled expansion over a wide velocity range.

Some bullets, such as the Remington Core-Lokt, Winchester Silvertip, and Nosler Partition, offer near-perfection with respect to expansion and penetration in big game. Other bullets have been designed to expand rapidly and violently when encountering the minimal resistance offered by a tiny prairie dog or a woodchuck. The hunter must always be aware of which bullet is designed for which game. Errors in bullet selection can be the cause of crippled but lost game.

The array of currently available centerfire cartridges is extensive—more than 90 different rifle cartridges are currently loaded in the United States. Some of these are available in but a single bullet weight, others in more than a half-dozen different weights. Some are quite obsolete, but shooter demand keeps the ammunition companies

Most cartridges fall into the bottlenecked, rimless category. *From left*: 300 Savage, 308 Winchester, and 30-06 Springfield.

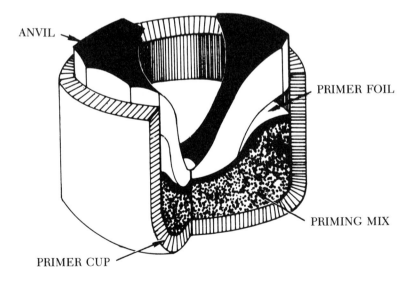

The tiny primer used in all of today's centerfire ammunition is a highly developed ignition system that supplies the necessary heat and fuel to ignite the powder charge in a cartridge case.

Magnum cartridges, such as this 350 Remington, often have a "belt" of brass around the case head.

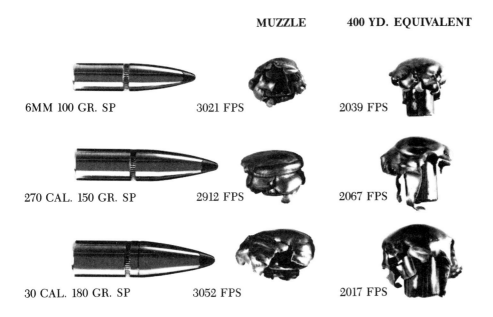

Hornady bullets of varying calibers showing expansion characteristics for points of impact at close and distant ranges.

manufacturing cartridges in calibers for which no firearm has been produced for 40 or more years. Some available calibers are unknown to the majority of shooters.

Faced with a seemingly endless selection of calibers and bullet weights, not to mention different brands and bullet styles, the shooter can easily overlook a cartridge that might suit his needs perfectly. It's also tempting to choose a cartridge just because it's new or currently popular in the press.

There are no shortcuts to caliber knowledge. If the shooter is unaware of a specific cartridge or loading, it might not matter because many cartridges have nearly identical performance levels. But a lack of awareness can just as likely lead to a poor cartridge choice or improper bullet application.

The purpose of this chapter is to inform the reader of all that is available for each given shooting purpose. How to select from the myriad choices will be treated in Chapter 7. Each cartridge will be described generally with reference to ascending bullet diameter and low-to-high ballistic level. Where appropriate and possible, the cartridge's name will be discussed with respect to any significant meaning, and alternate designations will be included. The reader interested in specific cartridges might be tempted to thumb past all the other cartridges, but doing so prevents many revealing comparisons and insights. A thoroughly useful knowledge of cartridges is built upon an overall understanding.

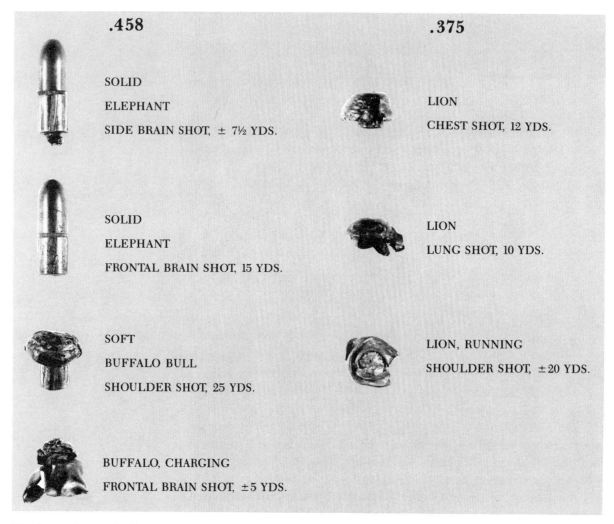

Fired Winchester bullets recovered from game.

Of course, we will discuss the appropriate applications of the various calibers and the bullet weights. The reader should note that appropriate bullet selection can make some cartridges suitable for shooting gophers or for shooting caribou. Bullet-weight selection will be treated by categories. The categories included are:

Varmint: Loads for off-season game, primarily small—such as prairie dogs, crows, woodchucks, and in some instances coyotes.

Furbearer: Loads for foxes, coyotes, bobcats, and the like, essentially a subcategory of varmint loads. Remember that whether a given cartridge is adequate for a coyote or bobcat may depend on hunting method—that is, whether the animal is spotted and taken across some wide canyon or called in close. A varmint load may also be a furbearer load, either with the same bullet or—more often—with a full-metal-cased bullet.

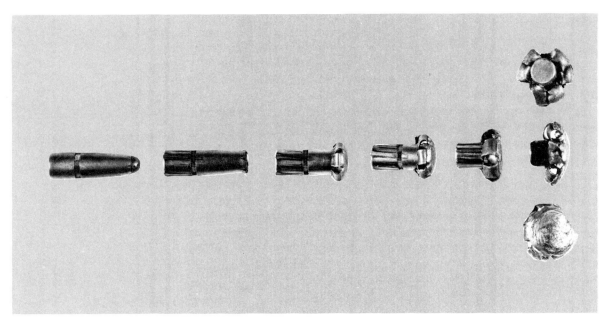

Perfect controlled (progressive) expansion is exhibited by this Winchester 180-grain Power Point fired from a 30-06 Springfield rifle.

Plinking: Loads for informal practice, usually at short range, with inexpensive ammunition of military origin, or generic packaging, or of promotional-type trademarks.

Target: Loads primarily intended for competitive shooting. Often, this ammunition must be handloaded, but in some instances special factory ammunition is loaded to a higher-than-normal level of accuracy.

Light Big Game: Loads generally and successfully used for game weighing up to 300 pounds.

Medium Big Game: Loads suitable for game weighing up to 500, perhaps even 700 pounds.

Heavy Big Game: Loads for the heaviest North American game, including large elk, moose, grizzly, and brown bear.

Dangerous Game: Loads useful for both heavy North American game and dangerous African game.

Unclassified: Loads generally for obsolete firearms. (These loads, used for specific purposes in the past, are often considered inadequate for such purposes today.)

Specific range limitations are often essential in light of a cartridge's trajectory or energy levels. In general, short range means 50 yards or less, medium range means 150 yards or less, and long range means up to 275 yards. An extra-long-range rating means a competent shooter could perhaps take shots to 350 or 400 yards. However, most often it is necessary to handload your ammunition to achieve the necessary accuracy at such protracted ranges.

Generally, Remington, Winchester, and Federal produce loads for the most popular cartridges. An attempt will be made to note where availability is limited. Included also will be cartridges and loads available only from some of the smaller ammunition producers such as A-Square and Hornady.

Cartridge popularity plays an important role in general availability. At this writing, Winchester manufactures loaded rounds for the 284 Winchester and 348 Winchester cartridges, but despite the major brand name, this ammunition would rarely be stocked by any but the biggest gun shops. Popularity (or probable availability) will be noted in connection with such cartridges.

Some of the author's comments will no doubt bring cries of anguish from shooters who have put cartridges to extreme, never intended, applications. There are those who insist that the 222 Remington is a fine cartridge for deer and those who insist that a 375 H&H is barely adequate for elk. After almost 35 years of full-time activity in the firearms and ammunition industry, the author shares no such extremist views. Recommendations in the following pages are based not only on extensive personal knowledge but—perhaps mostly—on the experience of thousands of shooters and hunters.

The reader should remember, too, that exceptions to all suggestions can occur. A recoil-shy shooter may be justified in using a 243 on large caribou, if he picks his shots carefully and hits where he aims. Equally, the one-gun owner may reasonably use a 30-06 for moose—with the proper ammo and sufficient expertise. All the same, after hearing all the arguments, from those of the smallbore fanatics to those of the bigbore extremists, I stand firmly behind the comments made for each cartridge and bullet.

17 CALIBER (.172" bullet diameter)

17 Remington

25-Grain Bullet—Varmint

This cartridge is loaded only by Remington and is anything but popular. Indeed, shooter use is so low that it is very difficult to find such staples as suitable small-diameter cleaning rods or bullets for reloading. Barrel-cleaning problems are particularly nettlesome because of the bullet-jacket fouling that seems unique to this cartridge.

The cartridge makes a fine varmint round on calm days at ranges up to perhaps 225 yards. However, even a slight breeze can cause the tiny 25-grain bullet to drift severely, making it difficult to score hits. This is the only factory cartridge ever loaded with the tiny 17-caliber bullet.

Cartridge nomenclature is obviously based on basic caliber and the manufacturer's name.

22 CALIBER (.224″ bullet diameter)
22 Hornet
45-Grain Bullet—Varmint

When used at ranges up to about 125 yards, the Hornet ranks among the all-time-great varmint cartridges with respect to accuracy. It would be difficult to find a factory gun/ammunition combination in this caliber that did not prove to be accurate, and groups of less than 1 inch are commonplace. This cartridge was being produced by the ammunition manufacturers long before commercial rifles were chambered for it.

Hunting in suburbia requires a relatively quiet and highly accurate cartridge. The Hornet fills this need very well, yet it is dying, the craze for ultra-high velocity and long-range shooting having all but driven it into obsolescence.

For those who have become bored with varmint shooting, as opposed to varmint *hunting*, the 22 Hornet will provide a great deal of satisfaction. Wherever varmints can be stalked to 125 yards or less is considered 22 Hornet country.

Another nice plus with the Hornet is very long barrel life. A good Hornet barrel seems to last forever (a result of the moderate velocity and powder charge). The shooter wishing to purchase an accurate Hornet rifle may need to find a used one or buy an import such as one

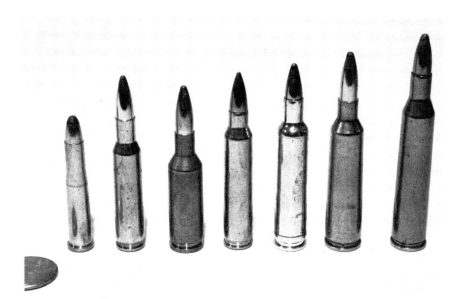

Typical of today's small-caliber cartridges are, *from left*: 22 Hornet, 222 Remington, 22 PPC, 223 Remington, 224 Weatherby Magnum, 22-250 Remington, and the 220 Swift.

of the Anschutz models. One American company, Kimber, currently makes fine, if expensive, rifles in this caliber.

In Europe this cartridge is known as the 5.6 × 35Rmm.

218 Bee

46-Grain Bullet—Varmint

Introduced in the late 1920s in a Winchester lever-action rifle, the 218 Bee is based on the 25-20 cartridge and originally was intended to supply a Hornet-like cartridge for lever-action rifle fans.

In lever-actions, the Bee did not satisfy the needs of varminting accuracy. However, in bolt-action guns it proved useful, though never quite as accurate as the Hornet. While it has slightly more velocity, its accuracy capability limits it to the same 125 yards as the Hornet. This cartridge is all but dead and it would not be surprising to see Winchester, the only current supplier, abandon this round.

The cartridge's nomenclature has no specific meaning and was simply an attempt to create another "Hornet" image.

221 Fireball

50-Grain Bullet—Varmint

Only Remington loads this round, which originally was designed as a shortened 222 Remington to be used in the Remington bolt-action single-shot handgun. Its name has no specific meaning (and the "221" may have been a ploy to suggest a short 222).

A few custom makers have chambered rifles for this cartridge, as has Kimber. The round is not very popular, though it is accurate and effective on varmints out to 150 yards, perhaps a bit more when used in a rifle-length barrel.

For those considering a Hornet rifle, a 221 Fireball might be a better choice today. The Fireball's case is considerably stronger than the Hornet's, perhaps a bit easier to come by, and equally accurate. The 221 duplicates Hornet rifle ballistics when fired from a handgun-length barrel, and exceeds the Hornet by several hundred feet per second in a rifle barrel. Furthermore, the 221's 50-grain bullet drifts less in a crosswind.

222 Remington

50-Grain Bullet—Target, Varmint
55-Grain Full-Metal-Jacket Bullet—Furbearer

The 222 had, for a good many years, the reputation of being the most accurate cartridge ever designed. It reigned supreme in benchrest competition for quite some time. Today, several cartridges are potentially more accurate, but the differences in performance are, for the most part, meaningless to the average shooter/hunter.

With good handloads and the right rifle, a capable person can group 10 shots into a ½-inch or smaller circle at 100 yards. Some lots of tested factory ammunition are fully capable of 1-inch or less 10-shot groups at the same range.

It has been popular to call the 222 Remington a 250-yard varmint cartridge. However, when the quarry may be a good-sized woodchuck, the 222 seems best restricted to 200 or perhaps 225 yards.

The 222 Remington was, at one time, one of the very most popular cartridges. While its fans have, for the most part, switched to the 223 Remington, it continues to be a useful cartridge for medium-range varminting.

Overseas, this cartridge is called the 5.7 × 43mm.

22 PPC

52-Grain Bullet—Target, Varmint

The 22 PPC, for many years available only to handloaders, is a wildcat cartridge named for its co-designers. Its parent cartridge, the 6mm PPC, is without a doubt the best-conceived cartridge ever de-

The 22 PPC (*left*) and the 6mm PPC (*right*) are the two most accurate factory-loaded cartridges in the world. The 10-shot groups shown are typical of factory-loaded Sako ammunition in these calibers.

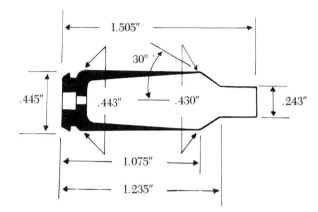

The 22 PPC cartridge has a small case with unique features to achieve very superior accuracy. Flash hole measures .06 inch instead of the usual .08 inch; its powder charge is completely consumed before the bullet exits.

---

signed with respect to accuracy. This 22-caliber version is simply a necked-down 6mm PPC case to appeal to those who favor 22-caliber loads.

The only factory ammunition currently available for this cartridge is made by Sako of Finland. It is distributed in the United States by Stoeger. While it's not an American factory-loaded cartridge, it is very highly regarded by benchrest shooters and is, indeed, today's most accurate factory-loaded 22-caliber cartridge. This author has fired many groups with factory Sako ammunition that resulted in 10 shots clustering into less than ⁴⁄₁₀-inch at 100 yards—and these were fired from an out-of-the-box Sako Varminter single-shot rifle.

American ammunition companies, suffering perhaps from a not-invented-by-us syndrome, have resisted the overwhelming superiority of the PPC cartridge. Hence, despite its virtues, the 22 PPC has not yet become very popular with shooters outside of the benchrest competitors' circle.

With a muzzle velocity of 3,400 feet per second, the 22 PPC is a fine cartridge for long-range varminting. Having more than ample accuracy and a very flat trajectory, this cartridge makes hitting at long ranges almost easy.

223 Remington

40-Grain Bullet—Varmint
55-Grain Bullet—Varmint, Target
55-Grain Full-Metal-Jacket Bullet—Furbearer, Plinking
64-Grain Bullet—see text

The 223 Remington is also known as the 5.56mm and (under the latter designation) is the official small-arms cartridge of the U.S. military forces. Undoubtedly it's one of the 10 most popular cartridges in current production. Federal is the only company to manufacture the 40-grain factory loads, but everyone produces the 55-grain loads. Paramilitary-style full-metal-jacketed 55-grain-bullet loadings, which are very inexpensive, are available from both U.S. and foreign manufacturers.

The 64-grain loading is a fairly new development, offered by Winchester as a light big-game load, specifically with mention of antelope. I fear this may prove to be an overextension of this cartridge's capability.

The 223 Remington, while perhaps not as accurate as the 222, is suitable for the most demanding of varmint-hunting situations and is proper for long-range shooting.

The ammunition companies have warned that military cartridges of this caliber can cause pressure increases of 5,000 to 8,000 pounds per square inch when used in sporting chambers. This is due to a difference in chamber-throat configuration and loading specifications.

Because the cartridge is accurate, readily available, and, in the FMC paramilitary type rounds, quite inexpensive, it is a great favorite with plinkers and other shooters interested in a "fun" cartridge. However, the 223 Remington is equally a cartridge for the serious varmint hunter who requires minute-of-angle accuracy.

The 223 Remington designation was perhaps an attempt on Remington's part to suggest a cartridge somewhat larger than the 222 Remington.

The 223 Remington (*left*) is the standard U.S. military cartridge today. It has been preceded in this honor by such rounds as the 45-70 Government, 30-40 Krag, 30-06 Springfield and 308 Winchester.

222 Remington Magnum

55-Grain Bullet—Varmint

The 222 Remington Magnum was an early attempt to supply the U.S. military with a new cartridge. As such, it never succeeded, but it was quickly marketed as a varmint round. Basically, it's an elongated 222 Remington, hence the name.

The 222 Remington Magnum makes quite a suitable long-range varmint round but has been completely overshadowed by the 223 Remington. Shooters who own both 222 Remington Magnum and 223 Remington rifles should take great care in keeping ammo and guns segregated. The ammo looks very much alike, but a 223 Remington shell fired in a longer 222 Remington Magnum chamber will burst and can cause serious property and personal injury.

The 222 Remington Magnum is an almost obsolete cartridge. It no longer has much purpose since the 223 Remington duplicates its ballistics and is somewhat more accurate.

225 Winchester

55-Grain Bullet—Varmint

This cartridge never gained any notable degree of popularity. Indeed, it has been the source of wildly varying opinions. It would seem that shooters have experienced a wide range of performance levels with respect to accuracy, ranging from excellent to near useless. Ballistics researchers also have reported wide ranges in ballistic uniformity. This sometimes hot and sometimes cold performance level is what undoubtedly kept the cartridge from becoming popular.

The 225 is dying; perhaps it already is dead. Its availability is extremely limited and there seems little reason to consider this round for any specific purpose. Handloaders have found it a particularly difficult cartridge.

224 Weatherby Magnum

55-Grain Bullet—Varmint

This cartridge has been available only from Weatherby, a company whose ammunition is loaded in Europe by Norma. The cartridge is

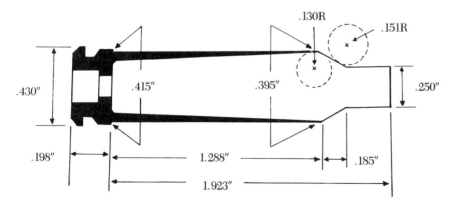

The 224 Weatherby Magnum case is the only commercial U.S. 22 caliber cartridge to use a belted case-head configuration.

capable of very fine accuracy and has a sufficiently flat trajectory to make it an ideal long-range varmint cartridge, perhaps even a very-long-range round. Ballistically, the 224 Weatherby Magnum is just slightly behind the 22-250 Remington.

Because only Weatherby has generally chambered rifles for this cartridge, it has never gained a great deal of popularity. Brass and ammunition are difficult to find and certainly expensive, compared to the 22-250 Remington. For the shooter, who can tolerate the inconvenience of difficult-to-find ammo and the expense, the 224 Weatherby will prove very satisfactory in all other areas. It is the only commercially available 22-caliber U.S. cartridge with a belted case.

The 224 designation is the true bullet diameter and the belted case would seem to help justify the Magnum nomenclature.

22-250 Remington

40-Grain Bullet—Varmint
53-Grain Bullet—Varmint
55-Grain Bullet—Varmint

This cartridge provides ample ballistics and accuracy to be used for very-long-range varminting. It has almost completely replaced the 220 Swift and, indeed, has a reputation as the ultimate very-long-range varmint round.

The 22-250 Remington started life as a wildcat long before Remington began to manufacture commercially available ammunition. Today, all major ammunition companies load this round. However, only Federal loads the 40-grain bullet.

The 22-250, originally also called the 22 Varminter, was based upon a 250 Savage cartridge necked down to 22 caliber. It is from this parent cartridge that the name was coined.

As with all 22-caliber cartridges, recoil is very low, but unlike all smaller-cased rounds, the noise level is notably high. Hence, it is not a cartridge for an inexperienced shooter.

220 Swift

50-Grain Bullet—Varmint
55/60-Grain Bullet—Varmint

This old-timer continues to have a small but devoted following. Today it is loaded only by Hornady and Norma. It's the fastest true 22-caliber cartridge ever made commercially. It is also quite accurate. However, the 22-250 Remington nearly duplicates its performance while using less powder and permitting notably increased barrel life.

The Swift cartridge has lost most of its former popularity. Today it is difficult to find, and only Ruger chambers new rifles for it.

24 (6mm) CALIBER (.243" bullet diameter)
6mm PPC

70-Grain Bullet—Target & Varmint

This is without debate the world's most accurate cartridge. It underwent extensive development by its creators, Ferris Pindell and Dr. Lou Palmisano, and PPC stands for Pindell, Palmisano Cartridge. It has established almost every possible benchrest record. And when a benchrest record is broken, it is invariably with the 6mm PPC. The phenomenal accuracy of this cartridge makes it no big task to put 10 shots into a group measuring less than ¼-inch at 100 yards. Indeed, its accuracy is so superior that it has almost excluded all others from competition.

For years, the 6mm PPC was strictly a handloading proposition. Specially manufactured 220 Russian cases were reformed into the 6mm PPC. (The 220 Russian case was derived from the 7.62 × 39 Russian.) These cases were produced with the required flash-hole diameter of .06-inch (instead of the usual .08-inch) only by Sako in

The 6mm PPC cartridge, the world's most accurate round, is shown (*left*) with the other popular 6mm cartridge—the 243 Win.

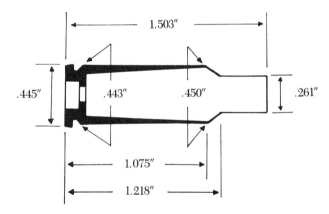

The 6mm PPC cartridge has a short, stubby case to insure that the powder charge is uniformly ignited. It is not only the very best benchrest cartridge ever designed, but also a fine medium- to long-range varmint round.

Finland. Despite its overwhelming superiority as a benchrest and target cartridge, U.S. manufacturers still refuse to produce this round. 'Tis a big shame!

With a muzzle velocity of 3,140 feet per second, the 6mm PPC—or simply "Six", as it is affectionately called—makes a fine medium- to long-range varmint round.

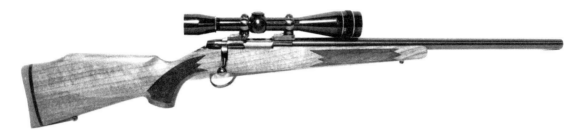

The world's most accurate factory centerfire hunting rifle and cartridge? No doubt about it—it's the Sako single-shot Varminter and the 6mm PPC.

243 Winchester

80-Grain Bullet—Varmint
85-Grain Bullet—Varmint
100-Grain Bullet—Light Big Game

This cartridge is easily included among the 10 most popular rounds in the United States. Named for its nominal bullet diameter, the 243 Winchester was an instant success. It is based on a necked-down 308 Winchester cartridge, is very accurate, and makes a superb very-long-range varmint cartridge.

With 100-grain bullets, it has been described by my late friend, outdoor writer and guide Les Bowman, as the ideal deer cartridge. Indeed, a great many thousands of folks agree. For use as a long-range

Popular small-bore cartridges, larger than 22 caliber, in current production include, *from left*: 6mm PPC, 243 Winchester, 6mm Remington, 240 Weatherby Magnum, 250 Savage, 257 Roberts, 25-06 Remington, and 257 Weatherby Magnum.

antelope and whitetail cartridge, the 243 leaves little to be desired. And its low recoil makes it popular with novices and recoil-shy but well-experienced riflemen.

The 243 is one of the very best selections for the one-rifle hunter who wishes to hunt both varmints and light big game, especially if most of the shooting will be for varmints. This author feels, however, that if the emphasis is on light big game, a larger bore diameter might be a bit more appropriate.

The metric designation for this cartridge is 6.2 × 52mm.

6mm Remington

80-Grain Bullet—Varmint
100-Grain Bullet—Light Big Game

When originally introduced as the 244 Remington, this cartridge was combined with guns having a 1-in-12-inch rifling twist. As a result, bullets heavier than 90 grains were not practical. It never proved very popular. Remington tried to give it new life by switching to a 1-in-9½-inch twist and renaming it the 6mm Remington. Despite this effort, it has never become as popular as Winchester's 243. The slightly larger case capacity results in a very slight increase in velocity over the 243. The difference is not enough to be of any consequence.

The 100-grain loading should not be used in rifles marked 244 since the twist rate is inadequate to stabilize the longer bullet.

Gun for gun, the 243 will usually prove somewhat more accurate, and it's a lot easier to find a good-shooting reload for the Winchester round. These two cartridges produce almost identical ballistics, so it makes sense to select the smaller and more accurate 243.

240 Weatherby Magnum

70-Grain Bullet—Varmint
87-Grain Bullet—Varmint
100-Grain Bullet—Light Big Game

This is a proprietary cartridge for Weatherby rifles. Because of the limited number of rifles chambered for it, the 240 Weatherby Magnum has not gained any great popularity. Many of the folks who choose a 6mm cartridge can see little advantage to a bigger, belted magnum case with a bullet diameter of 24 caliber when, after all, the 243 Winchester accomplishes everything that can be done with a 24-caliber bullet. Still, this is a very useful long- to ultra-long-range cartridge.

As long as there are Weatherby rifles, the cartridge will probably remain alive. But don't expect to find ammo in any but the very largest of gun shops.

25 CALIBER (.257" bullet diameter)

25-20 Winchester

86-Grain Bullet—Small Game

This cartridge derived its name from its basic caliber and the fact that the case was originally charged with 20 grains of black powder. It is, for all practical purposes, obsolete. Originally it was designed as a small-game lever-action rifle cartridge, but a few bolt-action rifles were also chambered for it. The Winchester Model 43 bolt-action, clip-fed rifle in this caliber is still a highly favored turkey rifle among some hunters. This cartridge is much too small to be humanely used on any big game.

At one time, the 25-20 was loaded with a high-speed 60-grain jacketed bullet designed for short- to medium-range varminting.

25-35 Winchester

117-Grain Bullet—Light Big Game

This cartridge originated in the 1890s and derived its name from its caliber and the 35-grain powder charge used in its rimmed case. The case is basically the 30-30 Winchester necked down to 25 caliber.

The 25-35 Winchester was intended for light big game. However, the cartridge has a ballistic level that makes it barely suitable for that purpose, and the ranges must be kept short.

This round is very much obsolete and extremely difficult to find. Only Winchester continues to manufacture it.

250 Savage

100-Grain Bullet—Light Big Game

Originally called the 250-3000 (250 for its bore diameter and 3000 for the muzzle velocity of its original 87-grain varmint load), the 250 was popular in the Savage 99 lever-action and a number of bolt-action rifles. The original 87-grain bullet was intended as a high-velocity big-game load. When it was quickly realized that this weight was insufficient for the purpose, a 100-grain loading was introduced. The 87-grain bullet was loaded until quite recently, when many of the ammo factories began to drop varmint-weight bullets in many calibers.

Remington, Ruger, and, to a lesser extent, Winchester firearms are still chambered for this cartridge. The Remington Model 700 Classic is still available for this cartridge in many gun shops, although the chambering has been discontinued. There is nothing to give the 250 an advantage over the 243 Winchester. Indeed, the latter has superior ballistics, so the 250 is no longer popular.

257 Roberts

100-Grain Bullet—Light Big Game
117-Grain Bullet—Light Big Game
120-Grain Bullet—Light Big Game

Originally, this round was called the 25 Roberts, named after Ned Roberts, its designer. It is basically a 7 × 57mm necked down to 25 caliber. Some chamber variations, which occurred during its wildcat days, caused Remington to rename it when they standardized dimensions and added it to their line of factory ammo.

Its larger case capacity makes it vastly superior to the 250 Savage. The 117- and 120-grain bullets perform better on light big game than 100-grain bullets of either 25 or 6mm diameter. The Federal 120-grain load using the Nosler Partition bullet is especially well suited for light big game. At one time, factory loadings were available in 87-grain weight.

During recent years the ammunition companies have increased the ballistics of factory loads. These loads are sometimes designated +P, the +P standing for added chamber pressure. Despite any merits, the 243 Winchester is far more popular. The 257 is a semi-obsolete cartridge, though Ruger continues to chamber rifles for this round. It is not an easy caliber to find, especially in rural ammunition outlets. It is useful over medium to long ranges.

Bullet expansion of the 257 Roberts.

25-06 Remington

87-Grain Bullet—Varmint
90-Grain Bullet—Varmint
100-Grain Bullet—Light Big Game
117-Grain Bullet—Light Big Game
120-Grain Bullet—Light Big Game

The 25-06 Remington was named for its caliber and for its parent cartridge, the 30-06 Springfield. As might be assumed, it is a 30-06 Springfield necked down to 25 caliber. The 25-06 was around for a great many years as a wildcat, in sometimes varying forms, before it was "legitimized" by Remington. This is a very fine extra-long-range cartridge.

It is well suited to the entire range of light big game, with the 120-grain bullet as the correct choice for animals over 200 pounds. It also performs well as a long-range varmint cartridge, sometimes being used at ranges up to 400 yards.

Due to the very large case capacity (over-bore), barrel life is somewhat short in comparison to other 25-caliber rifles. Noise level is quite high, and the muzzle blast prevents some shooters from doing their very best. Accuracy is usually good if the shooter is able to handle the noise. Recoil, while moderate, really makes this a less than ideal choice for youngsters or most women.

257 Weatherby Magnum

87-Grain Bullet—Varmint
100-Grain Bullet—Light Big Game
117-Grain Bullet—Light Big Game
120-Grain Bullet—Light Big Game

For years this was a proprietary cartridge, with firearms and ammunition available only from Weatherby. Recently, the Korean ammunition manufacturer, PMC, has announced that it will sell the Weatherby caliber in the U.S. However, since the 25-06 Remington cartridge closely matches the performance of this round, it is doubtful that the 257 Weatherby Magnum will ever become even remotely popular.

The cartridge was named for the bullet's nominal diameter and incorporates a belted case. It is very suitable for extra-long-range shooting.

26 (6.5mm) CALIBER (.264" bullet diameter)

6.5 Remington Magnum

120-Grain Bullet—Light Big Game

This is one of only two cartridges now manufactured in the U.S. using a .264-inch bullet diameter. Even in Europe, where the 6.5s first appeared, this diameter has never been popular.

The 6.5 Remington Magnum is a very short cartridge, by magnum nomenclature standards, but it does have a belted case head of the same dimensions as many other "magnum" rifle cartridges. The case head on this round is identical to the 300 Holland & Holland (H&H) Magnum.

Chambered only by Remington, and only in short-action rifles, the 6.5 Remington Magnum never achieved even a modicum of popularity. Remington has always been the only manufacturer of the cartridge, which now is rarely found on ammunition dealers' shelves.

Originally, Remington also offered a 100-grain varmint-weight load in this cartridge. Remington chose to use the metric designation of the bullet diameter when naming it.

264 Winchester Magnum

140-Grain Bullet—Light & Medium Big Game

The 264 Winchester Magnum is a dying cartridge. The 100-grain factory varmint load has long been discontinued. The factory 140-grain load will accomplish almost any task that can be done with a 270 Winchester using 130- or 150-grain bullets, but barrel life with the 264 Winchester Magnum is notably shorter.

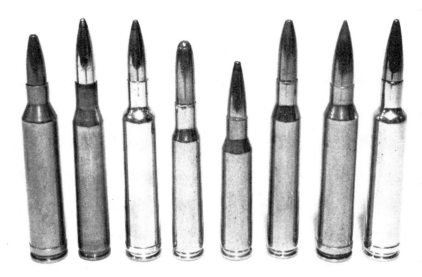

Medium-bore cartridges currently available in the U.S. include the following, *from left*: 264 Winchester Magnum, 270 Winchester, 270 Weatherby Magnum, 7mm Mauser, 7mm-08 Remington, 280 Remington, 7mm Remington Magnum, 7mm Weatherby Magnum.

While the 264 attained more popularity in the U.S. than any other 6.5mm cartridge, it never gained enough momentum to keep it going. Indeed, the 270 had already long been established and the 264 offered no real advantages. When introduced, the only thing really new about this 6.5mm-diameter cartridge was the novelty of its bore diameter.

Nonetheless, the 264 is an effective big-game cartridge and it has been successfully used on game as large as elk. However, it's good for such use only at medium ranges.

The 264 was named for its bullet diameter and its belted "magnum"-style case. It is a useful cartridge for extra-long-range hunting of light big game.

27 CALIBER (.277" bullet diameter)

270 Winchester

100-Grain Bullet—Varmint
130-Grain Bullet—Light Big Game
150-Grain Bullet—Medium Big Game

The 270 Winchester is based on a 30-06 case necked to 27 caliber, although its case is slightly longer than its parent cartridge. From the beginning it has been a very successful cartridge. Many consider, perhaps rightly, that 27 caliber is about as small a bullet diameter as will prove really ideal for medium big game. This author agrees. The 270 has taken countless scores of game, from tiny varmints to elk and a heap of African plains game. It is an ideal cartridge for long-range shooting as it has a very flat trajectory when used with spitzer bullets.

One of the great virtues of the 270 Winchester is its noticeably lighter recoil than the ubiquitous 30-06 Springfield cartridge, and it is at least as accurate. Though this is a subjective judgment, the author believes the 270 is even superior to the 30-06 for accuracy.

While the factories offer a 100-grain varmint load, many shooters will find noise and recoil a trifle more than ideal for that purpose. Yet for the one-rifle hunter, the 270 is an ideal way to bridge the gap from tiny varmint to small elk. With 150-grain bullets, the 270 will prove adequate for 400-pound animals at 200 yards, or 300-pound critters at 300 yards.

The 270 was the first commercial cartridge to use a .277-inch-diameter bullet. Only one other factory-produced round uses this diameter—the 270 Weatherby Magnum. Winchester named the 270 for its bore diameter. In Europe this cartridge is known as the 6.9 × 64mm.

The 270 surely qualifies as a very-long-range cartridge. This writer made the longest big-game shot of his career using a 270 Winchester and 130-grain bullet. It accounted for a very large caribou standing just over 400 yards away, and one shot did the job.

For most hunters, the 270 Winchester represents the upper level of comfortable recoil. Thus, for many applications it is a better choice than the somewhat more versatile 30-06 Springfield. The 30-06, however, should be favored for heavy big game. The 270 Winchester is the second-most-popular big-game cartridge.

270 Weatherby Magnum

110-Grain Bullet—Varmint
130-Grain Bullet—Light Big Game
150-Grain Bullet—Medium Big Game

Due to its extra velocity and resulting higher levels of kinetic energy and Optimum Game Weight ratings, this cartridge is preferable over the 270 Winchester for medium big game. It is an especially fine extra-long-range cartridge, though its availability has been limited and, hence, its popularity is low.

Recently, manufacturers have announced they will begin chambering standard firearms, such as the Ruger No. 1 and the Winchester Model 70, for the 270 Weatherby Magnum. This may lead to increased popularity for the cartridge, which is quite a good one. The 270 Weatherby Magnum, because of its greatly enlarged powder charge, will prove slightly less accurate than the 270 Winchester.

However, a careful handloader should be able to obtain 1¼-inch groups without undue difficulty.

The noise level and recoil do not make this round an ideal choice for varminting, despite the availability of suitable bullets. It is, however, a near-perfect choice for a one-rifle hunter. Its major drawback, compared to the 270 Winchester, 280 Remington, or 30-06 Springfield, is (somewhat) increased recoil and shorter barrel life. The cartridge is well up to the taking of 700-pound game at 200 yards or perhaps 600-pound animals at 300 yards, giving it an edge of about 200 pounds of quarry weight over the 270 Winchester.

28 (7mm) CALIBER (.284" bullet diameter)

7mm BR

140-Grain Bullet—Target & Light Big Game

This cartridge was originally intended to fit the needs of benchrest target shooters. The BR designation is an abbreviation of bench rest, though some shooters quibble and insist it's an abbreviation of benchrest and Remington.

No generally available rifles are chambered for this cartridge, it being a caliber found in semi-custom guns. However, Remington does chamber its single-shot XP-100 handgun for this caliber. Remington advertises a 2,215 fps velocity with a 15-inch barrel.

This cartridge is capable of very fine accuracy and is a serious candidate for many forms of target shooting. This author has watched a number of deer killed with the 7mm BR in a Remington XP-100 pistol. At ranges up to 100 yards it is, indeed, very effective. Field experience and ballistic evaluation would suggest that the cartridge is ample (when used with a 15-inch or longer barrel) for game weighing up to 225 pounds when the range does not exceed 100 yards.

7mm Mauser

140-Grain Bullet—Light Big Game
145-Grain Bullet—Light Big Game
175-Grain Bullet—Light Big Game

In factory loadings, this cartridge is a relatively mild performer. U.S. factory loads are deliberately loaded to low pressure levels in deference to a great many less-than-strong firearms that have been chambered for the 7mm Mauser. Handloaders can boost ballistics and make this cartridge suitable for medium big game, but any such undertaking should be done only with great care by a fully competent person.

The 7mm Mauser is so called for the bore diameter and the type of firearm originally chambered for it, as well as the designer's name. In Europe, where the cartridge originated, it is known as the 7 × 57mm. The 57mm portion of the nomenclature refers to the case's length in millimeters. As loaded by U.S. ammo makers, it is a useful cartridge at medium ranges. Solid-bullet ammunition for this cartridge is manufactured by A-Square.

7 × 30 Waters
120-Grain Bullet—Light Big Game

Only a very few Winchester Model 94 variations have been chambered for this cartridge which, basically, is a necked-down 30-30 Winchester. It was designed by Ken Waters. The cartridge has less potential with respect to game size than the 30-30 Winchester, and its use on small deer should perhaps be limited to medium ranges. It has been loaded only by Federal and is extremely difficult to locate in retail outlets.

7mm-08 Remington
120-Grain Bullet—Varmint
140-Grain Bullet—Light Big Game

This cartridge is based on a necked-down 308 round and the -08 in its nomenclature came from 308. It is a superb light big-game cartridge, quite suitable for long-range shooting. And it is a very accurate round.

As yet, the 308 Winchester continues to remain the favored big-game cartridge in short-action rifles. However deserving, the 7mm-08 Remington has not been able to make great inroads into the parent cartridge's popularity. Nonetheless, the 7mm-08 is a dandy cartridge and offers the advantage of notably less recoil. Popularity is sufficient to keep it available in most of the better-stocked ammunition outlets.

284 Winchester
125-Grain Bullet—Varmint
150-Grain Bullet—Light Big Game

This round is a suitable long-range light big-game cartridge, but is far from popular. Winchester is the only ammunition manufacturer ever to produce it. The 284 is almost unique among current American cartridges, being one of a very few to use a rebated head. This means the rim diameter is actually considerably smaller than the case's base diameter, a design which allows a very fat cartridge case to be used in conjunction with bolt faces of standard dimensions. Some shooters complain that this feature can cause feeding problems. Though this appears to be valid, all conclusions seem to be based on subjective observations.

The 284 Winchester, named for its bullet diameter, is very difficult to locate in most ammo outlets. Firearms chambered for it are also rare.

280 Remington

120-Grain Bullet—Varmint
140-Grain Bullet—Light Big Game
150-Grain Bullet—Light Big Game
165-Grain Bullet—Medium Big Game

This cartridge was originally introduced by Remington presumably to compete with the 270 Winchester. Initial market success was less than overwhelming. Remington, deciding that a nomenclature change might help, began calling it the 7mm Express Remington. When that did not work, they reverted to the original nomenclature. The 280 designation is based on bore diameter.

To boost the 280's popularity, Remington introduced the 140- and 120-grain bullets. The 280 Remington will do anything the 270 will, and almost anything the 30-06 can accomplish. It is a fine extra-long-range cartridge for light big game and is suitable for medium-sized North American game if the ranges are not too long. More than a few shooters have collected elk and moose with it, though I would not so recommend it.

7mm Remington Magnum

140-Grain Bullet—Light Big Game
150-Grain Bullet—Light Big Game
165-Grain Bullet—Medium Big Game
175-Grain Bullet—Heavy Big Game

The 7mm Remington Magnum is perhaps third in popularity among big-game cartridges, and therefore readily available in most places catering to hunter's needs. In the field, it will perform much like a 30-06, and with the heaviest bullets it can therefore be used for elk, moose, and even grizzly. However, most experienced hunters consider both it and the 30-06 bare minimums for heavy game. Accuracy and trajectory are easily good enough to qualify this cartridge as suitable for extra-long range. However, when used on heavy game, ranges should be reduced accordingly.

Perhaps one of the features that made this cartridge such a success was its being a "magnum" with 30-06 recoil. One of the driving forces to bring this cartridge into being was the late Les Bowman, who felt there was a real need for a potent big-game round without the recoil of larger magnum cartridges.

One disadvantage is the fact that bore wear is greater in the 7mm Remington Magnum than in the 30-06.

7mm Weatherby Magnum

139-Grain Bullet—Light Big Game
140-Grain Bullet—Light Big Game
154-Grain Bullet—Medium Big Game
160-Grain Bullet—Heavy Big Game
175-Grain Bullet—Heavy Big Game

There is almost no difference between this proprietary round and the 7mm Remington Magnum with respect to actual field performance. However, due to limited availability of rifles and ammo, the Weatherby round has never become popular. All the comments on performance made for the 7mm Remington Magnum apply to this cartridge.

30 CALIBER (.308" bullet diameter)

30 Carbine

110-Grain Bullet—Plinking

The 30 M1 U.S. Carbine was designed to replace the 1911 Model 45 automatic pistol for specific military personnel during World War II. The 30 Carbine offered greater firepower (15 or 30 rounds compared to 7), better accuracy because of the rifle configuration, and, in some models, even full-automatic fire.

The cartridge is very low-powered, about on par with a 32-20 Winchester, rendering it totally inappropriate even for light big game and not nearly accurate enough for small game or varmints. It makes a fine plinking cartridge, and perhaps has use for personal defense in the home.

303 Savage

190-Grain Bullet—Light Big Game

This cartridge is at best a medium-range light big-game cartridge. Its ballistics are on equal footing with the 30-30 Winchester. It is an obsolete cartridge and is currently loaded only by Winchester.

Some have suggested that its 303 designation was a ploy to make shooters think it had the punch of the more powerful 303 British cartridge. Others feel it was merely an attempt to suggest something bigger than the 30-30 Winchester. History has clouded any certainty regarding the motive behind the nomenclature.

30 Remington

170-Grain Bullet—Light Big Game

This is a rimless variant of the 30-30 designed to be used in pump-action and semiautomatic rifles. It is no more or less effective than the 30-30 Winchester—a medium-range light big-game cartridge. The 30 Remington is obsolete and is now loaded only by Remington.

30-30 Winchester

55-Grain Bullet—Varmint
125-Grain Bullet—Varmint
150-Grain Bullet—Light Big Game
170-Grain Bullet—Light Big Game

One of the most popular cartridges ever designed, the 30-30 has been in continuous production (and demand) since the 1890s. Finally,

Cartridges in 30 caliber are numerous and vary widely in sizes and applications. Among 30 caliber cartridges are, *from left*: 30-30 Winchester, 300 Savage, 30-40 Krag, 307 Winchester, 308 Winchester, 30-06 Springfield, 300 H&H Magnum, 300 Winchester Magnum, and 300 Weatherby Mag.

after a full century of use, it seems as if the 30-30 may have started to fall from the position of immense popularity it has enjoyed for so long.

The 30-30 designation stood for 30 caliber and 30 grains of smokeless powder. (It was the first sporting cartridge loaded with smokeless powder.) This cartridge is considered by many of today's experts as the minimum for use at medium ranges on light big game. But the fact that it has taken a million or more deer cannot be denied.

The 55-grain varmint load is manufactured only by Remington. This load uses a 22-caliber bullet seated in a 30-caliber plastic sabot. Only Federal loads the 125-grain varmint load. Varmint hunting with the 30-30 usually means short range due to accuracy limitations.

Properly used—within the constraints of accuracy, range, and game size—the 30-30 Winchester will probably be used successfully for another century.

The metric designation for this cartridge is 7.62 × 51Rmm.

300 Savage

150-Grain Bullet—Light Big Game
180-Grain Bullet—Light Big Game

This cartridge was designed as a shortened 30-06 to fit the Savage 99 lever-action rifles. It is a fine round for deer-sized game at medium to almost long ranges—*when spitzer bullets are used.*

Named for its bore diameter, the 300 Savage is now nearly obsolete. No firearms have been chambered for it for some time. Still, the owner of a Savage 99 featherweight chambered for this cartridge has one of the most delightful deer rifles ever produced.

The 300 Savage has been used frequently for medium big game, but such use is really stretching its ballistic capability. It's at its best when game weights do not exceed 300 pounds and ranges are no more than 225 yards.

30-40 Krag

180-Grain Bullet—Light Big Game

Despite the Krag's greater size, it is about equal to the 300 Savage with respect to field performance. At one time, it was the official U.S. military cartridge (in the Krag rifle). This cartridge is very obsolete, though not too many years ago a number of Ruger No. 3 single-shot rifles were chambered for it. Ammo has become very difficult to locate.

The 30-40 Krag was named for its bore diameter (30 caliber), the weight of its powder charge (40 grains) and the rifle in which it was used (Krag).

307 Winchester

150-Grain Bullet—Light Big Game

With respect to size, the 307 cartridge case is a rimmed 308 Winchester. Indeed, it can be reloaded in most 308 Winchester dies. The name was as close to 308 Winchester as one could come without using a designation like 308 Rimmed. This cartridge, however, should *not* be loaded using 308 Winchester data because it is meant to operate at considerably less pressure.

Designed for use in lever-actions, the 307 Winchester is a giant step ahead of the 30-30 in ballistics, but is chambered only in 30-30-type firearms (Winchester 94 and Marlin 336 lever-actions). Unlike the 30-30 Winchester, it is a classic example of a cartridge that failed almost at its inception. There were a lot of marketing reasons and a few technical ones for the lack of interest in the 307. But it chiefly boils down to the fact that when folks see a need for a more potent round than the 30-30, they also see a need for the increased accuracy levels of a bolt-action rifle, so why not choose the 308?

I suspect that finding 307 Winchester ammunition might well tax the patience of most hunters.

308 Winchester

55-Grain Bullet—Varmint
150-Grain Bullet—Light Big Game
165-Grain Bullet—Light Big Game
168-Grain Bullet—Target
180-Grain Bullet—Medium Big Game

This cartridge operates at a velocity of 100 to 200 feet per second (depending on bullet weight) less than the 30-06 Springfield. Thus, under most conditions it will serve as well as its longer brother.

Named for its bullet diameter, the 308 was for some years the standard U.S. military cartridge. As such, it was known as the 7.63 × 61mm NATO cartridge.

The 55-grain varmint load is made only by Remington. It's of Remington's Accelerator loadings, using a 22-caliber bullet in a 30-caliber plastic sabot.

The 308 Winchester is extremely accurate, even more so than the 30-06 Springfield, so it easily qualifies as a long- to extra-long-range cartridge. Its limitations, compared to the 30-06, matter only when heavy game and 180-grain bullets are being considered. The 30-06's 180-grain loads are considered marginal for heavy game by most authorities. Some even advise against such use. Thus, because the 308 is ballistically inferior, though only slightly so, it is not considered a heavy-game cartridge by most experts.

All the same, the 308 Winchester easily makes it into the top 10 most popular cartridges. It will handle game up to about 350 pounds

Remington loads a unique cartridge called the Accelerator in 30-30 Win, 308 Win (shown), and 30-06 Springfield cartridges. These all use a 55-grain 22-caliber bullet encased in a 30-caliber plastic sabot.

at 300 yards. Take the range down to 200 yards and a 500-pound animal is fair-sized quarry when using 180-grain bullets. For the 150-grain bullet at 300 yards, a game weight of about 275 pounds is the upper limit.

30-06 Springfield

55-Grain Bullet—Varmint
125-Grain Bullet—Varmint
150-Grain Bullet—Light Big Game
165-Grain Bullet—Light & Medium Big Game
180-Grain Bullet—Heavy Big Game
220-Grain Bullet—Unclassified

This is our most popular big-game cartridge. Known as the 7.62 × 63mm in Europe, the 30-06 has been used successfully on game as small as gopher and as large as brown bear. (Both extremes are probably stretching things a bit.)

The 55-grain load is a Remington 22-caliber bullet in a plastic sabot. Accuracy with this type of load can vary substantially from rifle to rifle. The 125-grain bullet will often give quite satisfactory varmint accuracy out to 200 yards.

Big-game loads for light and medium animals all are well qualified as long- to extra-long-range rounds. The use of 180-grain bullets on large elk, moose, and grizzly bear is marginal. The shooter who selects a 30-06 for such applications should limit range and be very careful with bullet placement. Difficult angles should not be attempted.

We have left the 220-grain loads, which usually are very accurate, unclassified. This is because the 220-grain bullets will deliver notably less energy to the quarry at all ranges than the 180-grain or the now discontinued 200-grain loads. Thus, the big bullet is less suitable for heavy game than the 180-grain weight. And it makes little sense to use such a heavy bullet on light or medium game. The 220-grain bullets are best ignored by most hunters.

Solid bullets of 180 grains are available in this caliber from A-Square.

The 30-06 is somewhat more versatile than the 270 Winchester or 280 Remington since it is marginally better suited to heavy game. It has enough power to handle 400-pound animals at 300 yards or 550-pound game at 200 yards when 180-grain bullets are used. However, recoil is heavy. If the shooter is not going to hunt heavy game, and shoots better with less recoil, the 270 can prove as good or perhaps a bit better. But any one-rifle hunter who selects a 30-06 Springfield will never regret the choice.

The 30-06 Springfield was named for its bore diameter (.30"), the year it was introduced (1906) and the rifle for which it was introduced (1906 Springfield).

The cartridge by which most sportsmen judge all others is the 30-06 Springfield (*center*). It is flanked by the two most popular medium-bore magnums, the 338 Win Magnum (*left*), and the 375 H&H Magnum.

300 H&H Magnum

180-Grain Bullet—Light to Heavy Big Game
220-Grain Bullet, Solid—See text

For the most part, this cartridge has been made obsolete by the 300 Winchester Magnum. It was named for its bore diameter. The H&H designation stands for Holland & Holland, the British firm that originated the cartridge. Ballistics of the H&H Magnum and the Winchester are, for all practical purposes, identical.

This is an extremely accurate cartridge and has been very popular with long-range match competitors. It is the minimum cartridge I would suggest if heavy North American big game will be hunted. It can be used equally well for our smallest big game and is a very fine extra-long-range cartridge. When game weights are high, keep ranges modest.

Recoil is somewhat heavy, and a novice would no doubt find it objectionable, yet this is a cartridge easily mastered by an experienced shooter.

The 220-grain loading is available only from A-Square. Of course, this solid bullet has limited, specialized uses.

The metric designation for this cartridge is 7.63 × 72mm.

300 Winchester Magnum

150-Grain Bullet—Light Big Game
180-Grain Bullet—Medium to Heavy Big Game
200-Grain Bullet—Heavy Big Game
220-Grain Bullet—Heavy Big Game

This cartridge uses a belted magnum case head of the same size as the 300 H&H Magnum, but has a shorter overall length and does not have the heavy taper of the Holland & Holland. It is an extremely versatile cartridge, suitable for all North American big game, from light to heavy. The 300 Winchester Magnum has seen some use by target shooters and is an excellent extra-long-range hunting cartridge.

This is a fine choice for all-around use. It is entirely adequate for any moose or elk, though some shooters prefer its bigger brother, the 338 Winchester Magnum. The wide range of available bullet weights in factory ammo and the relative popularity of this cartridge make it, for most shooters, a better choice than the 300 H&H.

As with all 30-caliber or larger magnums, it is not a cartridge for a recoil-sensitive shooter or a novice. But it is not so punishing as to cause difficulty for the experienced person who has accustomed himself to recoil.

A-Square supplies solid-bullet ammunition in this caliber.

300 Weatherby Magnum

110-Grain Bullet—Varmint (see text)
150-Grain Bullet—Light Big Game
180-Grain Bullet—Medium to Heavy Big Game
220-Grain Bullet—Heavy Big Game

This 300 uses a very large case and is really more cartridge than would normally ever be needed for hunting in North America. Recoil is quite severe compared to the 300 Winchester Magnum.

The 110-grain—varmint-weight—bullet is useful for no other purpose than varminting, but it certainly isn't practical to hunt varmints with a cartridge burning 90 grains of powder per shot. And perhaps the same consideration applies to this cartridge's use on light big game.

Nonetheless, for a shooter who wants the highest ballistic figures possible from a 30-caliber rifle, this round is it. It makes good sense to select Nosler Partition bullets to prevent bullet failures due to very high velocities.

At one time, this was a proprietary cartridge, and rifles and ammo were available only from Weatherby or custom sources. PMC (Korea) and Remington now load this cartridge, and Ruger and Winchester rifles are now being chambered for it.

However, because of its abusive recoil and muzzle blast, the 300 Weatherby Magnum probably will never see widespread use.

31 CALIBER (.310″ and .311″ bullet diameter)

32-20 Winchester

100-Grain Bullet—Unclassified

This is a low-powered cartridge, long since obsolete, although Winchester and Remington currently load ammunition. It was designed as a small-game lever-action rifle cartridge and, as such, exhibited only short-range accuracy. In the few bolt-action rifles made for it (Winchester Model 43) it was a useful pest-species and turkey cartridge for short to medium ranges. This cartridge uses a 0.310-inch-diameter bullet. Marlin is the only current firearm producer.

303 British

180-Grain Bullet—Light Big Game

This cartridge was at one time the British service cartridge. The 303 designation is that of the bore diameter, while the bullet (and groove) diameter is nominally 0.311-inch. Ballistically, as loaded in the U.S., this cartridge is slightly superior to the 300 Savage and about

160 feet per second slower than the 308 Winchester with a bullet of similar weight. Range can be stretched to about 250 yards, at least theoretically, but most of the bolt-action SMLE service rifles chambered for this cartridge are considerably worn, which means suitable accuracy is a real problem.

32 CALIBER (.320" and .323" bullet diameter)
32 Winchester Special
170-Grain Bullet—Light Big Game

The 32 Winchester Special is the ballistic twin of the 30-30, but not quite as accurate. No firearms are currently chambered for this dying cartridge.

The only purpose the 32 Winchester Special ever served has not been valid for many years. When the 30-30 was first introduced as a smokeless cartridge, reloaders were able to obtain only black powder. Due to the twist rate of the 30-30 and the lower velocities of black-powder loads, reloading produced poor accuracy. The 32 Winchester Special was introduced with a twist rate that would provide acceptable accuracy with black powder.

The cartridge uses a 0.320-inch bullet. It was named for its caliber, its company of origin, and its special purpose.

8mm Mauser
170-Grain Bullet—Light Big Game
220-Grain Bullet—Unclassified

This cartridge originated in Europe as a military round for the Mauser rifle. It is also known as the 8 × 57mm and the 7.9 × 57mm. It uses a 0.323-inch-diameter bullet.

The 8mm Mauser is loaded to very low pressure in this country because of the weakness of some of the early rifles chambered for it, and to prevent undue hazard should it be improperly (and unsafely) used in a rifle chambered for the 8 × 57J cartridge, which uses a 0.318-inch bullet diameter.

For all practical purposes, U.S. ammunition for this cartridge duplicates 300 Savage ballistics. European ammo is loaded to levels more like those of the 30-06. At one time the great number of military rifles available caused this to be a very popular cartridge. Today, interest in it is relatively low.

8mm Remington Magnum

180-Grain Bullet—Light to Medium Big Game
220-Grain Bullet—Heavy Big Game

This cartridge, which uses a 0.323-inch-diameter bullet, was introduced by Remington to compete with the 300 Winchester Magnum, 300 H&H Magnum, and perhaps the 338 Magnum. It uses the longer case length of the 300 H&H Magnum, but it has less body taper. It is very suitable as an extra-long-range cartridge and is capable of handling any quarry found in North America.

Despite its merit, the 8mm Remington has never become popular, and ammunition is extremely hard to find. Ammunition loaded with solid bullets is available from A-Square.

33 CALIBER (.338" bullet diameter)

338 Winchester Magnum

210-Grain Bullet—Light to Medium Big Game
225-Grain Bullet—Medium Big Game
250-Grain Bullet—Heavy Big Game

This cartridge is both potent and accurate and qualifies for big game at extra-long ranges. Naturally, on heavy big game, ranges should be shortened somewhat. The cartridge is an ideal selection for African plains game. It, and perhaps the 416 Remington Magnum, would get everything done in Africa, elephant including.

The 338 Winchester Magnum, while delivering somewhat less energy than the 375 H&H Magnum over short to medium ranges, will actually deliver more energy to the quarry than the larger cartridge when ranges exceed 200 yards. This is due to a sharper bullet profile and, hence, better velocity retention.

The Federal Premium ammo using the 210- and 250-grain Nosler Partition bullets supplies very positive performance and outstanding accuracy. The Remington 250-grain loading also is an outstanding performer.

Recoil and noise can be abusive with the 338 Winchester Magnum, the smallest of the true heavy cartridges. However, a rifle of ample proportions and weight will tame it sufficiently for most experienced shooters.

This cartridge is the most popular bigbore magnum in the U.S., and is slowly becoming a true classic. Popularity continues to grow with each year.

340 Weatherby Magnum

210-Grain Bullet—Light to Medium Big Game
250-Grain Bullet—Heavy Big Game

This is a big cartridge that will deliver about 150 feet per second more velocity than the 338 Winchester Magnum, with which it shares similar applications. However, because this round has been available only from Weatherby and A-Square, it has never become very popular. Indeed, it is quite difficult to locate ammo, brass, or reloading dies for the 340 Weatherby.

338 A-Square

250-Grain Bullet—Medium to Heavy Big Game

This cartridge is loaded only by A-Square. It's available with 250-grain solids, rapid-expanding soft-points (called the Lion Load), and slow-expanding soft-points (called the Dead Tough). The case for this round is a shortened 378 Weatherby Magnum, necked to 33 caliber. Because of very high velocities, bullet selection for reloading must be made carefully in order to avoid premature bullet break-up (disintegration) at short to medium ranges.

Recoil is very stout, and this is not a cartridge for any but a very experienced shooter. It is a very effective extra-long-range cartridge for heavy big game.

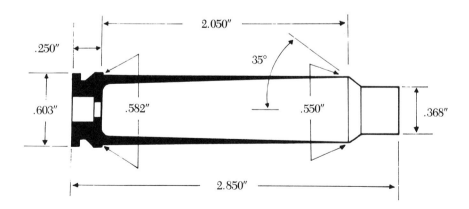

Technical specifications of the 338 A-Square.

34 CALIBER (.348″ bullet diameter)
348 Winchester
200-Grain Bullet—Light to Medium Big Game

This cartridge has been obsolete for quite some time. The original Winchester Model 71 was the only rifle ever chambered for the 348 until 1987, when Browning made a limited number of Model 71 copies. Winchester produced a lot of "commemorative" 200-grain loads for these Browning rifles. It is unknown if the company will ever do so again.

Because of the flat-nosed bullet used in this cartridge (required for the tubular magazine), it is for short- to medium-range applications. Accuracy potential would suggest a maximum range of about 150 to perhaps 175 yards.

Ammunition is extremely difficult to locate. This is the only commercial U.S. cartridge ever to use this bullet diameter.

35 CALIBER (.351″, .357″, .358″ bullet diameters)
351 Winchester Self-Loading
180-Grain Bullet—Unclassified

This cartridge is very obsolete, though Winchester still offers it. It is a tiny, straight-walled cartridge intended only for the Winchester Model 07 (1907) semiautomatic rifle. The 351 Winchester SL is actually underpowered for most deer-hunting situations.

Since ammunition is too expensive for plinking and not accurate enough for target shooting, this cartridge receives a non-classified listing. It would be a marginal choice for small deer at ranges less than 50 yards.

Ammo is almost impossible to locate. This is one of two U.S. sporting cartridges ever to use a .351-inch-diameter bullet; the other was the earlier and less powerful 35 Winchester Self-Loading cartridge.

The 351 Winchester Self-Loading Model 07—often simply called the 351 SL—saw its greatest use as a police firearm and was often used for prison-guard applications.

357 Magnum
158-Grain Bullet—Unclassified

The 357 Magnum is a handgun cartridge, introduced by Smith & Wesson, but more than just a few lever-action rifles have been chambered for this cartridge. Such firearms are best suited to plinking or perhaps personal defense. The cartridge is frequently far less accurate in lever-action rifles than it is when fired from a good target-grade revolver.

Because of often poor rifle accuracy and comparatively low power (far too little to be sporting on deer), the 357 Magnum is left unclassified for rifle use. It is, however, a superb handgun cartridge. Ammunition is readily available in a great range of bullet weights. The 158-grain weight listed here is perhaps the best choice in a rifle-length barrel.

The 357 Magnum was named for its nominal barrel-groove diameter, and was originally called the 357 Smith & Wesson Magnum.

35 Remington

150-Grain Bullet—Light Big Game
200-Grain Bullet—Light Big Game

This is a very old but very popular cartridge. Its low velocity makes it a short- to medium-range cartridge. Accuracy in Marlin 336 carbines is usually quite good, especially for a lever-action rifle. Although the 35 Remington is a dying cartridge, ammo is relatively easy to locate.

Many shooters report lack of bullet expansion when ranges exceed 100 yards.

356 Winchester

200-Grain Bullet—Light Big Game

This cartridge is basically a rimmed 358 Winchester with ballistics adjusted downward to allow for its use in lever-action rifles. Only comparatively few Winchester Model 94 and Marlin 336 rifles have been chambered for this cartridge. It was intended to give lever-action rifle fans a bunch more punch, but it failed to gain popularity with hunters.

Because of the blunt-nosed bullets (required for tubular-magazine rifles) velocity fall-off is rapid. Thus, range is limited to medium. Lever-action accuracy levels also limit the cartridge's maximum effective range to about 150 yards, perhaps a bit more.

Despite its drawbacks, the 356 Winchester is the best light big-game cartridge ever designed for use in Winchester 94 and Marlin 336 rifles and carbines.

Ammo is very scarce and is loaded only by Winchester.

358 Winchester

200-Grain Bullet—Light & Medium Big Game

As most industry insiders would agree, it is very difficult to achieve popularity with larger-than-30-caliber cartridges. Winchester had hoped that by necking up the 308 Winchester to accept a .358-inch-diameter bullet, they would have a successful 35-caliber cartridge. Shooters never responded accordingly.

This is quite a powerful medium-range cartridge and it deserves far greater popularity. But the fact remains that it is a dying cartridge. Most rifles chambered for it were semiautomatics (Winchester Model 100) or lever-actions (Winchester 88). However, Winchester and Ruger both offered a limited number of bolt-action rifles chambered for the 358 Winchester. These are very fine medium-range rifles. Any medium-size North American game may be taken if ranges are kept moderate.

350 Remington Magnum

200-Grain Bullet—Light to Medium Big Game

In terms of popularity, this big cousin of the 6.5mm Remington Magnum also proved to be a loser from the very first. However, it is quite a powerhouse in the 20-inch carbines made for it. Ballistics are adequate for any big game up to 200 yards. And for smaller animals, the range can be stretched to 300 or more yards.

Originally, a 250-grain bullet was available but, due to lack of popularity, the cartridge is now offered in only the 200-grain bullet weight, and ammunition is very difficult to find.

35 Whelen

200-Grain Bullet—Light Big Game
250-Grain Bullet—Light to Medium Big Game

For many years, this cartridge was available only as a wildcat. It was simply a 30-06 necked up to 35 caliber and was named for one of its originators—Colonel Townsend Whelen.

Remington recently "legitimized" the cartridge by making it available as a factory-loaded cartridge, while simultaneously offering a number of rifles so chambered. Its ultimate fate with regard to popularity has not yet been tested.

The 35 Whelen, as factory-loaded, does not deliver any more long-range punch than a 180-grain 30-06 bullet. Handloaded with projectiles having a sharper profile, its downrange ballistics can be improved.

36 (9.3mm) CALIBER (.366" bullet diameter)

9.3 × 62mm
9.3 × 64mm
9.3 × 74Rmm

286-Grain Bullet—Light to Medium Big Game

These cartridges are loaded in the U.S. only by A-Square. Ballistics are similar for the 9.3 × 62 and 9.3 × 74R, each with a 100-yard kinetic energy of about 2,800 foot-pounds. They both are adequate for long-range shooting. The 9.3 × 64 is notably more potent.

In the U.S., there are comparatively few European firearms chambered for these cartridges. Ammo is at best very difficult to locate.

37 CALIBER (.375", .376" bullet diameter)

38-55 Winchester

255-Grain Bullet—Unclassified

This is a very obsolete cartridge. It has a rim with 30-30-style dimension but uses a fairly straight case accepting .376-inch-diameter bullets. It was named for its approximate caliber (38) and the original charge weight of black powder (55 grains). The cartridge is quite dead and relatively low-powered, hardly suitable for short-range deer hunting in today's woods—hence the non-classified listing.

375 Winchester

200-Grain Bullet—Light Big Game
250-Grain Bullet—Light Big Game

This cartridge is a modern version of the 38-55, loaded to much higher pressures and using a .375-inch-diameter bullet. Case dimensions differ somewhat from the 38-55.

First introduced during the late 1970s in a Winchester Model 94, it never gained much popularity. It is, nonetheless, a suitable light big-game cartridge for short to medium range. However, ammo is extremely difficult to locate.

375 H&H Magnum

270-Grain Bullet—Medium to Heavy Big Game
300-Grain Bullet—Medium to Heavy Big Game

At one time, the 375 H&H (Holland & Holland) was a fairly popular elk and big-bear cartridge. However, the 338 Winchester Magnum has all but replaced it, and perhaps rightly so.

Many American sportsmen have thought of the 375 H&H as an ideal African dangerous-game cartridge. This opinion is seldom shared by those who have hunted in Africa. The 375 H&H, however, is very suitable for use on most African plains game. And its use for elk, moose, or grizzly cannot be faulted. Yet, when shooting beyond 200 yards, the 338 Winchester Magnum will deliver more punch. On the other hand, if the required task is to stop a charging grizzly bear at short range, the 375 H&H will prove vastly superior to the smaller 338 Winchester Magnum.

This is an extremely accurate cartridge, but it is not for everyone. The recoil is nothing less than brutal. For those who can handle it, the 375 will take everything from deer to many African species. Yes, it's more gun than needed on animals of less than 1,000 pounds, but it is one of the best all-around heavy big-game cartridges ever to come down the pike.

The 375 is truly one of the all-time cartridge greats. It will be with us for a long, long time and it is possible that it will never be exceeded as the ideal choice for the one-gun, worldwide big-game hunter, though some would favor the 338 Winchester Magnum for the same purpose.

In Europe this cartridge is known as the 9.5 × 72mm.

375 Weatherby Magnum

300-Grain Bullet—Heavy Big Game

This cartridge is currently loaded only by A-Square, so ammunition is quite scarce. Long ago it was dropped by Weatherby in favor of the much larger-cased 378 Weatherby Magnum. This round delivers ballistics very similar to the 375 H&H Magnum, and all of the comments concerning that cartridge also apply here.

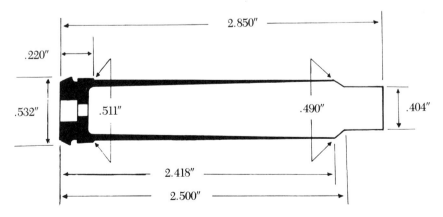

Technical specifications of 375 Weatherby Magnum.

378 Weatherby Magnum

270-Grain Bullet—Dangerous Big Game
300-Grain Bullet—Heavy Big Game

Currently, ammo is offered by both Weatherby and A-Square. This cartridge is a giant of a round. It uses the 460 Weatherby Magnum case, necked down to accept a .375-inch bullet. The 378 nomenclature may have been an attempt to avoid confusion with the smaller-cased 375 Weatherby Magnum.

Recoil is fierce—unmanageable by any but the most experienced shooters. Because of the high velocities achieved, bullet selection is very critical. Indeed, only the solid bullets seem suitable. If there is a need for great power (for dangerous African game), the shooter would be best advised to consider a larger-bore rifle for which suitable bullets are available. Popularity is very low, as this cartridge seems not to be ideal for any purpose.

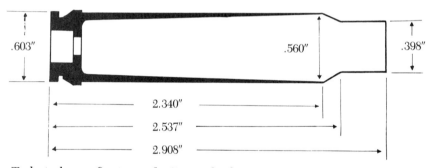

Technical specifications of 378 Weatherby Magnum.

40 CALIBER (.400" and .409" bullet diameter)

38-40 Winchester

180-Grain Bullet—Unclassified

This cartridge, loaded only by Winchester, is of handgun-case size, though at one time it was a popular short-range deer cartridge, used primarily in the Winchester Model 92 carbines. The 38-40 derives its name from an incorrectly designated caliber diameter (.38 instead of .40) and its original charge of 40 grains of black powder. It is very obsolete and fills no real need by today's standards. The 38-40 uses a .400-inch bullet.

450/400–3″

400-Grain Bullet—Heavy Big Game & Dangerous Game

This cartridge was a British development, used primarily for African hunting. It is loaded in the U.S. only by A-Square using .409-inch bullets. While it has been extremely popular in Africa, its use in the United States has been almost non-existent. A-Square loads three styles of 400-grain bullets for this cartridge: a rapidly expanding soft-point (Lion Load) a slow-expanding soft-point (Dead Tough), and a solid trademarked Monolithic.

41 CALIBER (.416″ bullet diameter)
416 Hoffman

400-Grain Bullet—Heavy Big Game & Dangerous Game

The 416 Hoffman is loaded only by A-Square. This cartridge was designed by Mr. Hoffman, a Texan, to gain 416 Rigby ballistics with a more readily available cartridge case. It employs a blown-out and necked-up 375 H&H Magnum case. The Hoffman has a great deal more punch than the original parent cartridge and is perfectly suitable for African dangerous game such as buffalo.

This is an ideal African dangerous-game cartridge for those who are not used to excessive recoil. It is adequate but not overpowerful. Indeed, I chose it and a 338 Winchester Magnum for my first African safari and never regretted the selections.

The 416 Hoffman obviously derived its name from its bullet diameter and its designer. It's very accurate, adequate for game up to 2,000 pounds, and can do yeoman service for anyone wishing to hunt elk, moose, or grizzly with a bigbore rifle.

Of course, ammo is not available in every gun shop, but bullets and cases, as well as loaded rounds, can be obtained from A-Square.

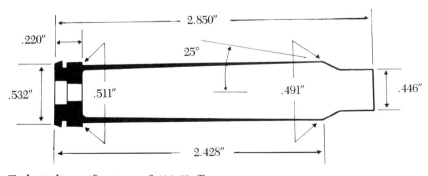

Technical specifications of 416 Hoffman.

416 Rigby

400-Grain Bullet—Heavy Big Game & Dangerous Game

This cartridge was designed by the English gunmaking firm of Rigby. Ballistics are excellent though not as impressive as the huge case might suggest. This is due to the fact that Rigby sought to provide hard punch with relatively mild pressures, which was accomplished by using a very large case. Comments for the 416 Hoffman apply fully to the 416 Rigby.

Ammo is loaded in the U.S. only by A-Square. The Rigby, the 416 Hoffman, and the 404 Jeffrey are the biggest cartridges that make any sense in North America (and are more than needed).

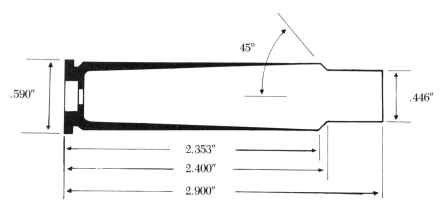

Technical specifications of 416 Rigby.

42 CALIBER (.423" bullet diameter)
404 Jeffrey

400-Grain Bullet—Heavy Big Game & Dangerous Game

This cartridge, designed by the British firm of Jeffrey, does not deliver as much punch as either of the 416s, but it has been extremely popular in Africa. The only U.S. manufacturer is A-Square, and ammo is very difficult to locate unless your dealer is willing to special-order it.

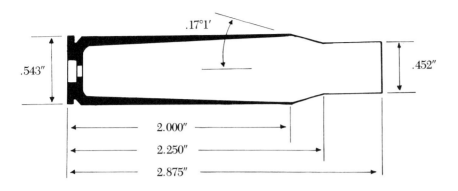

Technical specifications of 404 Jeffrey.

44 CALIBER (.427", .429" bullet diameter)
44-40 Winchester
200-Grain Bullet—Unclassified

Obsolete for quite some time, this cartridge has a .427-inch diameter bullet and was popular at one time for very short-range deer hunting. However, by today's standards it is not potent enough to be a sporting selection.

Ammunition has become mighty scarce. Some handguns were chambered for this cartridge.

44 Remington Magnum
240-Grain Bullet—Unclassified

This cartridge is a powerhouse handgun round, but when used in a rifle it is very low-powered compared to true rifle cartridges. Besides, most rifles chambered for this round (semiautomatics and lever-actions) are poor performers with respect to accuracy.

All in all, the 44 Magnum is at best a very short-range deer cartridge, and not nearly as efficient as a 30-30. Quite a few bullet weights are available. But for those who insist on hunting deer with this round, the 240-grain soft-point bullets are the best selection, though barely adequate.

444 Marlin

240-Grain Bullet—Light Big Game
265-Grain Bullet—Light Big Game

This is a fine short- to medium-range light big-game cartridge. It has a lot of up-close punch, but its flat-nosed bullet quickly loses velocity and energy. It is not a very popular cartridge, and ammunition is difficult to locate.

45 CALIBER (.458" bullet diameter)

45-70 Government

300-Grain Bullet—Light Big Game
405-Grain Bullet—Light Big Game

This cartridge was the U.S. service cartridge from 1873 until 1892, when it was replaced by the 30-40 Krag. All of those antique "Trapdoor" Springfield single-shot 45-70 rifles should no longer be considered safe for use with modern ammunition, being some 100 years old.

A great many Winchester lever-actions were also chambered for the 45-70 Government as were a number of other types of firearms, even including modern, safely shootable replicas of the Trapdoor Springfield. Perhaps because of nostalgic and romantic appeal, 45-70 rifles have had at least a modest revival by several manufacturers. This round was originally known as 45-70-300 and 45-70-405. The first two digits were the caliber designation, the second two were the black-powder charge weight in grains, and the last three digits were the bullet's weight in grains. The Government designation was to indicate the first official military cartridge.

The 45-70 has remained popular for more than 100 years, and firearms probably will be so chambered for a while longer. It is a very low-velocity cartridge using blunt bullets. Because of its rather poor trajectory, its practical range limit is about 125 yards.

In modern Ruger No. 1 single-shot rifles, many hunters enjoy taking game with this very old cartridge. Ammo is found in all but the smaller or poorly stocked gun shops.

458 Winchester Magnum

*465-Grain Bullet—Heavy Big Game (see text) &
  Dangerous Game*
*500-Grain Bullet— Heavy Big Game (see text) &
  Dangerous Game*
*510-Grain Bullet—Heavy Big Game (see text) &
  Dangerous Game*

This cartridge has been both maligned and praised by African hunters. Much of the negative comment has arisen from the failure of certain factory-loaded solid bullets, with respect to penetration and straight-line tracking in game. This problem disappears when 465-grain Monolithic A-Square solids are used.

The 458 Winchester Magnum (named for its bullet diameter) provides ballistics about on a par with such cartridges as the 416 Hoffman, 416 Rigby, and 450 Nitro Express–3¼-inch. Thus, it offers no great advantage with respect to ballistics. However, it does offer two other advantages over the 416s and the 450/400, as well as the 450 #2—or, for that matter, the 470 Rigby and the 475 #2. These advantages are availability and cost per round. Many good gun shops will have at least a few boxes of 458 Winchester Magnums on the shelves, whereas they may have none of those other calibers. And the cost will often be half that of the ballistically similar rounds.

With good solids and a plentiful supply of satisfactory soft-points, the 458 Winchester Magnum is deserving of the Africa-bound U.S. sportsman's consideration. With the right bullets, it's a very good performer, though not delivering the punch of some other large-caliber cartridges.

This cartridge is actually too big for any North American application unless handloaded to ballistic levels somewhat below factory performance—a not uncommon practice.

With full-power loads I would not be uncomfortable in Africa, except perhaps if faced with an angry elephant.

Recoil is best described as gruesome.

450 Nitro Express–3¼"

465-Grain Bullet—Dangerous Game
500-Grain Bullet—Dangerous Game

This is an English cartridge originally intended for use in Africa and India. It is quite scarce in the U.S. and is loaded here only by A-Square. Its ballistics are on par with the 458 Winchester, though it is a much larger cartridge.

450 #2

465-Grain Bullet—Dangerous Game
500-Grain Bullet—Dangerous Game

Ballistics of this English cartridge are identical to the 450 Nitro Express and the 458 Winchester, hence all applications and general comments under these headings pertain here. This round is loaded in the U.S. only by A-Square.

450 Ackley Magnum

500-Grain Bullet—Dangerous Game

This cartridge was designed by the famous gunsmith P.O. Ackley. It's a blown-out and necked-up version of the 375 H&H Magnum and was named for the nominal bore diameter and its originator.

A potent cartridge, it delivers almost as much energy at 200 yards as the 458 Winchester Magnum provides at 100 yards. For many shooters, the recoil level is beyond belief. Free recoil in a 10-pound rifle is on the order of 80 foot/pounds—about like four 30-06s at once.

The 450 Ackley is a fine dangerous-game cartridge. It is loaded commercially only by A-Square. While 375 H&H brass can be necked up, it is best when forming cases to use the cylindrical 375 H&H cases sold by A-Square, as these require none of the difficult necking-up steps. Simply run them into a 450 Ackley sizing die and trim as necessary.

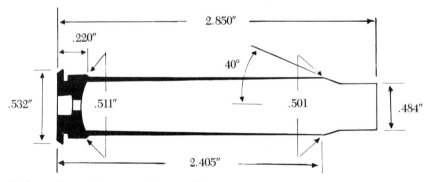

Technical specifications of 450 Ackley.

460 Short A-Square

500-Grain Bullet—Dangerous Game

This is a shortened 460 Weatherby Magnum and will deliver all the punch that can be had when using a standard-length bolt-action. At

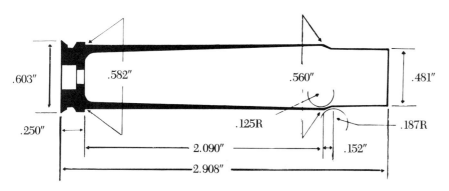

Technical specifications of 460 Weatherby Magnum.

the same time, it's an extremely efficient cartridge possessed of great accuracy.

This cartridge is loaded only by A-Square, and its disadvantage, besides recoil, is the difficulty in forming cases. A number of very expensive cases will be ruined during the initial case-forming operation.

460 Long A-Square
460 Weatherby Magnum

500-Grain Bullet—Dangerous Game

These two cartridges are grouped together, as they deliver almost identical ballistics. Even when fired in the massive A-Square rifles,

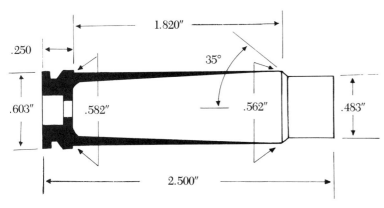

Technical specifications of 460 Short A-Square.

recoil is horrendous—too much for most shooters. A 12-pound rifle has about 90 foot/pounds of recoil. Lighter rifles, say 9 pounds, would develop 120 foot/pounds of recoil!

But if stopping a hostile elephant is on the agenda, nothing, except the 500 A-Square, will deliver more punch. The muzzle energy of the 460 Weatherby Magnum is almost 7,400 foot/pounds, and the 460 A-Square, with a velocity advantage of 50 feet per second, has almost 7,700 foot/pounds of kinetic energy.

46 CALIBER (.468" bullet diameter)
500/465 Nitro Express

480-Grain Bullet—Dangerous Game

This old English round comes up slightly behind the 458 Winchester with respect to ballistic punch. For practical purposes, all comments concerning the Winchester cartridge apply here. This round is loaded in the U.S. solely by A-Square and can be considered very rare.

47 CALIBER (.475" bullet diameter)
470 Nitro Express
475 #2

480-Grain Bullet—Dangerous Game
500 Grain Bullet (470 only)—Dangerous Game

These two English rounds perform alike and are on a par with the 458 Winchester Magnum. They are loaded in the U.S. solely by A-Square. One is named for the nominal bore diameter and the other for actual bullet (or groove) diameter. Both are seldom seen in the U.S.

50 CALIBER (.505" bullet diameter)
505 Gibbs

525-Grain Bullet—Dangerous Game

This cartridge delivers notably more punch than the 458 Winchester. Muzzle energy is just over 6,100 foot/pounds. Originating in England, this round is loaded in the U.S. only by A-Square. It is popular in Africa and is suitable for any dangerous game. However, the 505 Gibbs is surpassed in performance by the 460 Short A-Square.

51 CALIBER (.510" bullet diameter)
500 Nitro Express—3"
600-Grain Bullet—Dangerous Game

As loaded in the U.S. by A-Square, this cartridge gives muzzle energies similar to the 505 Gibbs, but because of its great bullet weight it is superior when ranges exceed 150 yards. Somewhat popular in Africa, it is almost unknown in the U.S.

495 A-Square
600-Grain Bullet—Dangerous Game

Despite its misleading nomenclature, this cartridge employs a .510-inch-diameter bullet. Its name was an effort to prevent confusion with the 500 A-Square. This is a very powerful cartridge, with a muzzle energy of over 6,900 foot/pounds. It is ballistically subordinate only to the 460 Weatherby Magnum, 460 Long A-Square, 500 A-Square—and about on a par with the 577 Nitro Express at short range. It is notably superior to the 577 when ranges are long. This cartridge is loaded only by A-Square.

500 A-Square
600-Grain Bullet—Dangerous Game
707-Grain Bullet—Dangerous Game

This is the most potent cartridge in current U.S. production, outpacing even the monster-mashing 460 Weatherby Magnum. The 500 A-Square (loaded only by A-Square) develops an amazing 7,947 foot/

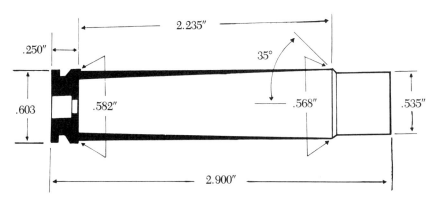

Technical specifications of 500 A-Square.

pounds of muzzle energy with the 707-grain bullet. The 600-grain bullet has 7,546 foot/pounds of muzzle energy. The difference between this cartridge and the 460 Long A-Square or the 460 Weatherby is not monumental, but the 500 is our most potent cartridge. The faint of heart should not even consider firing this powerhouse.

Irate elephant are about the only reason such power is needed, though some hunters use it for lesser African game.

57 CALIBER (.585″ diameter bullet)
577 Nitro Express
750-Grain Bullet—Dangerous Game

This is the largest-diameter cartridge currently loaded by A-Square. It is of British origin and was intended for use only in heavy double-barreled rifles. With 6,998 foot/pounds of muzzle energy, it is nothing short of monstrous, though it delivers less punch than the 460 Weatherby Magnum, 460 Long A-Square, and 500 A-Square. Rifles chambered for this cartridge are rare and very expensive. So is the ammo.

6

Exterior Centerfire Rifle-Cartridge Ballistics

As mentioned in connection with rimfire ammunition, published ballistic tables merely furnish averages with test barrels, not always in agreement with a shooter's chronograph, and shot-to-shot variations also occur with respect to velocity. In the case of centerfire ammunition it is common to encounter extreme velocity spreads of 75 feet per second between the slowest and fastest round in a 10-shot string. Sometimes an extreme spread of as much as 150 feet per second may be encountered during a test. Yet ammunition of extraordinary uniformity may show extreme velocity spreads of only 30 feet per second, or less, in a 10-shot test.

Thus, each shot can produce not only a muzzle-velocity variation but a different velocity at all downrange points. Energy, trajectory, wind drift, and Optimum Game Weight ratings will also vary.

All of these variations, however, do not negate the value of ballistics tables. When the variations occur within a normal dispersion above and below the listed values, the actual field-performance variation will be undetectable or nearly so.

Barrel lengths notably affect centerfire rifle-cartridge ballistics. For the most part, sporting barrels are too short to take full advantage of maximum potential velocity. Indeed, each inch of barrel length causes a measurable velocity change. Ballistic tables generally show external ballistics based on an assumed velocity from a 24-inch barrel. The major exceptions in test barrel lengths are:

Caliber	Standard Test-Barrel Length Used For Tables
7mm BR	15"
30 Carbine	20"
350 Remington Magnum	20"
351 Winchester Self Loader	20"
357 Magnum	20"
44 Remington Magnum	20"
All Weatherby Magnum calibers	26"

The 24-inch barrel used for the development of ballistic tables often does not conform to the barrel length used by the shooter. The majority of sporting rifles in non-magnum calibers have barrels of 22 inches. This means the shooter will seldom obtain the published ballistics; his muzzle velocity and all downrange ballistics will be somewhat lower than advertised.

The shooter can, however, make a reasonable estimate of the actual muzzle velocity he will get when his barrel length differs from the test standards. To do so, refer to Table 6.1. Find the velocity nearest to the advertised velocity of the load being used and then check the column of barrel-length change to obtain the anticipated velocity change. If your barrel is shorter than the advertised length, subtract from the advertised value; if your barrel length exceeds the advertised length, add to the advertised value.

TABLE 6.1

BARREL LENGTH AND VELOCITY

Barrel-Length Change in Inches	VELOCITIES (FPS)						
	1000	1500	2000	2500	3000	3500	4000
	Add or subtract:						
1	5	10	15	20	25	30	35
2	10	20	30	40	50	60	70
3	15	30	45	60	75	90	105
4	20	40	60	80	100	120	140
5	25	50	75	100	125	150	175
6	30	60	90	120	150	180	210
7	35	70	105	140	175	210	245
8	40	80	120	160	200	240	280

TABLE 6.2
BALLISTIC VARIATIONS CAUSED BY BULLET SHAPE

Bullet Weight (gr)	Bullet Shape	VELOCITIES (FPS) AT:				
		muzzle	100 yds	200 yds	300 yds	400 yds
180	round-nose	2700	2350	2025	1725	1465
180	semi-spitzer	2700	2470	2250	2040	1845
180	spitzer	2700	2485	2280	2085	1900

Bullet Weight (gr)	Bullet Shape	ENERGY (FT/LBS) AT:				
		muzzle	100 yds	200 yds	300 yds	400 yds
180	round-nose	2915	2205	1640	1190	860
180	semi-spitzer	2915	2440	2025	1165	1360
180	spitzer	2915	2470	2075	1740	1445

Downrange velocities depend greatly on bullet shape. Naturally, so do downrange energy, trajectory, and wind drift. Sharp-nose bullets retain velocity well, while blunt- and flat-nose bullets lose velocity rapidly, due to air resistance.

The ability to retain velocity is reflected by the ballistic coefficient of a bullet. A bullet with a high ballistic coefficient (.48) will exhibit higher retained ballistics than a bullet having a low ballistic coefficient (.22). Reloading catalogs and data sources often list the ballistic coefficient for various bullets. Ammunition manufacturers seldom do, but they list separate lines of ballistic data for bullets of varying configurations. Table 6.2 shows the effect of bullet shape on downrange performance.

Note how three bullets of varying shape but identical weight, starting at the same 2,700 fps muzzle velocity, will vary over distances of 100, 200, 300, and 400 yards. By the time the round-nose bullet reaches 400 yards it has lost 1,235 feet per second. The spitzer bullet loses only 800 feet per second over the same distance, giving it almost 600 foot/pounds of additional energy at 400 yards. This is a substantial amount.

Tables 6.3–6.6 show values obtained with the most common bullet shapes for a given caliber. For widely varying bullet shapes, the reader should consult the manufacturers' catalogs.

The first column in each table shows a load number. Use this reference number to locate the same load in another ballistic table. Where the load number cannot be located, the pertinent data were not available at press time.

The trajectory tables use several common points of impact at 100 yards for all cartridges—for example; either 2 inches high for varmint loads or 2.5 inches high for big-game loads. This allows the reader to see the optimum trajectory for every load and to compare it with similar loads. The random numbers used in factory-supplied data make such a comparison difficult. A few low-velocity cartridges assume a dead-on point of impact at 100 yards. When the bullet's line of flight falls more than 3 feet below point of aim, no trajectory data will be given as it is impractical to attempt such long-range shooting. Trajectories at 300 and 400 yards are rounded to the nearest inch.

Additionally, where available, the ballistic coefficient for the bullet used to obtain the data is shown in Table 6.6.

Keep in mind that barrel lengths used for the testing may produce data that could be misleading. For example, most of the 30-30 rifles in use have 20-inch barrels and will provide a velocity some 60 feet per second less than the data shown, which is for a 24-inch barrel. The 460 Weatherby's kinetic energy at the muzzle appears slightly higher than the somewhat more potent 500 A-Square data, again due to barrel-length differences. All Weatherby data are based on use of a 26-inch barrel, while the A-Square data are based on use of a 24-inch barrel.

(Text continues on page 133)

TABLE 6.3

AVERAGE FACTORY RIFLE-CARTRIDGE BALLISTICS

Velocity and Energy

Load No.	Cartridge	Bullet Weight (gr)	VELOCITY (FPS) AT:					ENERGY (FT/LBS) AT:				
			-0-	100 yds	200 yds	300 yds	400 yds	-0-	100 yds	200 yds	300 yds	400 yds
1	17 Rem	25	4040	3284	2644	2086	1606	906	599	388	242	143
2	22 Hornet	45	2690	2042	1502	1128	948	723	417	225	127	90
3	218 Bee	46	2760	2102	1550	1155	961	788	451	245	136	94
4	221 Fireball	50	2800	2137	1580	1180	988	870	507	277	155	109
5	222 Rem	50	3140	2602	2123	1700	1350	1094	752	500	321	202
6	222 Rem	55	3020	2562	2147	1773	1451	1114	801	563	384	257
7	22 PPC	52	3400	2930	2510	2130	NA	1335	990	730	525	NA
8	223 Rem	40	3650	3010	2450	1950	1530	1185	805	535	340	265
9	223 Rem	55	3240	2748	2305	1906	1556	1282	922	649	444	296
10	223 Rem	64	NA	NA	NA	NA	NA	NA	NA	NA	NA	NA
11	222 Rem Mag	55	3240	2748	2305	1906	1556	1282	922	649	444	296
12	225 Win	55	3570	3066	2616	2208	1838	1556	1148	836	595	412
13	224 Wea Mag	55	3650	3192	2780	2403	2057	1627	1244	943	705	516
14	22-250 Rem	40	4000	3320	2720	2200	1740	1420	980	660	430	265
15	22-250 Rem	55	3680	3137	2656	2222	1832	1654	1201	861	603	410
16	220 Swift	50	4110	3610	3135	2680	NA	1875	1450	1090	800	NA
17	6mm PPC	70	3140	2750	2400	2070	NA	1535	1175	895	665	NA
18	243 Win	80	3350	2955	2593	2259	1951	1993	1551	1194	906	676

EXTERIOR CENTERFIRE RIFLE-CARTRIDGE BALLISTICS

Load No.	Cartridge	Bullet Weight (gr)	VELOCITY (FPS) AT:					ENERGY (FT/LBS) AT:				
			-0-	100 yds	200 yds	300 yds	400 yds	-0-	100 yds	200 yds	300 yds	400 yds
19	243 Win	85	3320	3070	2830	2600	2380	2080	1770	1510	1280	1070
20	243 Win	100	2960	2697	2449	2215	1993	1945	1615	1332	1089	882
21	6mm Rem	80	3470	3064	2694	2352	2036	2139	1667	1289	982	736
22	6mm Rem	100	3100	2829	2573	2332	2104	2133	1777	1470	1207	983
23	240 Wea Mag	87	3500	3202	2924	2663	2416	2366	1980	1651	1370	1127
24	240 Wea Mag	100	3395	3106	2835	2581	2339	2559	2142	1785	1478	1215
25	25-20 Win	86	1460	1194	1030	931	858	407	272	203	165	141
26	25-35 Win	117	2230	1866	1545	1282	1097	1292	904	620	427	313
27	250 Savage	100	2820	2504	2210	1936	1684	1765	1392	1084	832	630
28	257 Roberts	100	2980	2661	2363	2085	1827	1972	1572	1240	965	741
29	257 Roberts	117	2780	2411	2071	1761	1488	2009	1511	1115	806	576
30	257 Roberts	120	2780	2560	2360	2160	1970	2060	1750	1480	1240	1030
31	25-06 Rem	87	3440	2995	2591	2222	1884	2286	1733	1297	954	686
32	25-06 Rem	90	3440	3043	2680	2344	2034	2364	1850	1435	1098	827
33	25-06 Rem	100	3230	2893	2580	2287	2014	2316	1858	1478	1161	901
34	25-06 Rem	117	2990	2770	2570	2370	2190	2320	2000	1715	1465	1246
35	25-06 Rem	120	2990	2730	2484	2252	2032	2382	1985	1644	1351	1100
36	257 Wea Mag	87	3825	3456	3118	2805	2513	2826	2308	1870	1520	1220
37	257 Wea Mag	100	3555	3237	2941	2665	2404	2806	2326	1920	1576	1283
38	257 Wea Mag	120	3300	3056	2823	2599	2388	2902	2489	2124	1800	1520
39	6.5 Rem Mag	120	3210	2905	2621	2353	2102	2745	2248	1830	1475	1177
40	264 Win Mag	140	3030	2782	2548	2326	2114	2854	2406	2018	1682	1389
41	270 Win	100	3430	3021	2649	2305	1988	2612	2027	1557	1179	877
42	270 Win	130	3060	2776	2510	2259	2022	2702	2225	1818	1472	1180
43	270 Win	150	2850	2585	2336	2100	1879	2705	2226	1817	1468	1175
44	270 Wea Mag	100	3760	3380	3033	2712	2412	3139	2537	2042	1633	1292
45	270 Wea Mag	130	3375	3119	2878	2649	2432	3287	2808	2390	2026	1707
46	270 Wea Mag	150	3245	3036	2837	2647	2465	3507	3070	2681	2334	2023
47	7mm BR	140	2215	2012	1821	1643	1481	1525	1259	1031	839	681
48	7mm Mauser	140	2660	2435	2221	2018	1827	2199	1843	1533	1266	1037
49	7mm Mauser	145	2690	2442	2206	1985	1777	2334	1920	1568	1268	1017
50	7mm Mauser	175	2440	2137	1857	1603	1382	2313	1774	1340	998	742
51	7×30 Waters	120	2700	2300	1930	1600	1330	1940	1405	990	685	470
52	7mm-08 Rem	120	3000	2725	2467	2223	1992	2398	1979	1621	1316	1058
53	7mm-08 Rem	140	2860	2625	2402	2189	1988	2542	2142	1793	1490	1228
54	284 Win	125	3140	2829	2538	2265	2010	2736	2221	1788	1424	1121
55	284 Win	150	2860	2595	2344	2108	1886	2724	2243	1830	1480	1185
56	280 Rem	120	3150	2866	2599	2348	2110	2643	2188	1800	1468	1186
57	280 Rem	140	3000	2758	2528	2309	2102	2797	2363	1986	1657	1373
58	280 Rem	150	2890	2624	2373	2135	1912	2781	2293	1875	1518	1217
59	280 Rem	165	2820	2510	2220	1950	1701	2913	2308	1805	1393	1060
60	7mm Rem Mag	140	3175	2923	2684	2458	2243	3133	2655	2240	1878	1564
61	7mm Rem Mag	150	3110	2830	2085	2320	2085	3221	2667	2196	1792	1448
62	7mm Rem Mag	165	2950	2800	2650	2510	2370	3190	2865	2570	2300	2050
63	7mm Rem Mag	175	2860	2645	2440	2244	2057	3178	2718	2313	1956	1644
64	7mm Wea Mag	140	3400	3163	2939	2726	2522	3593	3110	2684	2309	1978
65	7mm Wea Mag	154	3260	3023	2799	2586	2382	3539	3044	2609	2227	1890
66	7mm Wea Mag	160	3200	3004	2816	2637	2464	3637	3205	2817	2469	2156
67	7mm Wea Mag	175	3070	2879	2696	2520	2351	3662	3220	2824	2467	2147

VELOCITY AND ENERGY (continued)

Load No.	Cartridge	Bullet Weight (gr)	VELOCITY (FPS) AT:					ENERGY (FT/LBS) AT:				
			-0-	100 yds	200 yds	300 yds	400 yds	-0-	100 yds	200 yds	300 yds	400 yds
68	30 Carbine	110	1990	1567	1236	1035	923	977	600	373	262	208
69	303 Savage	190	1890	1612	1372	1183	1055	1507	1096	794	591	469
70	30 Rem	170	2120	1822	1555	1328	1153	1696	1253	913	666	502
71	30-30 Win	55	3400	2693	2085	1570	1187	1412	886	521	301	172
72	30-30 Win	125	2570	2090	1660	1320	1080	1830	1210	770	480	320
73	30-30 Win	150	2390	1973	1605	1303	1095	1902	1296	858	565	399
74	30-30 Win	173	2200	1895	1619	1381	1191	1827	1355	989	720	535
75	300 Savage	150	2630	2354	2094	1853	1631	2303	1845	1462	1143	886
76	300 Savage	180	2350	2137	1935	1754	1570	2207	1825	1496	1217	985
77	30-40 Krag	180	2430	2213	2007	1813	1632	2360	1957	1610	1314	1064
78	307 Win	150	2760	2321	1924	1575	1289	2530	1795	1233	826	554
79	308 Win	55	3770	3215	2726	2286	1888	1735	1262	907	638	435
80	308 Win	150	2820	2533	2263	2009	1774	2648	2137	1705	1344	1048
81	308 Win	165	2700	2440	2194	1963	1748	2670	2180	1763	1411	1199
82	308 Win	168	2680	2493	2314	2143	1979	2678	2318	1998	1713	1460
83	308 Win	180	2620	2393	2178	1974	1782	2743	2288	1896	1557	1269
84	30-06 Spfd	55	4080	3485	2965	2502	2083	2033	1483	1074	764	530
85	30-06 Spfd	125	3140	2780	2447	2138	1853	2736	2145	1662	1279	953
86	30-06 Spfd	150	2910	2617	2342	2083	1853	2820	2281	1827	1445	1135
87	30-06 Spfd	165	2800	2534	2283	2047	1825	2872	2352	1909	1534	1220
88	30-06 Spfd	180	2700	2469	2250	2042	1846	2913	2436	2023	1666	1362
89	30-06 Spfd	220	2410	2130	1870	1632	1422	2837	2216	1708	1301	988
90	300 H&H Mag	180	2880	2640	2412	2196	1990	3315	2785	2325	1927	1583
91	300 H&H Mag	220	2550	2267	2002	1756	NA	3176	2510	1958	1508	NA
92	300 Win Mag	150	3290	2951	2636	2342	2068	3605	2900	2314	1827	1424
93	300 Win Mag	180	2960	2745	2540	2344	2157	3501	3011	2578	2196	1859
94	300 Win Mag	200	2830	2680	2530	2380	2240	3560	3180	2830	2520	2230
95	300 Win Mag	220	2680	2448	2228	2020	1823	3508	2927	2424	1993	1623
96	300 Wea Mag	110	3900	3441	3028	2652	2305	3714	2891	2239	1717	1297
97	300 Wea Mag	150	3600	3307	3033	2776	2533	4316	3642	3064	2566	2137
98	300 Wea Mag	180	3300	3077	2865	2663	2470	4352	3784	3280	2834	2438
99	300 Wea Mag	220	2905	2498	2126	1787	1490	4122	3047	2207	1560	1085
100	32-20 Win	100	1210	1021	913	834	769	325	231	185	154	131
101	303 British	180	2460	2124	1817	1542	1311	2418	1803	1319	950	687
102	32 Win Special	170	2250	1921	1626	1372	1175	1911	1393	998	710	521
103	8mm Mauser	170	2360	1969	1622	1333	1123	2102	1464	993	671	476
104	8mm Mauser	220	2300	2033	1785	1561	NA	2584	2019	1557	1191	NA
105	8mm Rem Mag	185	3080	2761	2464	2186	1927	3896	3131	2494	1963	1525
106	8mm Rem Mag	220	2830	2581	2346	2123	1913	3912	3254	2688	2201	1787
107	338 Win Mag	210	2830	2590	2370	2150	1940	3735	3130	2610	2155	1760
108	338 Win Mag	225	2780	2572	2374	2184	2003	3860	3305	2845	2383	2004
109	338 Win Mag	250	2660	2456	2261	2075	1898	3927	3348	2837	2389	1999
110	338 Wea Mag	210	3250	2991	2746	2515	2295	4924	4170	3516	2948	2455
111	338 Wea Mag	250	3000	2806	2621	2443	2272	4995	4371	3812	3311	2864
112	338 A-Square	250	3120	2799	2500	2220	1958	5403	4348	3469	2736	2128
113	348 Win	200	2520	2215	1931	1672	1443	2820	2178	1656	1241	925

EXTERIOR CENTERFIRE RIFLE-CARTRIDGE BALLISTICS

Load No.	Cartridge	Bullet Weight (gr)	VELOCITY (FPS) AT:					ENERGY (FT/LBS) AT:				
			-0-	100 yds	200 yds	300 yds	400 yds	-0-	100 yds	200 yds	300 yds	400 yds
114	351 Win SL	180	1850	1556	1310	1128	1012	1368	968	686	508	409
115	357 Mag	158	1830	1427	1138	980	883	1175	715	454	337	274
116	35 Rem	150	2300	1874	1506	1218	1039	1762	1169	755	494	359
117	35 Rem	200	2080	1698	1376	1140	1001	1921	1280	841	577	445
118	356 Win	200	2460	2114	1797	1517	1284	2688	1985	1434	1022	732
119	358 Win	200	2490	2171	1876	1619	1379	2753	2093	1563	1151	844
120	350 Rem Mag	200	2710	2410	2130	1870	1631	3261	2579	2014	1553	1181
121	35 Whelen	200	2675	2378	2100	1842	1606	3177	2510	1958	1506	1145
122	35 Whelen	250	2400	2066	1761	1492	1269	3197	2369	1722	1235	893
123	9.3×62mm	286	2360	2089	1844	1623	NA	3538	2771	2157	1670	NA
124	9.3×64mm	286	2700	2505	2318	2139	1968	4629	3984	3411	2906	2460
125	9.3×74Rmm	286	2360	2089	1844	1623	NA	3538	2771	2157	1670	NA
126	38-55 Win	255	1320	1190	1091	1018	963	987	802	674	587	525
127	375 Win	200	2200	1841	1526	1268	1089	2150	1506	1034	714	527
128	375 Win	250	1900	1647	1424	1239	1103	2005	1506	1126	852	676
129	375 H&H Mag	270	2690	2420	2166	1928	1707	4337	3510	2812	2228	1747
130	375 H&H Mag	300	2530	2171	1843	1551	1307	4263	3139	2262	1602	1138
131	375 Wea Mag	300	2700	2420	2157	1911	1685	4856	3901	3100	2432	1891
132	378 Wea Mag	270	3180	2976	2781	2594	2415	6062	5308	4635	4034	3495
133	378 Wea Mag	300	2929	2576	2252	1952	1680	5698	4419	3379	2538	1881
134	38-40 Win	180	1160	999	901	827	764	538	399	324	273	233
135	450/400-3″	400	2150	1932	1730	1545	1379	4105	3316	2659	2119	1689
136	416 Hoffman	400	2380	2145	1923	1718	1529	5031	4087	3285	2620	2077
137	416 Rigby	400	2400	2164	1941	1734	1544	5115	4159	3346	2670	2118
138	404 Jeffrey	400	2150	1924	1716	1525	NA	4105	3289	2614	2064	NA
139	44-40 Win	200	1190	1006	900	822	756	629	449	360	300	254
140	44 Rem Mag	240	1760	1380	1114	970	878	1650	1015	661	501	411
141	444 Marlin	240	2350	1815	1377	1087	941	2942	1753	1001	630	472
142	444 Marlin	265	2120	1733	1405	1160	1012	2644	1768	1162	791	603
143	45-70 Govt	300	1810	1497	1244	1073	969	2182	1492	1031	767	625
144	45-70 Govt	405	1330	1168	1055	977	918	1590	1227	1001	858	758
145	458 Win Mag	465	2220	1999	1791	1601	NA	5088	4127	3312	2646	NA
146	458 Win Mag	500	2040	1823	1623	1442	1237	4620	3689	2924	2308	1839
147	457 Win Mag	510	2040	1770	1527	1319	1157	4712	3547	2640	1970	1516
148	450 NE-3¼″	465	2190	1970	1765	1577	NA	4952	4009	3216	2567	NA
149	450 NE-3¼″	500	2150	1920	1708	1514	NA	5132	4093	3238	2544	NA
150	450 No. 2	465	2190	1970	1765	1577	NA	4952	4009	3216	2567	NA
151	450 No. 2	500	2150	1920	1708	1514	NA	5132	4093	3238	2544	NA
152	450 Ackley Mag	500	2320	2081	1855	1649	NA	5975	4085	3820	3018	NA
153	460 Short A-Sq	500	2420	2175	1943	1729	NA	6501	5250	4193	3319	NA
154	460 Long A-Sq	500	2630	2372	2130	1901	NA	7679	6248	5036	4013	NA
155	460 Wea Mag	500	2700	2404	2128	1869	1635	8092	6416	5026	3878	2969
156	500/465 NE	480	2150	1917	1703	1507	NA	4926	3917	3089	2419	NA
157	470 Nitro Ex	480	2190	1954	1735	1536	NA	5111	4070	3210	2515	NA

VELOCITY AND ENERGY (continued)

Load No.	Cartridge	Bullet Weight (gr)	VELOCITY (FPS) AT:					ENERGY (FT/LBS) AT:				
			-0-	100 yds	200 yds	300 yds	400 yds	-0-	100 yds	200 yds	300 yds	400 yds
158	470 Nitro Ex	500	2150	1912	1693	1494	NA	5132	4058	3182	2478	NA
159	475 No. 2	480	2200	1942	1705	1492	NA	5158	4020	3099	2371	NA
160	505 Gibbs	505	2300	2008	1741	1501	NA	6166	4702	3532	2625	NA
161	500 NE-3″	600	2150	1927	1721	1531	NA	6158	4947	3944	3124	NA
162	495 A-Square	600	2280	2050	1833	1635	NA	6925	5598	4478	3562	NA
163	500 A-Square	600	2380	2144	1922	1766	NA	7546	6126	4920	3922	NA
164	500 A-Square	707	2250	2040	1841	1567	NA	7947	6530	5318	4311	NA
165	577 Nitro Ex	750	2050	1793	1562	1360	NA	6990	5356	4065	3079	NA

Notes: NA = Data not available from manufacturer
Wea Mag = Weatherby Magnum
Spfd = Springfield
A-Sq = A-Square
NE = Nitro Express

TABLE 6.4

AVERAGE FACTORY RIFLE-CARTRIDGE BALLISTICS

Optimum Game Weight and Trajectory

Load No.	Cartridge	Bullet Weight (gr)	Muzzle Vel. (fps)	OPTIMUM GAME WEIGHT (LBS) AT:					TRAJECTORY IN INCHES AT:					
				Muzzle	100 yds	200 yds	300 yds	400 yds	100 yds	150 yds	200 yds	250 yds	300 yds	400 yds
1	17 Rem	25*	4040	21	11	6	3	1	+2.0	+2.4	+1.7	−0.2	−4.0	−17.0
2	22 Hornet	45*	2690	18	9	3	1	0	0.0	−2.4	−7.7	−16.9	−31.0	—
3	218 Bee	46*	2760	22	10	4	2	1	0.0	−2.3	−7.2	−15.8	−29.0	—
4	221 Fireball	50*	2800	27	12	5	2	1	0.0	−2.0	−7.0	−15.0	−28.0	—
5	222 Rem	50*	3140	39	22	12	6	3	+2.0	+1.6	−0.4	−4.3	−11.0	−33.0
6	222 Rem	55*	3020	42	25	15	8	5	+2.0	+1.6	−0.4	−4.3	−11.0	−32.0
7	22 PPC	52*	3400	53	34	21	13	NA	+2.0	NA	+1.4	−1.0	−5.0	NA
8	223 Rem	40*	3650	40	22	12	6	3	+2.0	+2.0	+1.0	−1.6	−6.0	−22.0
9	223 Rem	55*	3240	51	31	19	11	6	+2.0	+1.5	−0.2	−3.5	−9.0	−27.0
10	223 Rem	64	NA	NA	NA	NA	NA	NA	NA	NA	NA	NA	NA	NA
11	222 Rem Mag	55*	3240	51	31	19	11	6	+2.0	+1.5	−0.2	−3.5	−9.0	−27.0
12	225 Win	55*	3570	69	44	27	16	9	+2.0	+2.2	+1.0	−1.5	−5.0	−20.0
13	224 Wea Mag	55*	3650	74	49	33	21	13	+2.0	+2.2	+1.2	−0.9	−4.0	−17.0
14	22-250 Rem	40*	4000	51	29	16	9	4	+2.0	+2.4	+1.8	0.0	−3.0	−16.0
15	22-250 Rem	55*	3680	75	47	28	17	9	+2.0	+2.2	+1.3	−0.7	−4.0	−17.0
16	220 Swift	50*	4110	87	59	39	24	NA	+2.0	NA	+2.8	−1.1	−7.0	NA
17	6mm PPC	70*	3140	76	51	34	22	NA	+2.0	NA	+1.4	−1.0	−5.0	NA
18	243 Win	80*	3350	120	83	56	37	24	+2.0	+2.0	+0.9	−1.5	−5.0	−19.0

Load No.	Cartridge	Bullet Weight (gr)	Muzzle Vel. (fps)	OPTIMUM GAME WEIGHT (LBS) AT:					TRAJECTORY IN INCHES AT:					
				Muzzle	100 yds	200 yds	300 yds	400 yds	100 yds	150 yds	200 yds	250 yds	300 yds	400 yds
19	243 Win	85*	3320	132	105	82	63	49	+2.0	+2.1	+1.2	−0.8	−4.0	−14.0
20	243 Win	100	2960	389	294	220	163	119	+2.5	+2.5	+1.2	−1.6	−6.0	−20.0
21	6mm Rem	80*	3470	134	92	63	42	27	+2.0	+2.1	+1.1	−1.0	−5.0	−17.0
22	6mm Rem	100	3100	447	340	256	190	140	+2.5	+2.7	+1.6	−0.8	−5.0	−17.0
23	240 Wea Mag	87*	3500	162	124	95	72	53	+2.0	+3.0	+2.0	0.0	−2.0	−12.0
24	240 Wea Mag	100	3395	586	449	342	258	192	+2.5	+3.4	+2.8	0.0	−2.0	−11.0
25	25-20 Win	86*	1460	12	6	4	3	2	0.0	−8.2	−23.5	—	—	—
26	25-35 Win	117	2230	228	133	76	43	27	+2.5	+0.6	−4.3	−12.8	−26.0	—
27	250 Savage	100	2820	336	236	162	109	72	+2.5	+2.3	+0.4	−3.2	−9.0	−28.0
28	257 Roberts	100	2980	397	283	199	135	92	+2.0	+1.7	0.0	−3.3	−8.0	−25.0
29	257 Roberts	117	2780	441	288	182	112	68	+2.5	+2.1	−0.2	−4.5	−11.0	−33.0
30	257 Roberts	120	2780	464	362	284	218	165	+2.5	+2.2	+0.6	−2.7	−8.0	−23.0
31	25-06 Rem	87*	3440	154	102	66	42	25	+2.0	+2.2	+1.1	−1.2	−5.0	−18.0
32	25-06 Rem	90*	3440	165	114	79	52	34	+2.0	+2.1	+1.2	−1.0	−5.0	−13.0
33	25-06 Rem	100	3230	505	363	257	179	123	+2.0	+2.6	+0.8	−1.7	−6.0	−19.0
34	25-06 Rem	117	2990	548	436	349	273	216	+2.5	+2.5	+1.4	−1.1	−5.0	−18.0
35	25-06 Rem	120	2990	577	439	331	247	181	+2.5	+2.5	+1.2	−1.5	−6.0	−20.0
36	257 Wea Mag	87*	3825	213	156	115	84	60	+2.0	+3.4	+2.6	+0.5	−1.0	−7.0
37	257 Wea Mag	100	3555	674	509	328	284	208	+2.5	+4.0	+3.1	+1.2	0.0	−8.0
38	257 Wea Mag	120	3300	776	616	486	380	294	+2.5	+4.5	+3.5	+1.7	−1.0	−10.0
39	6.5 Rem Mag	120	3210	714	530	389	281	201	+2.5	+2.7	+1.7	−0.5	−4.0	−16.0
40	264 Win Mag	140	3030	818	633	486	370	278	+2.5	+2.5	+1.4	−1.2	−5.0	−18.0
41	270 Win	100*	3430	202	138	93	61	39	+2.0	+2.1	+1.0	−1.2	−5.0	−18.0
42	270 Win	130	3060	726	542	400	292	210	+2.5	+2.5	+1.4	−1.2	−5.0	−19.0
43	270 Win	150	2850	781	582	430	313	224	+2.5	+2.2	+0.6	−1.7	−8.0	−25.0
44	270 Wea Mag	100*	3760	266	193	140	100	70	+2.0	+3.2	+2.4	+0.4	−1.0	−8.0
45	270 Wea Mag	130	3375	975	769	604	471	365	+2.5	+4.1	+2.9	+1.3	−1.0	−8.0
46	270 Wea Mag	150	3245	1153	945	770	626	506	+2.5	+3.3	+2.7	+0.8	−2.0	−7.0
47	7mm BR	140	2215	319	239	178	130	96	+2.0	+0.3	−3.7	−10.4	−21.0	—
48	7mm Mauser	140	2660	553	425	322	242	179	+2.5	+2.0	0.0	−3.8	−10.0	−28.0
49	7mm Mauser	145	2690	614	459	339	247	177	+2.5	+2.8	+0.8	−3.1	−10.0	−28.0
50	7mm Mauser	175	2440	667	448	294	189	121	+2.5	+1.5	−1.7	−7.5	−16.0	—
51	7×30 Waters	120	2700	425	263	155	88	51	+2.5	+2.0	−0.8	−5.8	−14.0	—
52	7mm-08 Rem	120*	3000	194	146	108	79	57	+2.0	+1.7	+0.2	−2.8	−7.0	−22.0
53	7mm-08 Rem	140	2860	688	532	407	308	231	+2.5	+2.3	+0.8	−2.2	−7.0	−26.0
54	284 Win	125*	3140	242	177	128	91	63	+2.0	+1.9	+0.6	−2.1	−6.0	−20.0
55	284 Win	150	2860	790	590	435	316	226	+2.5	+2.4	+0.8	−2.4	−8.0	−23.0
56	280 Rem	120*	3150	225	170	126	93	68	+2.0	+1.8	+0.6	−2.0	−6.0	−19.0
57	280 Rem	140	3000	794	617	475	362	273	+2.5	+2.5	+1.4	−1.2	−5.0	−18.0
58	280 Rem	150	2890	815	610	451	328	236	+2.5	+2.3	+0.8	−2.3	−7.0	−23.0
59	280 Rem	165	2820	916	646	447	303	201	+2.5	+2.2	+0.4	−3.2	−9.0	−27.0
60	7mm Rem Mag	140	3175	941	734	568	437	332	+2.5	+2.8	+1.8	−0.2	−4.0	−15.0
61	7mm Rem Mag	150	3110	1015	765	572	421	306	+2.5	+3.2	+1.6	−0.8	−6.0	−17.0
62	7mm Rem Mag	165	2950	1048	896	760	646	534	+2.5	+2.5	+1.4	−1.0	−5.0	−16.0
63	7mm Rem Mag	175	2860	1074	850	667	519	400	+2.5	+2.4	+1.0	−2.0	−6.0	−21.0
64	7mm Wea Mag	140	3400	1155	930	746	596	472	+2.5	+4.1	+3.0	+1.4	−1.0	−9.0
65	7mm Wea Mag	154	3260	1233	983	780	615	481	+2.5	+4.0	+2.8	+1.9	−2.0	−11.0
66	7mm Wea Mag	160	3200	1258	1041	858	704	575	+2.5	+3.9	+2.7	+1.8	−2.0	−11.0
67	7mm Wea Mag	175	3070	1329	1096	900	710	597	+2.5	+3.4	+2.3	+0.2	−3.0	−13.0

OPTIMUM GAME WEIGHT AND TRAJECTORY (continued)

Load No.	Cartridge	Bullet Weight (gr)	Muzzle Vel. (fps)	OPTIMUM GAME WEIGHT (LBS) AT:					TRAJECTORY IN INCHES AT:					
				Muzzle	100 yds	200 yds	300 yds	400 yds	100 yds	150 yds	200 yds	250 yds	300 yds	400 yds
68	30 Carbine	110	1990	143	70	34	20	14	0.0	− 4.5	− 13.5	− 28.3	—	—
69	303 Savage	190	1890	366	227	140	90	64	+2.5	− 0.6	− 7.6	− 19.3	− 36.0	—
70	30 Rem	170	2120	413	262	163	102	66	+2.5	+ 0.4	− 4.7	− 13.4	− 26.0	—
71	30-30 Win	55*	3400	59	30	14	6	3	+2.0	+ 1.8	0.0	− 3.8	− 10.2	− 35.0
72	30-30 Win	125*	2570	137	71	36	18	9	+2.0	+ 0.4	− 2.4	− 8.5	− 19.0	—
73	30-30 Win	150	2390	460	259	140	75	44	+2.5	+ 1.0	− 3.2	− 10.8	− 22.0	—
74	30-30 Win	170	2200	462	295	184	114	73	+2.5	+ 0.7	− 3.8	− 11.8	− 23.0	—
75	300 Savage	150	2630	614	440	310	215	146	+2.5	+ 1.9	− 0.4	− 4.7	− 11.0	− 36.0
76	300 Savage	180	2350	630	474	352	258	188	+2.5	+ 1.0	− 1.6	− 7.6	− 15.0	—
77	30-40 Krag	180	2430	697	527	393	290	211	+2.5	+ 1.1	− 1.3	− 6.5	− 12.0	—
78	307 Win	150	2760	709	422	240	132	79	+2.5	+ 2.0	− 0.6	− 5.4	− 13.0	—
79	308 Win	55*	3770	81	50	31	18	10	+2.0	+ 2.2	+ 1.4	− 0.5	− 3.0	− 15.0
80	308 Win	150	2820	757	549	391	274	188	+2.5	+ 2.2	+ 0.4	− 3.1	− 9.0	− 26.0
81	308 Win	165	2700	804	593	431	309	218	+2.5	+ 2.1	0.0	− 3.9	− 10.0	− 29.0
82	308 Win	168	2680	815	656	525	417	328	+2.5	+ 2.0	+ 0.2	− 3.3	− 9.0	− 25.0
83	308 Win	180	2620	874	666	502	374	275	+2.5	+ 2.0	− 0.2	− 4.2	− 10.0	− 29.0
84	30-06 Spfd	55*	4080	103	64	39	24	14	+2.0	+ 2.4	+ 1.9	+ 0.5	− 2.0	− 12.0
85	30-06 Spfd	125*	3140	242	168	115	76	50	+2.0	+ 1.8	+ 0.4	− 2.5	− 7.0	− 22.0
86	30-06 Spfd	150	2910	832	601	436	305	211	+2.5	+ 2.4	+ 0.8	− 2.3	− 7.0	− 23.0
87	30-06 Spfd	165	2800	896	665	485	350	248	+2.5	+ 2.2	+ 0.4	− 3.1	− 8.0	− 26.0
88	30-06 Spfd	180	2700	957	732	554	414	306	+2.5	+ 2.1	+ 0.2	− 3.5	− 9.0	− 27.0
89	30-06 Spfd	220	2410	1016	702	475	316	209	+2.5	+ 1.5	− 1.7	− 7.4	− 16.0	—
90	300 H&H Mag	180	2880	1161	894	682	515	383	+2.5	+ 2.3	+ 0.8	− 2.2	− 7.0	− 22.0
91	300 H&H Mag	220	2550	1204	846	583	393	NA	+2.5	NA	− 0.2	− 4.7	− 12.0	NA
92	300 Win Mag	150	3290	1202	867	618	434	299	+2.5	+ 2.8	+ 1.9	− 0.2	− 3.0	− 15.0
93	300 Win Mag	180	2960	1260	1005	796	626	487	+2.5	+ 2.5	+ 1.2	− 1.4	− 6.0	− 18.0
94	300 Win Mag	200	2830	1360	1155	972	809	675	+2.5	+ 2.7	+ 1.6	− 0.8	− 5.0	− 17.0
95	300 Win Mag	220	2680	1397	1065	803	598	440	+2.5	+ 2.0	0.0	− 3.8	− 10.0	− 28.0
96	300 Wea Mag	110*	3900	359	247	168	113	74	+2.0	NA	+ 2.6	+ 1.2	− 1.0	− 9.0
97	300 Wea Mag	150	3600	1575	1221	942	722	549	+2.5	NA	+ 3.1	+ 1.9	0.0	− 8.0
98	300 Wea Mag	180	3300	1747	1416	1143	918	732	+2.5	NA	+ 2.8	+ 0.9	− 2.0	− 10.0
99	300 Wea Mag	220	2905	1780	1132	698	414	240	+2.5	NA	+ 0.9	− 4.6	− 8.0	− 29.0
100	32-20 Win	100*	1210	9	5	4	3	2	0.0	− 11.5	− 32.3	—	—	—
101	303 British	180	2460	724	466	292	178	106	+2.5	+ 1.0	− 1.8	− 8.2	− 17.0	—
102	32 Win Special	170	2250	494	307	186	112	70	+2.5	+ 0.9	− 3.5	− 11.2	− 23.0	—
103	8mm Mauser	170	2360	570	331	185	103	61	+2.5	+ 1.0	− 3.1	− 10.7	− 22.0	—
104	8mm Mauser	220	2300	883	610	413	276	NA	+2.5	NA	− 2.0	− 6.0	− 18.0	NA
105	8mm Rem Mag	185	3080	1500	1080	768	536	367	+2.5	+ 2.6	+ 1.4	− 1.3	− 6.0	− 20.0
106	8mm Rem Mag	220	2830	1646	1248	937	695	508	+2.5	+ 2.2	+ 0.6	− 2.7	− 7.0	− 21.0
107	338 Win Mag	210	2830	1499	1149	881	657	483	+2.5	+ 2.4	+ 0.8	− 2.3	− 7.0	− 23.0
108	338 Win Mag	225	2780	1632	1292	1016	791	610	+2.5	+ 2.2	+ 0.6	− 2.6	− 8.0	− 23.0
109	338 Win Mag	250	2660	1765	1389	1084	838	641	+2.5	+ 2.1	+ 0.2	− 3.5	− 9.0	− 26.0
110	340 Wea Mag	210	3250	2271	1770	1370	1052	800	+2.5	NA	+ 2.7	+ 1.8	− 2.0	− 11.0
111	340 Wea Mag	250	3000	2531	2071	1688	1367	1100	+2.5	NA	+ 2.0	− 0.2	− 4.0	− 15.0
112	338 A-Square	250	3120	2847	2056	1465	1026	704	+2.5	NA	+ 2.0	− 0.4	− 4.0	− 17.0
113	348 Win	200	2520	960	652	432	281	180	+2.5	+ 1.6	− 1.2	− 6.5	− 14.0	—

EXTERIOR CENTERFIRE RIFLE-CARTRIDGE BALLISTICS

Load No.	Cartridge	Bullet Weight (gr)	Muzzle Vel. (fps)	OPTIMUM GAME WEIGHT (LBS) AT:					TRAJECTORY IN INCHES AT:					
				Muzzle	100 yds	200 yds	300 yds	400 yds	100 yds	150 yds	200 yds	250 yds	300 yds	400 yds
114	351 Win SL	180	1850	307	183	109	70	50	0.0	− 4.7	−13.6	−27.6	—	—
115	357 Mag	158*	1830	77	36	18	12	9	0.0	− 5.5	−16.2	−33.1	—	—
116	35 Rem	150	2300	411	222	115	61	38	+2.5	+ 0.7	− 4.1	−12.9	−26.0	—
117	35 Rem	200	2080	540	294	156	89	60	+2.5	0.0	− 6.3	−17.1	−34.0	—
118	356 Win	200	2460	893	567	348	209	127	+2.5	+ 1.3	− 2.0	− 8.1	−17.0	—
119	358 Win	200	2490	926	614	396	250	157	+2.5	+ 1.5	− 1.6	− 7.2	−16.0	—
120	350 Rem Mag	200	2710	1194	840	580	392	260	+2.5	+ 2.0	− 0.2	− 4.3	−11.0	−31.0
121	35 Whelen	200	2675	1148	807	556	374	249	+2.5	+ 2.1	− 0.2	− 4.4	−11.0	−32.0
122	35 Whelen	250	2400	1296	827	512	311	192	+2.5	+ 1.3	− 2.2	− 8.6	−18.0	—
123	9.3×62mm	286	2360	1613	1119	769	525	NA	+2.5	NA	− 1.0	− 5.0	−14.0	NA
124	9.3×64mm	286	2700	2415	1929	1528	1200	935	+2.5	NA	+ 0.9	NA	− 7.2	−23.0
125	9.3×74Rmm	286	2360	1613	1119	769	525	NA	+2.5	NA	− 1.0	− 5.0	−14.0	NA
126	38-55 Win	255	1320	219	164	127	103	87	0.0	− 8.7	−23.4	—	—	—
127	375 Win	200	2200	639	374	213	122	78	+2.5	+ 0.6	− 4.4	−13.1	−26.0	—
128	375 Win	250	1900	643	419	271	178	126	+2.5	− 0.3	− 6.9	−17.7	−33.0	—
129	375 H&H Mag	270	2690	2129	1550	1111	784	544	+2.5	+ 2.1	0.0	− 3.9	−10.0	−29.0
130	375 H&H Mag	300	2530	2186	1381	845	504	301	+2.5	+ 1.5	− 1.6	−16.6	—	—
131	375 Wea Mag	300	2700	2657	1913	1354	942	646	+2.5	NA	+ 0.5	− 3.3	− 9.0	−28.0
132	378 Wea Mag	270	3180	3510	2882	2352	1909	1540	+2.5	NA	+ 2.6	+ 1.8	− 2.0	−11.0
133	378 Wea Mag	300	2929	3378	2308	1542	1004	640	+2.5	NA	+ 1.2	− 2.3	− 7.0	−25.0
134	38-40 Win	180	1160	80	49	36	28	22	0.0	−12.1	−33.9	—	—	—
135	450/400-3″	400	2150	2385	1730	1242	885	629	+2.5	NA	− 3.6	−21.3	—	—
136	416 Hoffman	400	2380	3236	2369	1707	1217	858	+2.5	+ 0.3	− 3.0	− 8.7	NA	NA
137	416 Rigby	400	2400	3318	2432	1755	1251	883	+2.5	+ 0.3	− 3.0	− 8.7	NA	NA
138	404 Jeffrey	400	2150	2385	1709	1213	851	NA	+2.5	NA	− 3.0	−11.8	−19.0	—
139	44-40 Win	200	1190	101	61	44	33	26	0.0	−11.8	−33.3	—	—	—
140	44 Rem Mag	240	1760	471	227	119	79	59	0.0	− 5.9	−17.6	−36.0	—	—
141	444 Marlin	240	2350	1121	517	226	111	72	+2.5	+ 0.6	− 4.8	−14.9	−31.0	—
142	444 Marlin	265	2120	1004	548	292	164	109	+2.5	0.0	− 6.0	−16.4	−32.0	—
143	45-70 Govt	300	1810	801	453	260	168	123	+2.5	− 0.0	−10.0	−23.0	—	—
144	45-70 Govt	405	1330	579	392	289	230	190	+2.5	− 4.7	−19.6	—	—	—
145	458 Win Mag	465	2220	3549	2591	1863	1331	NA	+2.5	NA	− 2.0	−10.0	−18.0	—
146	458 Win Mag	500	2040	3184	2272	1603	1124	710	+2.5	+ 0.4	− 4.2	−12.9	−25.0	—
147	458 Win Mag	510	2040	3312	2164	1389	860	604	+2.5	0.0	− 5.6	−14.9	−28.0	—
148	450 NE-3¼″	465	2190	3407	2480	1783	1272	NA	+2.5	NA	− 3.0	−12.2	−20.0	—
149	450 NE-3¼″	500	2150	3727	2654	1869	1301	NA	+2.5	NA	− 3.6	−13.5	−21.0	—
150	450 No. 2	465	2190	3407	2480	1783	1272	NA	+2.5	NA	− 3.0	−12.2	−20.0	—
151	450 No. 2	500	2150	3727	2654	1869	1301	NA	+2.5	NA	− 3.6	−13.5	−21.0	—
152	450 Ackley Mag	500	2320	4683	3380	2394	1682	NA	+2.5	NA	− 1.5	− 8.5	−16.0	—
153	460 Short A-Sq	500	2420	5315	3858	2751	1938	NA	+2.5	NA	− 0.8	− 5.5	−11.0	−32.0
154	460 Long A-Sq	500	2630	6822	5005	3623	2576	NA	+2.5	NA	0.0	− 4.0	−10.0	−30.0
155	460 Wea Mag	500	2700	7381	5210	3614	2448	1640	+2.5	NA	0.0	− 4.0	−10.0	−30.0
156	500/465 NE	480	2150	3435	2435	1707	1183	NA	+2.5	NA	− 4.0	−11.2	−22.0	—
157	470 Nitro Ex	480	2190	3630	2578	1805	1252	NA	+2.5	NA	− 3.2	−10.3	−21.0	—

OPTIMUM GAME WEIGHT AND TRAJECTORY (continued)

Load No.	Cartridge	Bullet Weight (gr)	Muzzle Vel. (fps)	OPTIMUM GAME WEIGHT (LBS) AT:					TRAJECTORY IN INCHES AT:					
				Muzzle	100 yds	200 yds	300 yds	400 yds	100 yds	150 yds	200 yds	250 yds	300 yds	400 yds
158	470 Nitro Ex	500	2150	3727	2621	1820	1251	NA	+2.5	NA	−3.6	−11.0	−22.0	—
159	475 No. 2	480	2200	3680	2531	1713	1148	NA	+2.5	NA	−3.4	−10.5	−21.0	—
160	505 Gibbs	505	2300	4654	3097	2019	1294	NA	+2.5	NA	−3.0	−9.8	−20.0	—
161	500 NE-3″	600	2150	5367	3858	2753	1938	NA	+2.5	NA	−3.6	−11.0	−22.0	—
162	495 A-Square	600	2280	6400	4652	3326	2360	NA	+2.5	NA	−1.8	−7.9	−17.0	—
163	500 A-Square	600	2380	7280	5322	3834	2974	NA	+2.5	NA	−1.0	−6.2	−14.0	—
164	500 A-Square	707	2250	8540	6365	4678	2885	NA	+2.5	NA	−1.0	−7.4	−17.0	—
165	577 Nitro Ex	750	2050	7269	4863	3216	2122	NA	+2.5	NA	−5.0	−13.8	−27.0	—

Notes: NA = Data not available from manufacturer
Wea Mag = Weatherby Magnum
NE = Nitro Express
Spfd = Springfield
A-Sq = A-Square
— = bullet drops more than 3 feet below line of sight. As hold-over of more than 3 feet is unrealistic, this data has not been included.
Optimum Game Weight—see text
Trajectory +/− indicates bullet's path above or below line of sight when rifle is zeroed at 100 yards as indicated.
0.0 = Bullet impact is at line of sight.
(*) = Varmint-style bullets which should never be used for big game.
 Optimum Game Weights shown for these bullets are for varmints—game that can be killed with highly frangible bullets (crow, prairie dog, woodchuck, coyote, etc.)

TABLE 6.5

AVERAGE FACTORY RIFLE-CARTRIDGE BALLISTICS

Wind Drift and Uphill/Downhill Hold

Load No.	Cartridge	Bullet Weight (gr)	Muzzle Vel. (fps)	DRIFT (INCHES) FOR 10 MPH WIND:				45° ANGLE UP- OR DOWNHILL HOLD (INCHES) UNDER TARGET			
				100 yds	200 yds	300 yds	400 yds	100 yds	200 yds	300 yds	400 yds
1	17 Rem	25	4040	1.4	6.3	15.7	31.5	0.4	1.7	4.5	9.7
2	22 Hornet	45	2690	2.9	13.5	34.9	66.8	0.8	4.2	12.2	28.2
3	218 Bee	46	2760	2.7	12.3	32.0	62.9	0.7	3.7	10.6	24.7
4	221 Fireball	50	2800	1.8	7.8	20.0	39.2	0.7	3.4	8.9	18.7
5	222 Rem	50	3140	1.7	7.8	18.3	36.4	0.6	2.7	7.1	15.1
6	222 Rem	55	3020	0.9	3.4	8.5	16.8				
7	22 PPC	52	3400	1.2	5.1	12.4	NA	NA	NA	NA	NA
8	223 Rem	40	3650	1.5	6.5	16.1	32.3				
9	223 Rem	55	3240	1.4	6.1	15.0	29.4	0.5	2.4	6.3	13.0
11	222 Rem Mag	55	3240	1.4	6.1	15.0	29.4	0.5	2.4	6.3	13.0
12	225 Win	55	3570	1.2	5.0	12.2	23.7	0.4	2.0	5.0	10.2
13	224 Wea Mag	55	3650	1.0	4.3	10.2	19.6	NA	NA	NA	NA

Load No.	Cartridge	Bullet Weight (gr)	Muzzle Vel. (fps)	DRIFT (INCHES) FOR 10 MPH WIND:				45° ANGLE UP- OR DOWNHILL HOLD (INCHES) UNDER TARGET			
				100 yds	200 yds	300 yds	400 yds	100 yds	200 yds	300 yds	400 yds
14	22-250 Rem	40	4000	1.3	5.7	14.0	27.9				
15	22-250 Rem	55	3680	1.2	5.1	12.3	23.9	0.4	1.8	4.7	9.5
17	6mm PPC	70	3140	1.2	4.8	11.6	NA	NA	NA	NA	NA
18	243 Win	80	3350	1.0	4.3	10.4	19.8	0.5	2.2	5.4	10.6
19	243 Win	85	3320	0.7	2.7	6.3	11.6	NA	NA	NA	NA
20	243 Win	100	2960	0.9	3.6	8.4	15.7	0.6	2.6	6.4	12.2
21	6mm Rem	80	3470	1.0	4.1	9.9	18.8	0.5	2.0	5.0	9.8
22	6mm Rem	100	3100	0.8	3.3	7.8	14.5	0.6	2.4	5.7	10.8
23	240 Wea Mag	87	3500	0.7	2.8	6.7	12.4	NA	NA	NA	NA
24	240 Wea Mag	100	3395	0.8	3.4	8.0	15.0	NA	NA	NA	NA
25	25-20 Win	86	1460	4.0	15.7	33.6	56.7	2.8	12.7	32.1	63.3
26	25-35 Win	117	2230	1.9	8.4	20.4	38.7	1.1	5.1	13.0	26.5
27	250 Savage	100	2820	1.1	4.9	11.7	22.2	0.7	3.0	7.4	14.6
28	257 Roberts	100	2980	1.2	5.3	12.9	24.7	0.7	2.9	7.3	14.4
29	257 Roberts	117	2780	1.5	6.5	15.8	30.5	0.8	3.6	9.0	18.1
30	257 Roberts	120	2780	0.8	3.3	7.7	14.3	NA	NA	NA	NA
31	25-06 Rem	87	3440	1.1	4.7	11.4	21.8	0.5	2.1	5.2	10.5
32	25-06 Rem	90	3440	1.0	4.1	9.8	18.7	0.5	2.0	5.0	9.0
33	25-06 Rem	100	3230	0.9	3.9	9.3	17.6	0.5	2.3	5.6	10.8
34	25-06 Rem	117	2990	0.8	3.5	8.2	15.3	0.6	2.5	6.0	11.4
35	25-06 Rem	120	2990	0.8	3.3	7.9	14.7	0.6	2.5	6.0	11.4
36	257 Wea Mag	87	3825	0.7	3.0	7.0	13.2	NA	NA	NA	NA
37	257 Wea Mag	100	3555	0.6	2.4	5.6	10.4	NA	NA	NA	NA
38	257 Wea Mag	120	3300	0.8	3.3	7.7	14.5	NA	NA	NA	NA
39	6.5 Rem Mag	120	3210	0.8	3.5	8.3	15.6	0.5	2.3	5.5	10.6
40	264 Win Mag	140	3030	0.8	3.2	7.4	13.8	0.6	2.5	6.0	11.3
41	270 Win	100	3430	1.0	4.2	10.1	19.2	0.5	2.0	5.0	9.8
42	270 Win	130	3060	0.8	3.5	8.3	15.6	0.6	2.4	5.8	11.2
43	270 Win	150	2850	0.9	3.8	9.0	16.8	0.6	2.8	6.7	12.8
44	270 Wea Mag	100	3760	0.8	3.2	7.6	14.1	NA	NA	NA	NA
45	270 Wea Mag	130	3375	0.7	2.6	6.1	11.2	NA	NA	NA	NA
46	270 Wea Mag	150	3245	0.6	2.2	5.3	9.6	NA	NA	NA	NA
47	7mm BR	140	2215	1.4	6.3	15.1	28.5	1.1	4.9	12.1	23.8
48	7mm Mauser	140	2660	1.1	4.8	11.5	21.7	0.8	3.4	8.2	16.0
50	7mm Mauser	175	2440	1.5	6.3	15.3	29.2	0.9	4.1	10.3	20.4
51	7×30 Waters	120	2700	1.6	7.2	17.7	34.5	NA	NA	NA	NA
52	7mm-08 Rem	120	3000	1.1	4.4	10.7	20.1	0.6	2.7	6.5	12.8
53	7mm-08 Rem	140	2860	1.1	4.3	10.4	19.4	0.7	2.9	7.1	13.7
54	284 Win	125	3140	0.9	3.8	9.0	16.9	0.6	2.4	5.8	11.2
55	284 Win	150	2860	0.9	3.9	9.2	17.2	0.7	2.8	6.9	13.2
56	280 Rem	120	3150	1.0	4.1	9.9	18.7	0.5	2.4	5.9	11.5
57	280 Rem	140	3000	1.0	4.0	9.7	18.0	0.6	2.6	6.4	12.3
58	280 Rem	150	2890	0.7	3.1	7.3	13.5	0.6	2.6	6.1	11.6
59	280 Rem	165	2820	1.1	4.8	11.4	21.7	0.7	3.0	7.4	14.5
60	7mm Rem Mag	140	3175	0.9	3.8	8.8	16.7	0.5	2.3	5.7	11.0
61	7mm Rem Mag	150	3110	0.7	3.1	7.2	13.3	0.7	2.8	6.6	12.5
62	7mm Rem Mag	165	2950	0.5	2.0	4.6	8.4	NA	NA	NA	NA
63	7mm Rem Mag	175	2860	1.2	5.0	12.0	23.0	0.7	3.0	7.3	14.4
64	7mm Wea Mag	140	3400	0.6	2.4	5.5	10.1	NA	NA	NA	NA

WIND DRIFT AND UPHILL/DOWNHILL HOLD (continued)

Load No.	Cartridge	Bullet Weight (gr)	Muzzle Vel. (fps)	DRIFT (INCHES) FOR 10 MPH WIND:				45° ANGLE UP- OR DOWNHILL HOLD (INCHES) UNDER TARGET			
				100 yds	200 yds	300 yds	400 yds	100 yds	200 yds	300 yds	400 yds
65	7mm Wea Mag	154	3260	0.6	2.6	6.0	11.0	NA	NA	NA	NA
66	7mm Wea Mag	160	3200	0.5	2.1	5.1	9.2	NA	NA	NA	NA
67	7mm Wea Mag	175	3070	0.5	2.3	5.4	9.8	NA	NA	NA	NA
68	30 Carbine	110	1990	3.4	15.0	35.5	63.2	1.5	7.3	19.7	41.6
69	303 Savage	190	1890	2.3	9.6	22.9	42.2	1.5	6.8	17.2	34.5
70	30 Rem	170	2120	2.0	8.4	20.3	38.3	1.3	5.6	14.2	28.6
71	30-30 Win	55	3400	2.0	8.7	22.5	45.8	0.5	2.5	6.9	15.5
72	30-30 Win	125	2570	2.2	10.1	25.4	49.4	NA	NA	NA	NA
73	30-30 Win	150	2390	2.2	9.8	24.4	46.7	1.0	4.7	12.4	26.1
74	30-30 Win	170	2200	1.9	8.0	19.4	36.7	1.2	5.2	13.1	26.4
75	300 Savage	150	2630	1.1	4.8	11.6	21.9	0.8	3.4	8.4	16.4
76	300 Savage	180	2350	1.6	7.2	17.5	34.0	0.8	3.7	9.4	19.2
77	30-40 Krag	180	2430	1.0	4.4	10.3	19.3	0.9	3.9	9.5	18.1
79	308 Win	55	3770	1.2	5.0	12.2	23.5	0.4	1.8	4.6	9.3
80	308 Win	150	2820	1.0	4.4	10.4	19.7	0.7	3.0	7.3	14.1
81	308 Win	165	2700	0.7	3.0	7.0	13.0	NA	NA	NA	NA
82	308 Win	168	2680	0.8	3.1	7.3	13.5	NA	NA	NA	NA
83	308 Win	180	2620	0.9	3.9	9.2	17.2	0.8	3.4	8.1	15.4
84	30-06 Spfd	55	4080	1.1	4.6	11.0	21.3	0.3	1.5	3.9	7.9
85	30-06 Spfd	125	3140	1.1	4.5	10.8	20.5	0.6	2.4	6.0	11.9
86	30-06 Spfd	150	2910	1.0	4.2	9.9	18.7	0.6	2.8	6.8	13.2
87	30-06 Spfd	165	2800	0.7	2.8	6.6	12.3				
88	30-06 Spfd	180	2700	0.9	3.7	8.8	16.5	0.7	3.2	7.6	14.5
89	30-06 Spfd	220	2410	1.4	5.9	14.3	27.1	1.0	4.2	10.3	20.3
90	300 H&H Mag	180	2880	0.8	3.4	8.0	14.1	0.7	2.8	6.6	12.6
91	300 H&H Mag	220	2550	1.0	4.3	10.2	19.1	0.8	3.5	8.5	16.3
92	300 Win Mag	150	3290	0.9	3.8	9.0	16.9	0.5	2.2	5.3	10.4
93	300 Win Mag	180	2960	0.8	3.4	8.0	14.9	0.7	2.8	6.6	12.6
94	300 Win Mag	200	2830	0.5	2.2	5.0	9.2	NA	NA	NA	NA
95	300 Win Mag	220	2680	1.2	5.1	12.2	23.1	0.8	3.3	8.2	16.1
96	300 Wea Mag	110	3900	0.9	3.7	8.8	16.6	NA	NA	NA	NA
97	300 Wea Mag	150	3600	0.6	2.6	6.2	11.4	NA	NA	NA	NA
98	300 Wea Mag	180	3300	0.6	2.3	5.5	10.0	NA	NA	NA	NA
99	300 Wea Mag	220	2905	1.4	6.2	15.1	29.3	NA	NA	NA	NA
100	32-20 Win	100	1210	4.3	15.5	32.4	54.8	4.0	17.7	43.6	84.1
101	303 British	180	2460	1.6	7.1	17.2	32.9	0.9	4.1	10.5	21.1
102	32 Win Special	170	2250	1.9	8.4	20.3	38.6	1.1	5.0	12.8	26.1
103	8mm Mauser	170	2360	2.1	9.3	22.9	43.9	1.0	4.7	12.3	25.7
105	8mm Rem Mag	185	3080	0.9	4.0	9.7	18.1	0.6	2.5	6.1	11.8
106	8mm Rem Mag	220	2830	0.9	3.6	8.8	16.1	0.7	2.9	7.0	13.2
107	338 Win Mag	210	2830	0.8	3.5	8.3	15.4	0.6	2.4	10.6	26.4
108	338 Win Mag	225	2780	0.8	3.1	7.4	13.6	0.7	2.9	7.0	13.2
109	338 Win Mag	250	2660	1.1	4.5	10.8	20.3	0.6	3.3	8.1	15.7
110	340 Wea Mag	210	3250	0.7	2.9	6.7	12.4	NA	NA	NA	NA
111	340 Wea Mag	250	3000	0.6	2.5	5.7	10.5	NA	NA	NA	NA

EXTERIOR CENTERFIRE RIFLE-CARTRIDGE BALLISTICS

Load No.	Cartridge	Bullet Weight (gr)	Muzzle Vel. (fps)	DRIFT (INCHES) FOR 10 MPH WIND:				45° ANGLE UP- OR DOWNHILL HOLD (INCHES) UNDER TARGET			
				100 yds	200 yds	300 yds	400 yds	100 yds	200 yds	300 yds	400 yds
112	338 A-Square	250	3120	0.4	1.6	3.8	7.0	NA	NA	NA	NA
113	348 Win	200	2520	1.4	6.0	14.4	27.5	0.9	3.8	9.6	18.9
114	351 Win SL	180	1850	2.6	11.1	26.2	47.3	1.7	7.6	19.5	39.3
116	35 Rem	150	2300	2.5	11.0	27.2	51.5	1.1	5.2	13.8	29.3
117	35 Rem	200	2080	2.8	12.4	29.8	54.3	1.4	6.7	17.7	36.9
119	358 Win	200	2490	1.5	6.5	15.7	30.0	0.9	4.0	20.0	19.9
120	350 Rem Mag	200	2710	1.2	5.0	12.0	22.7	0.7	3.3	8.0	15.7
121	35 Whelen	200	2675	1.1	5.1	12.1	23.3	0.8	3.4	8.2	16.2
122	35 Whelen	250	2400	1.1	4.6	10.8	20.2	0.9	4.0	9.8	18.7
123	9.3×62mm	286	2360	1.0	3.8	8.8	16.6	NA	NA	NA	NA
124	9.3×64mm	286	2700	0.7	3.1	7.3	13.4	NA	NA	NA	NA
125	9.3×74Rmm	286	2360	1.4	5.6	13.7	25.6	NA	NA	NA	NA
126	38-55 Win	255	1320	2.3	9.4	21.4	37.9	2.2	9.7	23.8	46.2
129	375 H&H Mag	270	2690	1.1	4.5	10.7	20.2	0.8	3.3	7.9	15.4
130	375 H&H Mag	300	2530	1.2	5.0	11.8	22.3	0.9	3.7	9.0	17.6
131	375 Wea Mag	300	2700	0.5	2.1	4.9	9.2	NA	NA	NA	NA
132	378 Wea Mag	270	3180	0.5	2.3	5.4	9.8	NA	NA	NA	NA
133	378 Wea Mag	300	2929	1.2	5.1	12.1	23.4	NA	NA	NA	NA
134	38-40 Win	180	1160	3.9	14.2	30.0	51.0	4.2	18.7	45.6	87.5
135	450/400-3"	400	2150	1.3	5.6	13.4	25.0	NA	NA	NA	NA
136	416 Hoffman	400	2380	1.3	5.5	11.9	22.3	NA	NA	NA	NA
137	416 Rigby	400	2400	1.3	5.5	11.7	22.1	NA	NA	NA	NA
138	404 Jeffrey	400	2150	1.3	5.9	14.0	26.2				
139	44-40 Win	200	1190	3.9	14.2	30.0	51.0	4.2	18.7	45.6	87.5
140	44 Rem Mag	240	1760	4.0	16.9	38.0	65.3	1.9	9.3	24.8	51.2
141	444 Marlin	240	2350	3.1	14.1	35.3	65.3	1.1	5.4	15.1	33.4
142	444 Marlin	265	2120	2.6	11.6	28.3	52.4	1.2	6.0	16.0	33.5
143	45-70 Govt	300	1810	1.7	7.6	18.6	35.7	NA	NA	NA	NA
144	45-70 Govt	405	1330	2.8	10.8	23.2	39.3	3.2	13.6	33.5	63.9
145	458 Win Mag	465	2220	1.4	5.3	12.9	23.9	NA	NA	NA	NA
146	458 Win Mag	500	2040	1.5	6.3	15.0	27.9	1.3	5.7	14.0	27.2
147	458 Win Mag	510	2040	1.9	8.2	19.6	36.5	1.3	6.0	15.0	29.9
148	450 NE-3¼"	465	2190	1.3	5.5	13.2	24.4	NA	NA	NA	NA
150	450 No. 2	465	2190	1.3	5.5	13.2	24.4	NA	NA	NA	NA
152	450 Ackley Mag	500	2320	1.2	4.7	11.5	21.4	NA	NA	NA	NA
153	460 Short A-Sq	500	2420	1.1	4.6	10.7	20.2	NA	NA	NA	NA
155	460 Wea Mag	500	2700	1.1	5.0	11.7	22.7	NA	NA	NA	NA
156	500/465 NE	480	2150	1.2	5.8	13.7	25.5	NA	NA	NA	NA
157	470 Nitro Ex	480	2190	1.3	6.0	14.2	26.7	NA	NA	NA	NA
158	470 Nitro Ex	500	2150	1.3	6.3	14.9	28.1	NA	NA	NA	NA
160	505 Gibbs	505	2300	1.3	5.3	13.1	24.0	NA	NA	NA	NA
161	500 NE-3"	600	2150	1.2	5.6	13.4	25.0	NA	NA	NA	NA

WIND DRIFT AND UPHILL/DOWNHILL HOLD (continued)

Load No.	Cartridge	Bullet Weight (gr)	Muzzle Vel. (fps)	DRIFT (INCHES) FOR 10 MPH WIND:				45° ANGLE UP- OR DOWNHILL HOLD (INCHES) UNDER TARGET			
				100 yds	200 yds	300 yds	400 yds	100 yds	200 yds	300 yds	400 yds
162	495 A-Square	600	2280	1.3	5.1	12.5	23.1	NA	NA	NA	NA
163	500 A-Square	600	2380	1.2	4.8	11.6	21.8	NA	NA	NA	NA
164	500 A-Square	707	2250	1.2	4.8	11.8	21.9	NA	NA	NA	NA
165	577 Nitro Ex	750	2050	1.5	7.1	16.5	30.3	NA	NA	NA	NA

Notes: NA = Data not available from manufacturer
Wea Mag = Weatherby Magnum
Spfd = Springfield
A-Sq = A-Square
NE = Nitro Express
Missing line # indicates data unavailable for this load.

TABLE 6.6

MAXIMUM RANGE FOR AVERAGE FACTORY RIFLE-CARTRIDGE BALLISTICS

(Omitted Load No. Line Indicates Data Not Available)

Load No.	Cartridge	Bullet Weight (gr)	Muzzle Vel. (fps)	Maximum Range (yds)	Velocity at Max. Range (fps)	Angle of Departure in Degrees to Reach Maximum Range	TIME OF FLIGHT IN SECONDS FOR:				Bullet Ballistic Coefficient
							100 yds	200 yds	300 yds	400 yds	
1	17 Rem	25	4040	2561	286	30.0	0.082	0.184	0.312	0.476	0.151
2	22 Hornet	45	2690	2084	260	30.3	0.128	0.300	0.533	0.826	0.130
3	218 Bee	46	2760	2095	261	30.2	0.120	0.280	0.497	0.777	0.130
4	221 Fireball	50	2800	2803	310	29.7	0.117	0.260	0.434	0.651	0.188
5	222 Rem	50	3140	2872	316	31.6	0.104	0.225	0.382	0.570	0.188
9	223 Rem	55	3240	3142	334	32.1	0.100	0.218	0.357	0.525	0.209
11	222 Rem Mag	55	3240	3142	334	32.1	0.100	0.218	0.357	0.525	0.209
12	225 Win	55	3570	3212	335	31.8					0.208
15	22-250 Rem	55	3680	3502	353	32.2	0.086	0.185	0.300	0.433	0.230
18	243 Win	80	3350	3697	370	33.0	0.096	0.206	0.334	0.483	0.255
20	243 Win	100	2960	4576	434	35.1	0.106	0.223	0.352	0.495	0.356
21	6mm Rem	80	3470	3731	371	32.9	0.092	0.156	0.316	0.453	0.255
22	6mm Rem	100	3100	4650	436	34.9	0.100	0.210	0.332	0.466	0.336
25	25-20 Win	86	1460	2446	307	33.6	0.228	0.500	0.808	1.144	NA
26	25-35 Win	117	2230	3183	351	33.8	0.146	0.317	0.511	0.758	NA
27	250 Savage	100	2820	3836	387	34.0	0.113	0.246	0.386	0.552	NA
31	25-06 Rem	87	3440	3810	377	33.1	0.093	0.197	0.317	0.453	0.263
32	25-06 Rem	90	3440	3768	374	33.0	0.093	0.168	0.318	0.455	0.259
33	25-06 Rem	100	3230	4057	396	33.8	0.098	0.208	0.332	0.471	0.292
34	25-06 Rem	117	2990	4552	431	35.9	0.103	0.216	0.341	0.479	0.349
35	25-06 Rem	120	2990	4657	438	35.1	0.104	0.219	0.345	0.482	0.362

EXTERIOR CENTERFIRE RIFLE-CARTRIDGE BALLISTICS

Load No.	Cartridge	Bullet Weight (gr)	Muzzle Vel. (fps)	Maximum Range (yds)	Velocity at Max. Range (fps)	Angle of Departure in Degrees to Reach Maximum Range	TIME OF FLIGHT IN SECONDS FOR: 100 yds	200 yds	300 yds	400 yds	Bullet Ballistic Coefficient
39	6.5 Rem Mag	120	3210	3771	416	34.3	0.098	0.207	0.328	0.473	0.324
40	264 Win Mag	140	3030	4875	452	35.4	0.103	0.216	0.339	0.475	0.385
41	270 Win	100	3430	3687	368	32.8	0.092	0.196	0.316	0.454	0.251
42	270 Win	130	3060	4793	445	35.2	0.101	0.211	0.332	0.465	0.372
43	270 Win	150	2850	4442	426	35.0	0.109	0.228	0.361	0.509	0.345
47	7mm BR	140	2215	3838	398	34.9	0.114	0.307	0.492	0.703	0.311
48	7mm Mauser	140	2660	4197	415	35.0	0.119	0.253	0.404	0.575	0.311
50	7mm Mauser	175	2440	3575	375	34.2	0.131	0.282	0.456	0.658	0.273
52	7mm-08 Rem	120	3000	3906	384	31.5	0.106	0.225	0.361	0.515	0.285
53	7mm-08 Rem	140	2860	4108	399	31.7	0.111	0.234	0.373	0.530	0.311
54	284 Win	125	3140	4216	407	34.2	0.101	0.213	0.338	0.478	0.311
55	284 Win	150	2860	4424	426	35.0	0.110	0.232	0.367	0.517	0.344
56	280 Rem	120	3150	3963	386	31.9	0.101	0.214	0.342	0.488	0.285
58	280 Rem	150	2890	4446	427	35.0	0.105	0.219	0.343	0.479	0.401
59	280 Rem	165	2820	3886	391	34.1	0.113	0.240	0.384	0.549	0.290
60	7mm Rem Mag	140	3175	4237	404	32.7	0.100	0.210	0.334	0.423	0.311
61	7mm Rem Mag	150	3110	4543	429	34.8	0.101	0.212	0.335	0.475	0.346
63	7mm Rem Mag	175	2860	5166	474	36.1	0.109	0.227	0.355	0.495	0.426
68	30 Carbine	110	1990	2509	303	32.6	0.170	0.339	0.654	0.962	0.166
69	303 Savage	190	1890	3182	356	34.4	0.167	0.364	0.594	0.858	0.252
70	30 Rem	170	2120	3298	360	34.2	0.153	0.331	0.540	0.783	0.254
71	30-30 Win	55	3400	2317	212	30.1	0.099	0.226	0.342	0.613	0.139
73	30-30 Win	150	2390	3011	335	33.1	0.137	0.299	0.495	0.730	0.218
74	30-30 Win	170	2200	3307	360	34.1	0.147	0.318	0.519	0.754	0.254
75	300 Savage	150	2630	4039	404	34.7	0.121	0.256	0.508	0.581	0.223
76	300 Savage	180	2350	4506	442	36.1	0.134	0.281	0.445	0.626	0.383
77	30-40 Krag	180	2430	4552	443	36.0	0.129	0.272	0.429	0.604	0.383
79	308 Win	55	3770	3120	322	29.3	0.086	0.188	0.308	0.453	0.197
80	308 Win	150	2820	4470	430	35.2	0.112	0.238	0.378	0.537	0.314
83	308 Win	180	2620	4655	446	35.8	0.120	0.251	0.396	0.556	0.383
84	30-06 Spfd	55	4080	3181	325	29.7	0.080	0.173	0.283	0.415	0.197
85	30-06 Spfd	125	3140	3710	378	33.4	0.102	0.217	0.348	0.499	0.286
86	30-06 Spfd	150	2910	4635	439	35.3	0.108	0.226	0.357	0.501	0.365
87	30-06 Spfd	165	2800	5473	494	36.6	0.112	0.236	0.372	0.525	NA
88	30-06 Spfd	180	2700	5659	508	37.1	0.115	0.238	0.371	0.513	0.499
89	30-06 Spfd	220	2410	4515	441	35.9	0.131	0.274	0.438	0.610	0.380
90	300 H&H Mag	180	2880	4790	449	35.5	0.109	0.228	0.358	0.502	0.383
91	300 H&H Mag	220	2550	4426	431	35.5	0.122	0.257	0.407	0.573	0.359
92	300 Win Mag	150	3290	4101	398	33.8	0.096	0.204	0.325	0.461	0.295
93	300 Win Mag	180	2960	5313	480	36.1	0.109	0.228	0.358	0.502	0.436
95	300 Win Mag	220	2680	4658	445	35.7	0.117	0.246	0.387	0.543	0.380
100	32-20 Win	100	1210	2122	284	33.4	0.272	0.584	0.928	1.303	0.166
101	303 British	180	2460	4715	457	36.3	0.117	0.267	0.420	0.588	0.407
102	32 Win Special	170	2250	3176	350	33.7	0.144	0.314	0.515	0.752	0.239
103	8mm Mauser	170	2360	2871	325	32.8	0.139	0.307	0.512	0.758	0.205
105	8mm Rem Mag	185	3080	4087	394	31.7	0.103	0.218	0.347	0.493	0.300
106	8mm Rem Mag	220	2830	4625	440	35.9	0.111	0.233	0.367	0.516	0.435

MAXIMUM RANGE (continued)

Load No.	Cartridge	Bullet Weight (gr)	Muzzle Vel. (fps)	Maximum Range (yds)	Velocity at Max. Range (fps)	Angle of Departure in Degrees to Reach Maximum Range	TIME OF FLIGHT IN SECONDS FOR: 100 yds	200 yds	300 yds	400 yds	Bullet Ballistic Coefficient
108	338 Win Mag	225	2780	5203	474	35.1	0.112	0.234	0.365	0.509	0.435
109	338 Win Mag	250	2660	4192	414	35.0	0.119	0.251	0.399	0.566	0.329
112	338 A-Square	250	3120	NA	NA	NA	0.100	0.200	0.310	0.420	0.619
113	348 Win	200	2520	3633	378	34.2	0.127	0.272	0.439	0.632	0.276
114	351 Win SL	180	1850	2977	342	34.1	0.177	0.387	0.635	0.917	0.233
116	35 Rem	150	2300	2633	308	32.4	0.145	0.323	0.546	0.814	0.184
117	35 Rem	200	2080	2648	313	32.9	0.165	0.368	0.615	0.903	0.193
119	358 Win	200	2490	3482	368	33.9	0.129	0.278	0.450	0.652	0.261
120	350 Rem Mag	200	2710	3878	392	34.3	0.117	0.250	0.400	0.572	0.294
121	35 Whelen	200	2675	3881	392	34.5	0.119	0.253	0.405	0.580	0.294
122	35 Whelen	250	2400	4485	438	35.7	0.131	0.276	0.436	0.615	0.375
123	9.3×62mm	286	2360	NA	NA	NA	0.130	0.280	0.430	0.600	0.417
124	9.3×64mm	286	2700	NA	NA	NA	0.120	0.240	0.370	0.520	0.417
125	9.3×74Rmm	286	2360	NA	NA	NA	0.140	0.290	0.460	0.650	0.417
126	38-55 Win	255	1320	3505	389	35.9	0.202	0.431	0.688	0.970	0.311
129	375 H&H Mag	270	2690	4172	412	34.9	0.118	0.249	0.395	0.561	0.326
130	375 H&H Mag	300	2530	4088	410	35.0	0.125	0.265	0.423	0.601	0.324
134	38-40 Win	180	1160	2147	288	33.7	0.281	0.598	0.946	1.324	0.171
135	450/400-3″	400	2150	NA	NA	NA	0.150	0.310	0.490	0.700	0.327
136	416 Hoffman	400	2380	NA	NA	NA	0.130	0.280	0.450	0.630	0.320
137	416 Rigby	400	2400	NA	NA	NA	0.130	0.280	0.440	0.630	0.320
138	404 Jeffrey	400	2150	NA	NA	NA	0.150	0.310	0.500	0.710	0.315
139	44-40 Win	200	1190	2063	279	33.3	0.281	0.598	0.946	1.324	0.160
140	44 Rem Mag	240	1760	2305	289	32.5	0.193	0.437	0.727	1.053	0.166
141	444 Marlin	240	2350	2222	275	31.2	0.145	0.336	0.583	0.882	0.146
142	444 Marlin	265	2120	2687	313	32.1	0.157	0.349	0.585	0.864	0.193
144	45-70 Govt	405	1330	3119	366	35.8	0.241	0.512	0.809	1.126	0.280
145	458 Win Mag	465	2220	NA	NA	NA	0.140	0.300	0.480	0.680	0.327
146	458 Win Mag	500	2040	4026	416	35.9	0.156	0.330	0.526	0.747	0.345
147	458 Win Mag	510	2040	3427	372	34.8	0.158	0.341	0.552	0.796	0.274
148	450 NE-3¼″	465	2190	NA	NA	NA	0.140	0.300	0.490	0.690	0.327
150	450 No. 2	465	2190	NA	NA	NA	0.140	0.300	0.490	0.690	0.327
152	450 Ackley Mag	500	2320	NA	NA	NA	0.140	0.290	0.450	0.640	0.342
153	460 Short A-Sq	500	2420	NA	NA	NA	0.130	0.270	0.430	0.610	0.342
156	500/465 NE	480	2150	NA	NA	NA	0.150	0.310	0.500	0.700	0.320
157	470 Nitro Ex	480	2190	NA	NA	NA	0.140	0.310	0.490	0.700	0.304
158	470 Nitro Ex	500	2150	NA	NA	NA	0.150	0.310	0.500	0.720	0.298
161	500 NE-3″	600	2150	NA	NA	NA	0.150	0.310	0.490	0.700	0.327
162	495 A-Square	600	2280	NA	NA	NA	0.140	0.290	0.470	0.660	0.327

Load No.	Cartridge	Bullet Weight (gr)	Muzzle Vel. (fps)	Maximum Range (yds)	Velocity at Max. Range (fps)	Angle of Departure in Degrees to Reach Maximum Range	TIME OF FLIGHT IN SECONDS FOR:				Bullet Ballistic Coefficient
							100 yds	200 yds	300 yds	400 yds	
163	500 A-Square	600	2380	NA	NA	NA	0.130	0.280	0.440	0.630	0.327
164	500 A-Square	707	2250	NA	NA	NA	0.140	0.290	0.470	0.660	0.347
165	577 Nitro Ex	750	2050	NA	NA	NA	0.160	0.330	0.530	0.760	0.288

Notes: NA = Data not available from manufacturer
Wea Mag = Weatherby Magnum
Spfd = Springfield
A-Sq = A-Square
NE = Nitro Express

Missing Line # indicates data unavailable from manufacturer(s)
IMPORTANT: Any change in bullet's ballistic coefficient will notably alter all data in table.

If the previous table of Barrel Length and Velocity is used to estimate velocity, a corrected kinetic energy figure can be obtained by using the following formula:

$$\text{Kinetic Energy (foot/pounds)} = \frac{\text{Velocity}^2 \times \text{Bullet Wgt. in grs.}}{450,240}$$

The ballistic tables include data for "hold-under" on a 45° hill. These figures may be computed for any other angle by using the following formula:

$$h \left(\frac{N^2}{45} \right) = \text{Hold-under for new angle}$$

In which:

h = Hold-under for a 45° angle. Obtain this number from ballistic tables for the caliber and bullet being used and under the column for the range desired.
N = New angle for which you wish to calculate hold-under.

For example, what is the hold-under with the 6mm Remington using an 80-grain bullet at 3,470 fps for a 30° angle at 100 yards? Referring to line 1 of the exterior ballistics tables we find that the hold-under for this combination is .5 inches for a 45° angle at 100 yards. Therefore:

$$h \left(\frac{N^2}{45} \right) = \text{Hold-under}$$

$$.5 \left(\frac{30^2}{45} \right) = \text{Hold-under}$$

$.5 \, (.6666)^2 = $ Hold-under
$.5 \times .4444 = $ Hold-under
$.2'' = $ Hold-under for new angle of 30°.

Please remember that the hold-under distance you arrive at from either the ballistic tables or your calculations does not mean you would aim that far below your target. Rather it means you would subtract the distance arrived at from the required normal hold-over. If your rifle is sighted-in at 100 yards and hits 5 inches low at 200 yards, on flat land you would hold 5 inches high to hit a 200-yard target However, the 200-yard target is up- or downhill at a 45° angle. Assume the hold-under listed in the table is 3 inches. This 3-inch hold-under is subtracted from the required flat-land (horizontal) hold-over of 5 inches. Thus, your actual hold-over is 2 inches.

The conditions that apply to the ballistic tables are:

Temperature = 59°F.
  Barometer = 29.53 inches of mercury
    Elevation = 0.0 feet (sea level)

Maximum-range tables are estimates based on normal conditions, disregarding the effects of wind and variations in velocity as they occur from shot to shot. Additionally, these estimates are based on a flat-based, pointed bullet of .8-caliber ogive. Under certain circumstances it is possible that the range shown may be exceeded. If such an occurrence might create a risk of injury, an appropriate allowance should be made.

OPTIMUM GAME WEIGHTS

Kinetic-energy figures, while giving some very sound bases for comparing cartridge performance, do not provide any real indication of the appropriate applications for a specific cartridge and bullet.

A catch-all approach to cartridge application has been repeated numerous times, but should be regarded with skepticism. It states that it takes 1,000 foot/pounds of kinetic energy to kill an deer, or 1,500 foot/pounds to kill elk, or 2,500 foot/pounds to kill a grizzly. The "exact" number of foot/pounds required for a specific task varies slightly—depending on the quoting expert.

The holes in such an approach are obvious. Does it take 1,000 foot/pounds of kinetic energy to kill a deer that weighs 80 pounds or does the number apply to one weighing 180 pounds, or perhaps to the rare monster of 250 pounds? Surely it cannot apply equally to all deer of all sizes. And what about elk? Is 1,500 foot/pounds needed for a 550-pound elk, or a 690-pound elk, or one weighing 802 pounds or . . .? And does the kinetic-energy requirement take into consideration difficult angles, where considerable extra penetration is required? Kinetic energy is not, by itself, a valid means of measuring any bullet's ability to work.

But the hunter, especially one without extensive game-taking experience, is left without a very exacting approach to a real problem. He

50-YARD EQUIVALENT

150-YARD EQUIVALENT

250-YARD EQUIVALENT

Bullet performance is geared to range (impact velocity) and game size. Shown are Winchester 30-06 Springfield 165-grain pointed soft-point bullets with typical expansion at three different ranges.

hunts game of all sizes at all ranges and takes shots at all types of angles, some difficult, some not so difficult.

Very experienced hunters, including many African hunters, feel there is more to killing power than simply kinetic energy. Indeed, these persons have often stated that they believe bullet frontal area (bullet diameter) and bullet weight are important aspects of a bullet's ability to transmit a lethal blow deep into the quarry's vitals. Accepted cartridges for dangerous game are often 40 caliber and larger, with bullets weighing 400 grains or more. The most favored rounds tend to have velocities approaching 2,400 feet per second or more.

When a shooter gains sufficient game-taking experience, he acquires knowledge that tells him which cartridges work adequately. Deer have been killed with the 22 Long Rifle and polar bear have been laid out with a 222 Remington, but such stunts tell nothing of the practical and sporting application of a cartridge. Most important for any purpose is the selection of an appropriate bullet. Basically there are three types of bullets:

(1) highly frangible, rapid-expanding;
(2) controlled, slow-expanding;
(3) non-expanding.

Because of its frangible construction and rapid-expanding characteristics, the first style of bullet will begin to open upon contact with the quarry (or any other surface) and expand violently, coming to a stop with only inches of penetration. Sometimes these bullets expand to a classic mushroom shape and sometimes they may completely

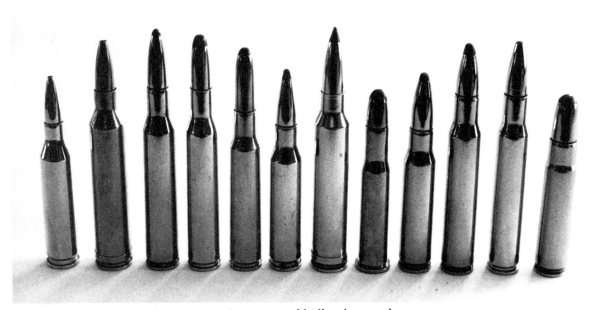

When selecting ammo, always choose sharp-pointed bullet shapes whenever possible to insure maximum down-range ballistics.

disintegrate. Either is perfectly acceptable for this bullet type's *appropriate* application, which is the hunting of small varmints.

The varmint-type bullet's construction is suitable for game up to perhaps 40 pounds in weight. Such bullets will destroy a great deal of tissue surrounding their rather shallow penetration paths. Sometimes varmint bullets also make good target bullets. However, attempts to use this type of bullet on larger game will result in hideous surface wounds which will not bring about a quick death. Indeed, even small deer will often escape, to suffer a protracted death.

Bullets providing slow, controlled expansion, the second type, are designed for hunting big game. These bullets are intended to reach deep into the vitals, sometimes exiting the far side of the game. Expansion should be at a maximum as the vital organs are reached. There are, of course, variations with respect to rate of expansion.

Naturally, since big game comes in sizes from 80 pounds to 1,000 pounds or more, not all big-game bullets will perform exactly alike. Ideally, the lighter and smaller-caliber bullets will expand more readily than the heavier and larger-caliber ones. Thus, a 243 deer bullet will prove unsatisfactory for applications best suited to a 338 moose bullet, and vice versa.

Any attempt to use a big-game bullet on varmints, or on game too light for the specific bullet, will most often result in little or no bullet expansion. The bullet will simply pass through the animal, creating only a small puncture wound and then expending most of its energy on the surrounding landscape.

The hunter must carefully balance range (impact velocity), bullet weight, and bullet construction to the intended quarry in order to accomplish swift, clean kills. An earlier chapter suggests general game size—varmint, light big game, medium big game, and heavy big game, for the different bullet weights available in each specific cartridge.

Non-expanding bullets, those fitting into the third bullet category, have a number of applications aside from military usage. These bullets are sometimes used for target work. They do not necessarily have a full jacket covering the nose. Some very fine target bullets are constructed with a small hollow point or with lead exposed on the nose, but are nevertheless non-expanding types.

When hunting small furbearers, some shooters favor non-expanding bullets so as not to needlessly destroy a valuable pelt. When hunting dangerous game in Africa, the use of non-expanding (solid) bullets is a common practice. For this type of hunting, it is often deemed best to use a bullet capable of extraordinary penetration through very thick hide and muscle as well as huge bone. But the shooter using the non-expanding type must always place his bullet very exactly. Such bullets kill quickly only by piercing the brain, spine, or heart muscle, or by causing massive, rapid hemorrhage.

No cartridge-application system, regardless of how exacting or elaborate, is of any value if the shooter attempts to use a varmint bullet on elk or a grizzly bullet on antelope, or any big-game bullet on var-

Cutaway of loaded rifle cartridge.

Cutaway of rifle bullets.

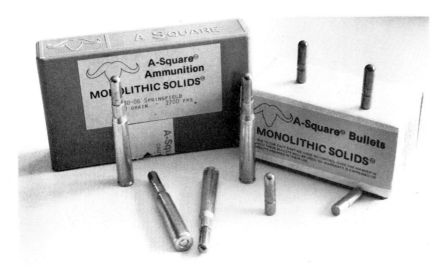

Nonexpanding bullets (such as these A-Square 30-06, 180-grain) have specific applications that include fur bearers and dangerous game. They are also useful for finishing shots.

mints, and so on. Only the shooter can ensure that he purchases ammunition containing suitable bullets. This point cannot be overstressed. When in doubt, consult the suggestions in the Centerfire Rifle Cartridge chapter.

Once the difference between varmint (rapid-expanding), big-game (controlled-expanding), and non-expanding bullets is recognized, the hunter can begin considering appropriate calibers and bullet-weights. Tables contained in this chapter list Optimum Game Weights for each load at distances of 0, 100, 200, 300, and 400 yards. These tables can make cartridge and bullet selection quite easy. But remember that a varmint bullet with a weight rating of 100 or more pounds is really never suitable for any game weighing more than 45 or 50 pounds because of its very quick and violent expansion on or near the surface of impact. Conversely, big game bullets often will fail to expand when the quarry is too light for the designed application.

When properly used, the Optimum Game Weight tables will prove an invaluable aid in selecting a cartridge well suited to the hunting of any chosen game. There is also a table of nominal (average) game weights which will be useful if you are uncertain of your intended quarry's weight.

Keep in mind that game weights vary notably from one geographic area to another. An average whitetail buck in one part of the country may well weigh only 80 pounds, while in another area 125 to 140 pounds might be representative, and in still other sections a buck may have to weigh 200 pounds to be considered average. This applies to almost all game, worldwide. Only among a few species, such as pronghorn antelope, do weights remain more or less constant from one area to another.

Thus, any listing of game weights must be rather arbitrary. Our tables list average weights suspected to be reasonably correct on a continental basis. But even the experts differ radically about game weights. It is therefore best to verify average species weight in the region of a hunt. Any hunter who then uses Table 6.4, Optimum Game Weights, will seldom, if ever, regret his selection of cartridge and bullet weight. Naturally, the Optimum Game Weight ratings must always allow for the longest shot you will attempt.

TABLE 6.7
NOMINAL WEIGHTS OF MALE ADULT GAME

Game	Average (lbs.)	Very Large (lbs.)	Extreme (lbs.)
African elephant		13,000	
white rhino	5,000	8,000	
giraffe	2,600		
black rhino	2,000	3,000	
American bison	1,600(800*)	2,200	3,000
African buffalo	700	1,800	
polar bear	700	1,000	1,550(900*)
moose	600	1,000	1,600+
musk ox	600(400*)		
zebra	550	775	
grizzly bear	500	1,000	1,600+
elk	500	800(600*)	1,000
kudu	550	720	
waterbuck		600	
wildebeest	500	600	
black bear	250	500	650+
hartebeest		450	
lion	330	500	
caribou	300(150*)	400(250*)	600(300*)
boar	200	350	450+
mule deer	200	300	400+
jaguar	200(150*)	250	310
sheep	175(125*)	275(175*)	325+
goat	175	250	310
impala	120	150	
wart hog	160	220	
cougar	140(90*)	200(140*)	225
whitetail deer	125	225	350+
feral pig	125	250	
reedbuck	115		
fallow deer	110		440
axis deer	110		
antelope	80(65*)	100	
grey wolf	60	100	170

Game	Average (lbs.)	Very Large (lbs.)	Extreme (lbs.)
javelina	50	65	
coyote	35	40	45
lynx	30	35	40
ocelot	24	35(30*)	
turkey	18(12*)	22	25
woodchuck	8	12	16
grey fox	8(7*)	12	15
red fox	6(5*)	11	15

(*weight of adult female)

NOTE: Listing of an aminal's weight does not mean it is necessarily huntable. Always consult local laws before hunting any game.

CALCULATING OPTIMUM GAME WEIGHTS

Handloaders and others who wish to calculate O.G.W. values for intermediate ranges, actual velocity as measured by chronograph, or any other reason can do so easily. The calculation, as I have developed it over the years, includes allowances for kinetic energy, bullet frontal area (diameter), bullet sectional density (length), impact velocity, and weight. Because of a varmint-type bullet's inability to penetrate deeply, the formula differs for this style of bullet as opposed to big-game and non-expanding bullets.

For big-game bullets (and solids) here's the formula:

$$\text{O.G.W. (in pounds)} = V^3 \times B^2 \times 1.5 \times 10^{-12}$$

For varmint bullets, this is the formula:

$$\text{O.G.W. (in pounds)} = V^3 \times B^2 \times 5 \times 10^{-13}$$

In these formulas, V is the velocity in feet per second (at the range for which you wish to calculate bullet effectiveness), and B is the bullet weight in grains.

Naturally, the Optimum Game Weight rating alone is insufficient to ensure cleanly killed game. The hunter must always use a suitable bullet and place it carefully so as to hit his quarry's vital organs.

Keep in mind that bullets do not necessarily penetrate in a straight line. Thus, any shot at an angle requiring the bullet to penetrate great distances (such as the stern end of a moose headed directly, or nearly so, away from the shooter) is seldom a sporting one. There is no way to predetermine what, if any, bullet divergence will occur from its entrance path.

Some bullets are better performers than others with respect to tracking true. And some shooters believe faster bullet spins (imparted by quicker rifling twists) also help a bullet to track true. But always, exceptional penetration requirements leave a lot to chance. This is a situation that a true sportsman will surely want to avoid on dangerous game. When shots requiring exceptional penetration cannot be avoided, the use of a solid bullet will optimize the chances of success.

The basic calculations for O.G.W. are best done on a calculator. The pocket type will work nicely. The following example will help you understand the needed steps.

Solve for a 30-06, 180-grain bullet at a velocity of 2,500 feet per second:

$$\text{O.G.W. (pounds)} = V^3 \times B^2 \times 1.5^{-12}$$

1. Enter velocity (V) 2500:   reads   2500
2. Enter y^x: reads   2500
3. Enter 3:   reads   3
4. Enter x: reads 1.5625^{10}

(Steps 2, 3 and 4 will cube the velocity.)

5. Enter 180:   reads   180
6. Enter $\times^2$:   reads   32400

(This squares the bullet weight.)

7. Enter $\times$:   reads 5.0625^{14}
8. Enter 1.5^{-12}:   reads 1.5^{-12}
9. Enter =:   reads   759.375

O.G.W. = 759 pounds

For those wishing to avoid calculations, the following table of selected bullet weights, bullet types, and velocities will be useful for obtaining O.G.W. values.

TABLE 6.8

GUIDE TO O.G.W. VALUES WITH SELECTED BULLET WEIGHTS, VELOCITIES, AND BULLET TYPES

Bullet Weight (gr)	Velocity (fps)	Bullet type	Optimum Game Weight (lbs)	Bullet Weight (gr)	Velocity (fps)	Bullet type	Optimum Game Weight (lbs)
25	4000	Varmint	20	50	3800	Varmint	70
	3600		15		3400		50
	3200		10		3000		35
	2800		5		2600		20
					2200		15
45	3400	Varmint	40		1800		5
	300		25				
	2600		20	55	3600	Varmint	70
	2200		10		3200		50
	1800		5		2800		35

EXTERIOR CENTERFIRE RIFLE-CARTRIDGE BALLISTICS

Bullet Weight (gr)	Velocity (fps)	Bullet type	Optimum Game Weight (lbs)
	2400		20
	2000		15
	1600		5
60	3600	Varmint	85
	3200		60
	2800		40
	2400		25
	2000		15
	1600		5
70	3600	Varmint	115
	3200		80
	2800		55
	2400		35
	2000		20
	1600		10
80	3500	Varmint	135
	3100		95
	2700		65
	2300		40
	1900		20
	1500		10
85	3500	Varmint	155
	3100		105
	2700		70
	2300		45
	1900		25
	1500		10
90	3400	Varmint	160
	3000		110
	2600		70
	2200		45
	1800		25
	1400		10
100	3400	Varmint	196
	3000		135
	2600		90
	2200		55
	1800		30
	1400		15
100	3400	Big Game	590
	3000		405
	2600		265
	2200		160
	1800		85
120	3400	Big Game	850
	3000		585
	2600		380
	2200		230
	1800		125
130	3300	Big Game	910
	2900		620
	2500		395
	2100		235
	1700		125
140	3200	Big Game	965
	2800		645
	2400		405
	2000		235
	1600		120
145	3100	Big Game	940
	2700		620
	2300		385
	1900		215
	1500		105
150	3200	Big Game	1105
	2800		740
	2400		465
	2000		270
	1600		140
165	3100	Big Game	1215
	2700		805
	2300		495
	1900		280
	1500		140
170	3000	Big Game	1170
	2600		760
	2200		460
	1800		255
	1400		120
175	3000	Big Game	1240
	2600		805
	2200		490
	1800		270
	1400		125
180	3000	Big Game	1310
	2600		855
	2200		520
	1800		285
	1400		135
200	3000	Big Game	1620
	2600		1055
	2200		640
	1800		350
	1400		165

O.G.W. VALUES (continued)

Bullet Weight (gr)	Velocity (fps)	Bullet type	Optimum Game Weight (lbs)	Bullet Weight (gr)	Velocity (fps)	Bullet type	Optimum Game Weight (lbs)
210	3000	Big Game	1785		1600		465
	2600		1165		1200		195
	2200		705				
	1800		385	285	2700	Big Game	2400
	1400		180		2300		1480
					1900		835
225	2800	Big Game	1665		1500		410
	2400		1050		1100		160
	2000		610				
	1600		310	300	2600	Big Game	2375
	1200		130		2200		1435
					1800		785
230	2800	Big Game	1820		1400		370
	2400		1145		1000		135
	2000		660				
	1600		340	400	2500	Big Game	3750
	1200		145		2100		2225
					1700		1180
250	2800	Big Game	2060		1300		525
	2400		1295		900		175
	2000		750				
	1600		385	500	2400	Big Game	5185
	1200		160		2000		3000
					1600		1535
275	2800	Big Game	2490		1200		650
	2400		1570		800		190
	2000		910				

BULLET MOMENTUM

Shooters have often sought to rate a bullet's potential performance on game by a better method than kinetic-energy figures. Some feel that a bullet's momentum is the best way to accomplish this. For those who do not wish to employ kinetic energy or O.G.W., here is the formula for momentum.

$$\text{Bullet Momentum (pounds)} = \frac{B \times V}{225{,}200}$$

In this formula, B is the bullet weight in grains and V is the bullet velocity in feet per second. Bullet-momentum figures are small numbers—2.2 pounds for a 180-grain bullet at 2,700 feet per second. The use of this method puts equal emphasis on the weight of the bullet and its velocity.

AMMUNITION PERFORMANCE BY LOT NUMBER

Many shooters fail to realize that ballistic performance can vary by ammunition lot. If you sight-in your rifle with one lot of a specific brand and bullet type, and actually hunt with ammunition from another lot, your point of impact may well be notably different with the second lot of ammo.

When purchasing cartridges, you can ensure that your sighting-in, practice, and hunting ammo all have similar points of impact and ballistics by buying ammunition of the same brand, bullet type *and* lot number.

Lot numbers are clearly indicated on the ammo box by all major manufacturers. Federal lists lot numbers on the back outside of each centerfire cartridge box. Winchester and Remington print lot numbers on one of the inside flaps of each box. Checking the lot number may take an extra minute when making your purchase, but it will pay big dividends in consistent points of impact.

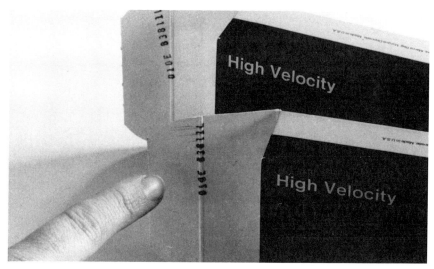

Manufacturers usually clearly mark lot numbers on each ammo package. The lot number represents a homogeneous group of ammunition produced on a specific date.

Doing so may give you another bonus, because if you find a lot of ammunition that proves exceptionally accurate in your rifle, you may wisely want to stock up with several years' supply. Lot numbers indicate a homogeneous group of ammunition made by the manufacturer on a specific date.

ACTUAL AMMUNITION VELOCITIES

This book has referred frequently to variations from advertised velocities, depending on barrel length, internal barrel dimensions, individual ammunition lot, etc. Table 6.9 lists a great many velocities actually measured 15 feet from the muzzle.

These velocities will not necessarily be duplicated with another firearm and another lot of ammunition, but they will show the scope of variations that might be incurred with typical firearms and ammunition.

Similar entries do not suggest duplicate lot numbers. Indeed, each line entry represents a separate ammunition lot.

TABLE 6.9
ACTUAL CHRONOGRAPHED VELOCITIES

Caliber	Bullet Weight (gr)	Brand	Advertised Velocity (fps)	Actual Velocity (fps)	Barrel Length (inches)
22 Hornet	45	Win.	2690	2700	26
22 Hornet	45	Win.	2690	2625	22
22 Hornet	45	Rem.	2690	2860	22
222 Rem	50	Rem.	3140	3040	26
222 Rem	50	Rem.	3140	2960	18½
222 Rem	50	Win.	3140	2949	18½
222 Rem	50	Norma	3140	2919	18½
222 Rem	50	PMC	3140	2937	18½
223 Rem	55	Rem.	3240	3067	20
223 Rem	55	Federal	3240	3014	18½
223 Rem	55	Rem.	3240	2855	18½
223 Rem	55	IMI	3240	3150	18½
223 Rem	55	Federal	3240	2878	18½
223 Rem	55	PMC	3240	2949	18½
225 Win	55	Win.	3570	3408	22
222 Rem Mag	55	Rem.	3240	3145	24
224 Wea Mag	55	Weatherby	3650	3727	26
224 Wea Mag	55	Weatherby	3650	3638	24
22-250 Rem	55	Rem.	3680	3788	26
22-250 Rem	55	Rem.	3680	3591	24
22-250 Rem	53	Norma	3680	3588	24
22 PPC	52	Sako	3400	3399	24
6mm PPC	70	Sako	3140	3138	24
243 Win	80	Rem.	3350	3267	22
243 Win	80	Win.	3350	3428	26
243 Win	80	Rem.	3350	3004	18½
243 Win	100	Rem.	2960	2838	26
243 Win	100	Win.	2960	2665	18½
243 Win	100	Rem.	2960	2690	18½
243 Win	100	Norma	2960	2754	18½

Caliber	Bullet Weight (gr)	Brand	Advertised Velocity (fps)	Actual Velocity (fps)	Barrel Length (inches)
6mm Rem	100	Rem.	3100	2689	18½
6mm Rem	100	Rem.	3100	3086	22
6mm Rem	100	Rem.	3100	3115	26
240 Wea Mag	100	Weatherby	3395	3360	26
25-20 Win	80	Win.	1460	1283	20
250 Savage	100	Rem.	2820	2826	24
257 Roberts	100	Win.	2980	2696	24
257 Roberts	100	Win.	2980	2710	22
257 Roberts	117	Win.	2780	2584	22
257 Roberts	117	Rem.	2780	2590	24
25-06 Rem	87	Rem.	3440	3343	26
257 Wea Mag	87	Weatherby	3825	3739	26
257 Wea Mag	100	Weatherby	3555	3526	26
257 Wea Mag	117	Weatherby	3300	3301	26
6.5 Rem Mag	120	Rem.	3210	2817	18½
264 Win Mag	140	Win.	3030	2966	24
270 Win	100	Rem.	3430	3123	22
270 Win	100	Win.	3430	3043	22
270 Win	100	Rem.	3430	3149	22
270 Win	100	Win.	3430	3032	22
270 Win	130	PMC	3060	2868	22
270 Win	130	Rem.	3060	2667	22
270 Win	130	Win.	3060	2860	22
270 Win	130	Win.	3060	2785	22
270 Win	130	Rem.	3060	2618	22
270 Win	130	Rem.	3060	2718	22
270 Win	130	Win.	3060	2831	22
270 Win	150	Federal	2850	2809	22
270 Win	150	PMC	2850	2624	22
270 Wea Mag	100	Weatherby	3760	3686	24
270 Wea Mag	100	Weatherby	3760	3802	26
270 Wea Mag	130	Weatherby	3375	3322	26
270 Wea Mag	150	Weatherby	3245	3144	26
7mm Mauser	175	Win.	2440	2538	29
7mm-08 Rem	140	Rem.	2860	2680	18½
284 Win	125	Win.	3140	3095	22
284 Win	150	Win.	2860	2793	22
280 Rem	150	Rem.	2890	2786	22
280 Rem	150	Norma	2890	2642	22
280 Rem	165	Rem.	2820	2732	22
7mm Rem Mag	175	Rem.	2860	2876	26
7mm Wea Mag	154	Weatherby	3260	3164	26
30 Carbine	110	Win.	1990	1945	20
303 Savage	190	Win.	1890	1934	26
30-40 Krag	180	Rem.	2430	2288	22
300 Savage	150	Win.	2630	2659	22
300 Savage	180	Rem.	2350	2336	22
307 Win	150	Win.	2760	2575	20
308 Win	150	Rem.	2820	2785	22
308 Win	165	Rem.	2700	2486	18½
308 Win	180	Rem.	2620	2525	22
308 Win	180	Win.	2620	2604	26
30-06 Spfd	125	Win.	3140	3174	22
30-06 Spfd	150	PMC	2910	2741	22

ACTUAL CHRONOGRAPHED VELOCITIES (continued)

Caliber	Bullet Weight (gr)	Brand	Advertised Velocity (fps)	Actual Velocity (fps)	Barrel Length (inches)
30-06 Spfd	150	Rem.	2910	2865	22
30-06 Spfd	150	Win.	2910	2837	22
30-06 Spfd	150	Win.	2910	2776	22
30-06 Spfd	180	PMC	2700	2638	22
30-06 Spfd	180	PMC	2700	2571	22
30-06 Spfd	180	Rem.	2700	2563	22
30-06 Spfd	180	Win.	2700	2588	22
300 H&H Mag	180	Rem.	2880	2779	24
300 Win Mag	150	Win.	3290	3247	24
300 Win Mag	180	Win.	2960	3048	24
300 Wea Mag	150	Weatherby	3600	3559	26
300 Wea Mag	180	Weatherby	3300	3164	26
300 Wea Mag	220	Weatherby	2905	2906	26
303 British	180	Winchester	2460	2440	25
32-20 Win	100	Win.	1210	1280	24
32 Win Spl	170	Win.	2250	2262	20
8mm Mauser	170	Rem.	2360	2335	23
338 Win Mag	210	Federal	2830	2775	24
338 Win Mag	250	Federal	2660	2586	24
340 Wea Mag	210	Weatherby	3250	3050	26
340 Wea Mag	250	Weatherby	3000	2730	26
348 Win	200	Win.	2520	2470	24
357 Mag	158	Speer	1830	1741	22
351 Win SL	180	Win.	1850	1830	20
35 Rem	150	Rem.	2300	2370	20
35 Rem	200	Rem.	2080	1990	20
356 Win	200	Win.	2460	2291	20
356 Win	200	Win.	2460	2327	20
358 Win	200	Win.	2490	2500	22
350 Rem Mag	200	Rem.	2710	2690	18½
375 H&H Mag	270	Win.	2690	2690	24
375 H&H Mag	300	Rem.	2530	2550	24
378 Wea Mag	270	Weatherby	3180	3050	26
378 Wea Mag	300	Weatherby	2925	2830	26
38-40 Win	180	Rem.	1160	1175	20
44-40 Win	200	Rem.	1190	1180	24
44 Rem Mag	240	Rem.	1760	1770	20
416 Hoffman	400	A-Square	2380	2439	23
460 Wea Mag	500	Weatherby	2700	2580	26

Win = Winchester
Wea = Weatherby
Rem = Remington
Spfd = Springfield
Mag = Magnum
Spl = Special
SL = Self Loading

7

Selecting Centerfire Rifle Cartridges

In the selection of rifle cartridges, no one can be totally objective. In defense of my opinions, let me say that they are based on 40 years of personal shooting and 35 years in the firearms industry. They have resulted from experience in the field in the U.S., as well as in such places as the sub-arctic tundra, tropical South American mountains, and African game fields. They are also based on considerable time spent in ballistic lab testing, plus the findings of literally thousands of shooters with whom I have spoken or corresponded during the last 40 years.

The cartridge selections shown in this chapter shrink the manufacturers' listings considerably. For the sake of brevity, only the best of the lot are listed, with an explanation of why the selection was made.

Many cartridges are capable of accomplishing a specific job. Those selected are felt to be superior to ballistically similar cartridges for reasons that include: potential accuracy; ballistics close to advertised claims; suitable bullets for the intended purpose; reasonably flat trajectory; ease of obtaining ammunition; recoil (in proportion to application); versatility of application; firearm availability; cost of ammunition, assuming there's a choice of comparable loads; and reloadability.

If the reader could own one firearm chambered for each cartridge in each basic category, he would have a firearms collection capable of hunting game of any size in any part of the world, or performing satisfactorily at any match.

About the only commercially produced rifle suitable for entry-level benchrest shooting, the Remington Model 40-XBBR is available on special dealer order.

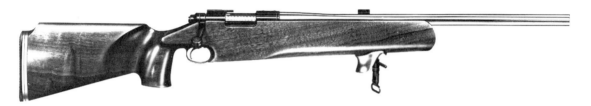

Not many U.S.-made target-grade rifles are manufactured. Remington's 40-XC is a first-class rifle suitable for the National Match Course and is chambered for the 308 Winchester.

TARGET SHOOTING
222 Remington, 7mm-08 Remington, 308 Winchester, 30-06 Winchester, and 300 H&H Magnum

Target-shooting disciplines come in many varieties. Some shooters never fire past 200 yards. For them the 222 Remington is adequate. The 7mm-08 Remington is a good choice for steel-silhouette shooting, while the 308 Winchester will work for almost any target shooting. The 30-06 continues to be popular, but the 308 is somewhat more accurate. The 300 H&H is among the most accurate of the large-capacity-case rounds used for target shooting at ultra-long ranges.

Important, and common to all of these, is the availability of suitable high-grade match bullets, though the 30-caliber choices are more varied and perhaps somewhat more refined than the 22 or 7mm types.

BENCHREST SHOOTING
6mm PPC

This is, as previously stated, the world's most accurate cartridge. Factory Sako ammunition in a factory-produced Sako single-shot rifle is capable of placing 10 shots in a half-inch space at 100 yards time after time. When carefully handloaded, this cartridge is capable of groups smaller than 0.2-inch. Almost every benchrest record possible has been set with the 6mm PPC, and if that record falls it is invariably to another shooter also using a "Six." This round also serves as a very fine varmint cartridge.

The Six has one major drawback—the availability of ammunition (and cases for reloading). But the cartridge's overwhelming accuracy makes it the first choice for this purpose, even though it is not currently an American factory-loaded cartridge.

A shooter could select a 222 Remington for benchrest shooting and thereby eliminate the difficulty of obtaining brass for the Six. However, despite the 222's fine accuracy, it would not be competitive. Benchrest shooting and the 6mm PPC are synonymous at this writing and it will most likely remain so for quite a few years.

PLINKING
223 Remington

Because of the unlimited quantities of paramilitary and military ammunition available at very low prices, this cartridge is a prime candidate for centerfire plinking.

Other important factors make it the only contender. The 223 Remington, known as the 5.56mm in military parlance, is a very accurate cartridge. In a good bolt-action rifle it is capable of minute-of-angle or better accuracy. Even in the popular semiautomatic Ruger Mini-14, the 223 will often deliver 2 m.o.a. with selected handloads. And, importantly, both recoil and muzzle blast are minimal.

Ruger Mini-14 chambered for the 223 Remington cartridge is perhaps the world's most popular centerfire plinking rifle.

Low cost, high accuracy, low recoil, and negligible muzzle blast are thus combined perfectly. No other contenders can offer such optimum levels of all four plinking requirements. And if all this weren't enough, the 223 Remington has a very flat trajectory, which helps to make hitting distant targets easy. One could ask no more from a cartridge for fun shooting. And, depending on the firearm selected, the 223 can double nicely for varmint hunting.

VARMINT HUNTING

223 Remington

For all the reasons given in the plinking category, the 223 Remington is also a fine choice for varmints. It is a fine cartridge for this purpose with sufficiently flat trajectory for 250- to 300-yard shooting. While it is ever so slightly less accurate than the 222 Remington, in a top-quality bolt-action rifle it is sufficiently accurate for even the smallest targets at a full 300 yards.

Since 300 yards is about as far away as most hunters can hit tiny targets in the field, the 223 Remington is an ideal selection for a great many shooters. Accuracy with factory ammo will limit varminting ranges to about 225 yards. You will need to reload for longer ranges.

22-250 Remington

This cartridge will stretch the varmint hunter's useful range to about 400 yards, but only if he is willing to reload. Factory loads seldom prove satisfactory for ranges beyond about 225 yards.

The reloader wishing to stretch his range might, however, do better with the 243 Winchester. Trajectory will be similar, but the effect of wind on the heavier 6mm bullets will be noticeably less. Nonetheless, the 22-250 is superbly accurate and the best 22 caliber for very-long-range varminting.

243 Winchester

The 243 Winchester is thought by many hunters to be the ultimate long-range varmint cartridge. Accuracy is superb (less than m.o.a. with good reloads in a tuned bolt-action rifle), trajectory is flat, and it delivers a devastating blow with varmint bullets. And wind drift is minimal with 80- or 85-grain bullets.

The 243 offers another advantage over any 22-caliber cartridge, because it can double nicely as an antelope or deer cartridge with 100-grain bullets. Reloaders will find that the Nosler 100-grain Partition bullet is the best possible choice for light big game.

Successful varminting demands the utmost in accuracy from cartridge, rifle, and shooter. Best cartridge choices include 223 Remington, 22-250 Remington, and 243 Winchester. This shooter is using a Remington 700 chambered for the 22-250 Remington.

Ruger Model 77 chambered for the 243 Winchester is an ideal rifle for hunting varmints, deer, and antelope.

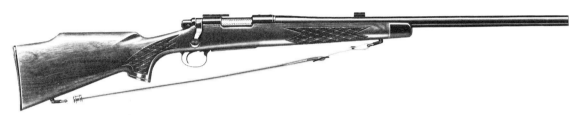

Remington Model 700 BDL is a fine varmint rifle. It is available in 223, 22-250, and 243 Winchester. It also comes chambered for the 222 Remington, 6mm Remington, 7mm-08 Remington, and 308 Winchester.

DEER-SIZED GAME

243 Winchester

The late Les Bowman was often quoted as saying the 243 Winchester was the very best cartridge ever designed for deer hunting for the average rifleman. Low recoil and high accuracy are two of the reasons. I can add only that the Nosler 95- and 100-grain bullets of the Partition style are necessary to make any 6mm rifle suitable for deer hunting.

The 243 is usually more accurate than its ballistic twin, the 6mm Remington. But despite all of its merits, the 243 has Optimum Game Weight ratings that generally rule out use on game larger than most deer and antelope. At 100 yards, the OGW is 294 pounds, at 200 yards it's 220 pounds, and at 300 yards it's 163 pounds. For antelope only—and for the capable shooter—the 243 Winchester will get the job done even at 400 yards, with an OGW rating of 119 pounds.

25-06 Remington

This is unquestionably the best available 25-caliber cartridge. It does double duty for varmints with 87- and 90-grain bullets, is well

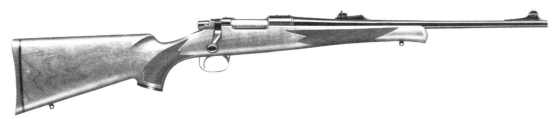

Remington Model Seven is one of the shortest and lightest big-game rifles available. Chambered for the 7mm-08 Remington, it is an ideal woods gun for deer-sized game. It's also a great mountain rifle for any game up to 300 yards. This same rifle is also available chambered for the 223 Remington, 243 Winchester, and 308 Winchester.

suited to light big game with 100-grain bullets, and is useful on game up to the size of caribou with 117-grain projectiles.

Because of its 117-grain bullet performance on game up to 300 pounds (to about 275 yards), the 25-06 Remington is more versatile than the 243 Winchester. The price of this added versatility is more muzzle blast, a tad more recoil, and a bit less accuracy, but it is a fine choice for any but the most recoil-shy shooters.

270 Winchester

If there is one best deer cartridge, it has to be the 270 Winchester. The 270 shoots flat, is very accurate, and hits hard. Still, recoil is easily manageable by most. Indeed, its lower recoil is what makes the 270 Winchester a better choice than the 30-06 for many riflemen.

The 130-grain bullet is the right selection for antelope, deer, goat, sheep, and caribou. But the 270's versatility goes even further with its 100-grain varmint bullet for off-season practice, and the 150-grain bullet will pinch-hit at modest ranges for game up to about 425 pounds if spitzer bullets are selected.

Because most deer hunters sooner or later have an opportunity to attempt a really long shot, or encounter a really big deer, or will hunt larger game in far-away places, the 270 Winchester is not only a good choice, but one of the very best.

7mm-08 Remington

Ballistically well-balanced for deer-sized game and very accurate, this cartridge is available in ultra-light and very short rifles, such as the Remington Model Seven. In such a tiny rifle, it is an ideal woods cartridge. In a rifle of more conventional length, the 7mm-08 makes a fine go-anywhere cartridge for deer and similar game up to 400 yards.

Popular and effective deer-hunting cartridges include, *from left*: 270 Winchester, 7mm Mauser, 7mm-08 Remington, 284 Winchester, 280 Remington, 300 Savage, 308 Winchester, 30-06 Springfield, and 358 Winchester.

Remington loads a 120-grain varmint bullet for this cartridge to make it possible, and fun, to get in some summertime varmint hunting.

The 7mm-08 cartridge also has become popular for silhouette shooting. Its high retained energy makes it ideal for toppling the steel targets at long ranges. The 7mm-08 is accurate, almost as accurate as its parent 308 Winchester round.

308 Winchester

One of the reasons for the popularity of 30-caliber cartridges is that with heavier bullets they lend themselves well to game sizes often notably larger than possible with smaller-diameter cartridges. With the appropriate light big-game bullet—150 grains—the 308 is capable of tackling any deer-sized animal at a full 400 yards. Perhaps it is potentially the most accurate of all big-game cartridges.

The deer hunter will get a great deal of versatility from any rifle chambered for the 308 Winchester. With 125-grain handloads, this round is an extremely accurate varmint cartridge. And, of course, with bullets from 125 to 168 or even 180 grains, it is a superb target round.

Importantly, the 308 doubles nicely for heavier game—up to 500 pounds at 200 yards or 375 pounds at 300 yards.

For all these reasons, few riflemen ever regret selecting the 308 Winchester. The availability of low-cost military-type ammunition makes it affordable to do a lot of practice shooting, as well.

30-06 Springfield

This is one of the most adaptable cartridges for the one-gun hunter. There are varmint loads (55-grain), deer and similar-sized game loads (150-grain), medium-game loads (165-grain) and even heavy-game loads (180-grain). The deer hunter will find the 30-06 up to any task, whatever the range. However, some hunters may find recoil just a bit more fatiguing than they like. For this reason many shooters avoid very light rifles when selecting this cartridge.

There is no reason to go to any larger cartridge for deer, or any game up to 300 pounds. The 30-06 will always be more than enough for any such applications and if you must use a deer rifle on medium to heavy game, then the 30-06 is your best selection from among the ideal half-dozen deer cartridges.

MEDIUM GAME

7mm Remington Magnum

This is a very versatile cartridge, with bullet weights available for light (140 or 150 grains), medium (165 grains), and heavy (175 grains) big game. Actually, many hunters prefer the 165-grain bullet for all hunting, as it delivers optimal ballistics.

The 7mm Magnum was long advocated by Les Bowman as ideal for hunting large game by shooters not accustomed to heavy recoil. Some claim the 7mm Remington Magnum is no more efficient than the 30-06 Springfield. This is a dubious generalization, as the 7mm Remington Magnum will do whatever the 30-06 Springfield can—at about 100 extra yards. The 165-grain bullet has an OGW rating for animals up to 645 pounds at 300 yards, and 534 pounds at 400 yards. And close in, at 100 yards, it delivers enough bone-crushing punch to anchor game up to 900 pounds.

300 Winchester Magnum

Game weighing 600 pounds is fair quarry at 300 yards. This cartridge is up to any medium-sized game. And when loaded with 200-grain bullets, it performs nicely on heavy game—up to 800 pounds at 300 yards. Its only real disadvantage is its somewhat heavy recoil. But if it's reserved for appropriate occasions, this is a very fine cartridge that duplicates the ballistics of the older and longer 300 H&H Magnum.

For occasional light big-game hunting, the shooter can use 150-grain loads, though he will be somewhat overgunned.

338 Winchester Magnum

This cartridge gets into the category of monster mashing. It reaches the upper limit of recoil for most experienced riflemen. But with 225- or 250-grain bullets, it's effective on game slightly over 600 pounds at a range of 400 yards. And back at 200 yards, it will handle game up to 1,000 or perhaps 1,100 pounds.

However, for medium game the Federal 210-grain Premium load using the Nosler Partition bullet will, with less recoil, handle most tasks—up to about 480 pounds at 400 yards or almost 900 pounds at 200 yards.

In a heavier rifle, such as an A-Square Hannibal, the 338 Winchester Magnum delivers recoil about on a par with a 30-06 lightweight rifle. Choosing this cartridge in a heavy rifle can make good sense unless you will be walking vertically most of the day.

The 338 Winchester Magnum is a fine cartridge for most of Africa, being less than suitable only on game the likes of rhino, hippo, buffalo, and elephant. It is certainly the most cartridge ever required for North American hunting, even though some shooters simply enjoy using larger calibers.

HEAVY BIG GAME
338 Winchester Magnum

This cartridge, as mentioned under medium game, is up to all the tasks of a heavy game load. Indeed, with 250-grain bullets, it is ideal for such applications. Its relatively flat trajectory makes it superb at long range, though heavy game should be approached as closely as possible before shooting. The Nosler Partition bullet is ideal for handloaders. At 250 grains, it is both very potent and very accurate.

Because the 338 bullet profile is most often superior, this cartridge will beat the 375 H&H Magnum with respect to delivered energy or OGW whenever the range exceeds 250 yards. The 338 Winchester Magnum is the ideal worldwide heavy-game cartridge.

375 H&H Magnum

This round delivers considerable up-close punch, with the 270-grain bullet preferred over the 300-grain weight. At 100 yards, it's up to game weighing 2,100 pounds, and even at 200 yards animals of 1,500 pounds can be bested. But all of this comes at the price of abusive recoil. A 9½-pound rifle in this caliber is barely heavy enough. More weight would be best to help keep recoil manageable.

Despite the misconceptions of many stateside hunters, the 375 H&H Magnum is far from ideal for rhino, hippo, buffalo, or elephant. It does not have the potential, even with solid bullets, to afford the necessary penetration on game that gets huge and tough.

DANGEROUS GAME

416 Hoffman and 416 Rigby

With a 100-yard Optimum Game Weight rating of about 2,400 pounds, both of these rounds are potent. The 416 Hoffman offers the advantages of easily obtainable brass for case forming (375 H&H) and one extra round in the magazine. The Rigby cartridge offers the advantage of relatively low chamber pressure. Both are generally suitable for all purposes except perhaps for white rhino and elephant. And not even the rhino and elephant are true exceptions, because carefully placed shots with solid bullets of good quality will get the job done.

458 Winchester Magnum

This cartridge has been both praised by some African hunters and condemned by others. Surely its ballistics are no better than either of the 416s. However, the 458 is far more readily available and is loaded

Not all solid bullets for dangerous game are up to the task. At left is an unfired .458-inch full-metal-jacket bullet. In the middle, the same bullet failed to penetrate due to the riveting of its nose. Such failure can also cause the bullet to veer from its intended course. The bullet on the right actually ruptured its jacket. It, too, failed to penetrate. Target was an elephant.

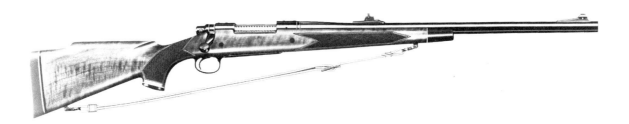

Chambered for both the 375 H&H and 458 Winchester Magnum cartridges, the Remington Safari grade 700 is popular with hunters of heavy and dangerous game. It will soon be available for a 416 Remington Magnum.

by both Winchester and Remington. (It is rumored that Remington will soon make available a 416 Magnum.)

When deep penetration is required, the 458 Winchester Magnum is at its best with the 465-grain A-Square Monolithic solid. This load also delivers a greater Optimum Game Weight rating than either the 500-or 510-grain bullet.

If the 458 Winchester Magnum has any faults, they are related to the use of poor bullets or the cartridge's relatively low velocity. But for all the controversy, the 458 makes a good choice, especially for the non-reloading hunter.

The 458 is sometimes recommended as a broad-application cartridge suitable even for deer when 300-, 350-, 400-, or 405-grain bullets are reloaded. The truth is that these short or blunt-nosed bullets seldom feed reliably through most bolt-action rifles. You will need round-nose bullets of 450-grains or more to get feeding reliability. If you want a commercial low-cost rifle, the 458 Winchester Magnum is currently the only choice in this category.

460 Short and Long A-Square, 460 Weatherby Magnum, 495 A-Square, and 500-A-Square

Each of these is a highly specialized cartridge of the type that should be chosen for elephant. However, recoil is in keeping with the 100-yard Optimum Game Weights for each, which are, respectively: 3,850 pounds, 5,000 pounds, 5,200 pounds, 4,650 pounds and 6,350 pounds. It takes a very skilled, experienced rifleman to handle such cartridges, and the rare need for such a rifle makes a specific single-caliber suggestion almost moot.

Each of the suggested cartridges is loaded by A-Square, and the 460 Weatherby is also available, naturally, from Weatherby. The 460s can be reloaded with generally available .458-inch bullets. The 495

A-Square Monolithic solid is a true solid, not a lead-core-jacketed bullet, and simply will not fail. At the left is an unfired .375-inch bullet and at the right is one recovered from a rhino. It is unmarked except for the grooves left by the rifling.

and 500 A-Square cartridges use .510-inch bullets best obtained directly from A-Square.

Only the 460 Weatherby rifle can be had as a standard-grade production gun, though A-Square custom-built rifles are only slightly more expensive.

CARTRIDGE SUMMARY

If I were forced to choose only three centerfire rifle cartridges for all of my hunting and shooting, the choices would be simple. I would use the 223 Remington, the 270 Winchester, and the 338 Winchester Magnum.

The 223 would be used as a varmint rifle. A Ruger single-shot rifle with Leupold 8x scope would seem about perfect, as would a Remington 700 in the same caliber. I'd choose 52- and 53-grain bullets—all reloads.

My 270 would be my light big-game cartridge. With 90- or 100-grain bullets, it could also serve as a back-up to my varmint rifle, the 223 Remington. I'd choose 130-grain Nosler Partition or Ballistic Tip bullets when reloading and Remington 130-grain Core-Lokt pointed soft-points for factory ammunition. With 150-grain Nosler Partition bullets in reloads or factory Federal Premium ammo, this rifle would serve as a back-up for my medium-game hunts.

The 338 Winchester Magnum, loaded with Federal factory or hand-loaded 210-grain Nosler Partitions, would be my choice for all medium game. When hunting for heavy game or African plains game, I'd use Remington or Federal factory loads with 250-grain bullets. If reloads were in order, they would be Nosler Partition types of the same 250 grains. Or, on some rare occasions, I would use A-Square 250-grain Monolithic solids.

It would be pleasant to assume that every reader's favorite cartridge has been included in this chapter, but that would be wishful thinking. The suggestions presented here certainly are not the only possible selections. I readily admit there are other suitable choices for each application. But on the basis of all my experience, after analyzing thousands of others' experiences and after firing more than a million rounds of centerfire ammunition, my suggestions for the best candidates are firm. I use other cartridges, and under extenuating circumstances I might even suggest something different. In general, however, it is my belief that a shooter who heeds the recommendations in this chapter will never regret his cartridge selections.

8

Rifle-Cartridge Reloading

The handloading of centerfire rifle cartridges offers many advantages, not the least of which is saving 50 percent or more of the cost of factory ammunition. In some instances, the saving can run as high as 70 percent of the price of factory ammunition. The money saved is most often used to purchase more components and, hence, enjoy more shooting. Indeed, in order to become a highly skilled marksman, undeterred by today's high cost of ammunition, loading one's own ammunition may be a necessity.

However, handloading is not for everyone. It requires meticulous care if accidents are to be prevented. When properly conducted, handloading is not dangerous. If undertaken with less than a mature approach, it could easily become a very dangerous pastime.

Apart from economy, handloading has another side to it: it can develop into an absorbing hobby. Those who are interested in maximum performance (outdoing the accuracy of factory loads) will find that their tools, accessories, and procedures very rapidly become highly sophisticated. A reasonable amount of sophistication is essential just to ensure factory-like performance. With each step of upgrading, the hobby interest grows.

All aspects of handloading cannot be covered in one chapter; the topic demands a lengthy book. Therefore, it is not the purpose of this chapter to teach you how to become an accomplished reloader, but rather to point out some of the advantages and disadvantages and to familiarize shooters with the basic steps of reloading a cartridge. Also, it is most important to be aware of some fundamental cautions.

For a basic understanding of how to handload, the author suggests the DBI publication entitled *Metallic Cartridge Reloading, Second*

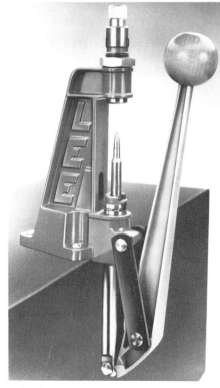

Reloading rifle cartridges can save a shooter 50 to 70 percent of the cost of ammunition and help achieve better accuracy than can be got with factory ammo.

Edition (1988). The studying of a detailed reloading handbook is a prerequisite for any attempt to handload ammunition.

COMPONENTS
Bullets

Be sure the bullets being used are of the recommended diameter and weight for the load you are using. Do not trust what the factory box indicates as its contents. Measure a sampling of bullets with a micrometer and also weigh a sampling on a powder scale. Factory errors, while rare, can occur.

Do not interchange brands or styles of bullets within the same load. Whenever any component change is made, you must return to the suggested starting load and work up, in small increments, to the maximum (or desired) load for your gun. Never exceed the powder manufacturer's maximum load. Use only the specific bullet listed in your data source.

The handloader has a wide choice of bullet selections, but bullet types and weights must be matched carefully to the intended application. The suggestions contained in an earlier chapter, with respect to bullet weights and game types, will serve as a basic guideline.

Handloading bullets come in several grades. Popular-priced, or standard, types are suitable for informal target shooting, plinking, and most deer hunting. Match-grade bullets are available for the serious target shooter. Popular styles of bullets are made by Nosler, Speer, Hornady, and Sierra.

Unique at the intermediate price level are the Nosler Ballistic Tip bullets. These feature a polycarbonate tip which will not deform in the magazine under recoil. The bullets are excellent at retaining velocity because of their very sharp profile and boattail. Ballistic Tip bullets are currently available only in 25, 26, 27, 28, and 30 caliber.

For medium and heavy game, many shooters wisely choose a premium-grade bullet. Such bullets offer superb expansion combined with high weight retention (meaning that they don't break up as they penetrate and expand). Premium-grade bullets are available from Speer (Grand Slam) and Nosler (Partition). Premium-grade bullets ensure the necessary transmission of shock on hard-to-stop game while ensuring the very deep penetration needed for large animals.

Powder

Powder should be kept in a cool, dry place, and always in the original container.

Use data only from the powder manufacturer or another reliable data source.

Never attempt to interpolate data. The use of so-called burning-rate charts for interpolation can be dangerous.

Always start with the suggested starting load and increase your powder charge in small increments, testing your loads before making each subsequent increase. Never exceed the listed maximum. If your combination of load and firearm shows pressure before you reach the maximum, reduce the charge a full 5 percent. If this 5 percent takes you below the suggested starting load, discontinue the use of that load. If trouble persists, look for the cause of the problem. Enlisting the aid of an experienced reloader is always a good double check.

Where your data source does not list a suggested starting load, reduce the maximum charge by 10 percent as a starting point, *except* where otherwise cautioned by the data source.

Always store powder out of reach of children and in an area free from potential fire hazards. Never use powder (or any component) whose identity is not certain. Do not purchase powder in paper bags, re-marked cans, etc.

Learn to identify deteriorating powder and discard it promptly and safely.

A booklet on smokeless powder is available from SAAMI, P.O. Box 838, Branford, CT 06405. Request the smokeless-powder pamphlet and supply a self-addressed, stamped No. 10 (business size) envelope. (A similar booklet is also available for primers.)

All powder charges should be checked with a good scale.

Primers

Inspect each primer for the presence of an anvil before seating. Be sure anvils are not cocked or tipped.

Primers are potentially dangerous. Be sure to keep only a minimum

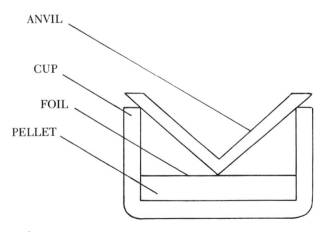

Typical primer construction.

amount on your workbench; it is wise never to exceed 100 primers. Store them in the original factory cartons only. Primers stored in bulk in containers, such as glass jars, amount to no less than bombs on their way to an explosion. Primers should be kept out of reach of children and stored in a cool, dry place.

Use only the specific primer listed in the powder manufacturer's data or other reliable data source. Never substitute large rifle primers for large pistol primers, etc.

The author strongly discourages the use of automatic primer feeds. Sooner or later a jam will be encountered. A careless moment could cause all the primers in the feed to explode and cause serious property and personal injury, or worse. Primers in a primer-feed tube can be mishandled in other ways and can cause an accident.

Cases

Do not mix case brands. Ideally, cases should be segregated into lots. When more than 4 or 5 percent of the cases in a lot show deterioration, the entire lot should be discarded.

One of the most common errors among beginning handloaders is failure to realize that cases must be kept trimmed to a fairly tight tolerance range. Experienced reloaders often err by not realizing that there is a limit to the number of times a case can be trimmed. After all, the brass removed by trimming has to come from someplace. That someplace becomes weaker as the brass is removed. In general, four trimmings from the maximum case length to the suggested trim length seem to be about right. When a fifth trimming is required, the brass should be discarded.

Cases should be carefully inspected before each loading for cracks, splits, stretch marks, or separations. Never load cases that have such damage.

Never load any case that has a loose primer pocket or one that shows evidence of gas leakage around the primer.

LOADING OPERATIONS

General

Avoid any and all distractions, no matter how slight, while reloading. This is not the time to enjoy your favorite music, chat with a friend, or have children playing about you.

Never smoke in the loading area.

Good housekeeping is a must. Clean up all spilled powder or primers immediately. Primers will dust during handling. Wipe this residue up after each loading session. Use an oily rag to wipe the bench area and tooling.

1. Case Inspection

Carefully wipe each case with a clean cloth and tap its mouth on the bench to dislodge any foreign material that may have gotten into the case on the ground at the range. Then inspect each case carefully for any abnormality.

Some of the more common signs of abnormalities include incipient case separation (which begins as a shiny mark around the head of the case), partial case separation, and cracked necks or bodies. But *any* sign of abnormality should disqualify a case from further use. Use only cases that were purchased new or were obtained by firing factory ammo in your rifle.

Properly loaded and cared-for brass can usually be reloaded three to twelve times before it needs to be discarded. After all cases have been inspected, brush the inside of the case neck, making three or four passes with an appropriate-size bronze bore brush.

2. Case Lubrication

Cases must be lubricated before they are run into the resizing die. This step is best accomplished by rolling the case across a pad saturated with the required lube. Such pads are available from several manufacturers.

Case lubrication.

3. Resizing and Decapping

The lubricated case is then run into a sizing die which will restore the fired case to its original dimensions (ensuring smooth feeding and chambering) and will remove the old primer.

4. Degreasing

After sizing the case, all traces of lubricant are removed by wiping it with a clean absorbent cloth. Any lubricant left on the case could result in unwanted, perhaps dangerous, increased thrust on the rifle's bolt when the cartridge is fired.

5. Case-Length Measuring and Trimming

Firing and resizing causes cases to stretch. When cases become too long, they may chamber with difficulty and cause dangerous pressure increases. Thus, after every sizing, the case must be measured to ensure that it falls between the maximum allowable length and the trim-to length.

When cases reach or exceed the maximum allowable length they are trimmed back to the required trim-to length in a small lathe-like tool called a case trimmer. After trimming, the case mouth must be deburred inside and out.

Resizing and decapping the case.

Trimming the case.

6. Priming

A new primer must now be inserted into the primer pocket of the case, and there are several kinds of tools designed to seat it properly. One popular method of accomplishing this step is to use a tool called a ram-prime. This is a shellholder-like device that mounts into the die station of the press. A primer is placed into the priming punch, a case slipped into position, and the press handle manipulated to cause the press ram to seat the primer into the case.

7. Powder Charging

A carefully weighed and balanced powder charge is next placed into the cartridge case, using a powder funnel. The exact powder charge is referenced from a reputable reloading manual.

8. Bullet Seating

Finally, using the appropriate die, a bullet is seated into the cartridge case. Bullets are normally held in place by friction seating. But for tubular-magazine rifles, semiautomatic rifles, and extremely heavy-recoiling cartridges, the case neck is crimped to the bullet by rolling its edge inward into a groove (cannelure) in the bullet. This crimping step requires that the bullet-seating die be adjusted some-

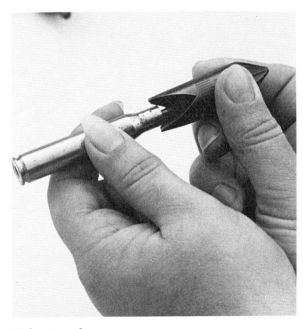

Deburring the case.

Positioning the primer.

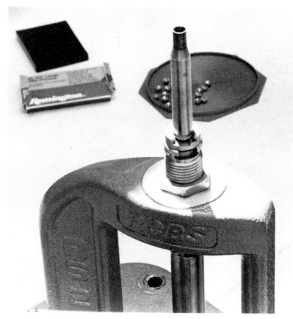
Seating the primer.

Powder charging the case.

what differently than when friction-seating.

Overall cartridge length must be carefully maintained to ensure smooth feeding and chambering.

That's all there is to it. With good reloads you can sometimes provide yourself with a better match of bullet to quarry. And on occasion, depending on caliber, it's possible to load ammunition to a higher velocity than available with factory rounds. Accuracy with carefully assembled reloads is normally quite superior to that of factory ammo. Benchrest shooters rely solely on reloads. And successful long-range hunters use reloads almost to the exclusion of factory cartridges.

The reloader must keep precise records and pay as much attention to matching cartridge and bullet to game as the user of factory cartridges. But the reloader has far more options available, especially in the search for accuracy. Being able to try a variety of powder types, powder-charge weights, and bullets will be a major factor in obtaining optimum accuracy.

HANDLOADING DO'S AND DON'TS

Do be safe rather than sorry.

Do throw out anything about which you have any doubt.

Do use only powder manufacturers or other reliable sources for your data.

Do have your gun carefully examined by a qualified gunsmith if there is any reason to believe you have fired loads that have exceeded the suggested pressure levels.

Do examine cases after each firing for telltale signs of excessive pressure or brass fatigue.

Do discontinue the use of any load that performs in an unexpected or unusual manner.

Do keep accurate and detailed records of all loads.

Do avoid wildcat cartridges for which no standard specifications are available.

Don't use data picked up in gun shops, via word of mouth, from magazines, etc.

Don't use reloads given to you by others. They may not be safe in *your* gun.

Don't use any round that will not chamber easily.

Don't use any component unless you are totally sure of its identity.

Don't use old or deteriorating components.

Don't use any components that have been stored under adverse conditions such as high temperature or high humidity.

Handloading can be fun, economical, and safe if done properly. Almost 4 million people in the United States are reloaders. As special skills are acquired, the benefits multiply. Start by following the powder manufacturer's recipes, take your time, be meticulous about details, and handloading will add a great deal of pleasure to your shooting.

PART II
HANDGUN AMMO

9

Centerfire Handgun Cartridges

Some of the oldest handgun cartridges are still with us. The 22 Short rimfire dates back to the Smith & Wesson "Lady Smith" revolver of 1854. The 45 Colt cartridge dates to the Colt Single Action Army revolver of the 1870s. The 45 Colt was originally a black-powder cartridge and, in its current smokeless-powder loading, is still popular after more than 100 years. The ubiquitous 45 Automatic, one of the most accurate handgun cartridges ever developed, has been around since 1911 and is still highly favored though the 9mm may soon overtake it.

For the most part, handgun cartridges have been developed primarily as loads for personal defense, anti-personnel military use, or for police use. Typical in these categories are the 380 Automatic, 9mm Luger, 45 Automatic, and 38 Special.

Some cartridges, of course, have been developed with the sportsman in mind. A few of these are the 22 Remington Jet Magnum, 221 Remington Fireball, 357 Remington Maximum, and 44 Remington Magnum.

Early handgun cartridges were extremely low-powered and not really adequate even for emergency personal defense. Through the years, cartridge developments have resulted in rounds that test the mettle of the shooter with respect to recoil and muzzle blast. Most notably, the 44 Remington Magnum is one that few handgunners can fully cope with. And there are also a lot of cartridges which, for all practical purposes, should have long ago been scrapped.

Currently, thirty true handgun cartridges are being loaded in the United States. The number is greatly multiplied by the wide range of bullet types that are loaded into these cartridges. There are the standard round-nose lead bullets, lead wadcutters, lead semi-wadcutters, lead hollow-points, jacketed soft-points, jacketed hollow-points, and full-metal-jacket bullets. Each of these projectiles has a particular area of application.

HANDGUN-BULLET STYLES

The shooter needs to give very careful consideration to the types of bullets selected for a specific use. The wrong bullet may well prove near useless under a given set of circumstances, while the correct bullet would have been ideal. A brief description of handgun-bullet styles is, therefore, justified.

Round-Nose Lead Bullets

This type of bullet is most common among revolver cartridges. Its use, despite past history, is best restricted to plinking and informal target shooting. The lead round-nose bullet is non-expanding. It simply cannot be driven fast enough to make it expand. Attempts to exceed approximately 900 feet per second invariably cause severe barrel leading and a resultant total lack of accuracy.

Wadcutter Lead Bullets

This projectile shape was designed for target shooting. The sharp shoulder on the front edge cuts cleanly and makes it easy to score holes in a paper target. Moreover, the wadcutter, especially the hollow-base type, tends to be extremely accurate, although its accuracy range is limited. When ranges approach 75 yards or so, many wadcutter bullets become unstable in flight, and if they hit the target at all, they often do so sideways or back end first because the bullet is tumbling through the air. Due to low velocity levels, wadcutter bullets are non-expanding.

Semi-Wadcutter Lead Bullets

This bullet style is most often credited to the late firearms author, Elmer Keith. Indeed, some ammunition specialists refer to it as the Keith style. This projectile is accurate at long and short ranges, and the transfer of energy is good. It makes a good target type for all ranges, and is to be preferred over round-nose types for personal defense or small-game hunting.

Hollow-Point Lead Bullets

The hollow-point style is often used in conjunction with a semi-wadcutter profile. When impact velocities are in excess of 850 to 950 feet per second, the hollow-point bullet will often provide good expansion. For this reason, it's the best possible type of lead bullet for personal defense or hunting. In some instances, carefully designed lead hollow-points will expand at velocities as low as 775 feet per second.

Handgun bullets come in many styles, each intended for specific applications. *From left*: jacketed hollow-point bullet, for rapid expansion at high velocity; semiwadcutter lead bullet (Keith style) with a hollow base, for accuracy at all ranges and good energy transfer; lead wadcutter with hollow base, very accurate target bullet for ranges to 50 yards.

Additional handgun bullet styles, *from left*: lead round-nose bullet with a hollow base, best for plinking and informal target shooting; full-metal-jacket bullet with hollow base, ideal for semiautomatic handguns; armor-piercing type, no longer legal for civilian use; jacketed soft-point bullet, combines deep penetration with expansion at high velocities.

Jacketed Soft-Point Bullets

This design is intended for higher velocities and for deep penetration combined with reliable expansion. The quality of these bullets varies widely; some of them expand well, some erratically, and some not at all. The shooter needs to select carefully to avoid disappointment. This type of bullet is well suited to the hunting of light game animals at short ranges.

Jacketed Hollow-Point Bullets

Designed for rapid expansion, some bullets of this type perform as expected, while others fail miserably. Once again, the shooter needs to select carefully and base his preferences on actual results. The jacketed hollow-point, when reliably designed and constructed, is excellent for home protection and the hunting of varmints, but it requires a higher-than-standard velocity level to function properly. Velocities in excess of 900 to 950 feet per second are a must, and even higher velocities are preferred.

Cutaway of handgun cartridge loaded with jacketed hollow-point bullet.

Full-Metal-Jacket Bullets

Bullets of this type were originally designed for military semi-automatic cartridges. In this type of handgun, the tough metal outer case helps avoid catastrophic jams that can occur with soft, easily deformed lead bullets. Today, many match-grade handgun bullets are made in the full-metal-jacket style, and they are often extremely accurate. Full-metal-jacket bullets also continue to be popular in

All handgun bullets do not expand properly, even though they're designed to do so. *From left*: jacketed hollow-point fired from a short-barreled revolver—failed to expand owing to low velocity; jacketed hollow-point 380 Auto bullet—failed to expand owing to poor design; jacketed hollow-point—failed to expand at an impact velocity of 850 feet per second; classic expansion—110-grain 38 Special +P bullet recovered from a target at 10 yards.

round-nose styles, as they provide maximum feeding reliability in semiautomatic pistols.

Non-Expanding Jacketed Soft-Point Bullets

These are specialized bullets intended for target shooting. Despite the exposed lead at the bullet nose, and regardless of velocity, this bullet will not expand on impact. Such projectiles are popular with some steel silhouette shooters.

To assist in the process of selecting a handgun cartridge and matching the bullet type to intended application, the following review of currently available centerfire handgun cartridges is offered, with specific application suggestions. For the most part, the list employs the same application categories that were explained in Chapter 5. However, the category of protection (home or self-defense) has been added here, and the benchrest category (applicable only to rifles) has been replaced by silhouette—an increasingly popular area of handgun competition.

22 CALIBER

22 Remington Jet Magnum

40-grain Bullet—Varmint

This is a nearly obsolete round as a great many years have passed since Smith & Wesson discontinued the revolver designed for it. The hope that it would be a popular varmint load soon faded. Because of excessive case taper, this cartridge, which is based on a 38 Special tapered to 22 caliber, tends to set back heavily in the chamber when fired. To avoid this, cartridges and chambers had to be almost surgically clean. Even a tiny trace of oil, grease, or cleaning solvent would result in this rearward shift when the revolver was fired, preventing the cylinder from turning for the next shot. This was always a nettlesome cartridge, and it is suffering a well deserved fate.

221 Remington Fireball

50-grain Bullet—Varmint

This is a superbly accurate round, designed for the Remington XP-100 bolt-action single-shot pistol. It is well suited to the task of long-range varmint hunting. The cartridge is based on the 222 Remington case in a somewhat shortened version. Remington is the sole manufacturer of this cartridge. The XP-100 is no longer being chambered for this cartridge.

25 CALIBER

25 Automatic (25 ACP)

45-grain Bullet—Unclassified
50-grain Bullet—Unclassified

The ballistics of this tiny cartridge are minimal. It was designed for small pocket semiautomatic handguns and was first made available in Europe, where it was known as the 6.35mm. Its use for self defense cannot be endorsed in view of the low ballistic level. However, many people who prefer minimum weight and bulk in a concealable firearm continue to favor the 25 ACP. The relatively poor accuracy provided by most of the handguns chambered for this cartridge eliminates any practical plinking use.

7MM

7mm BR

140-grain Bullet—Light Big Game

This Remington cartridge came to life as a competitor to the 6mm PPC and was intended to be a benchrest rifle cartridge. It commonly is necked to 6mm or 22 caliber for this application.

In 1988, Remington introduced factory-loaded ammunition to fit the Remington XP-100 handgun so chambered. This is an accurate and ballistically superior handgun cartridge for the hunter.

30 CALIBER

30 Luger

93-grain Bullet—Unclassified

This is an old cartridge, dating back to the early part of the century. It is for all practical purposes obsolete, and is currently loaded in this country only by Winchester. Its effectiveness as a military round was less than ideal and it was replaced by the very popular 9mm Luger.

30 Carbine

110-grain Bullet—Varmint

This round is currently chambered in a Ruger single-action revolver. It is an effective varmint cartridge when used with jacketed hollow-points. Full-metal-jacket bullets are sometimes used for furbearers. This cartridge has never been popular in handguns. It is a useful round for personal defense if one does not object to the large size of the Ruger S.A. revolver for such a purpose.

32 CALIBER

32 S&W

85-88-grain Bullets—Plinking

This cartridge's very low ballistic level makes it impractical for anything but plinking. Yet it is used by thousands for home protection, perhaps for no other reason than the availability of the firearm. A great many revolvers of widely varying quality have been produced for this cartridge.

32 S&W Long

98-grain Bullet—Plinking

Despite its 10-grain-heavier bullet and a 25 fps increase in muzzle velocity over the standard 32 S&W, this cartridge still remains a ballistic midget. Best application is for plinking.

In highly refined target-grade weapons, the 32 S&W Long is superbly accurate, at the same time offering distinct advantages over the 38 Special with respect to recoil and noise, both of which are very low with this cartridge. However, such target 32 S&W Long firearms are extremely rare and target-grade ammo is equally difficult to locate.

32 H&R Magnum

85-grain Bullet—Varmint, Small Game, Protection, Plinking
95-grain Bullet—Varmint, Small Game, Protection, Plinking

This cartridge was first made available in H&R revolvers. At this writing, only the Ruger single-action revolver is chambered for it.

The 32 H&R Magnum is great for small-game hunting or short-range varminting but is ballistically as light a cartridge as should be considered for personal protection. The cartridge has low recoil compared to a 38 Special and is therefore a good choice for an infrequent shooter. Ammunition is loaded only by Federal.

32 Short Colt

80-grain Bullet—Unclassified

This cartridge's performance is almost identical to the 32 S&W. Hence, it has little value to today's shooter and, indeed, is very nearly obsolete. No firearms have been chambered for this cartridge for quite some time. Ammo is very difficult to locate.

32 Long Colt

82-grain Bullet—Unclassified

With a bullet-weight increase of just 2 grains and a 10 fps velocity increase, the Long Colt is not a bit different from the 32 Short Colt. It is a nearly useless cartridge, though both of the 32 Colt rounds still see some use in home-defense revolvers.

32 Automatic

60-grain Bullet—Unclassified
71-grain Bullet—Unclassified

The fictional hero, James Bond, was highly enamored of the 32 Automatic and, indeed, if the quantity of ammunition sold is a criterion, so are a great many shooters. Nonetheless, the 32 Automatic does not offer any real advantage over the 32 S&W with respect to velocity or energy.

The 32 Automatic's main edge on the various 32 Smith & Wesson and Colt revolver cartridges is the fact that the 60-grain bullet, as loaded by Winchester with the Silvertip bullet, will reliably expand and therefore will better transfer energy. Because of the accuracy limitations of most semiautomatic handguns in this caliber, the 32 Automatic is not even much of a plinker's gun. Its most popular use is

Winchester 32-caliber Silvertip, showing typical expansion.

short-range personal defense, though this writer feels it to be inadequate.

38 CALIBER
38 Smith & Wesson
145/146-grain Bullet—Unclassified

The 38 Smith & Wesson represents a considerable ballistic gain over all the 32s except the 32 H&R Magnum. But still, ballistics are too light for the cartridge to be trusted for personal protection, an application that demands a minimum of 190 to 200 foot/pounds of energy at the muzzle.

38 Short Colt
125-grain Bullet—Unclassified

While this cartridge uses a lighter bullet than its S&W counterpart, its greater velocity makes it equal to the 38 S&W with respect to delivered energy—and an equally poor choice for any application. No handguns have been chambered for this hard-to-buy cartridge for a great many years.

380 Automatic
85-grain Bullet—Small Game, Protection, Plinking
88-90-grain Bullet—Small Game, Protection, Plinking
95-grain Bullet—Protection

This is a comparatively accurate cartridge and serves well for home or personal protection. The expanding bullets, especially the Win-

Winchester 380-caliber Silvertip, showing typical expansion.

chester 85-grain Silvertip, afford good energy transfer. Accuracy can vary widely, but with a good gun, such as a Walther PP or PPK, 2-inch groups at 25 yards are often the norm.

Many 38 Special users have belittled the 380 Auto, but the truth is that a 380 Auto with a 2¾-inch barrel will duplicate the performance of a 2-inch 38 Special revolver with standard-velocity ammunition. The choice of a 380 Auto for small critters or personal protection has made a great deal of sense to many thousands of shooters. In most brands, it is a reliably functioning round and affords sufficient energy to get these jobs done.

Due to grip design, many 380 semiautomatic handguns, such as the Walther, are somewhat uncomfortable to fire, at least for infrequent shooters.

9mm Luger

88-grain Bullet—Varmint, Plinking, Target
95-grain Bullet—Varmint, Plinking, Target
115-grain Bullet—Varmint, Protection
123/124-grain Bullet—Protection

This cartridge saw its start in the German Luger pistol and was used heavily during World War II. It was officially known then as the 9mm Parabellum cartridge. It has become extremely popular in this country, as U.S. shooters continue to show increasing interest in semiauto pistols. Its recent adoption as the official U.S. military handgun cartridge will further enhance its popularity.

The 9mm Luger is accurate and potent. When reliable expanding bullets are used, it is very effective for several handgun applications. It is, however, less than useful for light big game where a minimum impact energy of 500 foot/pounds is required (and much more is preferred).

Ballistically speaking, the 9mm Luger falls between the 38 Special +P loads and the 357 Magnum. Most shooters will find the 9mm a comfortable cartridge to shoot. It does yeoman service for police work and most sporting applications. There is plenty of inexpensive ammo available for plinking and target shooting.

38 Automatic

130-grain Bullet—Protection

This cartridge is obsolete, having been replaced by the 38 Super Automatic, which has a case of identical size and is simply loaded to higher pressure levels. The 38 Auto never gained any real popularity. Its performance duplicates that of the 9mm Luger.

38 Super Automatic

115-grain Bullet—Varmint, Protection
125-grain Bullet—Varmint, Protection
130-grain Bullet—Protection

The 38 Super is a less than popular cartridge. Its impressive ballistics are overshadowed by its being chambered in only one gun (Colt 1911-style auto) and by problems with blanked primers.

Nonetheless, it is a very accurate and efficient round, somewhat more potent than the 9mm Luger. Ammunition is very difficult to locate and undoubtedly most folks would be better served by a 9mm Luger handgun.

38 Special (Standard Pressure)

110-grain Bullet—Varmint, Small Game, Protection, Plinking
148-grain Bullet—Target, Small Game, Plinking
158-grain Bullet—Plinking, Protection
200-grain Bullet—Unclassified

This is the single most popular handgun cartridge. It is plentiful and available in a wide selection of bullet styles and even in the form of inexpensive paramilitary ammo. The 110-grain jacketed hollowpoint makes a fine selection for several applications. However, in fixed-sight revolvers this load has a point of impact that seldom coincides with the point of aim. Many times the 110-grain bullets strike 6 inches low at 25 yards.

The 148-grain wadcutter offers superb accuracy for target shooting or small game. The 158-grain bullets are available in round-nose or semi-wadcutter style, but round-nose lead bullets usually are a poor choice. The shooter should favor the semi-wadcutter type, and 158-grain bullets should be selected for guns with non-adjustable sights. The 200-grain bullet has very poor ballistics and no really practical application.

Shooters interested in the 38 Special should keep in mind that by selecting a 357 Magnum handgun they can use all 38 Special, 38 Special +P, and 357 Magnum ammunition in a single handgun. Plenty of low-cost ammo is available in this caliber.

38 Special +P

95/110-grain Bullet—Varmint, Small Game
125-grain Bullet—Small Game, Protection
150-grain Bullet—Protection
158-grain Bullet—Protection

This cartridge, as indicated by the +P designation, is loaded to higher pressure levels than standard 38 Special ammunition. Car-

Remington 38 Special 125-grain semijacketed soft-point bullet.

tridges marked with a +P on the head must never be used in firearms having aluminum frames or cylinders, or in any other revolver not specifically designated by the manufacturer as acceptable for +P ammo.

The +P cartridges add an effective amount of punch to the 38 Special, and therefore should be chosen for home or personal protection if the handgun is capable of handling the additional pressure. However, an infrequent or recoil-shy handgunner might shoot better with the lighter recoil and lower noise level of standard-pressure ammunition. This cartridge represents the upper limits of noise and recoil that can be readily tolerated by less than frequent shooters.

357 Magnum

110-grain Bullet—Varmint, Protection
125-grain Bullet—Varmint, Protection
140/145-grain Bullet—Varmint, Protection
158-grain Bullet—Protection, Light Big Game
180-grain Bullet—Silhouette

A 357 Magnum handgun is extremely versatile, as it will handle all 357 Magnum, 38 Special +P, and standard 38 Special ammunition. This gives the shooter the widest possible choice of available ammunition. The 357 Magnum has been used by some handgunners for short-range deer hunting, but shots must be carefully selected and exactly placed, and ranges should be held to 25 yards or less to make this a sporting caliber for light big game. This makes it a marginal choice for the purpose.

The 357 Magnum often proves to be too much cartridge for casual shooters, but it's quite easy to work one's way up through 38 Special and 38 Special +P ammo to develop the skill necessary to handle the heavier magnum loadings.

357 Remington Maximum

158-grain Bullet—Light Big Game, Silhouette
180-grain Bullet—Silhouette

This cartridge faltered almost at its introduction. The only generally available guns currently chambered for it are the Thompson/Center Contender single-shot and the Dan Wesson. Ammunition is very difficult to find.

The 357 Remington Maximum is an elongated 357 Magnum. It has been associated with premature barrel failure and other difficulties in some guns. A shooter who wants more than a 357 Magnum would do better to investigate the 41 Remington Magnum.

Remington 357 Maximum 180-grain semijacketed hollow point bullet.

41 CALIBER

41 Remington Magnum

170/175-grain Bullet—Plinking, Small Game, Varmint, Protection
210-grain Bullet—Target, Plinking, Small Game, Light Big Game, Protection

The 210-grain bullet is available as a semi-wadcutter lead bullet at a reduced velocity. This is the preferred bullet (and load) for target, plinking, and small game. The high-velocity jacketed 210-grain bullets are the appropriate choice for light big game. Either load is entirely adequate for personal protection.

Because the 41 Magnum never gained a great deal of popularity, ammo and reloading components are a bit hard to find. Perhaps most shooters feel that the 44 Magnum revolvers, built on the same-size frame, offer more versatility. Actually, the full-power 44 Magnum is too much cartridge for most shooters, myself included. For us, the 41 Magnum represents the upper level of ballistics combined with a cartridge that can be used accurately.

44 CALIBER

44 Smith & Wesson Special

200-grain Bullet—Varmint, Protection
246-grain Bullet—Target, Protection

At one time, this was a popular cartridge. It is quite obsolete today and survives perhaps solely because it serves well as a standard-velocity loading in handguns chambered for the 44 Remington Magnum.

44 Remington Magnum

180-grain Bullet—Varmint, Protection
200-grain Bullet—Varmint, Protection
210/220-grain Bullet—Varmint, Target, Protection
240-grain Bullet—Target, Small Game, Light Big Game, Silhouette, Protection

The 240-grain lead bullet in a standard-velocity (1,000 fps) loading is perhaps the most useful load in this otherwise overpotent cartridge. This bullet serves well for target, small game, and personal protection.

The highest-velocity loading is a 240-grain gas-check lead bullet at 1,350 feet per second, and this load makes a fine choice for light big game. The lower-velocity (1,150 fps) 240-grain jacketed bullets are also frequently selected for light big game. Shooters often favor the jacketed-bullet loads of this weight in order to avoid barrel leading.

This is an extremely potent cartridge whose recoil and noise often prove the undoing of otherwise fine pistol shots. Its use has caused many a shooter to develop an accuracy-destroying flinch. Yet silhouette shooters favor this round to help ensure that their hits will knock over the distant steel targets.

45 CALIBER

45 Automatic (45 ACP)

185-grain Bullet—Target, Varmint, Small Game, Protection
200-grain Bullet—Varmint, Protection
230-grain Bullet—Protection, Small Game

This extremely popular cartridge is capable of very high accuracy and possesses sufficient punch for most handgun applications. Accuracy is, of course, related to firearm quality, and there are a lot of old military 45 autos that, while reliable, are a good deal less than accurate. With most new commercial 45s, accuracy is quite good, even outstanding in the target-grade models.

For guns with fixed sights, the shooter would do best to use the 230-grain bullet. The 185-grain high-speed jacketed-bullet loads often shoot quite low, as much as 3 to 6 inches under point of aim. However, target loads using 185-grain bullets will often print within an inch or two of point of aim at 25 yards.

The 45 Auto serves admirably as a personal defense or police round. Recoil, while certainly not severe, is notably heavier than that of the 38 Special +P or the 9mm. However, occasional practice will enable most shooters to master this cartridge. In an accurate pistol, the 45 serves nicely for small game, and varmints too.

Handgun cartridges, in some calibers, are available in shot loads for use on small pests at close range. Shown is a Remington-loaded 45 Automatic shot loading.

The 45's major drawback is the cost of ammunition; even the paramilitary ammunition sells for about $10 per box of 50.

The cartridge will serve well for almost any application, but the shooter should keep in mind that some current variations of the original Colt 1911 pistol are not nearly as reliable as earlier models with respect to functioning.

45 Auto Rim

230-grain Bullet—Small Game, Protection

The 45 Auto Rim is the 45 ACP cartridge with a rim added. When the military could not get enough 45 ACP semiautomatic pistols, they had revolvers chambered for the 45 ACP cartridge. The rimless 45 case would not, of course, function with the standard ejection system then in use. Steel half-moon clips, which held three 45 ACP cartridges, were used to give the revolver's ejector system a purchase to remove the fired cases.

The 45 Auto Rim cartridge was designed to do away with the need for the steel half-moon clips. Typically, this cartridge is loaded with only a round-nose lead bullet. Ammunition is hard to find and is loaded only by Remington.

45 Colt

225-grain Bullet—Varmint, Protection
250-grain Bullet—Small Game, Target, Protection

This cartridge was the first official U.S. handgun cartridge, adopted in the late 1800s along with the Colt Single Action Army revolver. It is accurate and sufficiently powerful for most handgun applications. However, it has been abused by handloaders, who have attempted to use overly heavy loads to bring the cartridge up to light big-game potential. The very thin-walled 45 Colt case was not designed for this abuse.

Popularity has waned with the discontinuance of the Colt Single Action Army revolver. Nonetheless, the 45 Colt has been available for over 100 years and still has a small but ardent following. Both Smith & Wesson and Ruger chamber handguns for this cartridge.

45 Winchester Magnum

230-grain Bullet—Small Game, Protection

The 45 Winchester Magnum is an elongated 45 ACP and delivers ballistics that surpass many 44 Magnum loads. This cartridge and one other, the 9mm Winchester Magnum, were developed to be the rounds for which the Wildey gas-operated semiautomatic handgun was to be chambered. Few Wildey pistols ever made it to the marketplace, and Winchester has abandoned manufacture of the 9mm Magnum. Some Thompson/Center Contender single-shot pistols are chambered for the 45 Winchester Magnum, but ammunition is very difficult to find.

This round is potent and accurate, but little interest has been shown in it.

10

Exterior Centerfire Handgun-Cartridge Ballistics

Centerfire handgun ballistics are subject to all of the variations discussed in the chapters dealing with rimfire and centerfire rifle ballistics—even more so, because handgun barrels vary rather widely with respect to internal dimensions. As a result, ballistics obtained in one handgun are sometimes notably different from those obtained with the same ammunition in another handgun.

Further, handgun cartridges fired in the usual test barrels will reflect anticipated velocities only from a semiautomatic or single-shot pistol. Revolvers, with their cylinder-to-barrel gap, frequently deliver notably weaker ballistics than suggested by the pressure-and-velocity test barrels.

The revolver-cartridge ballistics listed in this chapter, where possible, show results of firing from specially vented barrels designed to duplicate revolver performance. Such ballistics are indicated by a "V" (for vented) after the barrel-length listing. Unfortunately, it has not been practical for the firearms industry to test many of the older handgun cartridges with these new barrels, as the sales of such ammunition don't warrant the effort or expense.

As in the earlier ballistics chapters, none of the listed numbers should be considered absolutes; rather they are suggestive of approximate levels of performance.

There is a trend toward the use of rifle cartridges in certain single-shot handguns. Cartridges such as the 30-30 Winchester, 35 Rem-

Handgun cartridges come in many sizes and shapes. Each has to be matched carefully to the intended task. *From left*: 22 Long Rifle, for target, plinking; 38 Special, for small game, protection, target, plinking; 357 Magnum, for small game, protection; 9mm Luger, for small game, protection, target, plinking; 45 Automatic, for small game, protection, target.

ington, and 222 Remington have been used in such firearms as the Remington XP-100 and Thompson/Center Contender handguns. But because such use is limited, no major efforts have been made to establish handgun ballistics for these rifle rounds. The shooter who delves into this area will find the use of a chronograph enlightening.

The conditions that apply to obtaining the listed average factory ballistics are:

Temperature:	59°F
Barometer:	29.53" of mercury
Elevation:	0.0 feet (sea level)
Midrange Trajectory:	Based on assumed use of iron sights

Generally speaking, cartridges that develop 200 foot/pounds of energy at the muzzle are considered adequate for personal protection. Most police departments now select cartridges that produce 250 to 300 foot/pounds of muzzle energy.

The hunting of deer is best undertaken with a cartridge that will provide a minimum of 500 foot/pounds at *impact* range. Many hunters feel that 700 foot/pounds should be the minimum. Keep in mind that

Shot loads are available for the 38/357 Mag., 44 Mag., 45 Auto.

bullet expansion is vital to the performance of many rounds. The shooter should undertake to determine if his bullets are expanding as expected.

An easy way to test expansion is to water-soak old telephone directories. They swell to about double thickness when totally saturated. You will need about 18 to 24 inches of water-soaked books to ensure complete expansion.

Positive expansion with handgun bullets will help increase effectiveness. Shown is the excellent performing Winchester Silvertip bullet in the 200-grain 44 Special loading.

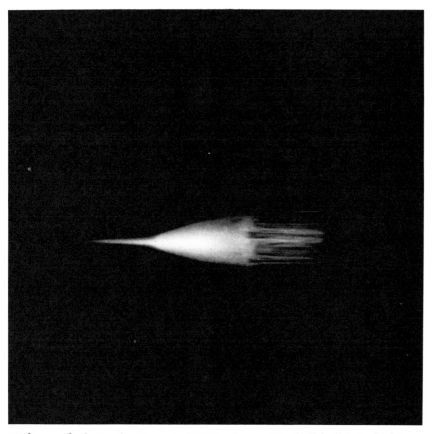
High-speed photo of a 50-grain 221 Remington Fireball bullet in flight.

Bullets that fail to expand may completely penetrate the test medium, so be sure to have a safe backstop. A good setup is a wooden box, sized to accommodate the wet books when stood with the flat side of a cover facing the shooter. The box should be lined with a large plastic garbage or leaf bag to prevent the water from draining out as the books are placed in the box. It is best to soak the books overnight in a tub or pail. Allow ample room for them to fully expand. Add water to the box after placing the phone books in it, in order to compensate for leakage which will occur during handling.

The Optimum Game Weight formulas discussed in Chapter 6 can be applied to handgun cartridges. It will be noted that handgun rounds develop relatively low weight ratings. This clearly points out why many handgun cartridges are so ineffective for hunting.

TABLE 10.1
AVERAGE EXTERIOR HANDGUN BALLISTICS

Caliber	Weight (gr)	VELOCITY (FPS) AT:			ENERGY (FT/LBS) AT:			MIDRANGE TRAJECTORY (INCHES) AT:		Barrel Length
		muzzle	50 yds	100 yds	muzzle	50 yds	100 yds	50 yds	100 yds	
22 Rem Jet Mag	40	2100	1790	1510	390	285	200	0.3	1.4	8⅜"
221 Rem Fireball	50	2650	2380	2130	780	630	505	0.2	0.8	10½"
25 Automatic	45	815	730	655	65	55	40	1.8	7.7	2"
25 Automatic	50	760	705	660	65	55	50	2.0	8.7	2"
7mm BR	140	2215	2135	2010	1525	1415	1255	—	0.5	15"
30 Luger	93	1220	1110	1040	305	255	225	0.9	3.5	4½"
30 Carbine	110	1790	1601	1430	785	625	500	0.4	1.7	10"
32 S&W	85/88	680	645	610	90	80	75	2.5	10.5	3"
32 S&W Long	98	705	670	635	115	100	90	2.3	10.5	4"
32 H&R Mag	85	1100	1020	NA	230	195	NA	1.0	NA	4½"
32 H&R Mag	95	1030	940	NA	225	190	NA	1.1	NA	4½"
32 Short Colt	80	745	665	590	100	80	60	2.2	9.9	4"
32 Long Colt	82	755	715	675	100	95	85	2.0	8.7	4"
32 Automatic	60	970	895	835	125	105	95	1.3	5.4	4"
32 Automatic	71	905	855	810	130	115	95	1.4	5.8	4"
38 S&W	145/146	685	650	620	150	135	125	2.4	10.0	4"
38 Short Colt	125	730	685	645	150	130	115	2.2	9.4	6"
380 Automatic	85	1000	920	860	190	160	140	1.2	5.1	3¾"
380 Automatic	88	990	920	870	190	165	150	1.2	5.1	4"
380 Automatic	90	1000	890	NA	200	160	NA	1.4	NA	3¾"
380 Automatic	95	955	865	785	190	160	130	1.4	5.9	4"
9mm Luger	88	1500	1190	1010	440	275	200	0.6	3.1	4"
9mm Luger	95	1300	1140	NA	355	275	NA	0.7	NA	4"
9mm Luger	115	1155	1045	970	340	280	240	0.9	3.9	4"
9mm Luger	123/124	1110	1030	970	340	290	260	1.0	4.1	4"
38 Automatic	130	1040	980	925	310	275	245	1.0	4.7	4½"
38 Super Auto	115	1300	1145	1040	430	335	275	0.7	3.3	5"
38 Super Auto +P	125	1240	1130	1050	425	355	305	0.8	3.4	5"
38 Super Auto +P	130	1215	1100	1015	425	350	300	0.8	3.6	5"
38 Spl	110	945	895	850	220	195	175	1.3	5.4	4"V
38 Spl	148	710	635	565	165	130	105	2.4	10.8	4"V
38 Spl	158	755	725	690	200	185	170	2.0	8.3	4"V
38 Spl	200	635	615	595	180	170	155	2.8	11.5	4"V
38 Spl	109 grs. #9 Shot	1000	—	—	—	—	—	—	—	6"
38 Spl +P	95	1175	1045	960	290	230	195	0.9	3.9	4"V
38 Spl +P	110	995	925	870	240	210	185	1.2	5.1	4"V
38 Spl +P	125	945	900	860	250	225	205	1.3	5.4	4"V
38 Spl +P	150	910	870	835	275	250	230	1.4	5.7	4"V
38 Spl +P	158	890	855	825	280	255	240	1.4	6.0	4"V
357 Mag	110	1295	1095	975	410	290	230	0.8	3.5	4"V
357 Mag	125	1450	1240	1090	585	425	330	0.6	2.8	4"V
357 Mag	140	1360	1195	1075	575	445	360	0.7	3.0	4"V
357 Mag	145	1290	1155	1060	535	430	360	0.8	3.5	4"V

EXTERIOR HANDGUN BALLISTICS (continued)

Caliber	Weight (gr)	VELOCITY (FPS) AT: muzzle	50 yds	100 yds	ENERGY (FT/LBS) AT: muzzle	50 yds	100 yds	MIDRANGE TRAJECTORY (INCHES) AT: 50 yds	100 yds	Barrel Length
357 Mag	158	1235	1105	1015	535	430	360	0.8	3.5	4″V
357 Mag	180	1145	1055	985	525	445	390	0.9	3.9	4″V
357 Rem Maximum	158	1825	1590	1380	1170	885	670	0.4	1.7	10½″
357 Rem Maximum	180	1555	1330	1115	965	705	530	0.5	2.5	10½″
41 Rem Mag	170	1420	1165	1015	760	515	390	0.7	3.2	4″V
41 Rem Mag	175	1250	1120	1030	605	490	410	0.8	3.4	4″V
41 Rem Mag	210	965	890	840	435	375	330	1.3	5.4	4″V
41 Rem Mag	210	1300	1160	1060	790	630	525	0.7	3.2	4″V
44 S&W Spl	200	1035	940	865	475	390	335	1.1	4.9	6½″
44 S&W Spl	246	755	725	695	310	285	265	2.0	8.3	6½″
44 Rem Mag	180	1610	1365	1175	1035	745	550	0.5	2.3	4″
44 Rem Mag	200	1420	1210	1055	895	650	495	0.6	2.7	6½″
44 Rem Mag	210	1495	1310	1165	1040	805	635	0.6	2.5	6½″V
44 Rem Mag	220	1390	1260	NA	945	775	NA	0.6	NA	6½″V
44 Rem Mag	240	1000	945	900	535	475	435	1.1	4.8	6½″V
44 Rem Mag	240	1180	1080	1010	740	625	545	0.9	3.7	4″V
44 Rem Mag	240	1350	1185	1070	970	750	550	0.5	2.3	4″V
44 Rem Mag	140 grs. #9 Shot	1000	—	—	—	—	—	—	—	6″
45 Automatic	185	770	705	650	245	205	175	2.0	8.7	5″
45 Automatic	185	940	890	845	365	325	295	1.3	5.5	5″
45 Automatic	200	975	915	860	420	370	330	1.4	5.0	5″
45 Automatic	230	835	800	765	355	325	300	1.6	6.8	5″
45 Automatic	117 grs. #9 Shot	1100	—	—	—	—	—	—	—	5″
45 Auto Rim	230	810	770	730	335	305	270	1.8	7.4	5½″
45 Colt	225	960	890	830	460	395	345	1.3	5.5	5½″
45 Colt	250	860	820	780	410	375	340	1.6	6.6	5½″
45 Win Mag	230	1400	1230	1105	1000	775	635	0.6	2.8	5″

WARNING: +P cartridges, with a +P stamped on the cartridge head, are loaded to higher than normal pressures. Such ammunition should be used only in firearms designated by the manufacturer as suitable for these extra-pressure rounds. Never use +P ammo in aluminum cylinders or aluminum-framed guns.

Abbreviations: Rem = Remington
Mag = Magnum
Win = Winchester
S&W = Smith & Wesson
H&R = Harrington & Richardson
V = Vented test barrel used to duplicate actual revolver velocities. Revolver cartridges tested in a solid barrel will show ballistics somewhat higher than actually possible to obtain in a revolver due to the gap between cylinder and barrel.
NA = Data not available

NOTE: All velocities and energies rounded to nearest 5 fps or 5 ft/lbs.

TABLE 10.2

APPROXIMATE MAXIMUM HORIZONTAL DISTANCE TO POINT OF FIRST IMPACT FOR SELECTED HANDGUN CARTRIDGES

Caliber	Bullet Weight (gr)	Muzzle Velocity (fps)	Distance* (yds)
22 Rem Jet Mag	40	2100	2334
221 Rem Fireball	50	2650	2667
25 Automatic	50	760	1400
30 Luger	93	1220	1900
32 S&W	88	680	1334
32 S&W Long	98	705	1434
32 Short Colt	80	745	1400
32 Long Colt	82	755	1400
32 Automatic	71	905	1467
38 S&W	146	685	1467
38 Automatic	95	955	1467
9mm Luger	115	1155	1867
9mm Luger	124	1110	1900
38 Super Auto +P	130	1215	2034
38 Spl +P	110	995	1800
38 Spl +P	150	910	2100
38 Spl	148	710	1634
38 Spl	158	755	1834
38 Spl	200	635	1934
41 Rem Mag	210	965	2234
41 Rem Mag	210	1420	2367
44 S&W Spl	246	755	1734
44 Rem Mag	240	1350	2500
45 Automatic	185	770	1467
45 Automatic	230	835	1700
45 Auto Rim	230	810	1634
45 Colt	250	860	1800

(*) These distances are calculated ranges, not the result of test firings, and are based on assumed use of bullets having tangent ogive noses of .8 caliber radius, cylindrical bearing, and flat base, with an angle of departure of approximately 35°.

(Tables continue on next page)

TABLE 10.3

OPTIMUM GAME WEIGHT RATINGS FOR SELECTED HANDGUN CARTRIDGES

Caliber	Bullet Weight (gr)	Muzzle Velocity (fps)	OPTIMUM GAME WEIGHT (LBS)	
			50 yds	100 yds
25 Automatic	45	815	1	—
25 Automatic	50	760	1	—
7mm BR	140	2215	285	240
30 Luger	93	1220	18	15
30 Carbine	110	1790	75	55
32 S&W	85	680	3	—
32 S&W Long	98	705	4	—
32 H&R Mag	85	1100	12	NA
32 H&R Mag	95	1030	11	NA
32 Short Colt	80	745	3	—
32 Long Colt	82	755	4	—
32 Automatic	60	970	4	—
32 Automatic	71	905	5	—
38 S&W	145	685	9	—
38 Short Colt	125	730	8	—
380 Automatic	85	1000	8	—
380 Automatic	90	1000	9	—
380 Automatic	95	955	9	—
9mm Luger	88	1500	20	12
9mm Luger	95	1300	20	NA
9mm Luger	115	1155	23	18
9mm Luger	123	1110	25	21
38 Super Auto	115	1300	30	22
38 Super Auto	125	1240	34	27
38 Super Auto	130	1215	34	27
38 Spl	110	945	13	11
38 Spl	148	710	12	—
38 Spl	158	755	14	12
38 Spl	200	635	14	12
38 Spl +P	95	1175	15	12
38 Spl +P	110	995	14	12
38 Spl +P	125	945	17	15
38 Spl +P	150	910	22	20
38 Spl +P	158	890	23	21
357 Mag	110	1295	24	17
357 Mag	125	1450	45	30
357 Mag	140	1360	50	37
357 Mag	145	1290	50	37
357 Mag	158	1235	50	39
357 Mag	180	1145	55	36

Caliber	Bullet Weight (gr)	Muzzle Velocity (fps)	OPTIMUM GAME WEIGHT (LBS)	
			50 yds	100 yds
357 Rem Maximum	158	1825	150	100
357 Rem Maximum	180	1555	115	75
41 Rem Mag	170	1420	70	45
41 Rem Mag	175	1250	65	50
41 Rem Mag	210	965	45	40
41 Rem Mag	210	1300	105	80
44 S&W Spl	200	1035	50	39
44 S&W Spl	246	755	35	30
44 Rem Mag	180	1610	125	80
44 Rem Mag	200	1420	105	70
44 Rem Mag	210	1495	150	105
44 Rem Mag	220	1390	145	NA
44 Rem Mag	240	1000	75	65
44 Rem Mag	240	1180	110	90
44 Rem Mag	240	1350	145	105
45 Automatic	185	770	20	14
45 Automatic	185	940	36	31
45 Automatic	200	975	45	38
45 Automatic	230	835	40	36

NA = Data not available

11

Selecting Centerfire Handgun Cartridges

The shooter who wants a practical handgun for personal protection or for hunting needs to consider relatively few cartridges. Experience shows that fewer than a dozen cartridges will fill all such uses. Naturally, any specific selections could be debated by anyone biased in favor of other rounds. All this notwithstanding, the selections listed in this chapter are tried and true. They have proved to be the best possible choices for many thousands of shooters.

221 Remington Fireball

This cartridge is generally available only in older Remington XP-100 single-shot pistols. The XP-100 has a good trigger as well as easily and accurately adjustable iron sights. It is also very accurate and lends itself to easy scope-mount installation. The cartridge itself is flat-shooting and has ample power for any type of varmint at all practical ranges. Finally, the 221 Remington Fireball is easy to reload for maximum accuracy.

All these features add up to exactly what is needed in a varmint-hunting handgun. Other cartridges may possess some or all of the mentioned attributes, but not nearly to the degree of the 221 Fireball. It is doubtful that anyone selecting the 221 Fireball and a used Remington XP-100 handgun would ever find reason to regret the choice.

(Those who do not use a single-shot pistol should consider the selection of a long-barreled 357 Magnum for varminting. This cartridge is discussed later.)

Custom Remington XP-100 has a wood stock and is available in rifle cartridge chamberings for such rounds as the 7mm-08 Remington.

The Fireball does have one drawback. Remington no longer chambers this round in the XP-100, so ammo may sooner or later become difficult to locate.

7mm BR

This cartridge is ideal for steel-silhouette target shooting. With 120-grain bullets it's also a fine varmint round. And its overall usefulness does not stop there—it's also a good choice for light big-game hunting at modest ranges.

The 7mm BR is extremely accurate. Its one drawback, if you consider it a drawback, is the fact that it's available only in the Remington XP-100 pistol.

32 H&R Magnum

This chambering is generally available only in the Ruger Single Six revolver. Because some shooters do not care for single-action revolvers, the 32 H&R is not for everyone.

This 32 cartridge is an ideal small-game round and will do nicely on varmints out to about 50 or even 75 yards. It is also the smallest-bore cartridge that should be considered for personal defense.

Cartridge availability is not good and this is a very real disadvantage. Loaded only by Federal, it will likely never become an easy cartridge to locate. For this reason, this is a round best reserved for reloaders.

For the recoil-shy, it's a fine starter cartridge. Recoil is notably lighter than with many 38 Special loads, and performance is up to the 38's level.

A 380 pocket auto is a fine choice for personal protection and small game but, owing to its small size and light weight, is not always comfortable to shoot.

380 Automatic

If a pocket semiautomatic is desired, the 380 is a fine choice as a personal-protection round. Accuracy can be second-rate in many 380s, but when the cartridge is combined with an accurate gun it also makes a fine short-range small-game cartridge.

Keep in mind that recoil can be bothersome with a small, light 380 pocket pistol. For example, the Walther PPK, which in every other way is a fine pocket gun, can actually draw blood as the slide travels rearward, passing over the web of the shooter's hand and lightly scratching it. A light glove will remedy the problem, of course. Many 380s are less than comfortable to shoot because they're so small. You may prefer one of the larger models, or at least a gun with a large enough tang to keep your hand low and prevent contact with the slide.

9mm Luger

This is the most versatile of all semiautomatic handgun cartridges. With light bullets, it does well as a varmint round. Small game can be taken with any bullet weight. And it is the best of the personal-defense rounds for semiauto handguns.

The 9mm also has the attributes of light recoil, easy reloadability, plenty of inexpensive plinking ammo, and great accuracy. This round is the very best choice for the single-gun semiauto user. Except for light big game, it will serve all purposes very well.

A wide variety of handguns can be found for the 9mm cartridge, ranging from guns small enough to be carried in the pocket to models large enough for effective target shooting or varminting.

38 Special, 38 Special +P

Our most popular handgun cartridge, the 38 is the undisputed king of revolver cartridges for paper-target shooting. It's also a fine small-game round. But in the standard-velocity loads it has proved less than perfect for personal defense or varminting. To meet these needs, the shooter should choose the higher-velocity 38 Special +P.

Keep in mind that +P cartridges develop their higher velocities with an increase in chamber pressure. They should never be used in revolvers with aluminum frames and/or aluminum cylinders. Alumi-

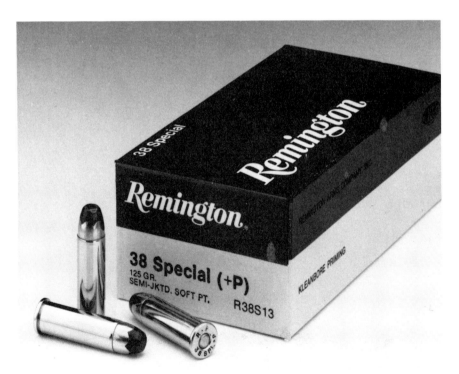

The 38 Special +P loads are very popular and extremely effective when used for small-game hunting or home defense.

num frames are standard on most revolvers bearing a lightweight designation. Aluminum cylinders were found on a small number of World War II Air Force service sidearms.

No +P cartridge should ever be used in any firearm, even of all-steel construction, unless the manufacturer designates its suitability for such use. When in doubt, contact the firearm manufacturer for recommendations. The high-pressure 38s can, of course, be used in 357 Magnum revolvers.

With the higher-velocity +P loads, the 38 Special is a fine varmint load. Bullets weighing 110 grains are often selected for this purpose. Heavier bullets, from 125- to 158-grain hollow-points, are quite suitable for personal defense.

Hollow-point loads often give extra performance to small handgun cartridges. Shown are 380 Auto rounds using an 88-grain jacketed hollow-point bullet.

357 Magnum

The 357 Magnum is basically an elongated 38 Special cartridge. All 357 Magnum revolvers will shoot 38 Special and 38 Special +P ammunition interchangeably. For many shooters who wish to use 38 Special ammo, a 357 Magnum revolver will broaden potential applications.

The 357 Magnum has, for most shooters, a notable amount of recoil and a startling degree of noise compared to all other handgun cartridges described up to this point. But this is not a serious drawback, as the shooter can gradually build up a tolerance for recoil by first using 38 Special, then 38 Special +P, and finally 357 Magnum cartridges.

The 357 has adequate power for personal protection, and trajectory is sufficiently flat to allow varminting as far out as 100 yards.

Accuracy is quite good with most factory loads. However, all-lead bullets at magnum velocities can cause serious barrel leading in many revolvers. This will quickly destroy any hope of accuracy, with bullets sometimes tumbling so badly as to miss a 25-yard, 1-foot-square target. Thus, jacketed bullets are favored by most shooters.

Handloaders often develop loads that will group into a 2-inch circle or less at 50 yards. This attribute, combined with those previously mentioned, make the 357 the most versatile of revolver cartridges. It is, however, not well suited to light big game except when used by an expert marksman who keeps shots to 25 yards or less.

41 Magnum

For the shooter who wants to hunt deer with a handgun, the 41 Magnum is a good choice. Its only major drawback is that ammo is semi-difficult to locate. Usually, only the largest gun shops stock a supply.

Recoil and noise are quite heavy, notably more than the 357 Magnum. Nonetheless, some dedicated shooters have little trouble mastering this cartridge. It affords a good deal more punch than the 357 and is suitable for light big game at modest ranges. The 41 Magnum is also a fine choice for steel-silhouette shooting.

Naturally, handgun hunting demands very precise bullet placement to be sporting. The handgunner must not shoot beyond the range at which he can consistently place all of his shots within a 3-inch circle.

44 Remington Magnum

This is a monster of a cartridge. It is often selected for light big game and silhouette shooting. Unfortunately, only a small percentage of those who choose a 44 Mag ever become proficient with it. Recoil and noise give all but the rare shooter a bad case of flinching.

However, for those who can handle generous servings of slam and bang, the 44 Mag provides as much power as is practical in a handgun. For a select few, it's ideal for silhouette-target competition, long-range varmints, and light big game.

45 Automatic (45 ACP)

This cartridge was, for nearly three-quarters of a century, the official U.S. military sidearm round. The 45 Automatic is very accurate and well fills the multiple demands of personal-defense, varmint, and small-game applications.

The 45 ACP has enough recoil so that some shooters are unable to master it. Yet the perceived recoil is lighter than that of the 357 Magnum.

The 45 ACP cartridge's reputation was solidified in the Colt 1911 pistol and many later versions thereof. These handguns were the epitome of reliability. While current commercial handguns are unquestionably more accurate than the military models, they are also a bit less reliable. This is due to closer-fitting parts—and also to the additional parts required in "Series 80" safety variations as opposed to earlier models.

CONCLUSION

The shooter who prefers semiautomatic pistols would have a very wide range of potential uses if he selected 380 Auto, 9mm Luger, and 45 Auto handguns. Back this all up with a 22 rimfire and all needs, except light big-game hunting, would be adequately covered.

Revolver fans selecting a 22 rimfire and a 357 Magnum would also have ammo choices to allow for all applications except light big game. For deer-sized animals, a 41 or 44 Magnum could be added. Or better still, a Remington XP-100 bolt-action pistol in 7mm BR or 7mm-08 could be added for big game.

12

Handgun-Cartridge Reloading

There are, of course, many similarities in the handloading process used for handgun cartridges and the reloading of rifle cartridges, described in Chapter 8. Hence, there is no need to repeat many of the statements made in that chapter. The reader is simply urged to review Chapter 8 and regard its cautions and advice as part of the following.

Handgun Bullets

Many bullet types and styles are available. There are lead alloy, lead-nosed jacketed, and full-metal-jacketed bullets. Generally, the all-lead bullets are best reserved for velocities not exceeding 800 feet per second. Lead bullets driven at higher velocities can leave lead in the bore. This accuracy-destroying condition will vary, depending on bullet speed, the smoothness of the gun bore, and the hardness of the lead alloy used to make the bullet. The softest alloys will lead the barrel at relatively low velocities. A few tested bullets proved unsatisfactory even at 750 fps.

Jacketed bullets with various nose shapes are extremely popular with handloaders. These offer freedom from leading, good accuracy, and sometimes controlled expansion. The reloader is cautioned, however, that the mere presence of a hollow point or soft lead nose is no guarantee of expansion. Testing bullets—using your load and handgun—is the only way to be certain of expansion.

Full-metal-cased bullets are often used for various types of target shooting. They are required to guarantee reliable feeding in many semiautomatics.

Powder

For the most part, the fastest-burning powders, such as Bullseye or 231, are best for most applications. Such powders often produce excellent accuracy and burn cleanly. Use the slow-burning powders only when you demand the highest possible velocity. Slow-burning powders sometimes leave a residue that can quickly jam or cause sluggish operation of both semiautos and revolvers.

Primers

Use standard handgun primers whenever practical. The use of magnum primers should be restricted to heavy charges of slow-burning powders in calibers such as the 357 Magnum, 41 Magnum, and 44 Magnum.

LOADING OPERATIONS

General

Because handgun cartridges are often consumed at a higher rate than rifle rounds, faster assembly methods are commonly employed when reloading. Also, because of the shooter's inability to shoot very tiny groups with a handgun, ammunition assembly for most purposes need not be as exacting. But this certainly does not mean that sloppy methods or inaccurate assembly will do.

The handgun reloader is well served with an automatic-indexing turret-style press. Such a press will cycle a cartridge through sizing, decapping, case expansion, powder charging, and bullet seating and crimping—all without removing the case from the shellholder. The dies and powder measure will rotate automatically into position as the reloader pumps the press handle.

One auto-indexing turret model, which is inexpensive and particularly easy to use, is the Lee A.I. Turret reloading press. The following outline of reloading operations is based on use of this press, along with Lee carbide dies and a Lee deluxe powder measure. Naturally, other tools can be used.

1. Case Inspection

Carefully wipe each case with a clean cloth and tap its mouth on the bench to dislodge any foreign material. Then inspect each case carefully for any abnormality. Discard any showing signs of abnormality (cracks, dents, leaky primer pocket, etc.). Also measure each case to ensure that it is at least 0.003-inch below maximum allowable length. If cases are to be crimped, the overall length must be reasonably

Lee auto indexing turret press is an ideal choice for reloading handgun shells, especially when it is equipped with carbide dies.

uniform to prevent crimped case mouths from failing to align with the cannelure on the bullet.

2. Case Lubrication

This step may be eliminated when using a carbide sizing die. If you use a steel sizing die (which is slightly less expensive) each case should be lightly lubricated by rolling it across a properly lubed pad or by anointing it lightly with a dab of grease on the finger tips.

3. Resizing and Decapping

Place the shell in the shellholder, with the sizing die in position directly over it. Stroke the press handle downward, running the case into the die. The shellholder should not quite contact the carbide die body; a gap of about 0.005-inch is right. During sizing, the fired primer is ejected and falls into the press base for later removal.

4. Priming

Place a primer of the correct type in the primer arm. Push the primer arm forward, holding it in place, and stroke the press handle upward, pulling the case from the sizing die and seating a new primer.

Case inspection.

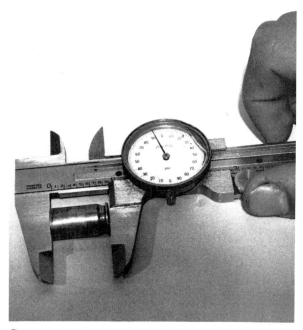

Case inspection: measurement.

The turret will automatically rotate to position the expanding die and the powder measure over the primed case for the next step.

5. Expansion and Powder Metering

Stroke the press handle fully downward. This will push the case into the expansion die, slightly belling the case mouth (for easy bullet starting) and will meter a powder charge into the case. Then stroke the press handle upward, removing the case from the die and automatically rotating the bullet-seating/crimping die into position for use after you verify your charge.

6. Verification of Powder Charge

Visually confirm the presence of the powder charge in the case, and carefully check that the powder height in the case is correct.

7. Bullet Seating and Crimping

Place a bullet in the case and stroke the press handle fully downward. This will raise the case and bullet into the die, seating the bullet to a predetermined depth.

Do not adjust dies to crimp cartridges that headspace on the case

Resizing and priming.

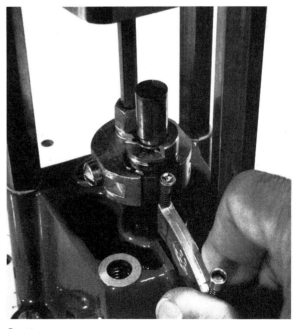

Seating a new primer.

Expansion and powder metering.

Verification of powder charge.

Bullet seating and crimping.

HANDGUN-CARTRIDGE RELOADING

mouth (25 Auto, 32 Auto, 380 Auto, 9mm Luger, 45 Automatic).

Revolver ammunition should be crimped. Bullets must have a cannelure—crimping groove—in order to be crimped, or else the case will buckle.

Finally, stroke the press handle upward and remove the loaded round. This handle stroke will rotate the sizing die into position to start the reloading of the next case.

8. Lubrication Removal

If you use a standard steel sizing die, wipe all grease from the cartridge case. This step is, of course, unnecessary when using a carbide die, which eliminates the need for case lubricant.

That's all there is to it. You can, after a bit of experience, load about 150 rounds per hour with an auto-indexing turret press. That's plenty of ammo, even for a dedicated shooter.

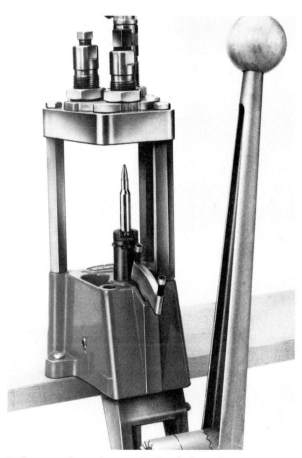

Rifle cartridges also can be loaded on the Lee press.

Entire turret, dies, and powder measure on Lee press are instantly removable and can be replaced with another setup for a different caliber. This allows the reloader to change from one caliber to another in a few moments.

PART III
SHOTSHELLS

13

The Confusing Dram Equivalent Rating System

When shotshells were loaded with black powder, the industry began a process of trying to convey to the consumer the relative power of specific shotshell loadings. Velocity alone was insufficient because the shot-charge weight might vary significantly. But it was not until the use of smokeless powder that the industry agreed on a generally accepted practice of rating shotshells. Regrettably, the chosen system was a throwback to black-powder use, and it caused more confusion than could have been imagined by those who concocted it. That system, unfortunately still used, was the dram equivalent rating.

Few shotgunners have ever understood dram equivalents; most sportsmen purchase shotshells simply by asking for a box of duck or squirrel loads. The more sophisticated request 1½ ounces of 4s or 1¼ ounces of No. 6s. Some readily recognize differences in brand names which suggest a high or standard velocity level. But few have any idea what a marking such as 3¾–1¼–6 or 3¾–1½–4 might mean—let alone MAX 1⅛–7½.

Here's the industry definition for the dram equivalent rating: "The accepted method of correlating relative velocities of shotshells loaded with smokeless propellant to shotshells loaded with black powder. The reference black-powder load chosen was a 3-dram charge with 1⅛ ounces of shot giving a muzzle velocity of 1,200 feet per second (fps). Therefore, a 3-dram (dr.) equivalent loading using smokeless powder

Manufacturers ought to use a simpler system. A velocity, shot-charge weight, and shot size would give the user all the info he needs.

would be one with 1⅛ ounces of shot having a velocity of 1,200 fps. Extending this, 1¼ ounces of shot at 1,165 fps would also be a 3-dram equivalent loading. A 3¼-dr. equivalent load might have 1⅛ ounces of shot and a velocity of 1,255 fps."

The foregoing definition is notable mainly for its flaws, and it creates as many questions as it answers.

It assumes, for example, that you understand the entire definition applies to 12-gauge loads only. It fails to mention the different velocities that would occur in 16- or 20-gauge loads when using identical charges of black powder and shot.

Not included, either, is any explanation of abbreviations or words used to replace numerical dram equivalent ratings—MAX., Maximum, MAG., Magnum, and so on. Of course, if one got into it deeply, it would become apparent that it is impossible to define such terms accurately, as they vary in application and use almost to the point of whim.

Astonishingly, no mention is made of the referenced black-powder granulation size (Fg, FFg, etc.) or, for that matter, the brand or manufacturer. Not every manufacturer's FFg black powder produced ballistics like every other manufacturer's product with a similar designation.

To assume the current ammunition user is familiar enough with black-powder shotshell loading to know what is being referenced is ridiculous. Indeed, why should today's shotgunner even care about this bewildering black-powder information?

To further heighten the absurdity, the dram equivalent rating system was developed, in its entirety, long after factory black-powder loads had passed into history. Ludicrous? You bet.

Unfortunately, today's ammunition user needs to have at least some understanding of all this gobbledygook if he is to sort all of the various loads into an understandable array of choices. Then the user can begin to think intelligently in terms of shot weight and velocity—as with rifle and handgun ammunition. It would seem logical, practical, and easy to list shotshells by gauge and shell length, shot-charge weight, and velocity. For example: 12-ga., 2¾", 1½ ozs., 1,260 fps—or simply 12–2¾–1½–1,260. What's confusing about that?

So why, then, after the industry has repeatedly gone through the exercise of trying to divest itself of dram equivalent ratings, has it failed to do so? Having served on one committee that attempted to do just this in the 1970s, I can say first-hand that the reasoning bears no more resemblance to common sense than the original concept of the dram equivalent. In fairness to some of those involved, perhaps part of the problem stems from the fact that most industry personnel can *speak* "dram" and *think* "feet per second." However, their ability does nothing to help the average ammunition user.

It would seem that the perpetuation of dram equivalent ratings is almost assured. In recent years, a slightly encouraging trend has surfaced. Manufacturers are beginning to list shotshell velocities in their catalogs.

Perhaps many accidents could have been avoided if the dram equivalent system had never been adopted. Some reloaders, failing to realize that the dram rating referred to black powder, loaded dram charges of smokeless powders with disastrous results, destroying their shotguns and suffering personal injury. This alone should have been sufficient reason to abandon the system.

The following dram equivalent tables list shot weights and approximate velocities for specific loads in each gauge. As this information is reviewed and compared with factory ratings, it becomes obvious that a 20-gauge 3-inch shell charged with 1¼ ounces of shot does not compare ballistically with any 12-gauge shell using the same 1¼ ounces of shot. Other misconceptions will be apparent. And when you are next exposed to someone's words of wisdom touting the 20-gauge 3-inch magnum as a waterfowl load, you will know better.

To interpret shotshell-box markings, shell gauge and length must, naturally, be isolated. Then it becomes a matter of breaking down a set of numbers containing three individual bits of information. For example: A 12-gauge 2¾-inch load may be marked 3¾–1¼–6. The first set of numbers refers to the dram equivalent. The second set of numbers is the shot-charge weight in ounces, and the third number is the shot size.

This chapter deals primarily with the first set of numbers. The second and third sets deal with shot, which is extensively covered in

Three drams of black powder compared to an amount of smokeless powder required to achieve ballistics that duplicate the black-powder charge.

the chapter on that topic. The reader should also be aware that the components of the three-digit dram equivalent rating are often shown separately on the ammo-box label.

The dram equivalent rating can be referenced to a specific velocity by using the appropriate table for gauge and then for the shot-charge weight. After a while, you will be able to think velocity when you know the gauge, shot weight, and dram equivalent rating, much as many shooters know that a 30-06, 180-grain factory load has an advertised velocity of 2,700 feet per second. Spaces in the tables filled with a hyphen indicate loads for which a specific velocity rating was never determined, although it would be easy to extrapolate a value.

Beyond the numerically valued dram equivalent ratings, you will need to put some value on the oft-used terms Maximum (MAX) and Magnum (MAG) as they are substituted for the first set of digits in the dram equivalent rating—for example: MAG–1½–2.

The word MAG means no more than a velocity level for this gauge, commonly loaded to the 1½ ounces of shot in the shell. The MAG in no way should be interpreted as meaning the maximum possible velocity, or the maximum possible powder charge, or even the maximum allowable pressure level. In the example just given, the MAG is a substitution for 3¾ (1,260 fps). Why? Perhaps to make the purchaser believe he's getting the greatest possible power. But in this example, a 4-dram equivalent is possible, practical, and loaded by at least one manufacturer.

The same type of translation applies to the term Maximum (MAX), as in: MAX–1¼–6. On a 12-gauge box, this dram rating would be

TABLE 13.1

APPROXIMATE VELOCITIES

10-GAUGE DRAM EQUIVALENT RATINGS

Shot Weight (oz)						DRAM EQUIVALENT RATING								
	3⅜	3½	3⅝	3¾	3⅞	4	4⅛	4¼	4⅜	4½	4⅝	4¾	4⅞	5
1¼	fps: 1200	1225	1250	1270	1295	1315	1340	1360	1385	1405	1430	1450	1475	1495
1⅜	—	1200	1225	1245	1265	1290	1315	1335	1360	1380	1405	1425	1450	1470
1½	—	1175	1200	1220	1245	1265	—	1310	—	1355	—	1400	—	1445
1⅝	—	1150	—	1195	—	1240	1265	1285	—	1330	—	1375	—	1420
1¾	—	1125	—	1170	—	1215	—	1260	—	1305	1330	1350	—	1395
1⅞	—	1100	—	1145	—	1190	—	1235	1260	1280	—	1325	—	1370
2	—	1075	—	1120	—	1165	—	1210	—	1255	—	1300	1325	1345
2⅛	—	1050	—	1095	—	1140	—	1185	—	1230	—	1275	—	1320
2¼	—	1025	—	1070	—	1115	—	1165	—	1205	—	—	—	—

12-GAUGE DRAM EQUIVALENT RATINGS

Shot Weight (oz)						DRAM EQUIVALMENT RATING								
	2½	2⅝	2¾	2⅞	3	3⅛	3¼	3⅜	3½	3⅝	3¾	3⅞	4	4⅛	4½
1	fps: 1130	1155	1180	1205	1235	1260	1290	1315	1345	1380	1400	1430	1455	—	1510
1⅛	1100	1120	1145	1170	1200	1225	1255	1280	1310	1335	1365	1390	1420	—	1475
1¼	1055	1080	1110	—	1165	1190	1220	—	1275	—	1330	—	1385	1410	1440
1⅜	—	—	1075	—	1130	—	1185	1210	1240	—	1295	—	1350	—	1405
1½	—	—	1040	—	1095	—	1150	—	1205	—	1260	—	1315	—	1370
1⅝	—	—	1005	—	1060	—	1115	—	1170	—	1225	—	1280	—	1335
1¾	—	—	970	—	1025	—	1080	—	1135	—	1190	—	1245	—	1300
1⅞	—	—	—	—	—	—	—	—	—	—	1155	—	1210	—	1265
2	—	—	—	—	—	—	—	—	—	—	1120	—	1175	—	1230

16-GAUGE DRAM EQUIVALENT RATINGS

Shot Weight (oz)				DRAM EQUIVALENT RATING					
	2¼	2⅜	2½	2⅝	2¾	2⅞	3	3⅛	3¼
⅞	fps: 1145	1170	1200	—	1255	—	1310	—	1365
1	1110	1135	1165	1190	1220	—	1275	1300	1330
1⅛	1075	1100	1130	1150	1185	1210	1240	—	1295
1¼	1040	—	1095	—	1150	—	1205	1230	1260

APPROXIMATE VELOCITIES *(continued)*

20-GAUGE DRAM EQUIVALENT RATINGS

Shot Weight (oz)	DRAM EQUIVALENT RATING								
	2	2⅛	2¼	2⅜	2½	2⅝	2¾	2⅞	3
¾	fps: 1145	—	—	—	—	—	—	—	—
⅞	1100	1125	1155	—	1210	1235	1265	—	1320
1	1055	—	1110	1135	1165	—	1220	—	1275
1⅛	1010	—	1065	—	1120	—	1175	1200	1230
1¼	—	—	—	—	1075	—	1130	—	1185

28-GAUGE DRAM EQUIVALENT RATINGS

Shot Weight (oz)	DRAM EQUIVALENT RATING					
	1¾	1⅞	2	2⅛	2¼	2⅜
¾	fps: 1115	1160	1205	1250	1295	—
⅞	1070	1115	1160	1205	1250	1295
1	1025	—	1115	1160	1205	1250

410 BORE DRAM EQUIVALENT RATINGS

Shot Weight (oz)	DRAM EQUIVALENT RATING		
	1⅜	1½	1⅝
½	fps: 1125	1200	1275
⅝	1050	1140	1210
¾	—	1080	1155

equivalent to 3¾ dram equivalent, or 1,330 fps. Thus, the code words used in the dram equivalent rating are more misleading than the number ratings.

Frequent reference to the nearby Dram Equivalent Ratings and the actual velocities for various factory loads (see also Chapter 15, on ballistics) will soon enable the ammunition student to recognize dram equivalents as specific velocity levels.

The velocity you obtain from a particular box of shells may not exactly duplicate the velocity suggested by the dram equivalent. The manufacturers do their best to duplicate the nominal velocity, but it is not uncommon for an average velocity level to vary by plus or minus

25 feet per second. The largest average deviation from nominal that I have chronographed in recent years was 35 feet per second. Of course, the velocity of any single round could vary even more than the average levels, as individual shots will obviously produce velocities above and below the average.

Do not give undue significance to extra velocity when all else is equal. Muzzle velocities diminish rapidly, and the downrange differences are not nearly as great as you might expect. Of course, when hunting game that is difficult to bag, every possible advantage, including velocity, is desired. For waterfowl hunting, where big wing bones need to be broken and deep penetration is essential, the highest possible velocities are usually desirable. But for partridge, rabbit, or squirrel, the differences in performance between high-velocity and standard-velocity shells are almost meaningless. Velocity increases make the most sense with the large shot sizes because larger pellets will retain more of the initial velocity. Generally, there is no need for high velocity with shot sizes of No. 6 or smaller.

The essential point here is that shotshell specifications are not impossible to understand. The ridiculous dram equivalents can be reduced to meaningful information on velocity, shot-charge weight, and pellet size. Velocities normally encountered will range from 1,145 to perhaps 1,330 feet per second. Shot-charge weights will range from ½ ounce in the tiny 410 to 2¼ ounces in the big 10-gauge magnum. And lead shot sizes normally encountered will be from No. 9 up to BB and buckshot sizes. First, select the appropriate shot-charge weight, then shot size, and last, an appropriate velocity level. Then the confusion will all but disappear.

The chapter on shot sizes will make it easy to select an appropriate size. The ballistics chapter should help eliminate any confusion that still remains.

14

What You Should Know About Lead Shot

Selecting the right kind of shot is simple in theory, sometimes bewildering in practice. As every shotgunner knows, the smaller the shot size is, the higher is its numerical designation. That's easy enough to remember, but for the very large pellet sizes there are "alpha" designations—a BB size in both lead and steel shot, as well as BBB, T, and F for the largest steel-shot sizes. Some steel waterfowl loads even combine two sizes in one shell—BB × 4, for example. (See Chapter 17 for steel-shot information.) Buckshot is numbered differently from other lead shot. No. 4 Buck has a pellet diameter of .24-inch—much larger than ordinary No. 4 (.13-inch). Target and wingshooting loads can be confusing since many shotgunners don't really understand whether there's any practical difference between No. 7½ and No. 8 or even 9, there being such slight differences in individual pellet size. Also, a single size is often available in soft, hard, and plated versions. Yet proper selection is vital to good performance.

Pattern density depends on pellet size. If you're hunting tiny targets, such as rail or woodcock, your pattern must contain a great many pellets. If the space between the pellets is too great in comparison to quarry size, the pattern will have "holes" which could result in the target being missed or receiving too few hits. But even as many as 10 hits with tiny pellets may not bring down a duck if the pellets fail to penetrate to the vitals. Pellet size and total pellet-charge weight need to be matched to game and range.

Pattern density is an important aspect of a load's effectiveness. Pattern density is governed by pellet count, which in turn is determined by pellet size and total shot-charge weight.

The first step in putting shot sizes to work for the gunner is to formulate some ideas as to which sizes are appropriate for various applications. Of course, you may base your selection of shot sizes on extensive personal experience. But if you haven't had extensive experience with every variety of shotgun quarry, Table 14.1 will help. This table is based on the experience of thousands of shotgunners. In using such recommendations, however, you must bear in mind that many states prohibit the use of certain shot sizes on certain types of game, or may specify permissible shot sizes. For example, three different sizes are listed for turkey, but turkey hunting is quite often restricted with respect to shot size.

Sometimes the restrictions are based on hunter safety. For this reason, many turkey-hunting and conservation groups advocate small pellet sizes. To offset the disadvantages of tiny pellets, the hunter must learn to call his quarry to close range and then restrict himself to head shots.

Please remember that Table 14.1, like the other information in this chapter, applies to lead shot only. And remember that for waterfowl in most American shooting locales, steel shot is mandated by law—and the recommended sizes for lead do *not* apply to steel.

TABLE 14.1

RECOMMENDED SIZES OF LEAD SHOT

Game Being Hunted	Suggested Shot Size
Turkey, fox, and game animals of similar size.	BB
Geese,* turkey, fox, and large ducks* such as blacks, mallards, white-winged scoter.	2
All ducks,* small geese,* pheasants, turkey, squirrels, and rabbits.	4
Large ducks* at ranges of 30 yards or less; small ducks* such as teal, oldsquaw, and bufflehead at all ranges. Also pheasants, rabbits, large grouse, and squirrels.	5
Pheasants at moderate to short range, grouse, partridge, rabbits, squirrels, crows, and doves.	6
Crows, woodcock, snipe, large rails (clapper), rabbits, doves, pigeons, grouse, partridge, quail, and trap shooting.	7½
Small grouse, partridge, woodcock, snipe, large rails (clapper), quail, and trap shooting.	8
Quail, woodcock, snipe, all rails, and skeet shooting.	9
Small rails (sora).	11

(*Applicable only where lead shot is legal for waterfowl.)

Naturally, if experience shows less than perfect results, due to your actual field conditions, it's reasonable to go one size larger or smaller than a suggested pellet size. If, for example, you have difficulty in bagging large birds, you might try the next-larger shot size. That also applies if you're finding too many pellet holes in your table fare. On the other hand, excessive tissue destruction would imply the need to use the next-smaller size. When in doubt, favor a larger pellet size as this often produces cleaner kills and fewer lost cripples.

You must select a pellet size capable of penetrating to the vital organs and/or breaking the wing or leg bones of the quarry. Having selected the appropriate pellet size, you must also make sure your charge of shot is heavy enough and will thus provide sufficient pellets in the pattern to make the required multiple hits. Large ducks, for instance, demand a minimum of five No. 4 lead pellets to ensure that they are consistently brought to bag. Therefore, when using large pellet sizes you must also use a sufficient total pellet-charge weight to get adequate pattern density.

Table 14.2 lists the minimum weight of shot found to be appropriate for the indicated shot sizes, along with a minimum muzzle velocity. Using a load that has a muzzle velocity equal to, or greater than, the listed velocity for each pellet size will ensure adequate penetration if game and shot size are matched correctly.

The use of very heavy shot charges with small pellets can produce excessive pattern density. The result of too many pellets will be a quarry that somewhat resembles a sieve.

The range at which you hunt will play an important part in deter-

TABLE 14.2
BALANCING SHOT SIZE, CHARGE WEIGHT, AND VELOCITY

Shot Size	Use	Minimum Charge Weight (oz)	Minimum Suggested Muzzle Velocity (fps)
BB	All recommended game (Table 14.1)	1½	1210
2	All recommended game (Table 14.1)	1⅜	1210
4	All recommended game (Table 14.1) except rabbit; for rabbit, a charge of 1⅛ ounces at 1135 fps is acceptable	1¼	1260
5	All recommended game (Table 14.1) except rabbit; for rabbit, a charge of 1⅛ ounces at 1135 fps is acceptable	1¼	1260
6	All recommended game (Table 14.1) except pheasant; for pheasant, 1¼ ounces is suggested; for rabbit, a charge of 1 ounce is acceptable	1⅛	1165
7½	All recommended game (Table 14.1) except crow; for crow, 1⅛ ounces is suggested; for rabbit, a velocity of 1135 fps is acceptable	1	1165
8	All recommended applications (Table 14.1)	⅞	1135
9	All recommended applications (Table 14.1)	¾	1135

mining the needed size and number of pellets. If you will be shooting ducks at maximum ranges with No. 4s, you may well want a shot charge of 1½ ounces, the 12-gauge "baby magnum" load. If all your shooting is at short ranges, you might well be satisfied with 1⅛ ounces. If the ranges encountered in the field frequently vary, you will be best served by the minimum suggested charge weights in the table.

The larger the diameter of the pellets, the smaller will be the number in a given weight of shot. Tables 14.3 and 14.4 indicate the relationship between size, diameter, and the number of pellets in a given charge weight. Table 14.3 gives this information for "soft" shot (0.5% antimony content) and Table 14.4 provides the same information for "hard" shot (4.0% antimony content). Variations occur in antimony content, but as a rule the figures in the tables will not be enormously altered by such variations.

Tables 14.3 and 14.4 bring out the point that there are differences in shot even when they are of the same physical size. These pellet differences have to do with alloy content and surface plating, if any.

Soft shot (also called drop shot)—manufactured from pure lead or with a trace of antimony (0.5% or less)—has the advantage of low cost.

TABLE 14.3

SOFT PELLETS: SIZES, WEIGHTS, AND COUNTS

Shot Size	Diameter (inches)	Approximate Pellet Weight* (gr)	½	¹¹⁄₁₆	¾	⅞	1	1⅛	1¼	1⅜	1½	1⅝	1⅞	2	2¼
							Pellet Count								
BB	0.180	8.75					50	56	62	68	75	81	91	100	112
2	0.150	5.03	43	59	65	76	87	97	108	119	130	141	163	174	195
4	0.130	3.37	65	89	97	113	130	146	162	178	195	211	243	260	292
5	0.120	2.57	85	116	127	148	170	191	212	233	255	276	318	340	382
6	0.110	1.99	110	151	165	192	220	247	275	302	330	357	412	440	495
7½	0.095	1.28	170	233	180	297	340	382	425	467	510				
8	0.090	1.09	200	275	300	350	400	450	500						
9	0.080	0.77	284	390	426	497	568	639							
11	0.060	0.32	675	928	1012	1181	1350								

(*) Assumes a "soft" lead pellet of 0.5% antimony

But soft shot deforms easily in its passage through the barrel's forcing cone, bore, and choke. The deformed pellets do not fly true but instead veer rapidly off course. As a result, soft shot gives very "open" patterns. Any velocity increase compounds the distortion.

Some enterprising reloaders use this deformation as an advantage by loading to very high velocities with soft shot. This gives them effective "spreader" loads which deliver very wide patterns at short ranges. But it's obvious that soft shot is not ideally suited to moderate-range, let alone long-range, shooting. It's simply an inexpensive, short-range type of shot.

Hard shot, sometimes called chilled shot, contains from 0.6% to 3.0% antimony to harden the pellets. Hard shot resists deformity, therefore gives better long-range patterns, and is used in most hunting shells. Due to its lower density (caused by the addition of the antimony), hard shot contains a few more pellets per ounce. This is clearly shown when comparing Tables 14.3 and 14.4.

Extra-hard shot, sometimes called magnum shot, contains from 3.1% to 6% antimony. This is the type of shot most often used in target loads. Its hardness further reduces pellet deformation and results in denser patterns. Extra-hard shot is quite costly to manufacture, so its

TABLE 14.4
HARD PELLETS: SIZES, WEIGHTS, AND COUNTS

Shot Size	Diameter (inches)	Approximate Pellet Weight* (gr)	SHOT CHARGE WEIGHTS (OZ)												
			½	11/16	¾	⅞	1	1⅛	1¼	1⅜	1½	1⅝	1⅞	2	2¼
							Pellet Count								
BB	0.180	8.58					51	57	63	70	76	82	95	102	114
2	0.150	4.92	44	61	66	77	89	100	111	122	133	144	166	178	200
4	0.130	3.19	68	94	102	119	137	154	171	188	205	222	256	274	308
5	0.120	2.51	87	119	130	152	174	195	217	239	261	282	326	348	391
6	0.110	1.94	113	155	169	197	226	254	282	310	339	367	423	452	508
7½	0.095	1.24	176	242	264	308	352	396	440	484	528				
8	0.090	1.06	207	284	310	362	414	465	517						
9	0.080	0.74	294	404	441	515	589	662							
11	0.060	0.31	699	961	1048	1223	1398								

(*) Assumes a "hard" lead pellet of 4.0% antimony content.

use in hunting loads is often restricted to the higher-priced premium-grade shotshells.

The fourth type of lead shot is plated. The plating is often copper, sometimes nickel. Plating can be added to soft, hard, or extra-hard shot. The purpose is to add even more hardness and thus make patterns still denser. Extensive tests suggest that the gain from plating is minor. Thus, the cost is seldom justified. Only the most demanding shooting by the most skilled shooters would seem to benefit from this extra manufacturing step. Nonetheless, much of the highest-priced shotgun ammo features plated, extra-hard shot combined with a buffering agent.

The buffering agent often used is a ground polyethelene material. The size of the granulation varies from fine to very fine, depending on the manufacturer's belief as to what granulation works best. The buffering material lessens the effect of the pellet being constricted by the other shot surrounding it. Thus, the buffer also helps prevent shot deformation and thereby increases pattern density. Because it is an added cost, buffering material is used only in top-of-the-line ammunition.

A review of the tables will reveal that some factory loads have little to recommend their use. For example, a ½-ounce load of No. 4 shot,

Premium shotshells often employ extra-hard plated shot combined with a granulated polyethylene "buffer" to provide maximum pattern density.

It will take hits from four to five pellets of the appropriate size to consistently bring game to bag.

contained in the 2½-inch 410-bore shells, could scarcely be recommended for any valid No. 4 shot application. With only 68 pellets in the pattern, one would be hard pressed to make the multiple hits required at any but the shortest ranges. None of this is to suggest that the owners of small gauges do not bring game to bag with light charges of heavy shot. The point is not whether it can be done, but rather that such ammunition is less than ideal for many applications, especially when the ranges are more than moderate.

The shooter's first concern about shot should be to choose an appropriate size for the intended application. The second concern should be to match the selected shot size with a minimum shot weight as suggested in the tables. For long ranges, shot charges should be increased. Maximum ranges call for maximum shot-charge weights.

For difficult shooting, switching from standard-velocity to high-velocity loads will enhance the pellet's penetration and energy-delivering capabilities. For more on the differences, refer to Chapter 15.

A shooter can often overcome the error of wrong velocity or wrong gauge. And sometimes even the error of a wrong shot-charge weight will be less of an obstacle than expected. But a serious miscalculation regarding shot-size selection will invariably lead to disappointments.

The shooter can often do a credible job of determining patterns before hunting by firing at 40″ × 40″ sheets of paper and then circling the 30-inch main pattern. Shooting should be done at the maximum practical hunting range. Patterns with holes that would allow a quarry to receive less than four or five hits indicate a need for a smaller pellet size (to increase pellet count), shorter ranges, or a tighter choke.

Patterning on paper before hunting will give some indication of field potential. This load of BB shot left holes big enough for a duck or goose to pass unharmed, or only crippled.

Shot charge weights vary widely. *From left*: charges of ¾-ounce, ⅞-ounce, 1-ounce, 1⅛-ounces, 1¼-ounces, 1⅜-ounces, 1½-ounces, 1⅝-ounces and 1⅞-ounces.

15

Exterior Shotshell Ballistics for Lead Pellets, Slugs, and Buckshot

As with all previous ballistic tables in this book, the figures in the shotshell ballistic tables should not be considered as absolute. While shotshell ballistics are, for the most part, fairly uniform from gun to gun, some variation will occur, due to ammunition-manufacturing processes and/or barrel length. But from a practical viewpoint, field performance at normal shotgun ranges will not noticeably differ whether the shooter employs a 21-inch or 32-inch barrel. The ballistic tables contained herein are based on common barrel lengths, as follows:

Gauge		Barrel Length
10	=	32"
12	=	30"
16	=	28"
20	=	26"
28	=	26"
410 bore	=	26"

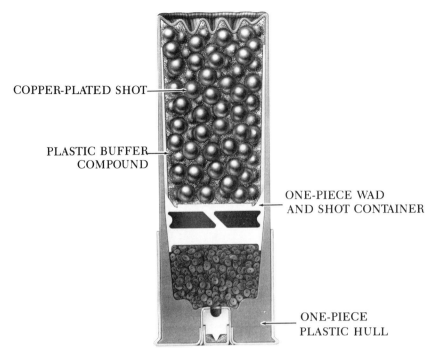

Cutaway of a loaded shotshell.

The nominal muzzle velocities for factory shotshells are shown in Table 15.1. On occasion, a manufacturer may decide to load to a somewhat different velocity than that shown. Steel-shot loads are listed separately in the chapter dealing with them.

The single most important determinant of downrange shotshell ballistics is pellet size. A No. 2 pellet that leaves the muzzle at 1,330 fps will arrive at the 60-yard mark at 735 fps. A No. 7½ pellet started at the same 1,330 fps will have a velocity of only 585 fps at 60 yards—about 150 feet per second less than the larger pellet.

Individual pellet energy also shows substantial differences. The larger the pellet is, the more kinetic energy it can transmit, both at the muzzle and downrange. If both a No. 2 and a No. 4 pellet are fired at a muzzle velocity of 1,330 fps, the respective muzzle energies will

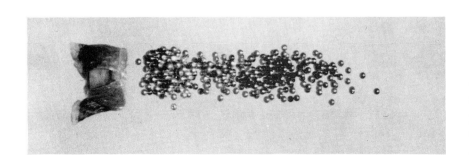

A Federal shot charge in flight showing the wad cup peel back as the wad drops away from the shot column.

TABLE 15.1

FACTORY-LOADED SHOTSHELL SPECIFICATIONS (LEAD SHOT)

Gauge	Shell Length (inches)	Listed Dram Equiv.	Shot-Charge Weight (oz)	Available Shot Sizes	Nominal Velocity (fps)
10	3½	4½	2¼	BB, 2, 4	1210
10	3½	4¼	2	BB, 2, 4, 5, 6	1210
10	3½	MAG	1¾	Slug	1280
10	3½	MAG	NA	18 pellets of 00 Buck	NA
10	3½	MAG	NA	54 pellets of #4 Buck	NA
10	2⅞	4¼	1⅝	4	1330
12	3	4	2	BB, 2, 4	1180
12	3	4	1⅞	BB, 2, 4, 6	1210
12	3	4	1⅝	2, 4, 6	1280
12	3	4	NA	10 pellets of 000 Buck	1225
12	3	4	NA	15 pellets of 00 Buck	1210
12	3	MAX	NA	24 pellets of #1 Buck	1040
12	3	4	NA	41 pellets of #4 Buck	1210
12	3	NA	1	Slug	1760
12	3	NA	1¼	Slug	1560
12	2¾	3¾	1½	BB, 2, 4, 5, 6	1260
12	2¾	3¾	1¼	BB, 2, 4, 5, 6, 7½, 8, 9	1330
12	2¾	3¼	1¼	6, 7½, 8, 9	1220
12	2¾	3½	1⅛	9 (special target)	1310
12	2¾	3¼	1⅛	4, 5, 6, 7½, 8, 9	1255
12	2¾	3	1⅛	7½, 8, 9 (target)	1200
12	2¾	2¾	1⅛	7½, 8, 8½, 9 (target)	1145
12	2¾	3¼	1	6, 7½, 8	1290
12	2¾	2¾	1	8, 9 (target)	1180
12	2¾	MAG	1¼	Slug	1490
12	2¾	MAX	1	Slug	1560
12	2¾	NA	1	Slug	1680
12	2¾	MAX	NA	34 pellets of #4 Buck	1250
12	2¾	3¾	NA	27 pellets of #4 Buck	1325
12	2¾	4	NA	20 pellets of #1 Buck	1075
12	2¾	3¾	NA	16 pellets of #1 Buck	1250
12	2¾	4	NA	12 pellets of 00 Buck	1290
12	2¾	3¾	NA	12 pellets of 0 Buck	1275
12	2¾	3¾	NA	9 pellets of 00 Buck	1325
12	2¾	3¾	NA	8 pellets of 000 Buck	1325
16	2¾	3¼	1¼	2, 4, 6	1260
16	2¾	3¼	1⅛	4, 5, 6, 7½, 9	1295
16	2¾	2¾	1⅛	4, 5, 6, 7½, 8, 9	1185
16	2¾	2½	1	4, 6, 7½	1165
16	2¾	MAX	⅘	Slug	1600
16	2¾	3	NA	12 pellets of #1 Buck	1225

Gauge	Shell Length (inches)	Listed Dram Equiv.	Shot-Charge Weight (oz)	Available Shot Sizes	Nominal Velocity (fps)
20	3	3	1¼	2, 4, 6, 7½	1185
20	3	MAX	NA	18 pellets #2 Buck	NA
20	2¾	2¾	1⅛	4, 6, 7½	1175
20	2¾	2¾	1	4, 5, 6, 7½, 8, 9	1220
20	2¾	2½	1	4, 5, 6, 7½, 8, 9	1165
20	2¾	2¼	⅞	6, 7½, 8, 9	1155
20	2¾	2¼	⅞	8, 9 (target)	1200
20	2¾	MAX	¾	Slug	1600
20	2¾	NA	⅝	Slug	1560
20	2¾	3	NA	20 pellets #3 Buck	1200
28	2¾	2¼	¾	6, 7½, 8	1295
28	2¾	2	¾	9 (target)	1200
410	3	MAX	¹¹⁄₁₆	4, 5, 6, 7½, 8, 9	1135
410	2½	MAX	½	4, 5, 6, 7½, 9	1135
410	2½	MAX	½	9 (target)	1200
410	2½	MAX	⅕	Slug	1830

NA = The nominal velocities of buckshot loads marked NA were not available. Shot-charge weights are not applicable to buckshot loads as the loads are assembled by pellet count, usually listed on the box. NA in dram-equivalent column indicates this value was not established.

be 19.8 foot/pounds and 13.2 foot/pounds, and at 60 yards the respective energy figures will be 6 foot/pounds and 3.6 foot/pounds.

Table 15.2 applies to lead shot only. Steel shot, due to its lower density, loses velocity more rapidly. While the velocity levels shown in Table 15.2 are restricted to a necessarily limited number, the table will supply sufficient data for a good understanding of velocity versus shot size. It should be obvious that shot size is more significant in maintaining downrange velocity than the initial velocity of the load. To cite another example, a No. 7½ pellet that leaves the muzzle at 1,330 fps arrives at the 40-yard mark traveling at 720 fps, while a No. 6 pellet started at 1,200 fps—130 fps slower—arrives at the 40-yard mark with a nearly identical velocity of 725 feet per second.

The trajectory of shot when rounded to the nearest inch is such that all shot sizes from No. 2 to No. 7½ have nearly identical drops when used at normal velocities of 1,150 to 1,330 fps. At 20 yards, pellet drop is 1 inch, at 40 yards 3 inches, and at 50 yards 7 to 10 inches. Obviously, pattern diameters are large enough so you can ignore the trajectory of shot until the range exceeds 40 to 45 yards.

From 45 to 60 yards you might wish to hold from 6 inches to a full foot high if you're certain you can judge range and estimate the re-

TABLE 15.2

EXTERIOR PELLET BALLISTICS (LEAD SHOT)

Shot Size	VELOCITY (FPS)				ENERGY PER PELLET (FT/LBS)			
	Muzzle	20 yds	40 yds	60 yds	Muzzle	20 yds	40 yds	60 yds
2	1330	1050	865	735	19.8	12.3	8.6	6.0
	1295	1030	850	725	19.0	11.9	8.1	5.9
	1220	980	820	700	16.6	10.7	7.5	5.5
	1200	975	815	690	16.1	10.6	7.4	5.3
4	1330	1015	820	690	13.2	7.7	5.0	3.6
	1295	996	805	680	12.6	7.4	4.9	3.5
	1220	950	780	660	11.1	6.8	4.6	3.3
	1200	940	770	655	10.8	6.6	4.4	3.2
5	1330	995	795	665	10.1	5.7	3.6	2.5
	1295	975	785	655	9.6	5.4	3.5	2.4
	1220	935	755	635	8.5	5.0	3.3	2.3
	1200	920	745	630	8.2	4.8	3.2	2.2
6	1330	975	770	635	7.8	4.2	2.6	1.8
	1295	955	755	625	7.4	4.0	2.5	1.7
	1220	915	730	615	6.6	3.7	2.4	1.7
	1200	905	725	605	6.4	3.6	2.3	1.6
7½	1330	935	720	585	5.0	2.5	1.5	1.0
	1295	915	710	580	4.8	2.4	1.4	1.0
	1220	880	685	565	4.2	2.2	1.3	0.9
	1200	870	680	560	4.1	2.2	1.3	0.9

Note: To calculate total energy absorbed by the target, multiply the number of pellets you can place on a silhouette target at the range of interest by the listed energy. For example: If you place five No. 2 pellets on your target at 40 yards, the total energy transferred to the target is 8.6 (for one pellet started at 1,330 fps) × 5 (total number of pellets on target) = 43 foot/pounds.

quired hold-over without ruining your swing and/or "forward allowance" (how far you lead a moving target). However, even at extreme ranges most expert shotgunners simply ignore pellet trajectory. The errors in estimating range and hold-over would probably be greater than the amount of drop for which the shooter is trying to compensate.

Table 15.3 lists the changes in velocity that can be expected for specific barrel-length changes. The differences, you will note, are very small—ranging from 5 to 12½ fps per inch of barrel change. Table 15.4 shows time of flight and drop in inches for various pellet sizes at different muzzle velocities.

Table 15.5 lists downrange ballistics for some typical slug and buckshot loads. While a range of 100 yards is included in the slug data, that may exceed the practical accuracy limitations of any specific slug, barrel, and load combination. The maximum sporting range for slugs

If permitted by law, slugs are always preferred to buckshot loads for hunting big game.

is the distance at which you can keep all of your shots within a 6-inch circle. In Table 15.6, note that only 12-gauge slugs (and not all of those) delivered sufficient energy and accuracy for 100-yard shooting of deer. Naturally, when shooting slugs, rifle-type sights should be used.

When hunting deer, buckshot is never sporting (truly effective) at ranges past 25 yards. The 30- and 40-yard data should not be construed as a suggestion to use buckshot at those ranges.

Slug performance is frequently a topic of debate. However, such discussions can be reduced most simply to the figures in Table 15.6, showing actual performance in typical sight-equipped shotguns. The guns used for the testing were a Remington Model 870 and an Ithaca Model 37, both equipped with the factory-produced slug barrels using the supplied open sights. Comparative 100-yard figures for three rifle cartridges are included at the bottom of the table to give a reference to accuracy and delivered kinetic energy. Not every available slug was tested, but those shown are popular and representative of available ammunition.

It is important to try several brands and styles of slugs when testing for accuracy. Some shotguns will show a preference for one style of slug, even though another gun of the same make and model won't perform as well with the same load.

It's common knowledge that a string of pellets from a shotgun won't travel nearly as far as a rifle bullet, and even a rifled slug won't travel nearly as far before coming to earth. That's why shotgun hunting is sometimes permitted but rifle hunting prohibited in some flat or densely populated areas. Yet a string of pellets or a slug can be lethal at much longer distances than some gunners realize, and the same safety precautions are necessary as with any other firearm. The following table shows how far these projectiles will fly.

Typical slug group, fired at 50 yards, shows a 2½-inch group for five shots.

TABLE 15.3
SHOTSHELL VELOCITY AND BARREL LENGTH

Buckshot and Rifled Slugs

Gauge	Nominal Barrel Length (inches)	Range of Barrel Lengths to Which Data Applies (inches)	Loss or Increase in Velocity for each 1" Shorter or Longer Barrel (fps)
10	30	32-22	7½
12	30	32-22	7½
16	28	30-20	7½
20	26	30-20	7½
28	26	28-20	7½
410 bore	26	28-20	12½

Pellets—No. 11 to BB

Gauge	Nominal Barrel Length (inches)	Range of Barrel Lengths to Which Data Applies (inches)	Loss or Increase in Velocity for each 1" Shorter or Longer Barrel (fps)
10	30	32-22	6
12	30	32-22	5
16	28	30-20	7½
20	26	30-20	7½
28	26	28-20	12½
410 bore	26	28-20	12½

To get the best accuracy, slug guns need special cylinder or improved-cylinder barrels with scope sights.

TABLE 15.4

EXTERIOR SHOTGUN BALLISTICS—TIME OF FLIGHT AND TRAJECTORY

Shot Size	Muzzle Velocity (fps)	TIME OF FLIGHT (SECONDS) TO:			DROP (INCHES) AT:		
		20 yds	40 yds	60 yds	20 yds	40 yds	60 yds
4	1360	.051	.117	.196	0.5	2.6	7.4
5	1360	.052	.119	.202	0.5	2.7	7.8
6	1360	.053	.122	.208	0.5	2.9	8.3
BB	1330	.050	.111	.182	0.5	2.4	6.4
2	1330	.051	.115	.191	0.5	2.6	7.0
4	1330	.052	.119	.199	0.5	2.7	7.7
5	1330	.053	.121	.205	0.5	2.8	8.1
6	1330	.054	.124	.211	0.6	3.0	8.6
7½	1330	.055	.129	.223	0.6	3.2	9.6
BB	1315	.051	.112	.183	0.5	2.4	6.5
2	1315	.052	.116	.192	0.5	2.6	7.1
4	1315	.053	.120	.201	0.5	2.9	7.8
5	1315	.053	.122	.206	0.6	2.9	8.2
6	1315	.054	.125	.212	0.6	3.0	8.7
2	1295	.053	.177	.194	0.5	2.6	7.8
4	1295	.053	.121	.203	0.6	2.8	8.0
5	1295	.054	.124	.208	0.6	2.9	8.4
6	1295	.055	.126	.215	0.6	3.1	8.9
7½	1295	.056	.132	.227	0.6	3.3	9.0
BB	1255	.053	.116	.189	0.5	2.6	6.9
2	1255	.054	.120	.199	0.6	2.8	7.7
4	1255	.055	.124	.207	0.6	3.0	8.3
5	1255	.056	.126	.213	0.6	3.1	8.7
6	1255	.056	.129	.219	0.6	3.2	9.2
8	1255	.058	.137	.236	0.6	3.6	10.7
2	1240	.055	.121	.201	0.6	2.8	7.8
4	1240	.056	.125	.209	0.6	3.0	8.4
5	1240	.056	.128	.215	0.6	3.1	8.9
6	1240	.057	.130	.221	0.6	3.3	9.4
7½	1240	.058	.136	.133	0.6	3.6	10.5
4	1235	.056	.127	.210	0.6	3.0	8.5
5	1235	.056	.128	.215	0.6	3.2	8.9
6	1235	.057	.131	.221	0.6	3.3	9.4
8	1235	.059	.138	.238	0.7	3.7	11.0
2	1220	.055	.123	.203	0.6	2.9	8.0
4	1220	.056	.127	.212	0.6	3.1	8.6
5	1220	.057	.129	.217	0.6	3.2	9.1
6	1220	.058	.132	.223	0.6	3.6	9.6
7½	1220	.059	.137	.235	0.7	3.6	10.2
8	1220	.059	.139	.240	0.7	3.8	11.1

EXTERIOR SHOTGUN BALLISTICS (continued)

Shot Size	Muzzle Velocity (fps)	TIME OF FLIGHT (SECONDS) TO:			DROP (INCHES) AT:		
		20 yds	40 yds	60 yds	20 yds	40 yds	60 yds
4	1200	.057	.128	.214	0.6	3.2	8.8
5	1200	.058	.131	.219	0.6	3.3	9.3
6	1200	.058	.137	.226	0.7	3.4	9.8
7½	1200	.060	.139	.238	0.7	3.7	10.9
8	1200	.060	.141	.242	0.7	3.8	11.3
9	1200	.062	.146	.254	0.7	4.1	12.4
4	1185	.058	.130	.216	0.6	3.2	9.0
6	1185	.059	.135	.227	0.7	3.5	10.0
8	1185	.061	.142	.244	0.7	3.9	11.5
4	1165	.059	.131	.219	0.7	3.3	9.2
5	1165	.059	.134	.224	0.7	3.5	9.7
6	1165	.060	.137	.230	0.7	3.6	10.2
8	1165	.062	.144	.247	0.7	4.0	11.8
9	1165	.063	.149	.258	0.8	4.3	12.9
4	1155	.059	.132	.220	0.7	3.4	9.3
5	1155	.060	.135	.225	0.7	3.1	9.8
6	1155	.060	.137	.231	0.7	3.6	10.3
8	1155	.062	.145	.248	0.8	4.0	11.9
9	1155	.064	.150	.260	0.8	4.3	13.0
9	1150	.064	.151	.260	0.8	4.4	13.1
7½	1145	.062	.144	.245	0.7	4.0	11.6
8	1145	.063	.146	.250	0.8	4.1	12.0
4	1135	.060	.134	.223	0.7	3.5	9.6
5	1135	.061	.137	.228	0.7	3.6	10.0
6	1135	.061	.139	.234	0.7	3.7	10.6
7½	1135	.063	.145	.246	0.8	4.0	11.7

Slugs come in a variety of weights and styles. Testing of several types is usually required to find best accuracy.

TABLE 15.5

RIFLED SLUGS—VELOCITY AND ENERGY

Gauge	Slug Weight (Oz)	VELOCITY (FPS)			ENERGY (FT/LBS)		
		Muzzle	50 yds	100 yds	Muzzle	50 yds	100 yds
12	1	1560	1175	977	2364	1342	928
16	4/5	1600	1175	965	1989	1073	650
20	5/8	1580	1240	1035	1515	932	648
410	1/5	1830	1335	1040	651	345	210

RIFLED SLUGS—TIME OF FLIGHT AND TRAJECTORY

Gauge	Slug Weight (Oz)	Muzzle Velocity (fps)	TIME OF FLIGHT (SECONDS) TO:				DROP (INCHES) AT:				MIDRANGE TRAJECTORY (INCHES) FOR A RANGE OF:			
			25 yds	50 yds	75 yds	100 yds	25 yds	50 yds	75 yds	100 yds	25 yds	50 yds	75 yds	100 yds
12	1	1560	.051	.110	.178	.254	.5	2.1	5.3	10.7	.1	.6	1.5	3.1
16	4/5	1600	.051	.110	.178	.254	.5	2.1	5.3	10.6	.1	.6	1.5	3.1
20	5/8	1580	.051	.110	.178	.254	.5	2.1	5.3	9.8	.1	.6	1.5	3.1
410	1/5	1830	.044	.096	.157	.226	.4	1.6	4.1	8.2	.1	.4	1.2	2.5

BUCKSHOT—VELOCITY AND ENERGY

Gauge	Buck Size	VELOCITY (FPS) AT:					ENERGY (FT/LBS) AT:				
		Muzzle	10 yds	20 yds	30 yds	40 yds	Muzzle	10 yds	20 yds	30 yds	40 yds
12	00	1325	1220	1135	1070	1015	210	180	155	135	125
12	00	1250	1160	1085	1030	985	185	160	140	125	115
12	0	1300	1200	1120	1055	1005	185	160	135	120	110
12	1	1250	1135	1050	990	935	140	115	100	90	80
12	4	1325	1195	1095	1020	960	80	65	55	50	45
16	1	1225	1115	1040	975	925	135	110	95	85	75
20	3	1200	1100	1025	970	915	75	65	55	50	45

BUCKSHOT—TIME OF FLIGHT AND TRAJECTORY

Gauge	Size	Muzzle Velocity (fps)	TIME OF FLIGHT (SECONDS) AT:						DROP (INCHES) AT:					
			10 yds	20 yds	30 yds	40 yds	50 yds	60 yds	10 yds	20 yds	30 yds	40 yds	50 yds	60 yds
12	00	1325	.024	.049	.076	.105	.135	.167	0.1	0.4	1.0	2.0	3.2	4.8
12	00	1250	.025	.052	.080	.110	.141	.174	0.1	0.5	1.2	2.2	3.5	5.2
12	0	1300	.024	.050	.078	.107	.137	.169	0.1	0.5	1.1	2.0	3.3	4.9
12	1	1250	.030	.063	.099	.136	.176	.217	0.2	0.7	1.7	3.2	5.2	7.8
12	4	1325	.024	.050	.078	.109	.141	.175	0.1	0.5	1.1	2.1	3.4	5.1
16	1	1225	.031	.064	.100	.138	.178	.220	0.2	0.7	1.8	3.3	5.4	8.0
20	3	1200	.026	.054	.085	.116	.150	.186	0.1	0.5	1.3	2.4	3.9	5.9

TABLE 15.6

ACTUAL SLUG PERFORMANCE

Type	Brand	Weight of Slug	VELOCITY (FPS) AT:			ENERGY (FT/LBS) AT:			Average Accuracy—five 5-shot groups at 100 yds
			muzzle	50 yds	100 yds	muzzle	50 yds	100 yds	
12 ga. HP	Winchester	1 oz (437 gr)	1448	1090	882	2037	1154	756	5″ with Rem. 870
12 ga. HP	Remington	1 oz (437 gr)	1472	1108	896	2105	1192	780	4.75″ with Rem. 870
12 ga. HP	Federal	1 oz (437 gr)	1485	1118	904	2142	1214	794	5.25″ with Rem. 870
12 ga. HP	Federal	1¼ oz (547 gr)	1384	1151	931	2327	1609	1050	6.5″ with Rem. 870
12 ga. Sabot	BRI (440)	1 oz (437 gr)	1234	1098	975	1478	1170	923	5.75″ with Rem. 870
12 ga. Sabot	BRI (Police)	1 oz (437 gr)	1219	1085	963	1442	1142	903	10″ with Rem. 870
12 ga. Pedestal	Worthy	1 oz (437 gr)	1425	1097	883	1971	1168	757	7.5″ with Rem. 870
12 ga. Solid	Brenneke	478 gr (incl. wads)	1350	1058	864	1935	1188	792	7.5″ with Ithaca 37
20 ga. HP	Winchester	⅝ oz (273 gr)	1524	1119	905	1408	759	497	7.5″ with Rem. 870
20 ga. HP	Remington	⅝ oz (273 gr)	1546	1135	918	1449	781	511	7.75″ with Rem. 870
20 ga. HP	Federal	⅝ oz (273 gr)	1559	1145	926	1474	794	520	8″ with Rem. 870
20 ga. Solid	Brenneke	370 gr (incl. wads)	1386	1086	887	1579	969	646	9.5″ with Ithaca 37
30-30 SP	Remington	150 gr	2350	—	1939	1840	—	1252	4.5″ with Win. carbine
44 Mag. HP	Remington	240 gr	1760	—	1330	1651	—	943	6.5″ with Ruger carbine
45-70 SP	Remington	405 gr	1300	—	1141	1520	—	1171	4.3″ with Marlin carbine

Notes: 1. 12-ga. ballistics obtained in 20″ slug barrels (improved cylinder)
      2. 20-ga. ballistics obtained in 26″ slug barrels (improved cylinder)
      3. All wads are screwed to the base of Brenneke slugs & therefore are part of the projectile weight.
      4. Ballistics of rifle cartridges included for comparison.

TABLE 15.7

EXTERIOR BALLISTIC, SHOTGUN

Approximate Maximum Horizontal Distance
to Point of First Impact for Leading Buckshot of the Shot String

Shot Size	1350 fps Distance (yds)	1275 fps Distance (yds)	1200 fps Distance (yds)	1125 fps Distance (yds)
00 Buck	610	604	597	587
0 Buck	590	580	574	567
1 Buck	567	557	550	544
2 Buck	527	517	510	504
3 Buck	497	490	484	477
4 Buck	480	474	467	460

LEAD PELLETS, SLUGS, AND BUCKSHOT

Approximate Maximum Horizontal Distance
to Point of First Impact for Rifled Slugs

Gauge	Slug Weight (oz)	Distance (yds)	fps
12	⅞	817	1600
16	⅘	817	1600
20	⅝	817	1600
410	⅕	844	1830

Approximate Maximum Horizontal Distance
to Point of First Impact for Leading Pellets of the Shot String*

Shot Size	1350 fps Distance (yds)	1275 fps Distance (yds)	1200 fps Distance (yds)	1125 fps Distance (yds)
FF	467	460	454	447
F	450	444	437	430
TT	434	427	420	414
T	420	414	407	400
BBB	404	397	390	384
BB	387	380	374	367
B	370	364	357	354
1	354	347	344	337
2	337	330	327	320
3	320	317	310	304
4	304	300	294	287
5	290	284	277	274
6	274	267	260	257
7	257	250	247	240
7½	247	244	237	234
8	240	234	230	224
9	224	217	214	207

(*No allowance for balled shot—that is, pellets clumped together, a possibility with soft shot)

16

Selecting the Right Gauge and Loads

Shotgunners aren't getting the help they need to select an appropriate gauge and load for a given use. Publication after publication features articles by "experts" who tout the great ballistic powers of the 20-gauge 3-inch magnum. Most of these writers point out that the 20-gauge 3-inch shell is available with a full 1¼-ounce load; hence, it supposedly equals the 12-gauge. Others declare that the only waterfowl load worth a hoot is the 10-gauge 3½-inch magnum with BB-size shot. And still others will make great claims for the tiny 28-gauge as an upland gun.

The reason for such extreme claims may simply be a need for something to write about, or it may be the author's prejudice, based on limited experience and feelings rather than facts.

Shotshells come in many gauges and shot sizes. Careful selection can make a big difference in field success.

However, selection of gauges and loads is not difficult or mysterious. Gauge selection and shell length, will be very quickly covered. Specific load selection is easy, too, as it's based on three simple factors—shot size, total shot weight, and velocity. But let's begin with gauges and shell lengths.

10-GAUGE 3½" MAGNUM

This shell has only one legitimate application—long-range waterfowling. Even turkey hunters have no need for this behemoth round. The monstrous recoil is seldom mastered by casual shooters. For those few who can handle abusive recoil, the 10-gauge has its place—with steel shot, particularly where geese must be taken at ranges beyond 50 yards. Most shooters would be better off to pass up the long-range shots and use a gun that would enable them to master the shotgunning art.

At one time, 10-gauge shells were also loaded in a 2⅞-inch length. Such ammo has now become rather obsolete and does not merit discussion here.

Waterfowl hunting with steel shot does fully justify the use of 10-gauge guns. Steel shot requires extra case volume to enable the less-dense steel pellets to be loaded in heavy charge weights. The 10-gauge supplies the needed volume. More on steel loads is included in Chapter 17.

12-GAUGE 3" MAGNUM

The 12-gauge 3-inch magnum shotgun is a very versatile gun. Almost all such models will accept standard 12-gauge 2¾-inch ammunition. The exceptions are some of the automatics that will function with high-velocity 2¾-inch loads but not with lighter loads.

The 12-gauge 3-inch shell is becoming extremely popular as steel-shot-only laws govern more and more waterfowl areas. The extra ¼-inch of length gives a lot of needed room for steel pellets.

Of course, the 3-inch shell offers no advantage for any shooting other than turkey hunting and long-range waterfowling. At that, the heaviest weight, a 2-ounce shot charge, is loaded only to the modest level of 1,180 fps. Most experienced waterfowlers have found that when the temperature drops to around 10°F, shot velocities begin to fall off noticeably. The 1⅞-ounce load may then fail to do the job it was designed to do—kill waterfowl cleanly at long ranges. Under these conditions, the lighter 1⅝-ounce load, at a muzzle velocity of 1,280 fps, seems to do a better job.

A standard 2¾-inch 12-gauge shell will push a 1½-ounce charge at 1,260 fps. Will an extra ⅛ ounce of shot and 20 fps really make it worthwhile for most hunters to buy the 3-inch shells. Except with steel pellets, the answer is no, it is simply not worth the extra ammunition cost for anyone but a turkey hunter or a purist waterfowler. A purist is the kind who seldom leaves the shoreline for upland cover; one whose waterfowling is so important that he or she will pay any premium for an extra few yards of range.

I was such a hunter, and for years a 3-inch gun was the only waterfowling gun for me. But now that I'm a bit older, I don't like the extra recoil. My ducks are still bagged just as regularly with 2¾-inch magnum shells. Ironically, now that I've learned that lesson, it becomes necessary to switch to steel pellets and once again to 3-inch shells.

As mentioned, turkey hunting is another valid application of 12-gauge 3-inch shells, especially with the higher-velocity 1⅝-ounce loads. Dense patterns are needed when head shots are taken, and smaller shells don't have sufficient pellet count to qualify as effective turkey loads.

12-GAUGE 2¾″

Until the advent of steel-shot requirements, this shell was truly the do-almost-everything round. The spectrum of loads goes from 1½ ounces to 1 ounce in pellet sizes from BB to No. 9. Also available are 000, 00, 0, 1 and No. 4 Buckshot as well as 1¼- and 1-ounce rifled slugs. Everything from tiny railbirds to deer and black bear have been successfully hunted with 2¾-inch 12-gauge shells.

16-GAUGE 2¾″

Until recently, this was a very dead gauge. Guns are often as heavy as 12-gauge guns and ballistics are always inferior. The 20-gauge offers nearly the same ballistics at reduced gun weight. Indeed, the 16 isn't even needed for skeet competition, which has classifications for 12, 20, 28, and 410 bore.

Upland birds can be hunted with 12-, 16-, or 20-gauge guns. The majority of hunters choose a 12-gauge, 2¾-inch shell with 1¼ ounces of the appropriate-size shot.

But recently a few firearm manufacturers have begun again to offer 16-gauge guns. I'm willing to bet such offerings will be comparatively short-lived, as the 16-gauge has no real area of superiority. (Sorry, 16-gauge fans, I've heard all the arguments and they won't stand close scrutiny.)

But this doesn't mean the 16 is a handicap for every purpose. A 16-gauge shotgun can do yeoman service in the uplands. Many shooters are consistently successful each fall using 16-gauge loads. In this bore size, the 1¼-ounce loads are the most effective for pheasant, while the 1⅛-ounce loads can be used for all other upland species.

20-GAUGE 3" MAGNUM

In a lightweight model, the 20-gauge 3-inch chambering provides a very versatile upland gun that, in a pinch, can double as a modest-range waterfowl gun—with lead shot—or pheasant tool. With steel shot, the 20-gauge is not, in this writer's opinion, a suitable waterfowl shell.

The heaviest 20-gauge 3-inch load—despite its 1¼ ounces of shot—is a ballistic midget compared to a 12-gauge shell. The 20-gauge velocity is but 1,185 fps, compared to a potential 1,330 fps in 12-gauge with the same 1¼ ounces of shot. And because of its longer shot column, the 20-gauge delivers a somewhat less dense pattern. However, when there is a need for occasional heavyweight punch, the 3-inch 20-gauge can do a fair job at some tasks normally best accomplished with a 12.

20-GAUGE 2¾"

A perennial favorite, the 2¾-inch 20-gauge is frequently abused. With its maximum loading, it moves a 1⅛-ounce charge at 1,175 fps. Whereas this is the 2¾-inch magnum load for the 20, the same shot charge and velocities are target loads and light upland loads in the 12-gauge. Obviously, the smaller gauge offers no magical powers, and the 2¾-inch 20-gauge is, at best, a good upland-bird, squirrel, or rabbit shell. It does not have enough punch to consistently take pheasants at ranges exceeding 40 yards, nor would a good sportsman think of it as a deer or bear gauge with either slug or buckshot.

The real delight of a 20-gauge in woodcock and grouse cover cannot be matched. In such habitat, the 20-gauge will get the job done when the right loads are used. And a lightweight 20 is a pleasure to carry and shoot. The standard 20-gauge is also the correct choice for any shooter who is sensitive to recoil.

The heaviest 2¾-inch loads are poor choices for waterfowl hunting except at extremely short ranges and under ideal conditions. Steel-shot loads further reduce the 2¾-inch shell's potential.

High-grade shotshells use extra-hard plated shot and a granulated polyethylene buffer to deliver the tightest possible pattern at the longest practical ranges.

28-GAUGE 2¾"

At very short ranges, the 28-gauge is capable of taking small upland birds, squirrels, and rabbits. However, if the range is more than about 25 yards, a great number of cripples will be likely. The 28 is at its best on a skeet field rather than in the game field. A number of hunters succeed in taking a fair share of quail, rabbits, woodcock, and other small upland game with this gauge, but at ranges longer than 75 feet even some of the great wingshooters I hunt with will often have trouble making clean kills.

410 BORE 3"

The 410 is often considered a stunt gun with respect to hunting. Actually, it is adequate for rabbits, squirrels, and small birds up to a maximum of 20 yards. Past this range, the average shooter will have great trouble making clean kills. The author used a 3-inch 410 on rabbits when he was a teenager. He never killed a rabbit past 20 yards without shooting twice. The first shot would invariably roll the rabbit, and I quickly learned that a second shot, while the rabbit was rolling, was required to accomplish a clean job.

410 BORE 2½"

The shell is useless except for making the game of skeet very difficult. No conscientious sportsman would ever go afield with this shell.

LOAD SELECTION

The selection of a suitable load in a given gauge and shell length is not difficult if approached with an understanding of the three-part selection process: shot size, shot weight, velocity.

The correct size is a vital key to success. Unfortunately, many gun writers tend to suggest the smallest possible shot size. They have done so in the belief that a dense pattern will help ensure hits—which is true as far as it goes. But no number of hits will bring game to bag unless the pellets are large enough to have the energy needed to penetrate vital organs. A big pheasant thoroughly dusted with a charge of No. 9 shot at 40 yards may well escape—perhaps to die a protracted death. Even if recovered, its flesh will have a great many blood-shot pellet holes to be "eaten around" at the table. The same pheasant, hit with a charge of No. 4 shot, will most often succumb instantly—and most of the pellets will pass through the bird, creating no dental hazard at the dinner table.

The correct shot size, of course, can be learned by trial and error. After a good number of game birds or other quarry escape, it becomes obvious that the shot size being used is incapable of penetrating to the vitals or breaking wing bones. A switch to one, two, or even *three* sizes larger might come about as a result of trial and error.

Indeed, at one time I raised 500 to 1,000 pheasants each year and was present when most of those birds were shot. In the beginning, almost all of my hunters used 7½'s. But I soon discovered that a great many "misses" were actually hits, although the bird showed only subtle signs of being shot. The number of dead birds later found in the cover was startling. Over the years, through a progression of 7½, 6, and 5, we finally settled on No. 4 shot as the ideal pheasant size.

The hunter is urged to apply the information and suggestions contained in Chapter 14 concerning shot sizes. The same advice applies to the selection of an appropriate shot-charge weight. If you select the

Ingredients of a successful shotshell include an appropriate powder charge, the proper wad, some granulated buffer, and copper-plated shot of suitable size.

right pellet size but use too light a shot charge, patterns will not be dense enough to assure the necessary multiple hits for clean kills. On the other hand, too heavy a shot charge could result in having your table fare "scrambled" unintentionally.

Finally, a selection of high- or standard-velocity shells is appropriate. Gear your selection to potential ranges. For short or medium range, select standard-velocity shells. For longer ranges, high velocity is appropriate. Some shot weights, such as those described as magnum, come only in one velocity level. Some basic velocity levels should go along with shot sizes. These are covered in detail in Chapter 14.

A range limitation applies to all shotshell loads. Basically, maximum practical range is established by pellet size (required penetration) and pattern density (necessary multiple hits). A paradox of shotshells is that the smallest pellets provide the greatest pattern density but are least able to penetrate at medium to long range. The following table lists maximum practical ranges for specific pellet sizes when combined with a minimum useful shot-charge weight.

TABLE 16.1
MAXIMUM PRACTICAL RANGES FOR VARIOUS SHOT SIZES IN APPROPRIATE CHARGES

Shot Size	Minimum Charge (oz)	Maximum Practical Range (yds)
BB	1½	60*
2	1⅜	55*
4	1¼	50*
5	1¼	47**
6	1⅛	45**
7½	1	40
8	⅞	37
8½ & 9	¾	35

(*) Add 5 to 10 yards when using premium ammo loaded with copper-plated shot and a granulated polyethelene filler.

(**) Add 3 to 6 yards when using premium ammo loaded with copper-plated shot and a granulated polyethelene filler.

NOTE: Table assumes use of hard shot and appropriate choke for range involved (modified choke for 35 to 40 yards, full choke for all ranges past 40 yards).

17

Steel-Pellet Shotshells

For several years, steel shot has been required for waterfowling in many regions. The U.S. Fish & Wildlife Service has ruled that beginning with the 1991–1992 hunting season all waterfowlers will use steel shot. Thus, all shotgunners who pursue waterfowl, as well as a great many upland-game shooters, must learn what's required to bag game with steel-shot loads.

The major difference in using steel shot, compared to lead shot, stems from its hardness. In the shotgun chamber and barrel, steel's hardness can cause some unique ballistic problems. But in general, ammunition manufacturers have overcome most of the early difficulties. Extensive use of steel-shot loads, especially with shot sizes

Sheel shot is available nonplated (darker shot) or copper-plated (lighter shot). The copper plating helps to prevent the pellets from rusting. Note in the close-up that steel pellets are not perfect spheres but have some surface imperfections.

larger than B, will eventually cause a very slight ringing of the barrel around the choke area, but no noticeable difference in the barrel's performance will occur. This ringing is more likely, and will occur sooner, in barrels with a full choke.

Steel-shot loads can be used without undue problems in most currently manufactured U.S. shotguns. However, older shotguns, manufactured prior to the advent of steel shot, often have thinner and/or softer barrels that are more readily deformed. If doubt exists, contact the manufacturer of your shotgun, being sure to state both model and serial number. Older guns of high value (either of a monetary or sentimental nature) should not be used with steel shot.

Much has been made of the fact that steel pellets, due to their approximately 30% lower density, deliver considerably less energy to the target than lead pellets. This, though true, is misleading. Simply selecting steel shot that is two sizes larger than the lead pellets normally used will enable the shooter to keep game-taking performance at an equal level. For example, instead of selecting No. 6 lead shot for teal, use No. 4 steel shot; or rather than selecting No. 4 lead shot for blacks and mallards, choose No. 2 steel. If No. 2 lead shot has been effective for geese substitute No. 1 or BB steel shot, and so on. For upland game, use No. 6 steel shot instead of the usual No. 8 or 7½ lead. Some jurisdictions impose regulations determining maximum pellet size, so check your state's hunting laws before purchasing ammo loaded with the largest steel-shot sizes.

It is not always possible to duplicate the weight of a lead charge when switching to steel shot. Because of steel's lower density, it requires about 30% more space to house a similar charge weight. Currently, the heaviest steel 12-gauge 3-inch load uses 1⅜ ounces of shot and the heaviest 12-gauge 2¾-inch steel load is 1¼ ounces. Compare this to 2 ounces of lead in some 3-inch 12-gauge loadings and 1½ ounces in 2¾-inch 12-gauge shells. Federal has introduced a 3½-inch 12-gauge shell loaded with 1 9/16 ounces of steel shot, and at least a couple of gun manufacturers supply shotguns chambered for this extra-long shell.

Steel shot does not impose a great handicap. The lower density of steel means there will be more pellets in a given weight compared to traditional lead pellets. For example, there are about 135 lead No. 4 pellets (depending upon shot hardness) in an ounce, while the same weight of steel 4s will have 192 pellets. Thus, while a 2¾-inch 12-gauge 1¼-ounce lead load of 4s might contain 168 pellets, a 1⅜-ounce load of No. 2 steel will have a similar count. A 1½-ounce magnum load of lead 2s might have 130 pellets, whereas it requires a 1¾-ounce load of steel BBs to have an almost equal count at 126 pellets.

Pattern density is accomplished by pellet count, not shot-charge weight. Thus, it is possible to select a steel-shot load employing pellets two sizes larger and still obtain satisfactory pattern density. You may, however, need to switch from 2¾-inch shells to 3-inch or 3½-inch shells, or even switch from 12- to 10-gauge to keep ammo performance equal.

Difficulty in loading steel pellets can easily be seen in this photo. The vial at the left contains the traditional 1½ ounces of No. 4 lead shot used by many waterfowlers. The vial at right contains 1⅜ ounces of No. 2 steel shot. It takes a lot of room in a case to load a heavy steel shot charge.

Waterfowlers need to use more open chokes for steel shot than for lead shot. Improved-cylinder and modified chokes are preferred over the traditional full choke. Those guns that accept screw-in chokes prove very adaptable to the switch to steel pellets.

There is another unique steel-shot characteristic that helps keep patterns quite dense. Unlike lead, steel shot is not noticeably deformed as it passes from shell through forcing cone, barrel, and choke. Thus, it flies truer. This means patterns remain denser with steel. Because of this tight patterning, a steel load might deliver a pattern up to one-third smaller in diameter than the pattern of a comparable lead-shot load when fired from barrels with similar chokes.

The density of steel-shot patterns is so great that less choke is required to obtain similar patterns. For waterfowl at ranges up to 30 yards, an improved-cylinder choke often provides optimum pattern density. For ranges of 30 to 40 yards, a modified choke is about perfect. Improved-modified or modified-trap choking is best for the longer ranges. With the possible exception of head shots on turkey, there appears to be no useful full-choke application when steel pellets are used. A fringe benefit of less barrel choke is that the ideal upland-game choke, improved cylinder (used in conjunction with lead shot loads), can be equally effective for waterfowl with steel shot.

Lead-shot strings (the distance from the most forward pellet in the pattern to the most rearward pellet) often run from 14 to 20 feet. Steel-shot strings are in the range of 7 to 10 feet. This is because some of the lead pellets are heavily deformed and tend to lose velocity rapidly, while the uniform roundness of steel allows all the pellets in the charge to retain nearly equal velocity. Because of the shorter steel-shot string, the need to properly lead a moving target—to swing ahead of it sufficiently and smoothly—is slightly exaggerated. Unfortunately, the small difference goes unnoticed by many shotgunners, though a shorter or longer lead is sometimes needed.

The muzzle velocities of steel shot loads are often higher than those of lead shot. At short ranges, to about 30 yards, the shooter doesn't need to lead a bird as much with these steel loads as with a lower-velocity lead-shot load. With these same steel-shot velocities, leads at 30 to 40 yards will approximate the leads used with most lead-shot loads. At ranges beyond 40 yards, forward leads with steel shot must be greater than those required with lead shot because, while many steel-shot loads start out faster, they lose velocity sooner. At approximately 40 yards, they have fallen below the velocity levels of lead. Using steel properly requires some practice and lead adjustment.

TABLE 17.1

STEEL-PELLET LEADS FOR TARGETS CROSSING AT RIGHT ANGLE

(calculated for a muzzle velocity of 1275 fps)

Target Speed (fps)	Distance in Yards to Crossing Target			
	20	30	40	50
	Lead in feet (approx.) for BBs			
50	2.6	4.2	6.0	8.0
70	3.7	5.9	8.4	11.3
90	4.7	7.6	10.8	14.5

Target Speed (fps)	Distance in Yards to Crossing Target			
	20	30	40	50
	Lead in feet (approx.) for No. 1 pellets			
50	2.7	4.3	6.2	8.3
70	3.7	6.0	8.6	11.6
90	4.8	7.7	11.1	15.0

This is not to suggest, as has been stated by at least one state game department, that the shooter should shorten the lead with *all* steel loads at short ranges, use identical lead at medium ranges, and lengthen the lead at long ranges. Nothing could be more misleading. The muzzle velocities of lead-shot waterfowl loads range from 1,185 feet per second to 1,330 feet per second, while those of steel-shot waterfowl loads currently range from 1,260 feet per second to 1,450 feet per second. If you've been using a 12-gauge 2¾-inch, 1½-ounce lead load at 1,260 fps, and switch to a steel shot load of 1⅛ ounces at 1,365 fps, the advice is valid. But if you've been using a 12-gauge 1¼-ounce lead load with 1,330 fps muzzle velocity and switch to a steel 1¼-ounce load with 1,275 fps muzzle velocity, the proper steel-shot lead will *always* be greater, regardless of the range.

The best advice is to shoot the steel loads as often as possible. Only practice will enable you to adopt the necessary leads as a natural,

Target Speed (fps)	Distance in Yards to Crossing Target			
	20	30	40	50
	Lead in feet (approx.) for No. 2 pellets			
50	2.7	4.3	6.3	8.5
70	3.7	6.0	8.8	11.9
90	4.8	7.8	11.3	15.3

Target Speed (fps)	Distance in Yards to Crossing Target			
	20	30	40	50
	Lead in feet (approx.) for No. 4 pellets			
50	2.7	4.5	6.5	8.9
70	3.8	6.3	9.1	12.5
90	4.9	8.0	11.7	16.0

reflexive part of your shooting. By beginning with an open choke and keeping ranges modest, you will reduce the learning period to the shortest possible time. Once you can bag birds at the short ranges, switching to a bit more choke and longer ranges will come quite naturally. Table 17.1 reflects typical lead requirements with steel shot of various sizes. Tables 17.2 and 17.3 suggest steel-shot sizes and compare ballistic performance to lead.

Some waterfowlers avoid the use of the heaviest lead-shot charges when temperatures dip into the single digits, because cold weather can reduce the already lower velocities of heavy shot charges to a point at which long-range penetration becomes a real problem. The same approach is wise when using steel shot. In the most severe weather, it's best to opt for a bit more velocity rather than an extra ⅛-ounce of shot. Indeed, in view of steel's tendency to lose velocity

TABLE 17.2
STEEL-SHOT SELECTOR GUIDE

Game	Range (yds)	Choke	Shot Weight (oz)	Shot Size
Geese	to 30	imp. cyl.	1¼ & up	2, 1, BB
Geese	30 to 40	modified	1¼ & up	1, BB
Geese	beyond 40	imp. mod.	1¼ & up	1, BB
Small ducks	to 30	imp. cyl.	1⅛ & up	4, 2
Small ducks	30 to 40	modified	1⅛ & up	4, 2
Small ducks	beyond 40	imp. mod.	1⅛ & up	2
Big ducks	to 30	imp. cyl.	1⅛ & up	2, 1
Big ducks	30 to 40	modified	1¼ & up	2, 1
Big ducks	beyond 40	imp. mod.	1¼ & up	1
Upland birds	to 30	imp. cyl.	1 & up	6, 4
Upland birds	30 to 40	modified	1 & up	4
Pheasants	to 30	imp. cyl.	1⅛ & up	4, 2
Pheasants	beyond 30	modified	1⅛ & up	4, 2

imp. cyl. = improved cylinder
imp. mod. = improved modified

TABLE 17.3
STEEL BALLISTICS VERSUS LEAD

Shot Type	Weight (oz)	Shot Size	Muzzle Velocity (fps)	Retained Energy (ft/lbs) 40 yds	Retained Energy (ft/lbs) 60 yds
lead	1¼	6	1330	2.3	1.3
steel	1⅛	4	1365	2.5	1.4
lead	1¼	4	1330	4.4	2.7
steel	1⅛	2	1365	4.4	2.6
lead	1½	4	1260	4.1	2.6
steel	1¼	2	1275	4.1	2.4
lead	1½	2	1260	7.0	4.6
steel	1¼	BB	1275	8.3	5.2

faster, this practice may be even more important than it has been with lead.

The advent of steel shot has led to the use of larger pellet sizes. Sizes of BBB, T, and F are now available in steel-shot factory loads and for reloading. Keep in mind, however, that very large steel pellets may score barrels and ring chokes much sooner than the smaller sizes. In my experience, there seems to be no real need for steel sizes larger than B. Larger pellets result in patterns that are too sparse even for the largest geese. Lead pellets of BB size have been shown to be less effective on geese than No. 2 shot, despite some beliefs to the contrary. Even with the need to use pellets two sizes larger, steel Bs will nicely replace the No. 2 lead shot which is so effective on high-flying geese. And the smaller steel No. 1 pellets are highly favored by many experienced goose hunters.

Steel-shot loads of an ounce or less will have very limited effective range for waterfowl. Thus, 12- and 10-gauge steel-shot loads are best for ducks and geese, while 20-gauge steel loads are suitable for upland shooting.

Maximum shotgun ranges are always a topic of debate. However, with careful selection, a practical shotgunner should be able to use steel shot effectively at 45 to 50 yards. Indeed, that's about as far as most of us should ever attempt to press a shotgun into use, regardless of the pellets employed. Admittedly, some experienced shotgunners bag geese at more than 50 yards, but doing so requires considerable skill and, for most hunters, results in fewer clean kills.

Table 17.4 lists many of the steel loads available at the time of this writing by brand, shot weight, shot size, and pellet count. Advertised muzzle velocities as well as corresponding dram equivalents are included. Table 17.5 lists the exterior ballistics of steel pellets at 3, 30, 40, and 50 yards, as well as the nominal pellet count of steel versus lead per ounce of shot. Pellet diameters (identical for steel and lead) are shown, as are steel pellet weights. Table 17.6 shows additional performance characteristics—time of flight, wind drift, and trajectory.

Additional loads have been and will be frequently introduced. Upland-game and target loads will eventually become commonplace, although we now have sufficient steel-shot loads to satisfy most shooters' needs.

TABLE 17.4

COMMONLY AVAILABLE STEEL-SHOT LOADS

Gauge	Brand	Shell Length (inches)	Shot Weight (oz)	Muzzle Velocity (fps)	Dram[1] Equiv.	Shot Sizes (& pellets per load)	Manufacturer's Product Code
10	Rem	3½	1¾	1260	4¼	BB (126), 2 (218), 3 (273)	STL10MAG
10	Win	3½	1¾	1260	4¼	BB (126), 2 (218)	X10SSM
10	Fed	3½	1⅝	1350	4½	BB (117), 2 (203)	W104
12	Fed	3	1⅜	1265	3¾	BB (99), 1 (141), 2 (171), 4 (264)	W149
12	Fed	3	1¼	1450	4¼	BB (90), 1 (128), 2 (156), 4 (240)	W140
12	Fed	3	1¼	1400	4	F (48)	W149F
12	Win	3	1¼	1375	4	T (66), BBB (76) BB (90), 1 (128), 2 (156), 4 (240)	X123SSM
12	Rem	3	1¼	1375	4	BB (90), 1 (128), 2 (156), 3 (191), 4 (240), 6 (393)	STL12MAG
12	Rem	3	1¼[2]	1375	4	BB×2 (126), BB×4 (195), 2×6 (321)	MRS12H
12	Rem	2¾	1¼	1275	3½	1 (128), 2 (156), 4 (240)	STL12S
12	Fed	2¾	1¼	1325	3¾	BB (90), 1 (128), 2 (156), 4 (240)	W148
12	Win	2¾	1¼	1275	3½	BB (90), 1 (128), 2 (156), 4 (240), 6 (393)	X12SSF
12	Rem	2¾	1⅛	1365	3¾	BB (81), 1 (115), 2 (140), 3 (175), 4 (216), 6 (354)	STL12
12	Rem	2¾	1⅛[2]	1365	3¾	BB×2 (120), BB×4 (171), 2×6 (282)	MRS12
12	Fed	2¾	1⅛	1365	3¾	2 (140), 4 (216), 6 (354)	W147
12	Win	2¾	1⅛	1365	3¾	1 (115), 2 (140), 4 (216), 6 (354)	X12SSL
12	Win	2¾	1	1375	NA	2 (125), 4 (192)	W12SD
12	Dan/Arms	2¾	1	1455	4	5 (242)	NA
12	Dan/Arms	2¾	⅞	1380	3½	4 (168)	NA
16	Fed	2¾	⁵⁄₁₆	1300	NA	2 (117), 4 (180)	W168
20	Win	3	1	1330	3¼	4 (192), 6 (315)	X20SSM
20	Fed	3	⁵⁄₁₆	NA	NA	2 (117)	W209-2
20	Fed	3	1	1330	3¼	4 (192), 6 (315)	W209
20	Rem	3	1	1330	3¼	2 (125), 3 (153), 4 (192), 6 (315)	STL20H
20	Fed	2¾	¾	1425	3¼	4 (144), 6 (236)	W208
20	Win	2¾	¾	1425	3¼	4 (144), 6 (236)	X20SSL

[1] to nearest ¼ dram
[2] "DuPlex" MultiRange Load (2 shot sizes)
NA = Not Available

TABLE 17.5

STEEL-PELLET BALLISTICS

Pellet Size	Nominal Pellet diameter*	Nominal Steel Pellet weight (gr)	VELOCITY (FPS) AT:				ENERGY (FT/LBS) PER PELLET AT:				Steel Nominal Pellet Count per oz.	Lead Nominal Pellet Count per oz.
			3 yds	30 yds	40 yds	50 yds	3 yds	30 yds	40 yds	50 yds		
F	0.220"	11.00	1400	1095	1030	985	48.0	29.0	26.0	24.0	39	27
BB	0.180"	6.08	1450	991	862	774	28.4	13.3	10.0	8.1	72	50
			1365	933	821	728	25.2	11.8	9.1	7.2		
			1350	923	813	721	24.6	11.5	8.9	7.0		
			1325	904	796	706	23.7	11.0	8.6	6.7		
			1275	887	784	697	22.0	10.6	8.3	6.5		
			1210	855	757	674	19.8	9.8	7.7	6.1		
1	0.160"	4.25	1450	935	810	710	19.8	8.3	6.2	4.8	103	73
			1365	896	779	684	17.7	7.6	5.7	4.4		
			1275	855	747	657	15.4	6.9	5.3	4.1		
			1210	819	718	633	13.7	6.3	4.9	3.8		
2	0.150"	3.50	1450	910	785	685	16.3	6.4	4.8	3.6	125	87
			1365	876	757	661	14.6	6.0	4.4	3.4		
			1350	870	752	657	14.2	5.9	4.4	3.3		
			1325	852	736	643	13.6	5.6	4.2	3.2		
			1275	837	726	635	12.7	5.4	4.1	3.1		
			1210	807	702	615	11.4	5.1	3.8	2.9		
4	0.130"	2.28	1450	865	730	630	10.6	3.8	2.7	2.0	192	135
			1365	831	707	608	9.5	3.5	2.5	1.8		
			1330	817	697	599	9.0	3.4	2.4	1.8		
			1275	795	679	585	8.2	3.2	2.3	1.7		
			1200	763	654	564	7.3	2.9	2.1	1.6		

(*) = lead or steel

(Tables continue on next page)

TABLE 17.6
STEEL-PELLET PERFORMANCE CHARACTERISTICS

Shot Size	Muzzle Velocity (fps)	TIME IN FLIGHT (SECONDS) AT:				10 MPH WIND DRIFT (INCHES[1]) AT:				DROP (INCHES[2]) AT:			
		20 yds	30 yds	40 yds	50 yds	20 yds	30 yds	40 yds	50 yds	20 yds	30 yds	40 yds	50 yds
BB	1350	.0498	.0802	.1150	.1541	1	2	4	8	½	1	2¼	3¾
	1275	.0524	.0841	.1201	.1608	1	2	5	8	½	1¼	2½	4
	1210	.0548	.0879	.1252	.1672	1	2	5	8	½	1¼	2½	4½
1	1365	.0500	.0812	.1172	.1584	1	3	5	9	½	1	2¼	4
	1275	.0530	.0858	.1234	.1662	1	3	5	9	½	1¼	2½	4¼
	1210	.0555	.0895	.1290	.1710	1	3	5	9	½	1¼	2¾	4¾
2	1365	.0504	.0822	.1190	.1617	1	3	5	9	½	1¼	2¼	4
	1350	.0508	.0829	.1201	.1629	1	3	5	9	½	1¼	2¼	4
	1275	.0534	.0863	.1253	.1695	1	3	5	9	½	1¼	2½	4½
	1210	.0559	.0905	.1305	.1762	1	3	6	9	½	1½	2¾	4¾
4	1365	.0514	.0847	.1239	.1697	1	3	6	11	½	1¼	2½	4¼
	1330	.0525	.0863	.1262	.1723	1	3	6	11	½	1¼	2½	4½
	1274	.0544	.0892	.1301	.1779	1	3	6	11	½	1¼	2¾	4¾
	1210	.0568	.0930	.1354	.1845	1	3	6	11	½	1½	3	5¼

[1] rounded to nearest inch
[2] rounded to nearest ¼ inch

18

Shotshell Reloading

A shotshell reloader can lower costs significantly by reloading fired factory shells. The cost of primers and wads will be fairly uniform, regardless of the gauge shell reloaded, but the cost of powder varies slightly from shell type to shell type. The major cost variance will depend on the shot-charge weight. Table 18.1 shows that savings of 61% to 82% are possible by reloading. Obviously, the load actually purchased or reloaded can cause some variation. All reload costs are based on current suggested list prices for primers, powder, and wads, and shot prices are calculated at the local current rate of $12.50 per 25-pound bag.

Versatility is another important reloading advantage. How many different 12-gauge shot weights are available in factory loads at your dealer? Two, three, maybe four? You can reload as many as nine different shot-charge weights, customizing your load to fit any specific application.

Of course, you can keep things simple by merely duplicating your favorite factory loadings. Reloading also gives you ready access to shot sizes that are hard to find in factory loads. Available lead-shot sizes include No. 11, 9, 8½, 8, 7½, 7, 6, 5, 4, 2, and BB.

Many shotgunners mistakenly believe reloading is complicated or dangerous. Actually, shotshell loading is easy, quick, and safe.

Shotshell assembly is quicker to accomplish than many shooters think. You need only a reloading press, a scale to check weights of shot and powder, a good reloading manual, several extra shot bars, and a number of powder bushings. If you want to load a second or third gauge, it's most convenient to purchase a complete press for each one because die changes can be nettlesome.

Steel-shot reloading entails the use of several other accessories and any number of unique cautions. But for the beginner, the assembly of lead-pellet shotshells will progress smoothly and effortlessly.

TABLE 18.1

COST OF FACTORY-LOADED SHOTSHELLS VS. RELOADS

Gauge	Length	Shot (oz)	Cost of Factory Shells per box	Cost of Reloads per box	Saving
10	3½"	2 Mag.	$28.00	$4.95	82%
12	3"	1⅞ Mag.	20.80	4.50	78%
12	2¾"	1½ Mag.	16.25	3.96	76%
12	2¾"	1¼ H.V.	12.60	3.59	71%
12	2¾"	1⅛ target	8.20	3.21	61%
12	2¾"	1 target	7.60	3.04	60%
16	2¾"	1⅛ H.V.	12.00	3.21	73%
20	3"	1¼ Mag.	16.50	3.45	79%
20	2¾"	1⅛ Mag.	15.70	3.21	79%
20	2¾"	1 H.V.	11.05	3.11	72%
20	2¾"	⅞ target	7.70	2.88	63%
28	2¾"	¾ target	9.00	2.82	69%
410	3"	11/16 H.V.	10.30	2.72	74%
410	2½"	½ target	7.50	2.56	66%

Since primers are explosive and powder is flammable, both must be treated with respect. Still, they are no more hazardous than the cleaning fluids, gasoline, solvents, and many similar items found in and around the home. When stored in the original containers in reasonable quantities, they do not present a hazard.

Most shotshell presses are self-contained units with separate stations for performing all seven of the necessary reloading steps, which will be described below. You must be very careful to use only the specified components in the specified quantities indicated in your data source. By so doing you ensure that your reloaded shells will be safe and ballistically uniform. To verify powder-charge weights you'll need a scale, which should also be capable of checking the shot-charge weight. A scale that will weigh up to 985 grains will be needed to weigh the heaviest shot charge of 2¼ ounces. Actually, you should purchase one of the scales that will accommodate 1,000 grains or more.

Every reloader should use a detailed shotshell-reloading manual and study it carefully before attempting to reload. Here are the seven simple assembly steps.

1. Resizing and Decapping

Slip a shell into the die at station one and push the handle of the press downward fully. You will feel some resistance as the brass of the case is resized and the fired primer is ejected from the case. Lift the press handle upward, and the resized and deprimed shell will be partially ejected from the die. Remove the shell and you are ready to reprime it.

2. Repriming

Place a new primer in the priming base. Then slip the shell onto the priming station and lower the press handle fully to seat the new primer. Raise the press handle and remove the shell, which is now ready for powder. Be certain to use the primer specified in the loading data.

Resizing and depriming the fired primer.

Repriming. New primer placed into priming base.

3. Powder Charging

Place the case under the powder and shot drop-tube. Then lower the press handle fully and hold it in the down position. Meter the powder charge by pushing the powder side of the metering bar inward fully. Return the press handle to its upward position—without letting it snap free. This is the point at which several powder charges should be verified on the scale for each loading session. Once verified, you need not normally do so again until the next loading session if you're using fixed-metering powder bushings.

4. Seating the Wad

Carefully place the specified wad onto the powder and shot drop-tube. Gradually lower the press handle while guiding the wad into the alignment fingers. Fully seat the wad until the press handle bottoms. Hold the press handle in its downward position. Note the wad-pressure gauge reading. It should be about 25 pounds for most loads, and will be specified in your load data. If it is not, adjust the rammer—downward to increase pressure or upward to decrease pressure.

Some loads may require a wad pressure of up to 100 pounds. Read

Repriming. Resized shell on priming station.

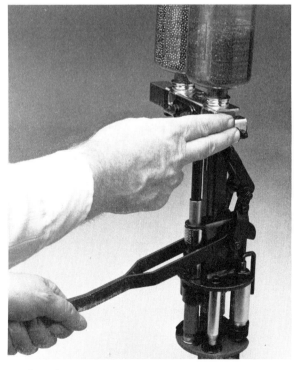

Powder charging.

the wad pressure each time a wad is seated to ensure that the tool has not gone out of adjustment. A pressure reading that is notably different from preceding ones may be an indication of an incorrect powder charge or the wrong case or wad being inadvertently used.

5. Shot Metering

While maintaining the press handle in its lowered position from step four, meter the shot charge by pressing inward on the shot end of the metering bar. A rapid motion will help prevent the bar from binding. Then slowly elevate the press handle to its uppermost position.

6. Starting the Crimp

Place the shell securely beneath the crimp starter. If your shell originally had a six-point crimp, then a six-point crimp starter should be in place. (Tools usually come with an eight-point crimp starter in position because most shells are originally so loaded.) Fully lower and raise the press handle to start the crimp. At this point in the procedure, the case will be partially closed, perhaps a third of the way.

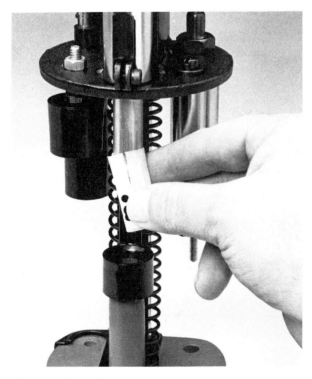

Seating the wad.

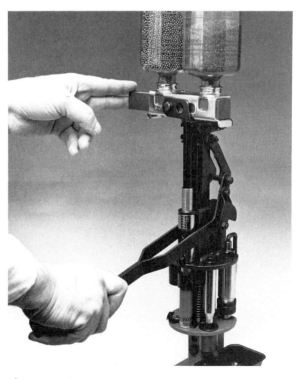

Shot metering.

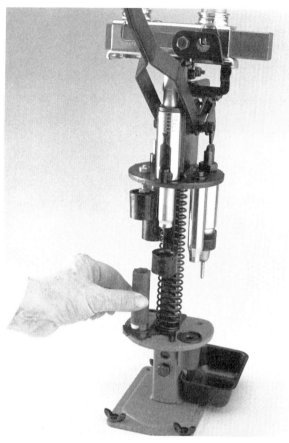
Starting the crimp. Place the shell underneath the crimp starter and depress the press handle fully.

Starting the crimp. Properly formed crimp start will close the case mouth about one-third of the way.

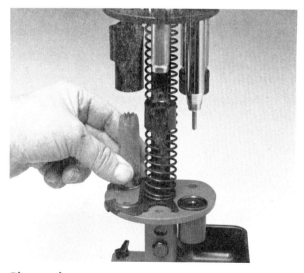
Closing the crimp.

Finished shell ready to fire.

7. Closing the Crimp

Place the shell below the final crimp die, then fully lower the press handle. When it is raised you will have a completely loaded shell that will perform perfectly if you've carried out each procedure carefully.

Describing the preceding steps takes a lot longer then the actual doing. I comfortably load four to five boxes of shells in an hour. And that time includes visually inspecting each case for defects before loading, as well as checking the loaded round. The initial inspection should be for splits or cracks on the body or neck, primer pockets that show the dark smudges of a gas leak and, if the case is so constructed, the integrity of the base wad. Discard any case that shows these or any other signs of deterioration.

After the case has been loaded, also check to be sure no cracks or splits occurred during the loading procedures. Another check should be made during loading—for a snug fit of the primer. If a primer goes into the primer pocket effortlessly, either the primer is undersized or the primer pocket is too large. Discard any such primer/case combination.

That's all there is to the basics. Naturally, you'll want to consult a complete loading manual before actually loading shotshells.

PART IV

AMMO MANAGEMENT AND SAFETY

19

Ammo Interchangeability

The material in this chapter was contained in the author's first book, *American Ammunition and Ballistics*. Because this information is both timeless and important, it is repeated here.

Most of us, probably since the time we were kids, have been aware of cartridge interchangeability in a given firearm—or rather, in certain firearms. After all, didn't we load up our 22 Long rifle plinker with Shorts because they were considerably less expensive to burn up on tin cans? And why not? The barrel was clearly labeled, "chambered for 22 Short, Long and Long Rifle." There were only a few exceptions—22LR guns that wouldn't function properly with the shorter rounds. But those firearms were clearly marked, "for 22 Long Rifle cartridges only."

Shooters are constantly concerned with interchangeability, especially when a cost reduction is possible for practice shooting. Some shooters seek lighter-recoiling loads, most noticeably perhaps in the big magnum handguns. This may cause problems. Just because a cartridge fits into a chamber does not ensure that it is interchangeable with the cartridge inscribed on the gun. In fact, some of these "fits" can cause serious damage to the firearm and, in certain instances, injure the shooter severely.

High-velocity cartridges should not be used in firearms manufactured prior to the introduction of such cartridges. When in doubt, consult the manufacturer.

The use of short cartridges in long chambers tends to cause erosion of the chamber. With continued use, such erosion may cause difficult extraction and, in extreme cases, ruin the chamber for further use of the longer cartridge.

The following cartridges can be interchanged safely. No other cartridge switching should ever be attempted. Further, no converse interchangeability should be attempted; in other words, you can use 32 Shorts in a firearm chambered for 32 Longs, but don't try to use Longs in a gun chambered only for Shorts.

CENTERFIRE RIFLE INTERCHANGEABILITY

Among centerfire rifle cartridges, the only interchangeability involves guns chambered for the 45-90 Winchester. These can be used with 45-70 Government rounds. Chamber erosion can occur with this short round and might cause difficult extraction with the longer shell. Due to the general unavailability of the longer shells, this is probably of no consequence.

Other centerfire combinations are sometimes described (and perhaps correctly) as being interchangeable. However, upon examination of such combinations, we find that different nomenclature came about in many ways, but primarily it was the result of firearms manufacturers' marketing policies. These interchangeable names are as follows:

SHOTSHELL INTERCHANGEABILITY

Interchangeability in shotgun shells is limited strictly to the use of short shells in long chambers. This means that 10-gauge 2⅞-inch shells can be used in 10-gauge 3½-inch chambers; 12-gauge 2¾-inch shells can be used in 12-gauge 3-inch chambers; 16-gauge 2 9/16-inch shells can be used in 16-gauge 2¾-inch chambers; 20-gauge 2¾-inch shells can be used in 20-gauge 3-inch chambers; and finally, 410 bore 2½-inch shells can be used in 410 bore 3-inch chambers.

Caution: One of the real problems in interchanging shells occurs when some neophyte or overzealous clerk "discovers" that a shell of one type fits a gun of another chamber type. The following list shows some of these so-called "discoveries," all of which create dangerous conditions. The author makes no claim that this list is complete. It merely represents those he is aware of at this time. It will serve to warn shooters who own guns of the calibers involved that they must guard against potentially dangerous situations.

If you own guns of such calibers, it pays to be doubly certain you have not grabbed the wrong ammo. Be sure to check if you accidentally have left a few rounds of one caliber or gauge in your pockets before loading with a new batch of shells for a gun of the other caliber. Be especially careful on outings to the range, where dangerous combinations of ammo and firearms may be on hand simultaneously.

TABLE 19.1

CARTRIDGE INTERCHANGEABILITY

Rimfire

Firearm marked for:	Can also be used with:
22 Short	22 BB Cap, 22 CB Cap, 22 Short Blank, 22 CB Short.
22 Long	22 BB Cap, 22 CB Cap, 22 Short Blank, 22 Short, 22 CB Short, 22 CB Long.
22 Long Rifle	22 BB Cap, 22 CB Cap, 22 Short Blank, 22 CB Short, 22 CB Long, 22 Long, 22 LR Shot
22 Win Mag RF	22 Win RF, 22 Rem Spl
22 Rem Spl	22 Win RF
22 Win RF	22 Rem Spl
25 Stevens	25 Stevens Short
32 Long	32 Short

Centerfire Handgun

Firearm marked for:	Can also be used with:
32 S&W Long	32 S&W, 32 S&W Blank, 32 Colt New Police
32 Colt New Police	32 S&W, 32 S&W Blank, 32 S&W Long
32 Long Colt	32 Short Colt
38 Long Colt	38 Short Colt
38 S&W	38 Colt New Police, 38 S&W Blank
38 Spl	38 Short Colt, 38 Long Colt, 38 Spl Blank
357 Mag	38 Short Colt, 38 Long Colt, 38 Spl Blank, 38 Spl, 38 Spl +P
38-40 Win	5 in 1 Blank
38 Super Auto	38 Auto Colt
44 S&W Spl	44 S&W Russian
44 Rem Magnum	44 S&W Spl
44-40 Win	5 in 1 Blank
45 Colt	5 in 1 Blank

NOTE: 38 Special +P ammo should be used only in .38-caliber guns that have been designated or recommended by the firearm manufacturer as suitable for such use.

TABLE 19.2

INTERCHANGEABLE NAMES

Centerfire Handgun Cartridges

Full or primary name:	Also called:
25 Automatic	25 Auto, 25 ACP, 25 C.A.P., 6.35mm Auto, 6.35mm Browning (Auto)
30 Luger	7.65 Luger, 7.65 Parabellum
32 Automatic	32 Auto, 32 ACP, 32 C.A.P., 7.65 Auto, 7.65mm Browning (Auto)
9mm Luger	9mm Parabellum
380 Automatic	9mm Corto, 9mm Kurtz, 9mm Short
38-40 Win	38-40, 38 WCF, 38 Win, 38-40 Rem, 38-40 Marlin
44-40 Win	44-40, 44 WCF, 44 Win, 44-40 Rem, 44-40 Marlin

Centerfire Rifle Cartridges

Full or primary name:	Also called:
6mm Rem	(formerly) 244 Rem
25-20 Win	25-20, 25 WCF, 25-20 Marlin
280 Rem	7mm Express Rem
30-30 Win	30-30, 30 Win, 30 Marlin, 30 Savage, 30 WCF
32-20 Win	32-20, 32 Win, 32 Marlin, 32 Rem, 32 WCF, 32 Colt LMR
38-40 Win	38-40, 38 WCF, 38 Win, 38-40 Rem, 38-40 Marlin
44-40 Win	44-40, 44 WCF, 44 Win, 44-40 Rem, 44-40 Marlin
45-70 Gov	45-70, 45-70 Marlin, 45-70-405, 45-70-500

TABLE 19.3
DANGEROUS ARMS AND AMMUNITION COMBINATIONS

Centerfire Handguns

Chambered for	Dangerous ammo
32 S&W	32 Auto 32 Short Colt 32 Long Colt
38 Auto	38 Super Auto 38 Super Auto +P
32-20 Win	32-20 High Velocity
38 S&W	38 Auto 38 Short Colt 38 Long Colt 38 Spl 38 Spl +P
38 Spl	380 Auto 357 Mag 38 Spl +P
45 Auto	44 S&W Spl 44 Rem Mag
45 Colt	44 S&W Spl 44 Rem Mag
38-40 Win	38-40 High Velocity
44-40 Win	44-40 High Velocity

Centerfire Rifles

Chambered for	Dangerous ammo
17 Rem	221 Rem Fireball 30 Carbine
17-223 Rem	17 Rem 221 Rem Fireball 30 Carbine
223 Rem	222 Rem 5.56 Military
243 Win	250-3000 (250 Savage) 225 Win 300 Savage
6mm Rem (244 Rem)	250-3000 (250 Savage)
257 Roberts	250-3000 (250 Savage)
6.5mm Rem Mag	300 Savage
264 Win Mag	270 Win 284 Win 308 Win 303 British 350 Rem Mag 375 Win
270 Win	30 Rem 30-30 Win 300 Savage 32 Rem 308 Win 7mm Mauser (7×57mm) 375 Win
7mm Mauser (7×57mm)	300 Savage
7mm Rem Mag	7mm Weatherby Mag 270 Win 280 Rem 35 Rem 350 Rem Mag
280 Rem	270 Win 30 Rem 30-30 Win 300 Savage 308 Win 7mm Mauser (7×57mm) 375 Win
284 Win	300 Savage 7mm Mauser (7×57mm)
30-40 Krag	303 Savage 303 British 32 Win Spl

AMMO INTERCHANGEABILITY

Chambered for	Dangerous ammo
30-06 Springfield	8mm Mauser (8 × 57mm)
	32 Rem
	35 Rem
	375 Win
300 H&H Mag	30-06 Springfield
	8mm Mauser (8 × 57mm)
	30-40 Krag
	375 Win
300 Weatherby Mag	338 Win Mag
300 Win Mag	8mm Mauser (round-nose bullet)
	303 British
	350 Rem Mag
	38-55 Win
303 British	32 Win Spl
303 Savage	32 Win Spl
	32-40 Win
308 Win	300 Savage
338 Win	375 Win
348 Win	35 Rem
38-55 Win	375 Win
375 Win	38-55 Win
	41 Long Colt

Rimfires

Chambered for	Dangerous ammo
22 Win RF	22 BB Cap
	22 CB Cap
	22 Short
	22 Long
	22 Long Rifle
	22 Long Rifle Shot
22 Win Mag RF	same as 22 Win RF
22 Win Auto	same as 22 Win RF
5mm Rem RF Mag	same as 22 Win RF
25 Stevens Long	5mm Rem RF Mag

Shotguns

Chambered for	Dangerous ammo
410 Bore	219 Zipper
	30-30 Win
	303 British
	32 Win Spl
	32-40 Win
	35 Win
	38-40 Win
	44 S&W Spl
	44-40 Win
	44 Rem Mag

Except as noted earlier, a firearm should be used only with the ammunition for which it was designed. The combinations in the following list are typical of those in which a cartridge of one caliber will generally fire in a firearm of another caliber. Such errors can result in split or ruptured cartridge cases. Far worse, they can lead to possible serious injury to the shooter and/or bystanders. The possibility of leaving a bullet stuck in the bore, thus forming an obstruction, also exists.

Note: It is, of course, always dangerous to shoot shotshells of any gauge in a shotgun of a different gauge. Also, the use of any shotshell longer than the chamber can be dangerous. That is to say, 3-inch shells should never be used in 2¾-inch chambers, 2¾-inch shells should never be used in 2 9/16-inch chambers, and so on.

It is not always possible to emphasize a warning strongly enough. The misuse of ammunition can lead to serious consequences. Be certain always, never sorry.

20

Ammo Storage and Handling

Ammunition is not unduly dangerous to store or handle. However, it is not an innocuous substance to be carelessly chucked onto some shelf and ignored until needed. Sometimes, federal, state or local regulations govern storage methods. Where no such regulations apply, this chapter will provide safe guidelines.

Properly manufactured ammunition is a rather stable commodity, well suited to normal commerce. Inventories of modern sporting ammunition will not explode en masse, despite any hoopla presented on television. If a single round in a conglomeration of many rounds is caused to fire, it will not cause surrounding cartridges to simultaneously explode. Generally, therefore, no limits are imposed on factory-packaged ammunition which may be shipped, stored, or displayed in commercial warehouses or sales establishments.

Packaged ammunition that is dropped will not generally fire due to shock if the packaging material remains intact and undamaged. Properly packed ammunition will withstand normal handling encountered in commerce and will withstand appropriate drop, vibration, and rotation testing.

However, loose or bulk ammunition might, under certain conditions, permit a discharge of a single cartridge or several. For example, a 45 Automatic cartridge tossed underhand into an open wooden box of cartridges, from a distance of 20 feet, resulted in the detonation of a single cartridge. The fired cartridge's ruptured case landed near the person who threw the original cartridge. (It is unknown whether the fired cartridge was the one thrown or another in the box of loose ammunition.) The fired case showed clear evidence across the primer (which was partially backed out) of the impact of another cartridge's rim. It is, of course, unknown whether this impact crease in the primer occurred before or after ignition, although it would be reasonable to think it was the actual cause of ignition.

The moral is that a primer impacted by any object can, under specific circumstances, ignite even though ignition was not intended. Thus, ammunition stored loose and in bulk, or individual rounds stored where they may be subject to primer impact from other objects or due to falling, are needless storage hazards. However, the likelihood of serious or lethal harm, in the event that a cartridge ignites in the open, is limited. Indeed, in one test, ammunition deliberately ignited in a cardboard box failed to penetrate the box.

The author is unaware of any serious injury, let alone a fatality, caused by fully unsupported rounds of ammunition being ignited, whether due to fire or primer impact.

The primer in sporting ammunition contains explosive compounds, but both the primer and the propellant are insensitive to normal periods of storage as long as excessive temperature and/or humidity are avoided. Ammunition can be safely stored in tropic or arctic regions, but extremely high or low storage temperatures should be carefully avoided.

Moisture is a great enemy of proper ammunition storage. The other great enemy is heat. When in doubt about conditions of storage, do not use the ammunition for any critical application. Widely varying temperatures during storage can adversely affect ammunition performance, as can any corrosive atmosphere (from chemical plants, stables, seashore, etc.).

Ammunition should never be subjected to immersion in water or exposed to any organic solvent, paint thinner, petroleum product, ammonia, or similar material. Anything that could potentially affect the integrity of primer or propellant, or weaken the cartridge case, must always be avoided. Ammunition exposed to potentially deteriorating conditions should not be fired, but rather disposed of in a safe manner.

Keep in mind that any round of ammunition that results in a weak firing may leave a bullet, shot, or wad lodged in the barrel of the firearm. Always carefully inspect for bore obstructions after any firing that seems even slightly less than normal in force, recoil, or report. Shooting any firearm with any barrel obstruction can cause the barrel to burst, causing injury or death to shooter and bystander alike.

Ideally, home storage should be in a locked closet or cabinet, in a room where extreme temperature changes will not occur. Avoid attic storage where extreme temperatures often occur during summer and winter. Do also avoid storage in unusually damp locations.

Naturally, ammunition should be stored out of reach of children and incompetent persons. Pets that chew on shotshells could be fatally injured since an ingredient in some smokeless powders can be toxic to them.

Ammunition may, by law, be required to be locked in an automobile trunk when in transit—it may simply be convenient to do so.

But extreme temperatures may occur in such storage, so ammunition should be removed promptly at the end of a journey. A back shelf in a car (or any other place in the passenger compartment) can also be subject to extreme summertime temperatures. Don't expose ammo to such conditions. Keeping it in a styrofoam cooler can help avoid extreme temperatures during auto transportation.

Blank cartridges use rapidly burning propellants. These may cause very loud noise during any detonation. Also, their ignition may be quite violent. Blank cartridges demand great respect.

Instances have been reported of ammunition performing satisfactorily after 50 years of storage. This helps confirm that there is no maximum storage period for modern, high-quality ammunition that is properly cared for. Yet any ammunition to be used for critical purposes, such as self-protection, the protection of others, or for the hunting of dangerous game, should be kept in storage for only relatively short periods. Under proper conditions of storage, a five-year period would not be considered excessive.

Centerfire or rimfire ammunition, properly stored, should remain ballistically satisfactory for a period of 10 or more years. Ammunition should be loaded only into firearms that have clean, dry bores and chambers. Contamination by oil or solvents can be ruinous to ammunition. Care should be taken to prevent any physical damage to ammunition during loading or unloading procedures. When used for any critical purpose, ammunition in loaded firearms should be replaced every six months, the old ammo being used for practice.

Cartridges carried in belt loops can be affected by oils from the leather or by wetness from rain, snow, perspiration, and so on. Prolonged exposure to such conditions should be avoided, and ammunition carried that way should be replaced frequently.

Any ammunition that shows signs of deterioration should be discarded. This may be evident as a corrosive discoloration on bullet, primer, or case. It also includes any physical deformity that occurs during handling.

It would be impossible to anticipate or suggest all the possible abnormalities that might be encountered during storage and handling of ammunition. Only ammunition stored under good conditions and in a proper physical state should ever be used. Treat all ammunition with the respect due to any potentially hazardous material.

Ammunition improperly used can cause great property damage, physical harm, or even accidental death. Caution should always prevail. Each user is the ultimate controller of a potentially lethal commodity. Treat ammunition accordingly and avoid disaster.

Should a misfire ever be experienced, always keep any firearm pointed in a safe direction for at least 30 seconds. The problem could be a "slow" fire caused by a malfunctioning firearm or delayed cartridge ignition. After waiting 30 seconds, and while keeping the firearm pointed in a safe direction, carefully unload the cartridge involved. Do not attempt to re-use the cartridge, but dispose of it in a safe manner.

Additional information is provided in a pamphlet entitled "Properties of Sporting Ammunition and Recommendations for its Storage and Handling." The pamphlet is available from Sporting Arms and Ammunition Manufacturers Institute (SAAMI), P.O. Box 838, Branford, CT 06405. You must include a stamped, self-addressed No. 10 (business-size) envelope with your request.

21
Shooting and Ammo Safety

Throughout this book, I have stressed safety, and I'm going to conclude with a few more thoughts on the subject. Any book related to shooting would be less than complete without safety warnings.

Any fired cartridge represents a potential for serious injury or death, as well as extensive property damage. Only the shooter can serve as the ultimate safety factor. All firearms are mechanical contraptions, and a firearm may malfunction because of a worn or broken part, poor design, or shooter error. Thus, any loaded firearm must be treated with all the respect and care necessary to ensure that any bullet fired, whether intentionally or unintentionally, will strike a safe backstop somewhere downrange.

On several occasions I have seen a shooter continue to operate a firearm even though it was not feeding cartridges smoothly from magazine to chamber. On two occasions, the vigorous manipulation of the bolt resulted in the muzzle of the firearm being pointed upward at a rather steep angle. In the first instance the shooter's finger struck the trigger as the bolt was slammed forward, causing the firearm to discharge. The bullet cleared the downrange backstop and the small hill beyond. Subsequent reports and a visit to the range by state police confirmed that the bullet made it all the way through a very distant kitchen window.

In the other instance, the gun had a military-style action in which the firing pin and its spring were cocked as the bolt was shoved forward. The vigorous manipulation of the bolt, combined with a very light trigger pull (with a trigger system unsuited to such a pull) caused the striker to slip from the sear and fire the cartridge just as the bolt was engaging the lugs. The bolt was driven rearward with great force into the shooter's palm. In this instance, the bullet was adequately contained by overhead range baffles—but barely so.

Guns that are difficult to operate can be dangerous. When encountering a firearm that functions less than smoothly, it is best not to proceed with its use.

The shooter should also be alert for any ammunition problem that might cause difficult firearm manipulation. Bullets that are deformed, bent, crooked, or seated to an improper depth can cause difficulty. Each round should be carefully inspected. This can be done just before loading the gun or at home after an ammunition purchase. Checking at both points will help double your safety.

Any abnormal cartridge should be returned to the box and ultimately to the place of purchase or manufacture. (Please keep in mind that cartridges cannot be sent to anyone via the U.S. mail.)

High primers, often associated with poorly assembled reloads, are a needless risk. A primer protruding beyond the end of a case may be impacted or impinged upon by some portion of the firearm's action during functioning of the gun. This could result in ignition of the cartridge, which is especially hazardous when the cartridge is partially contained within the firearm, but not fully chambered.

Ammunition should never be subjected to any misuse or abuse that would weaken its ability to contain the forces of propellant ignition or that might physically alter it so as to interfere with smooth firearm functioning. Ammunition that shows any signs of corrosion should not be used.

Once ignition occurs, ammunition performance can sometimes be less than expected. Weak or "punky" sounds, abnormally light or heavy recoil, noticeably poor accuracy, or difficult extraction of the fired cartridge case can all be signals of faulty ammunition and/or firearm condition. Immediately cease the use of any box of ammunition that shows any signs of unusual or abnormal performance.

Proper safety, of course, demands more than simply being alert or keeping the muzzle pointed at a safe backstop. It also means handling and storing ammunition safely, as described in Chapter 20.

Still more is involved in safety. Perhaps the two easiest steps to take in the prevention of injury are always to wear safety glasses and hearing protection when shooting. Shooting glasses can prevent eye injury in the event of an accident. The loss of an eye easily occurs and is easily prevented. Remember that hearing loss due to shooting is cumulative. Always wear ear protection even when shooting 22 rimfire cartridges.

The ten basics of shooting safety are as follows:

1. Treat every gun with the respect due a loaded firearm.
2. Be absolutely positive of your target before you even begin to think about pointing the gun or pulling the trigger.
3. Always be sure that the barrel and action are free of obstructions. Such obstructions could cause the gun to burst on firing.

4. Never point any gun at any time at any target you do not wish to "kill."
5. Never set a loaded gun aside, whether briefly or for storage. Don't put it down until it's unloaded.
6. Avoid intoxicating beverages or any medication that might affect your ability to think clearly and quickly when shooting.
7. Never attempt to climb, jump, run, or proceed at any rate other than a walk when carrying a loaded firearm.
8. Never shoot at any flat or hard surface, or any other surface that might result in a ricochet; this includes water.
9. Take only empty and preferably disassembled firearms into home, car, or camp.
10. Always store ammunition and firearms out of reach of children or incompetent persons.

With care, a lifetime of enjoyment can be had in the shooting sports. A careless moment may make the shooter wish he had spent a lifetime without firing a shot.

APPENDIX

Historical Exterior Ballistic Tables

Some of the information on exterior ballistics presented in this chapter was taken from an old Winchester sales guide and three early Winchester catalogs. The tables will be of special interest to ammunition historians, cartridge collectors, and, of course, anyone whose curiosity may be aroused.

It's interesting to compare the ballistics of cartridges of the early 1900s with those of cartridges that are popular today. Many of the cartridges that have been discontinued for a great number of years took game cleanly and quickly in the hands of the skilled woodsman of yesteryear. You will find listed a great many of the old favorites, including the 6mm Lee Navy, 33 Winchester, 38-55 High Velocity, 38-56 Winchester, 38 Express, 40-82 Winchester, 45-70-350, 50-90 Winchester Express, 50-110-300 Winchester High Velocity, and many more.

The first three tables are taken from Winchester catalogs dated from 1900 to 1925. Tables A.4 and A.5 are taken from a Winchester sales guide, printed in the early 1940s. The collecting of old ammunition catalogs and related promotional literature is a fascinating pastime. For further reference, I suggest that you contact local cartridge and/or catalog collectors.

For clarity, some table headings have been modified from the original catalog pages. It's interesting to note that some of the figures are carried out to tenths of a foot/pound or tenths of a second.

About two-dozen cartridges and loadings have been discontinued during the years since the publication of the author's first ammunition book. Many of those cartridges and loads are still available on dealers' shelves, and many will continue to be used in the years to come. Table A.6 is offered to assist shooters with continuing interest in these loads.

TABLE A.1

VELOCITY, PENETRATION, AND TRAJECTORY OF WINCHESTER BULLETS

(from #66 Winchester Catalog, 1900)

Penetration[1] at 15 feet from muzzle

Rifle Used	Barrel Length (inches)	Cartridge	Bullet Weight (grains)	Muzzle Velocity (fps)	Plain Lead bullets	Metal-Patched bullets	MIDRANGE TRAJECTORY (INCHES) AT: 100 yds	200 yds	300 yds
Model 1890	24	22 Win. R.F.	45	1137	4		4.0		
Single Shot	26	22 Win. S.S.	45	1481	5		2.7	12.6	33.7
Lee Stgt. Pull	28	6mm U.S. Navy	112	2500		60	0.8	3.6	9.4
Model 1892	24	25-20 W.C.F.	86	1300	9		3.3	13.8	34.7
Single Shot	28	25-20	86	1304	9		3.4	13.6	34.7
Model 1894	26	25-35 W.C.F.	117	1925		36	2.4	5.1	13.9
Model 1894	26	30 W.C.F.	160	1885		35	2.1	5.2	13.6
Savage Rifle	26	303 Savage	180	1840		33	1.2	6.3	16.4
Model 1895	28	30 U.S. Army	220	1960		58	1.5	5.1	14.1
Model 1892	24	32 Winchester	115	1177	6½		3.5	15.4	37.2
Single Shot	30	32-40	165	1385	8½	18	2.7	11.3	28.3
Model 1892	24	38 Winchester	180	1268	7½		3.2	14.4	35.7
Single Shot	30	38-55	255	1285	9½	17	3.0	12.9	32.0
Express S.S.	30	38-90 Win. Exp.	217	1546	9		2.2	8.6	22.8
Model 1886	26	38-56 Winchester	255	1359	11	14½	2.8	12.2	30.1
Model 1886	26	38-70 Winchester	255	1449	10	19	2.6	10.6	27.2
Model 1895	26	38-72 Winchester	275	1443	16	25	2.2	10.6	27.7
Single Shot	26	40-70 Sharp's Stgt.	330	1229	11½		3.3	13.4	32.9
Marlin Rifle	28	40-60 Marlin	260	1419	8½		3.0	11.8	29.4
Single Shot	28	40-60 Winchester	210	1475	9½		2.6	11.7	30.1
Model 1895	26	40-72 Win. B.P.	330	1359	13	23	2.6	12.2	30.5
Model 1895	26	40-72 Winchester	300	1386		22	2.4	11.6	28.5
Single Shot	30	40-90 Sharp's Stgt.	370	1357	16	22	2.7	10.8	26.9
Model 1886	26	40-65 Winchester	260	1325	9	14½	2.9	12.0	30.7
Model 1886	26	40-70 Winchester	330	1349	13	19½	2.8	11.8	29.4
Model 1886	26	40-82 Winchester	260	1445	12	17½	2.6	11.9	30.3
Express S.S.	30	40-110 Win. Exp.	260	1555	12¼		2.1	9.0	23.6
Model 1892	24	44 Winchester	200	1245	9		3.4	15.3	37.4
Single Shot	30	45-75 Winchester	350	1343	14½		3.0	12.4	30.6
Single Shot	30	45-60 Winchester	300	1271	11½		3.2	13.7	33.1
Model 1886	26	45-70-500	500	1179	18		3.7	14.4	34.4
Model 1886	26	45-70-5 = 405	405	1271	14	16½	3.3	13.1	32.4
Model 1886	26	45-70-405 Smokeless	405	1286		20	4.1	12.3	29.0
Model 1886	26	45-70-350 Win.	350	1307	13		2.8	13.1	32.4
Model 1886	26	45-70-330 Gould	330	1338	10		2.8	12.7	31.8
Model 1886	26	45-90 Winchester	300	1480	13	19	2.4	10.3	27.3
Express S.S.	30	45-125 Win. Exp.	300	1633	9½		2.2	9.0	25.1
Model 1886	26	50-110 Win. Exp.	300	1536	11		2.5	11.9	33.5
Model 1886	26	50-100-450 Win.	450	1383	16		2.9	11.9	30.7
Express S.S.	30	50-95 Win. Exp.	300	1493	10		2.6	12.6	33.5

[1]Penetration of bullets in dry pine boards ⅞ inch thick

TABLE A.2

BALLISTICS OF WINCHESTER CARTRIDGES AND RECOIL OF WINCHESTER RIFLES

(From #81 Winchester Catalog, 1918)

Penetration is not the measure of striking energy. As an illustration, take the figures in our table for the 30 Winchester Centerfire Cartridge. With the soft-point bullet, the penetration is but 11 boards, whereas that cartridge with the full-patch bullet will penetrate 42 boards. The energies of both are the same. All other things being equal, the bullet which resists deformation will give the maximum penetration. The soft-point bullet, which generally stops inside the skin of the animal, delivers its whole energy; while the full-patch bullet, which passes through the animal, may make a less severe wound. Penetration, therefore, is not a good test of killing power. If the target is harder or softer than that described in our table, the results obtained will not be the same; nor will the comparative results show corresponding differences. The rifles used in determining the following ballistics were equipped with barrels of standard lengths.

Cartridge	Bullet Weight (grains)	VELOCITY (FPS) muzzle	VELOCITY (FPS) 100 yds	ENERGY (FT/LBS) muzzle	ENERGY (FT/LBS) 100 yds	PENETRATION[1] AT 15 FEET BULLETS Lead	PENETRATION[1] AT 15 FEET BULLETS SP	PENETRATION[1] AT 15 FEET BULLETS FMC	MIDRANGE TRAJECTORIES (INCHES) AT: 100 yds	MIDRANGE TRAJECTORIES (INCHES) AT: 200 yds	MIDRANGE TRAJECTORIES (INCHES) AT: 300 yds	FREE RECOIL (FT/LBS) Smokeless	FREE RECOIL (FT/LBS) Black Powder
6mm	112	2562.0	2231.5	1632.8	1239.1		12	60	0.8	3.5	9.1	7.1	
22 Win. C.F.	45	1541.2	1126.0	237.4	126.7	8			2.6	13.7	38.3	0.4	0.5
25-20 S.S	86	1411.9	1132.6	380.8	245.0	9	8	11	2.7	13.5	35.8	0.5	0.7
25-20 Win.	86	1376.3	1108.6	361.8	234.7	9	8	11	2.9	14.1	41.0	0.8	0.8
25-20 W.H.V.	86	1728.1	1407.9	570.4	378.6		10	20	1.9	8.9	24.3	1.4	
25-35 Win.	117	1973.0	1698.1	1011.6	749.6		11	36	1.3	6.1	16.0	3.4	
30 Winchester	170	2003.4	1753.0	1515.5	1160.2		11	42	1.2	5.7	14.8	7.2	
30 Army Ptd.	150	2557.9	2331.7	2179.8	1811.3				0.7	3.3	8.2		
30 Army Ptd.	180	2345.5	2167.4	2199.3	1878.0				0.9	3.7	9.1		
30 Army	220	1993.5	1798.4	1941.8	1580.3		13	58	1.2	5.4	13.5	11.6	
30 Govt. '03	220	2198.9	1989.7	2362.5	1934.3		18	68	1.0	4.4	11.0	15.0	
30-06 Govt.	150	2700.0	2465.1	2428.6	2024.5		14	75	0.6	2.9	7.9	11.4	
30-06 Govt.	180	2499.4	2313.1	2497.5	2139.1				0.8	3.3	7.9	12.6	
30-06 Govt.	220	2198.9	1989.7	2362.5	1934.3		18		1.0	4.4	11.0	15.0	
303 British	215	1999.1	1775.7	1908.3	1505.7		13	56	1.2	5.5	14.1	11.0	
32 Win. S.L.	165	1392.0	1167.0	710.1	499.1		10	17	2.7	12.5	33.3	1.9	
32 Winchester	115	1222.2	1010.9	381.5	261.0	6.5	6.5	10	3.6	16.9	43.6	1.1	1.2
32 Win. Special	170	2104.4	1792.7	1672.0	1213.5		12	45	1.2	5.6	14.6	7.7	
32 W.H.V.	115	1636.0	1304.3	683.6	434.5		7	17	2.0	10.4	28.0	2.7	
32-40	165	1427.7	1194.5	747.0	522.9	8.5	8.5	18	2.5	12.2	31.9	3.1	
32-40 W.H.V.	165	1748.5	1476.9	1120.4	799.4		10	30	1.7	8.1	21.5	5.5	
33 Winchester	200	2050.3	1761.7	1867.3	1378.7		13	39	1.2	5.6	15.0	11.4	
35 Win. S.L.	180	1396.0	1151.0	779.1	529.6		9	17	2.7	13.1	34.4	2.8	
35 Winchester	250	2192.7	1945.3	2669.6	2101.1		15	56	1.0	4.6	11.8	19.8	
351 Win. S.L.	180	1856.4	1541.7	1377.8	950.1		13	26	1.5	7.4	20.2	5.6	
38 Winchester	180	1324.0	1053.3	700.8	433.5	7.5	10	12	3.2	15.5	41.7	3.2	4.7
38 W.H.V.	180	1770.0	1389.6	1252.5	771.9		10	20	1.8	9.3	25.6	6.7	
38-55	255	1321.0	1131.6	988.3	725.2	9.5	13.5	14	2.9	13.6	34.4	6.0	8.4
38-55 W.H.V.	255	1590.1	1364.2	1432.0	1054.0		10	23	2.0	9.4	24.4	9.4	
38-56 Win.	255	1397.0	1189.2	1105.3	800.9	11	12	17	2.6	12.3	31.0	5.8	8.1
38-70 Win.	255	1489.5	1262.9	1256.5	903.3	10	12	19	2.1	11.8	28.7	7.2	10.2
38-72 Win.	275	1476.6	1286.1	1331.7	1010.2	16	15	25	2.3	10.6	27.1	8.7	9.4
38 Express	217	1595.8	1313.7	1227.4	831.8	9			2.1	10.2	27.5		9.6
40-60 Win.	210	1532.7	1220.3	1095.7	694.6	9.5			2.3	11.8	32.0		6.9

BALLISTICS AND RECOIL (continued)

Cartridge	Bullet Weight (grains)	VELOCITY (FPS) muzzle	VELOCITY (FPS) 100 yds	ENERGY (FT/LBS) muzzle	ENERGY (FT/LBS) 100 yds	PENETRATION[1] AT 15 FEET BULLETS Lead	PENETRATION[1] AT 15 FEET BULLETS SP	PENETRATION[1] AT 15 FEET BULLETS FMC	MIDRANGE TRAJECTORIES (INCHES) AT: 100 yds	MIDRANGE TRAJECTORIES (INCHES) AT: 200 yds	MIDRANGE TRAJECTORIES (INCHES) AT: 300 yds	FREE RECOIL (FT/LBS) Smokeless	FREE RECOIL (FT/LBS) Black Powder
40-65 Win.	260	1367.2	1145.1	1079.4	757.7	9	11	14.5	2.6	13.2	33.4	6.8	8.7
40-70 Win.	330	1382.8	1196.7	1401.5	1049.6	13	11	19.5	2.7	12.2	33.9	9.2	13.0
40-72 Win.	330	1373.0	1190.6	1381.6	1063.2	13			2.8	12.1	33.9		14.6
40-72 Win.	300	1423.8	1214.6	1350.7	983.0		14	22	2.5	11.8	30.6	10.0	
40-82 Win.	260	1492.1	1236.9	1285.6	883.5	12	11	17.5	2.4	11.3	29.9	8.8	12.2
401 Win. S.L.	200	2132.7	1749.2	2020.3	1359.1		14	34	1.2	5.8	16.1	11.5	
401 Win. S.L.	250	1869.9	1562.2	1941.5	1355.1		12	27	1.5	7.2	19.6	12.2	
405 Winchester	300	2197.5	1923.1	3217.6	2464.2		13	48	1.0	4.7	12.3	28.2	
44 Winchester	200	1300.6	1034.6	751.4	475.5	9	10	13	3.3	15.9	42.4	3.9	5.4
44 W.H.V.	200	1563.9	1226.1	1086.3	667.8		10	19	2.3	11.6	31.2	6.0	
45-60 Win.	300	1314.6	1091.8	1151.5	794.2	11.5			3.0	14.5	37.4		9.3
45-70 W.H.V.	300	1882.9	1559.0	2362.4	1619.5		13	25	1.5	7.2	19.9	16.2	
45-40-350	350	1343.8	1139.1	1403.8	1008.6	13	11	17	2.9	15.0	34.3	10.3	14.6
45-70-405 Govt.	405	1317.6	1143.3	1561.7	1175.8	13	12	18	2.9	13.3	33.6	12.3	16.2
45-70-500 Govt.	500	1201.1	1081.6	1602.1	1317.2	18	15	20	3.5	14.8	36.1	15.2	18.4
45-75 Win.	350	1382.7	1168.2	1485.1	1060.8	14.5			2.7	13.0	32.9		13.6
45-90 Win.	300	1531.7	1247.8	1563.3	1037.5	13	15	19	2.3	11.2	30.2	11.4	16.5
45-90 W.H.V.	300	1985.7	1643.2	2627.2	1798.7		14	26	1.3	6.5	18.0	19.0	
50-95 Win. Exp.	300	1556.8	1214.2	1614.8	982.3	10			2.3	11.9	32.7		17.5
50-100-450 Win.	450	1422.1	1206.6	2021.2	1455.2	16	14	20	2.5	12.0	32.1	21.5	25.2
50-110 Win. Exp.	300	1605.8	1250.2	1718.2	1041.4	11	12	20	2.2	11.0	31.2	11.3	19.8
50-110-300 W.H.V.	300	2230.1	1779.4	3313.7	2109.8		14	26	1.1	5.6	16.2	25.6	

[1]Penetration at 15 feet in ⅞ inch soft pine boards.

TABLE A.3

BALLISTICS OF WINCHESTER CARTRIDGES AND RECOIL OF WINCHESTER RIFLES

(From #83 Winchester Catalog, 1925)

Penetration is not the measure of striking energy. As an illustration, take the figures in our table for the 30 Winchester Centerfire Cartridge. With the soft-point bullet, the penetration is but 11 boards, whereas that cartridge with the full-patch bullet will penetrate 42 boards. The energies of both are the same. All other things being equal, the bullet which resists deformation will give the maximum penetration. The soft-point bullet, which generally stops inside the skin of the animal, delivers its whole energy; while the full-patch bullet, which passes through the animal, may make a less severe wound. Penetration, therefore, is not a good test of killing power. If the target is harder or softer than that described in our table, the results obtained will not be the same; nor will the comparative results show corresponding differences. The rifles used in determining the following ballistics were equipped with barrels of standard lengths.

Cartridge	Bullet Weight (grains)	VELOCITY (FPS) muzzle	VELOCITY (FPS) 100 yds	ENERGY (FT/LBS) muzzle	ENERGY (FT/LBS) 100 yds	PENETRATION[1] AT 15 FEET BULLETS Lead	PENETRATION[1] AT 15 FEET BULLETS SP	PENETRATION[1] AT 15 FEET BULLETS FMC	MIDRANGE TRAJECTORIES (INCHES) AT: 100 yds	MIDRANGE TRAJECTORIES (INCHES) AT: 200 yds	MIDRANGE TRAJECTORIES (INCHES) AT: 300 yds	FREE RECOIL (FT/LBS) Smokeless	FREE RECOIL (FT/LBS) Black Powder
6mm	112	2560	2230	1635	1240		12	60	0.7	3.5	9.0	7.0	
22 Win. C.F.	45	1540	1125	240	125	8			2.5	13.5		0.4	0.5
25-20 S.S	86	1410	1135	380	245	9	8	11	2.5	13.5		0.5	0.7
25-20 Win.	86	1375	1110	360	235	9	8	11	3.0	14.0		0.8	0.9
25-20 W.H.V.	86	1730	1410	570	380		10	20	2.0	9.0		1.5	
25-35 Win.	117	2175	1880	1230	920		11	44	1.0	5.0	13.0	4.5	
270 Winchester	130	3160	2970	2880	2550		17		0.5	2.0	4.5		
30 Winchester	170	2200	1930	1825	1410		11	50	1.0	4.5	12.0	9.0	
30 Army, Ptd.	150	2560	2330	2180	1810				0.7	3.5	8.0		
30 Army, Ptd.	180	2345	2165	2200	1880				0.8	3.5	9.0		
30 Army	220	1995	1800	1940	1580		13	58	1.0	5.5	13.0	11.5	
30 Govt. '03	220	2200	1990	2365	1935		18	68	1.0	4.5	11.0	15.0	
30-06 Govt.	150	2700	2465	2430	2025		14	75	0.6	3.0	7.0	11.5	
30-06 Govt.	180	2500	2315	2500	2140				0.7	3.5	8.0	12.5	
30-06 Govt.	180	2700	2505	2915	2505		17		0.5	2.5	7.0	16.5	
30-06 Govt.	220	2400	2185	2810	2340		17		1.0	4.0	9.0	16.0	
303 British	215	2000	1775	1910	1505		13	56	1.0	5.5	14.0	11.0	
32 Win. S.L.	165	1390	1165	710	500		10	17	2.5	12.5	33.0	2.0	
32 Winchester	115	1225	1010	380	260	7	7	10	3.5	17.0		1.1	1.2
32 Win. Spl.	170	2250	1925	1910	1395		12	52	1.0	4.5	12.0	9.5	
32 W.H.V.	115	1635	1305	685	435		7	17	2.0	10.5	28.0	2.5	
32-40	165	1430	1195	745	525	9	9	18	2.5	12.0	32.0	3.0	4.1
32-40 W.H.V.	165	1750	1475	1120	800		10	30	1.5	8.0	21.0	5.5	
33 Winchester	200	2200	1895	2150	1580		13	45	1.0	5.0	13.0	13.5	
35 Win. S.L.	180	1395	1150	780	530		9	17	2.5	13.0	34.0	3.0	
35 Winchester	250	2195	1945	2670	2100		15	56	1.0	4.5	12.0	20.0	
351 Win. S.L.	180	1855	1540	1380	950		13	26	1.5	7.5	20.0	5.5	
38 Winchester	180	1325	1055	700	445	8	10	12	3.0	15.5	41.0	3.0	4.5
38 W.H.V.	180	1770	1390	1255	770		10	20	2.0	9.5	25.0	6.5	
38-55	255	1320	1130	990	725	10	14	14	3.0	13.5	34.0	6.0	8.5
38-55 W.H.V.	255	1590	1365	1430	1055		10	23	2.0	9.5	24.0	9.5	
38-56 Win.	255	1395	1190	1105	800	11	12	17	2.5	12.5	32.0	5.5	8.0
38-72 Win.	275	1475	1285	1330	1010	16	15	25	2.5	10.5	27.0	8.5	9.5
40-60 Win.	210	1533	1220	1095	695	10			2.5	11.5	32.0		7.0

BALLISTICS AND RECOIL (continued)

Cartridge	Bullet Weight (grains)	VELOCITY (FPS)		ENERGY (FT/LBS)		PENETRATION[1] AT 15 FEET BULLETS			MIDRANGE TRAJECTORIES (INCHES) AT:			FREE RECOIL (FT/LBS)	
		muzzle	100 yds	muzzle	100 yds	Lead	SP	FMC	100 yds	200 yds	300 yds	Smokeless	Black Powder
40-65 Win.	260	1370	1145	1080	760	9	11	15	2.5	13.0	33.0	7.0	8.5
40-72 Win.	300	1425	1215	1350	985		14	22	2.5	12.0	30.0	10.0	
40-82 Win.	260	1490	1235	1285	885	12	11	18	2.5	11.0	30.0	9.0	12.0
401 Win. S.L.	200	2135	1750	2020	1360		14	34	1.0	5.5	16.0	11.5	
401 Win. S.L.	250	1870	1560	1940	1355		12	27	1.5	7.0	19.0	12.0	
405 Winchester	300	2200	1925	3220	2465		13	48	1.0	4.5	12.0	28.0	
44 Winchester	200	1300	1035	750	475	9	10	13	3.0	16.0	42.0	4.0	5.5
44 W.H.V.	200	1565	1225	1085	670		10	19	2.5	11.5	31.0	6.0	
45-60 Win.	300	1315	1090	1150	795	12			3.0	14.5	37.0		9.5
45-70 W.H.V.	300	1885	1560	2365	1620		13	25	1.5	7.0	20.0	16.0	
45-70-405 Govt.	405	1320	1145	1560	1175	13	12	18	3.0	13.0	33.0	12.0	16.0
45-75 Win.	350	1385	1170	1495	1060	15			3.0	13.0	33.0		13.5
45-90 Win.	300	1530	1250	1565	1040	13	15	19	2.5	11.0	30.0	11.5	16.5
45-90 W.H.V.	300	1985	1645	2630	1800		14	26	1.5	6.5	18.0	19.0	
50-110 Win. Exp.	300	1605	1250	1720	1040	11	13	20	2.0	11.0	31.0	11.5	19.5

[1]Penetration at 15 feet in ⅞ inch soft pine boards.

RIFLE SIGHTING TABLES FOR WINCHESTER CARTRIDGES

(From "Sales Guide of Winchester Metallic Ammunition and Shotshells," issued and used during early 1940s)

To help the shooter to quickly adapt his holding to various ranges, Winchester has developed the following tables showing the approximate actual positions of the bullets at the ranges given. These are based on the rimfire rifle being zeroed at 50 yards and the centerfire rifle at 100 yards—in many cases 200 yards also. These figures show the distance in inches above or below the line of sight. In the centerfire tables, positions above the line of sight are indicated by a plus sign, those below by a minus sign. It must be understood, of course, that due to wind conditions and other factors there are bound to be variations in the flight of bullets, which cannot be avoided. Therefore, these figures in all cases must be read as indicating *approximate* positions. The rifles used in determining these ballistics had standard-length barrels. This new presentation was developed because it makes it simpler and quicker for the shooter to adapt his holding to any ranges.

TABLE A.4
RANGE TABLE FOR WINCHESTER RIMFIRE CARTRIDGES

Cartridge	Bullet Type	Bullet Weight (gr)	DROP OF BULLET (INCHES) ZERO AT 50 YARDS		
			100 yds	150 yds	200 yds
Leader 22 Short	Lead	29	9.5		
Super Speed 22 Short	KK	29	7.0	31.0	67.0
Super Speed 22 Short	KK, HP	27	7.0	31.5	68.0
Leader 22 Long	Lead	29	8.0		
Super Speed 22 Long	KK	29	5.5	24.5	54.0
Super Speed 22 Long	KK, HP	27	6.0	25.0	58.0
Leader 22 Long Rifle	Lead	40	6.5		
EZXS, 22 Long Rifle	Lead	40	7.5		
All-X Match 22 L.R.	Lead	40	6.5		
Super Speed 22 L.R.	KK	40	5.0	24.0	50.5
Super Speed 22 L.R.	KK, HP	37	5.5	22.5	50.0
22 Extra Long	Lead	40	9.0		
22 W.R.F.	Lead	45	6.5		
22 W.R.F.	KK	45	6.5		
Super Speed 22 W.R.F.	KK	45	5.0	22.5	46.0
Super Speed 22 W.R.F.	KK, HP	40	5.0	22.5	47.5
22 Automatic	Lead	45	8.0		
22 Automatic	KK	45	8.0		
22 Automatic	KK, HP	45	8.0		
25 Stevens	Lead	65	6.0		
25 Short Stevens	Lead	65	9.5		
32 Short	Lead	80	9.0		
32 Long	Lead	90	8.5		
41 Swiss	Lead	310	9.0		

KK = Kopperklad
HP = Hollow-Point

TABLE A.5

RANGE TABLE FOR WINCHESTER CENTERFIRE CARTRIDGES

Path of Bullet (inches) Above or Below Line of Sight

Cartridge	Bullet Type	Bullet Weight (gr)	50	100	200	300	400	500
SS 218 Win. Bee	HP	46	+0.70	0	−6.0	−26.5		
				+3.5	0	−19.0		
SS 219 Win. Zipper	HP	46	+0.40	0	−4.0	−18.0		
				+2.5	0	−13.0		
SS 219 Win. Hornet	HP	56	+0.60	0	−4.5	−19.0		
				+2.5	0	−13.5		
SS 22 Win. Hornet	SP	45	+0.80	0	−7.5	−32.0		
				+4.0	0	−22.5		
SS 22 Win. Hornet	HP	46	+0.80	0	−6.5	−31.5		
				+3.5	0	−22.5		
SS 22 High Power	PSP	70	+0.60	0	−4.5	−17.0		
				+3.0	0	−11.0		
SS 220 Win. Swift	PSP	48	+0.30	0	−2.5	−9.0	−24.0	−50.5
				+1.5	0	−6.0	−19.5	−46.0
SS 220 Win. Swift	PSP	55	+0.35	0	−2.5	−11.0	−27.0	−56.0
				+1.5	0	−7.0	−22.0	−49.0
25-20 Winchester	Lead	86	+2.60	0	−18.5	−76.0		
25-20 Winchester	FP	86	+2.60	0	−18.5	−76.0		
25-20 Winchester	SP	86	+2.60	0	−18.5	−76.0		
SS 25-20 W.H.V.	SP	86	+1.90	0	−15.5	−62.0		
SS 25-20 Win.	HP	60	+1.20	0	−11.0	−48.0		
25-20 Single Shot	SP	86	+2.70	0	−22.0	−80.5		
25 Remington Auto	SP	117	+0.90	0	−6.5	−26.0		
6.5mm Mannlicher	SP	145	+0.90	0	−6.5	−24.5	−58.0	−116.5
SS 25-35 Win.	FP	117	+1.00	0	−7.5	−29.5		
SS 25-35 Win.	SP	117	+1.00	0	−7.5	−29.5		
SS 257 Win. Roberts	PSP	87	+0.49	0	−3.5	−13.0	−31.0	−60.0
				+2.0	0	−10.5	−24.0	−51.0
SS 257 Win. Roberts	PE	100	+0.59	0	−3.5	−15.0	−36.0	−70.0
				+2.5	0	−9.5	−27.5	−50.0
SS 250-3000 Savage	FP	87	+0.50	0	−3.5	−14.5	−34.5	−69.0
				+2.5	0	−9.0	−26.5	−58.0
SS 250-3000 Savage	SP	87	+0.50	0	−3.5	−14.5	−24.5	−69.0
				+2.5	0	−9.0	−26.5	−58.0
SS 250-3000 Savage	PE	100	+0.60	0	−4.5	−16.0	−38.5	−73.5
				+2.5	0	−10.0	−29.5	−62.0
SS 270 Win.	PE	130	+0.50	0	−3.5	−12.5	−30.0	−54.5
				+2.0	0	−7.5	−23.0	−46.0
SS 270 Win.	SP	150	+0.60	0	−4.5	−18.0	−44.0	−86.5
				+2.5	0	−11.0	−33.5	−72.5
SS 270 Win.	PE	100	+0.40	0	−3.0	−10.5	−24.5	−47.0
				+1.5	0	−6.5	−18.5	−40.5
SS 7mm Mauser	SP	175	+0.80	0	−5.5	−22.0	−52.0	−100.0
SS 7mm Mauser	PE	150	+0.60	0	−4.5	−15.5	−34.5	−67.0
				+2.5	0	−9.5	−26.0	−56.0
7.62mm Russian	HCP	145	+0.60	0	−3.5	−14.0	−40.5	−78.0
Super Speed 30 Win.	FP	170	+1.00	0	−7.5	−28.0		

APPENDIX

Cartridge	Bullet Type	Bullet Weight (gr)	50	100	200	300	400	500
Super Speed 30 Win.	SP	170	+1.00	0	− 7.5	−28.0		
Super Speed 30 Win.	HP	110	+0.70	0	− 6.0	−24.5		
Super Speed 30 Win.	HP	150	+0.90	0	− 6.5	−26.0		
30 Remington Auto	SP	170	+1.10	0	− 7.5	−29.5		
SS 300 Savage	PSP	150	+0.70	0	− 4.5	−17.5	−41.5	− 79.5
				+3.0	0	−11.0	−32.0	− 67.0
SS 300 Savage	SP	180	+0.90	0	− 7.5	−26.5	−58.0	−114.5
303 Savage	SP	190	+1.50	0	− 7.5	−35.0		
SS 303 British	SP	215	+1.00	0	− 7.0	−28.5	−69.5	−130.0
30 Army (30-40 Krag)	FP	220	+1.00	0	− 7.0	−27.0	−65.5	−127.5
30 Army (30-40 Krag)	SP	220	+1.00	0	− 7.0	−27.0	−65.5	−127.0
SS 30 Army Ptd. (30-40 Krag)	PE	150	+0.70	0	− 4.0	−17.5	−41.5	− 79.5
				+3.0	0	−10.0	−32.0	− 67.0
SS 30 Army Ptd. (30-40 Krag)	PE	180	+0.80	0	− 4.5	−19.5	−46.0	− 87.0
				+3.5	0	−11.5	−35.0	− 73.0
SS Army (30-40 Krag)	SP	180	+0.80	0	− 5.5	−22.5	−55.0	−108.0
				+3.5	0	−14.0	−42.5	− 92.5
SS 30-06 Govt.	PE	150	+0.50	0	− 3.5	−14.0	−33.0	− 63.0
				+2.5	0	− 9.0	−25.0	− 53.0
30-06 Govt.	FP	180	+0.60	0	− 4.5	−16.0	−43.5	− 78.5
				+3.0	0	− 9.0	−32.5	− 65.0
SS 30-06 Govt.	PE	180	+0.60	0	− 4.5	−16.5	−38.0	− 71.5
				+3.0	0	− 9.5	−28.0	− 59.0
SS 30-06 Govt.	SP	180	+0.70	0	− 4.5	−16.5	−44.5	− 88.5
				+3.0	0	− 9.5	−35.0	− 76.0
SS 30-06 Govt.	SP	220	+0.80	0	− 5.5	−22.0	−52.0	−102.5
				+3.5	0	−13.5	−36.5	− 87.0
30-06 Govt. Boattail Precision	FP	172	+0.60	0	− 4.5	−16.0	−38.0	− 73.0
				+3.0	0	− 9.5	−28.5	− 61.0
30-06 Govt. Wimbledon Cup	FP	180	+0.60	0	− 4.5	−16.5	−38.0	− 71.5
				+3.0	0	− 9.5	−28.0	− 59.0
300 H&H Mag. Match	FP	180	+0.50	0	− 3.5	−12.5	−29.0	− 55.0
				+2.0	0	− 7.5	−22.0	− 45.5
SS 300 H&H Magnum Boattail	HP	180	+0.55	0	− 4.5	−15.0	−38.0	− 76.0
				+2.5	0	− 9.5	−29.5	− 65.0
SS 300 H&H Magnum Boattail	SP	220	+0.70	0	− 4.5	−18.0	−44.5	− 86.0
				+3.0	0	−11.0	−34.5	− 73.0
8mm (7.9mm)	SP	236	+1.10	0	− 7.5	−29.0	−70.5	−136.5
SS 8mm Mauser BT	SP	170	+0.80	0	− 5.5	−23.0	−58.0	−116.0
32 Winchester	Lead	100	+3.10	0	−24.5	−98.0		
32 Winchester	FP	115	+3.10	0	−23.5	−90.5		
32 Winchester	SP	115	+3.10	0	−23.5	−90.5		
[1]SS 32 W.H.V.	SP	115	+2.20	0	−17.0	−67.5		
[1]SS 32 Win.	HP	80	+1.30	0	−13.5	−59.0		
SS 32 Win. Spl.	SP	170	+1.00	0	− 7.5	−28.5		
SS 32 Win. Spl.	HP	110	+0.80	0	− 5.5	−28.5		
32 Win. Self-Loading	SP	165	+2.60	0	−21.0	−74.0		
32 Remington Auto	SP	165	+1.00	0	− 7.5	−31.0		
32-40	SP	165	+2.60	0	−19.5	−66.0		
33 Winchester	SP	200	+1.10	0	− 8.0	−32.5		
SS 348 Win.	SP	150	+0.60	0	− 5.5	−21.5	−70.0	−143.0
				+3.0	0	−14.5	−58.0	−128.0

RANGE TABLE (continued)

Cartridge	Bullet Type	Bullet Weight (gr)	50	100	200	300	400	500
SS 348 Win.	SP	200	+0.80	0	− 6.5	−24.0	−73.0	−147.5
				+4.0	0	−16.0	−58.5	−129.5
35 Winchester	SP	250	+1.10	0	− 7.5	−29.0		
35 Win. Self-Loading	SP	180	+2.50	0	−22.0	−74.0		
35 Remington Auto	SP	200	+1.10	0	− 8.5	−32.0		
351 Win. Self-Loading	FP	180	+1.50	0	−12.5	−45.5		
351 Win. Self-Loading	SP	180	+1.50	0	−12.5	−45.5		
SS 375 H&H Magnum	SP	270	+0.70	0	− 4.5	−17.5	−41.5	− 82.5
				+3.0	0	−10.5	−32.0	− 70.5
SS 375 H&H Magnum	SP	300	+0.70	0	− 5.5	−21.0	−49.0	− 94.5
SS 300 H&H Magnum	PE	150	+0.50	0	− 3.0	−13.0	−29.0	− 57.0
				+2.0	0	− 8.0	−22.0	− 48.0
SS 300 H&H Magnum	PE	180	+0.50	0	− 4.5	−13.5	−32.0	− 59.5
				+2.5	0	− 8.0	−24.0	− 49.0
SS 300 H&H Magnum	HP, BT	180	+0.55	0	− 4.5	−15.0	−38.0	− 76.0
				+2.5	0	− 9.5	−29.5	− 65.0
SS 300 H&H Magnum	SP, BT	220	+0.70	0	− 4.5	−18.0	−44.5	− 86.0
				+3.0	0	−11.0	−34.5	− 73.0
38 Winchester	SP	180	+3.30	0	−26.0	−90.5		
[1]38 W.H.V.	SP	180	+1.70	0	−15.5	−61.0		
38-55	SP	255	+3.00	0	−22.0	−76.0		
38-56 Winchester	SP	255	+2.70	0	−17.5	−67.5		
38-72 Winchester	SP	275	+2.40	0	−15.5	−63.0		
40-65 Winchester	SP	260	+2.90	0	−19.5	−72.0		
40-82 Winchester	SP	260	+2.30	0	−18.0	−64.0		
401 Win. Self-Loading	SP	200	+1.20	0	− 9.5	−41.0		
405 Winchester	SP	300	+1.00	0	− 7.0	−31.0		
44 Winchester	SP	200	+3.30	0	−31.0	−91.0		
[1]44 W.H.V.	SP	200	+2.20	0	−19.5	−73.5		
45-70-405 Govt.	SP	405	+2.80	0	−21.0	−76.0		
45-90 Winchester	SP	300	+2.20	0	−18.5	−63.5		

SS = Super Speed   HP = Hollow-Point   PE = Pointed Expanding   BT = Boattail
SP = Soft-Point   FP = Full-Patch   HCP = Hollow Copper Point   [1]Not adapted to pistols or revolvers or to Winchester Model 73 rifle.

TABLE A.6
BALLISTICS OF RECENTLY DISCONTINUED RIFLE AMMUNITION

Cartridge	Bullet Weight (gr)	VELOCITY (FPS) AT:				ENERGY (FT/LBS) AT:			
		muzzle	100 yds	200 yds	300 yds	20 yds	100 yds	200 yds	300 yds
5mm Rem RF Mag	38	2105	1609	1229	—	374	218	127	—
22 Savage	70	2760	2404	2076	1775	1184	898	670	490
6mm Rem	90	3190	2886	2558	2273	2033	1638	1307	1032
256 Win	60	2760	2097	1542	1148	1015	586	317	176
250 Savage	87	3030	2673	2342	2036	1773	1380	1059	801
257 Roberts	87	3170	2802	2462	2147	1941	1516	1171	890
6.5×54 Mann. Schoen.	160	2010	1803	1611	1439	1435	1155	922	736
6.5 Rem Mag	100	3390	2998	2639	2308	2551	1995	1546	1183
264 Win Mag	100	3320	2926	2565	2231	2447	1901	1461	1105
30-40 Krag	220	2160	1956	1765	1587	2279	1869	1522	1230
308 Win	110	3180	2666	2206	1795	2470	1736	1188	787
308 Win	200	2450	2208	1980	1767	2665	2165	1741	1386
30-06 Spfd	110	3380	2843	2365	1936	2791	1974	1356	915
300 H&H Mag	150	3130	2822	2534	2264	3262	2652	2188	1707
32 Rem	170	2140	1785	1475	1228	1728	1203	821	569
32-20 Win	115	1490	1226	1054	951	567	384	284	231
32-40 Win	170	1530	1325	1164	1052	883	663	551	418
338 Win Mag	300	2430	2152	1893	1655	3933	3084	2387	1824
350 Rem Mag	250	2400	2180	1971	1776	3197	2638	2156	1751
358 Win	250	2230	1988	1762	1557	2760	2194	1723	1346

Glossary

Many of the terms defined in this glossary appear in the preceding text. Many others are used nowhere in this book, but they should be clearly understood by anyone interested in ammunition and ballistics in fact, by every shooter. They are terms commonly used in connection with ammunition, ballistics, firearms, military and police ordnance, and sport shooting. They are presented here not only to clarify any details in the text that may require explanation for some readers, but as a general service to shooters.

Ambient Temperature Prevailing temperature at a test range or facility, preferably between 65° and 70°F.

Angle of Departure Angle transcribed by the center line of the bore and a horizontal line at the instant a projectile leaves the muzzle of a firearm.

Angle of Elevation Angle formed between the line of sight to the target and the axis of the barrel bore.

Annulus Ringlike space between the top of a primer and the case, created by the bevel of the primer pocket.

Anvil Portion of the primer which rests against the bottom of the primer pocket and against which the primer pellet is crushed when a firing pin strikes. Anvils are most often strips of two- or three-legged construction.

Backthrust Force that squeezes a cartridge case rearward in a chamber. In revolvers, when the case is forced rearward, the rear section of the case will sometimes expand into the gap between cylinder and standing breech, and will impede the turning of the cylinder.

Ball Ammunition Military small-arms ammunition with full-metal-jacket bullets. Sometimes called "hard ball."

Balled Shot Shot pellets which fuse into a cluster of two or more as a result of forces encountered during passage through the forcing cone, bore, and choke.

Ballistic Coefficient Ratio of a projectile's sectional density to its coefficient of form. It is an index of the rate at which the projectile decelerates in flight due to resistance and drag of the atmosphere. A low ballistic coefficient (such as .220) indicates a quick loss of velocity while a high ballistic coefficient (such as .468) indicates better velocity retention.

Ballistics Science of projectiles in motion, generally divided into categories: interior ballistics, dealing with motion and forces while the projectile is still in the chamber or barrel of a firearm; exterior ballistics, dealing with the projectile's flight through the atmosphere; and terminal ballistics, dealing with the projectile's characteristics and performance at impact.

Barrel Corrosion Barrel damage caused by chemicals or oxidation (rusting). At one time, corrosive primers caused such damage, but modern primers are non-corrosive.

Barrel Erosion Wearing, or physical deterioration, of the bore or throat of a barrel as a result of hot propellant gases and projectile friction.

Barrel Life Usually expressed as the number of rounds that can be fired through a barrel before it is so eroded as to cause a loss in accuracy. Barrel life generally may be about 5,000 rounds, depending on caliber, whether the barrel is fired while excessively hot, and the bearing surface of the bullet.

Barrel Time (Ignition Barrel Time) Elapsed time from ignition of the primer to the exit of the projectile(s) from the barrel, measured in micro-seconds.

Barrel Vibration Oscillations of a barrel which occur as a result of firing.

Barrel Walk Change in the point of impact, due to internal stress(es), as a barrel heats from repeated firings.

Barrel Whip Somewhat circular movement of a barrel's muzzle end as the projectile leaves. Some authorities believe barrel whip is greatest with high velocities, long bullets, or rapid twist rates.

Battery Cup Flanged metallic cup in a shotshell primer assembly that provides rigid support for the primer cup and anvil.

BB Air-rifle projectile of .177-inch diameter or a shotgun pellet of .18-inch diameter. A misnomer for a shotgun pellet in general.

BBB Shot Shotgun pellet of .19-inch diameter.

Belted Case Cartridge case with an enlarged section that encircles the head, directly in front of the extractor groove. Such cases use the front edge of the belt to headspace the cartridge in the chamber.

Big Bore In this country, any firearm or cartridge of .30 caliber or larger.

Blow Back Leakage of gas rearward between the case and chamber wall, originating at the mouth of the case. *Blowback operation* refers to a semiautomatic cycling system in which the barrel does not move and locking is accomplished by inertia. Today's rimfire autoloading rifles and pistols, and some low-powered centerfire handguns, are blowback-operated.

Boattail The tapered portion at the rear of a bullet that reduces the bearing surface down to a smaller diameter than the flat base. This tapering end streamlines airflow at subsonic velocities (below approximately 1,080 fps). It has no notable beneficial exterior ballistic effect when velocity is above the speed of sound.

Body Portion of a metallic cartridge case that contains the propellant. In shotshells it is the tubular section that contains the propellant, wad, and shot.

Bottleneck Tapered shoulder of a case from the body to the neck, giving the cartridge a bottle shape.

Brisance Shattering power of high explosives or the ignition feature of a primer.

Buckshot Lead pellets ranging in size from .20-inch to .36-inch diameter. A misnomer sometimes applied to any shotgun pellet.

Bullet Creep Movement of a bullet out of the cartridge case while in the cylinder or chamber, due to recoil of the gun and the inertia of the bullet. Sometimes called bullet starting or popping.

Cannelure Grooved section around the circumference of a bullet to allow crimping the case to the bullet.

Cap Obsolete term referring to a primer. Properly used in reference to a percussion cap.

Case Capacity Amount or weight of a particular type of powder that can be placed in a cartridge case with the bullet fully seated, without compressing the powder charge.

Case Life Number of times a case can be reloaded and fired before it needs to be discarded.

Chilled Shot Shot pellets containing at least 0.5% of antimony to harden the alloy. Also called hard shot.

Chronograph Instrument to measure elapsed time and to convert that time to feet per second. With some chronographs, tables must be used to convert the measured period to feet per second.

Coefficient of Form Numerical term indicating the general profile of a projectile.

Cook-Off Firing of a cartridge caused by overheating in a hot firearm chamber. Usually associated with machine guns.

Crimp Rolling of a metallic cartridge-case mouth into a bullet's cannelure to prevent bullet creep or keep the bullet from being forced deeper into the case when it impacts against receiver surfaces during the feeding cycle. Also the section of a shotshell that closes the mouth of the case.

Cycle Time Time elapsed from the beginning to end of a specific function. The cycle time in a semiautomatic is the time elapsed from pulling the trigger until a freshly chambered round is ready for another firing.

Delayed Fire Any abnormal delay in ignition or discharge of a cartridge. This implies that firing does eventually occur.

Dispersion Greatest horizontal or vertical distance between any two bullet holes on a target, normally measured center to center.

Double-Base Powder Propellant composed of colloided nitrocellulose and nitroglycerin as its base, as opposed to a single-base powder which employs only colloided nitrocellulose as base material.

Doubling Unintentional firing of a second shot, as when a malfunction causes both barrels of a double-barreled shotgun to fire on a single trigger pull.

Drop Shot Shotshell pellets containing less than 0.5% antimony. Also called soft shot.

Duplex Load Shotshell containing pellets of two different sizes or a metallic cartridge containing two or more projectiles. At one time, this term referred to experimental use of two propellants in a case.

Dust Shotgun pellets smaller than No. 11; therefore, shot of 0.04-inch or smaller diameter.

Effective Range Maximum distance at which a projectile can be expected to be lethal.

F Shot Shotgun pellet of 0.22-inch diameter.

Five-in-One Blank Blank cartridge that was designed for use in firearms of three different calibers: 38-40, 44-40, and 45 Colt. The Five-in-One designation was most likely a promotional device based on 38-40 and 44-40 applications in rifles and handguns.

Flash Hole Hole pierced or drilled through the center of the primer pocket in a metallic cartridge case. Also the hole in the end of a battery-cup primer in shotshells.

Flash Inhibitor Material added to a propellant for the purpose of reducing muzzle flash.

Folded Crimp Closure of a shotshell by folds of the case mouth into pie-wedge segments to hold the shot in place.

Fouling Accumulation of bullet-jacket metal in a firearm bore. Such deposits reduce accuracy. Sometimes also applied to lead accumulation. (See *Leading*.)

Full Metal Jacket (FMJ) Bullet whose jacket completely encloses the nose and whose base usually has some lead exposed.

Fusing Balling of lead shot due to a gas leakage. Also the melting of a jacketed bullet's core, or the melting of a lead-alloy bullet.

Gas Check Cup, made of jacket-type material, affixed to the base of a lead bullet.

Gauge Term used to identify the diameter of a shotgun bore, related to the number of bore-diameter lead balls needed to weigh one pound.

Grain Unit of weight (avoirdupois): 7,000 grains per pound.

Group Measurement Determination of the center-to-center distance between the two bullet holes farthest apart on a target. This distance is also called the group extreme spread.

Hardball Slang term for full-metal-jacketed bullets, most often applied to 45 ACP ammunition.

Head End of the cartridge case at which the primer is inserted.

Heel Rear portion of a bullet.

Heel Cavity Recess in the base of a bullet.

Hull Slang term for a cartridge or shotshell case.

High Velocity Level of velocity exceeding the standard level for a specific type of cartridge. Sometimes used to designate any cartridge with a velocity greater than 2,000 fps.

Hyper Velocity Level of velocity for 22 rimfire ammunition that exceeds the range of velocities employed for high velocity cartridges.

Jacket Envelope enclosing the lead core of a compound bullet.

Keyhole Oblong or oval hole in a target, produced by an unstable bullet striking the target at an angle to the bullet's longitudinal axis. (See *Yaw*.)

Leading Accumulation of lead in the bore of a firearm from the passage of lead shot or bullets.

Loading Density Amount of space available taken up by a propellant charge in a cartridge case with the bullet seated. A 98% density indicates that there is still room, equal to 2% of the potential volume, for more powder. A 101% density would indicate a compressed powder charge.

Lot Number Number applied to a homogeneous group of ammunition (or component) produced at one time with identical raw materials or components.

Match-Grade Ammunition Ammunition loaded with special care to achieve a high level of accuracy.

Metal Fouling See *Fouling*.

Midrange Load Reduced-velocity centerfire cartridge used principally for target shooting.

Midrange Trajectory Trajectory at halfway point in the flight of a bullet toward a target at a specified distance—that is, at half the distance from the firearm to the target.

Minute of Angle (m.o.a.) Angular measurement to describe accuracy. One minute of angle is $1/60$-degree and subtends 1.047-inch at 100 yards—which, for the purpose of shooting, is rounded to 1 inch. A minute-of-angle group, therefore, subtends ½-inch at 50 yards, 1-inch at 100 yards, 2 inches at 200 yards, and so on.

Misfire Failure of the priming pellet to ignite after the primer receives an adequate blow from the firing pin; or failure of the primer to ignite the propellant.

Mushroom Expansion of a bullet to a larger diameter.

Muzzle Blast Noise occurring at the muzzle of a firearm as a projectile and hot gases are released from the barrel.

Neck Portion of a cartridge case that holds the bullet in place. On a bottlenecked case, that portion lying forward of the shoulder.

Necked Down Reduced in diameter at the neck—describing a cartridge case formed by squeezing down the neck to a smaller caliber (for example, from 308 to 243).

Necked Up Enlarged in diameter at the neck—describing a cartridge case formed by expanding the neck to a larger caliber (for example, from 308 to 358).

Non-corrosive Containing no chemicals that will cause corrosion (rusting) of the bore. All primers were at one time corrosive, but today's primers are non-corrosive.

Ogive Curved section of a bullet that forms the nose profile and begins at the forward end of the bearing surface.

Overbore Capacity Powder-charge capacity of a cartridge that holds more powder than can normally be burned efficiently in that bore diameter and volume.

Paramilitary Having military characteristics or style—said of cartridges that are of military style (full-metal-cased bullet) and are often sold at prices well below that of commercial soft-point ammunition.

Parent Cartridge Original cartridge from which, through some modification, a new cartridge was formed. For example, the 308 is the parent cartridge of the 243 (a necked-down 308) and the 358 Winchester (a necked-up 308) cartridges.

Pattern Distribution of shot fired from a shotgun, generally measured as a percentage of pellets striking within a 30-inch circle at 40 yards.

Pellet Small spherical projectile (shot) loaded in shotshells.

Percussion Cap Explosive caplike priming unit used with a percussion muzzleloading firearm. When struck by the hammer, the primer in the percussion cap explodes and ignites the black powder in the barrel.

Pie Crimp Six- or eight-segment folded crimp used to close the mouth of a shotshell.

Plinking Informal shooting at inanimate objects located at arbitrary or indefinite distances from the firing point.

Plus P (+P) Higher than normal pressure—describing a standard cartridge that has been loaded to generate higher than normal pressures at firing in order to increase ballistic performance. Ammunition so stamped should never be used in any firearm that has not been designated suitable for Plus P ammunition.

Plus P Plus (+P+) Extra-high pressure—a designation for ammunition that generates even higher pressures than Plus P ammunition, making it unsuitable for most firearms. Generally not sold to civilians, such cartridges are intended for special-purpose police use.

Point of Aim Point on which the shooter aligns the firearm's sights.

GLOSSARY

Point of Impact Point at which a bullet strikes a target.

Powder Propellant in a cartridge or shotshell.

Powder-Burning Rate Speed at which a propellant burns. It is determined by both physical and chemical characteristics.

Powder Deterioration Chemical decomposition of smokeless propellants, usually occurring with improper storage conditions over a long period of time.

Powder Fouling Powder residue left in a firearm after firing.

Pressure Force developed in the cartridge (and in the gun) by the expanding gases generated by the combustion of the propellant.

Pressure Barrel Barrel used to measure firing pressures. Such barrels may be set up to use copper or lead crushers for such measurement, or they may employ electronic strain gauges to measure pressure in true pounds per square inch. Barrels using copper or lead crushers produce recordings which are termed c.u.p. (copper units of pressure) or l.u.p. (lead units of pressure).

Pressure Curve Graph of the relationship of chamber pressure to time of bullet travel in a firearm when a cartridge or shell is fired.

Primer Dust Minuscule bits of priming material. Primers may "dust" when handled or agitated. That is, they may leave behind minute particles of priming compound. Accumulations of primer dust are explosive and can be hazardous.

Primer Pocket Portion of a cartridge case into which the primer is seated.

Projectile Rotation Spinning motion imparted to a projectile by engagement with the rifling in a firearm's barrel. The rate of rotation depends on the rifling's rate of twist and the velocity. The barrel twist (left or right) determines the clockwise or counterclockwise direction of the rotation.

Proof Load Shell loaded to elevated pressures to test a firearm's strength and integrity after the manufacture of the firearm. Such a cartridge (sometimes called definitive proof) should never be used except for this initial test, and then only when the firearm is adequately shielded to prevent property or physical injury.

Propellant Powder used in a cartridge case to propel a projectile.

Reduced Velocity Any velocity below the speed normally produced by a specific cartridge and bullet weight.

Reference Ammunition Carefully loaded, assembled, and controlled ammunition designed and tested to produce a specific velocity and pressure, used to calibrate ballistic laboratory instrumentation.

Residual Pressure Pressure level that remains in the cartridge case or the shell within the firearm's chamber and in the bore, after the projectile leaves the muzzle of the firearm.

Rifled Slug Shotgun projectile with "rifling" grooves swaged into its bearing surface, usually employed for hunting deer or other medium game with a smoothbore.

Rimless Case Case whose rear end has the same basic diameter as the case head (area directly forward of the extractor groove), inclusive of any body taper.

Rimmed Case Case whose rear end is notably enlarged over the diameter of the case head to form a rim. This enlarged area serves as a control for headspace dimension and affords a purchase area—in effect, a flange—for the firearm's extractor.

Rolled Crimp Shotshell crimp formed by placing a thin wad over the shot and then turning over the edge of the case to hold this wad in place. This is an obsolete form of crimp, used today in a modified form for loading some rifled-slug ammunition and for a few specialized target loads.

Round Complete metallic cartridge or (less frequently) shotshell.

Sabot-Type Projectile Sub-caliber projectile centered in a lightweight carrier (sabot) to permit firing it in a larger-caliber firearm.

Sectional Density Ratio of a bullet's weight to its diameter, calculated by the following formula:

$$\text{Section Density} = \frac{\text{Weight of bullet in pounds}}{\text{Diameter of bullet in inches}}$$

Semi-Rimmed Case Cartridge case having the rim area slightly enlarged. This rim is not used for headspace control (as with a rimmed cartridge) but does enhance extractor purchase on the case.

Semi-Wadcutter Handgun bullet designed by the late Elmer Keith, which has an elongated, flat-tipped nose and a sharp (not rounded) shoulder at the front of the bearing surface.

Shocking Power Colloquial term describing (but not specifying in terms of measurement) a bullet's ability to incapacitate a quarry.

Shoulder Portion of a case that angles away from the body to the neck. Also the portion of a bullet such as a semi-wadcutter that angles inward from the bearing surface to the nose.

Shot Buffering Granulated polyethylene used to cushion pellets and improve pattern density and uniformity.

Small-Arms Ammunition In the U.S., ammunition of any caliber smaller than 1 inch in diameter.

Small Bore In the U.S., most often a term for 22 rimfire; less often, any caliber smaller than 0.308-inch in diameter.

Soft Shot Shotgun pellets containing an antimony content of 0.5% or less.

Spitzer Sharp-pointed bullet, or the nose of such a bullet.

Squib Load that produces sub-standard velocity.

Standard Velocity Velocity level common to a specific cartridge (but exceeded in high-velocity loadings of the same cartridge).

Star Crimp Fold crimp of six or eight segments used to close a shotshell case; also called folded or pie crimp.

Steel Shot Shot formed of metal alloy not exceeding 90 Diamond Pyramid Hardness, designed as a non-toxic substitute for lead shot.

Straight Case Cartridge case having no shoulder section or taper.

Suppressed Temperature Artificially reduced temperature, used for ammunition testing.

Swage Method of forming lead bullets under pressure from short pieces of lead wire.

T Shot Steel-shot size used to indicate a diameter of 0.20-inch.

Trajectory Path of a bullet's (or shot string's) flight, which forms a curve rising above the line of sight (because of the slightly upward-tilting barrel—the angle of elevation between the bore axis and line of sight) and then dropping below the line of sight (because of gravity's constant pull, exerted from the instant of projectile emergence to impact).

Twist, or Twist Rate Distance for one complete turn of a barrel's rifling, usually expressed as a ratio of one turn—for example, 1 in 10 inches.

Varmint Bullet Bullet designed for high frangibility to ensure rapid expansion or disintegration on striking the quarry. This characteristic also minimizes the chance of ricochets when the bullet impacts the earth, as in the case of a miss.

Wadcutter Flat-nosed handgun bullet designed for high accuracy and the ability to cut clean, easy-to-score holes in a paper target.

Web Solid portion of a centerfire cartridge case between the inside of the case, at the head end, and the bottom of the primer pocket; also the smallest dimension of a smokeless-powder granule.

Wildcat Cartridge designed by other than an ammunition factory and not produced as standard, commercially available ammunition.

Yaw Angle between the longitudinal axis of a projectile and a line tangent to the trajectory at the center of the projectile. In layman's terms, the tilt of a projectile that is not flying straight but is wobbling.

Index

Accuracy
   handguns, 30
   lead shooting adjustment, 248–250
   muzzle blast and, 61
   recoil and, 51
   rimfire ammunition, generally, 26–30
   22 Long cartridge, 22
   22 Long Rifle cartridge, 22
   22 Short cartridge, 21
   22 Winchester Magnum rimfire, 24

Ballistic coefficient, 117
Ballistics
   cartridge similarities, 5
   centerfire handgun-cartridge, 187–195
   centerfire rifle-cartridge, 115–246
   dram-equivalent rating system, 211–217
   historical tables of, 277–287
   rimfire, 36–50
   shotshell, 226–237
   spitzer/round-nose bullets compared, 3–4, 6–8
   steel shot, 251–254
   See also Centerfire handgun-cartridge ballistics; Centerfire rifle-cartridge ballistics; Rimfire ballistics; Shotshell ballistics
Barrel length
   centerfire rifle-cartridge ballistics, 115–118, 133–134
   rimfire ballistics, 48–50
   shotshell ballistics, 226, 232
   velocity and, 10–12
BB cap designation, 17
Benchrest shooting, 149
Big game, 155–156. *See also* Dangerous game; Game considerations; Optimum Game Weights
Bottleneck cartridge case, 64
Bowman, Les, 13
Browning semiauto rifle, 20
Buckshot, 235
Bullet(s)
   centerfire handgun cartridges, 173–175
   centerfire rifle cartridges, 66, 117
   dangerous game, 156–157
   game considerations, 135–142
   handgun cartridge reloading, 202, 205, 207
   rifle cartridge reloading, 160, 165–166
   spitzer/round-nose bullet compared, 3–4, 6–8, 117
   22 Long Rifle cartridge, 22
Bullet expansion, 188–190
Bullet momentum calculation, 142

Centerfire handgun cartridge(s), 171–186
   bullet styles, 173–175
   historical development of, 171–172
   interchangeability of, 267, 268

7mm, 176
22 caliber, 175
25 caliber, 176
30 caliber, 176–177
32 caliber, 177–179
38 caliber, 179–183
41 caliber, 183
44 caliber, 183–184
45 caliber, 184–186
Centerfire handgun-cartridge ballistics, 187–195
  bullet expansion, 188–190
  conditions in, 188
  maximum horizontal distance table, 193
  Optimum Game Weight, 190, 194–195
  table of, 191–192
  variability, 187
Centerfire handgun-cartridge selection, 196–201
  7mm BR, 197
  9mm Luger, 198–199
  32 H&R Magnum, 197
  38 Special and 38 Special +P, 199–200
  41 Magnum, 200–201
  44 Remington Magnum, 201
  45 Automatic (45 ACP), 201
  221 Remington Fireball, 196–197
  357 Magnum, 200
  380 Automatic, 198
Centerfire rifle cartridge(s), 63–114
  availability, 70
  bullet/game selection, 67–69
  handgun use, 187–188
  historical development of, 63–64
  interchangeability, 266, 267, 268–269
  primer, 64–66
  17 caliber, 70
  shapes of, 64
  22 caliber, 71–77
    22 Hornet, 71–72
    22 PPC, 73–74
    22-250 Remington, 77
    218 Bee, 72
    220 Swift, 77
    221 Fireball, 72
    222 Remington, 72–73
    222 Remington Magnum, 75–76
    223 Remington, 75
    224 Weatherby Magnum, 76–77
  24 caliber, 78–80
    6mm PPC, 78–79
    6mm Remington, 80
    240 Weatherby Magnum, 80
    243 Winchester, 79–80
  25 caliber, 81–83
    25-06 Remington, 82
    25-20 Winchester, 81
    25-35 Winchester, 81
    250 Savage, 81
    257 Roberts, 82
    257 Weatherby Magnum, 83
  26 caliber, 83–84
    6.5 Remington Magnum, 83
    264 Winchester Magnum, 83–84
  27 caliber, 84–86
    270 Weatherby Magnum, 85–86
    270 Winchester, 84–85
  28 caliber, 86–89
    7mm BR, 86
    7mm Mauser, 86–87
    7mm Remington Magnum, 88–89
    7mm Weatherby Magnum, 89
    7mm-08 Remington, 87
    7x30 Waters, 87
    280 Remington, 88
    284 Winchester, 87–88
  30 caliber, 89–95
    30 Carbine, 89
    30 Remington, 90
    30-06 Springfield, 93
    30-30 Winchester, 90–91
    30-40 Krag, 91
    300 H&H Magnum, 94
    300 Savage, 91
    300 Weatherby Magnum, 95
    300 Winchester Magnum, 94
    303 Savage, 89–90
    307 Winchester, 92
    308 Winchester, 92–93
  31 caliber, 95–96
    32-20 Winchester, 95
    303 British, 95–96
  32 caliber, 96–97
    8mm Mauser, 96
    8mm Remington Magnum, 97
    32 Winchester Special, 96
  33 caliber, 97–98
    338 A-Square, 98
    338 Winchester Magnum, 97
    340 Weatherby Magnum, 98
  34 caliber, 99
  35 caliber, 99–101
    35 Remington, 100
    35 Whelen, 101
    350 Remington Magnum, 101
    351 Winchester Self-Loading, 99

INDEX

356 Winchester, 100
357 Magnum, 99–100
358 Winchester, 101
36 caliber, 102
37 caliber, 102–104
    38-55 Winchester, 102
    375 H&H Magnum, 102–103
    375 Weatherby Magnum, 103
    375 Winchester, 102
    378 Weatherby Magnum, 104
40 caliber, 104–105
    38-40 Winchester, 104
    450/400-3″, 105
41 caliber, 105–106
    416 Hoffman, 105
    416 Rigby, 106
42 caliber, 106–107
44 caliber, 107–108
    44 Remington Magnum, 107
    44-40 Winchester, 107
    444 Marlin, 108
45 caliber, 108–112
    45-70 Government, 108
    450 Ackley Magnum, 110
    450 Nitro Express—3¼, 109
    450 #2, 110
    458 Winchester Magnum, 109
    460 Long A-Square/460 Weatherby Magnum, 111–112
    460 Short A-Square, 110–111
46 caliber, 112
47 caliber, 112
50 caliber, 112
51 caliber, 113–114
    495 A-Square, 113
    500 A-Square, 113–114
    500 Nitro Express—3″, 113
57 caliber, 114
Centerfire rifle-cartridge ballistics, 115–146
  actual velocities, 144–145
  ammunition lot and, 143
  barrel length and, 115–118, 133–134
  bullet momentum, 142
  hold-under calculations, 133–134
  maximum range, 130–133
  Optimum Game Weight, 122–126, 134–142
  tables of, 118–122
  variability in, 115
  wind drift and uphill/downhill hold, 126–130
Centerfire rifle-cartridge selection, 147–158
  benchrest shooting, 149
  considerations in, 147

  dangerous game, 156–158
  deer-sized game, 151–154
  heavy big game, 155–156
  medium game, 154–155
  plinking, 149–150
  recommendations, 158
  target shooting, 148
  varmint hunting, 150–151
Choke, 246, 247
Chronograph, 43
Civil War (U.S.), 15
Crimping, 259–261

Daisy caseless cartridge, 63
Dangerous game, 156–158
Dead Tough, 98
Deer-sized game, 151–154
Down-/uphill angle. *See* Up-/downhill angle
Dram equivalent rating system, 211–217

8mm Mauser, 96
8mm Remington Magnum, 97
Extra-hard shot, 223–224

Firing pin pattern, 31
5mm rifle, 18–19
Folbert BB Cap, 15
40 caliber centerfire rifle cartridges, 104–105
41 caliber centerfire handgun cartridges, 183
41 caliber centerfire rifle cartridges, 105–106
41 Magnum, 200–201
41 Remington Magnum, 183
41 Short Remington derringer ammunition, 25
41 Swiss Rimfire, 16–17
42 caliber centerfire rifle cartridges, 106–107
44 caliber centerfire handgun cartridges, 183–184
44 caliber centerfire rifle cartridges, 107–108
44 Remington Magnum
  described, 107, 184
  selection of, 201
44 Smith & Wesson Special, 183
44-40 Winchester, 107
45 Auto cartridge, 62
45 Automatic (45 ACP)
  described, 184–185
  selection of, 201
45 Auto Rim, 185
45 caliber centerfire handgun cartridges, 184–186
45 caliber centerfire rifle cartridges, 108–112
45 Colt cartridge, 171, 185
45 Winchester Magnum, 185–186
45-70 Government, 108

46 caliber centerfire rifle cartridges, 112
47 caliber centerfire rifle cartridges, 112
50 caliber centerfire rifle cartridges, 112
51 caliber centerfire rifle cartridges, 113–114
57 caliber centerfire rifle cartridges, 114
404 Jeffrey, 106–107
410 bore 2½", 242
410 bore 3", 242
416 Hoffman
  dangerous game and, 156
  described, 105
416 Rigby
  dangerous game, 156
  described, 106
444 Marlin, 108
450 Ackley Magnum, 110
450 Nitro Express—3¼, 109
450 #2 cartridge, 110
450/400—3" cartridge, 105
458 Winchester Magnum
  dangerous game and, 156–157
  described, 109
460 Long A-Square
  dangerous game and, 157–158
  described, 111–112
460 Short A-Square
  dangerous game and, 157–158
  described, 110–111
460 Weatherby Magnum
  dangerous game and, 157–158
  described, 111–112
470 Nitro Express, 112
495 A-Square
  dangerous game and, 157–158
  described, 113
500 A-Square
  dangerous game and, 157–158
  described, 113–114
500/465 Nitro Express, 112
505 Gibbs, 112
577 Nitro Express, 114
Full-metal-jacket bullet(s), 174–175

Game considerations
  big game, 155–156
  bullets, 66, 67–69
  cartridge selection, 14
  centerfire handgun ballistics, 188–189
  dangerous game, 156–158
  deer-sized game, 151–154
  lead shot, 218, 219, 220
  medium game, 154–155
  steel shot, 245, 246, 251
  22 Long Rifle cartridge, 22–23, 24
  22 Winchester Magnum rimfire, 25
  varmint hunting, 150–151
  See also Optimum Game Weights
Gyro-Jet cartridge, 63

Handgun(s)
  accuracy, 30
  barrel length variations, 49–50
  range and, 24
  recoil and, 61–62
  rimfire ballistics, 39, 43, 45–46, 49–50
Handgun cartridge(s). *See* Centerfire handgun cartridges
Handgun-cartridge reloading, 202–207
Hard shot, 223
Hearing protection, 275
Henry rifle, 15–16
Historical ballistics, 277–287
Hold-under calculations
  centerfire ammunition, 133–134
  rimfire ammunition, 40–42
Hollow-point ammunition, 43, 173
Hornady bullets, 67–68
Hypervelocity ammunition
  accuracy, 26–27
  Long Rifle cartridge, 23, 43

Interchangeability, 265–269
  centerfire rifle cartridges, 266, 267, 268–269
  cost considerations, 265
  shotshells, 266, 269

Jacketed bullets, 66
Jacketed hollow-point bullets, 174
Jacketed soft-point bullets, 174

Kimber rifle, 29
Kinetic energy, 5–6

Lead shooting adjustment, 248–250
Lead shot
  ballistics tables, 228–229, 230
  designations of, 218
  game considerations, 218, 219, 220
  pattern density/pellet size, 218, 221
  pattern determination, 225
  range, 221–222
  selection of, 224–225
  size/weight/count relationships, 222–223
  steel shot compared, 246, 247–249, 251

INDEX

types of, 222–224
See also Steel shot
Leupold scope, 29
Lever-action rifle, 27
Load selection, 243–244
Long rifle, 20–21
Lots (ammunition), 143

Magnum terminology, 12–14
Medium game, 154–155
Mossberg rifle, 29
Muzzle blast, 61

NATO cartridge, 92
9mm Luger
  described, 180
  selection of, 198–199
Non-expanding jacketed soft-point bullets, 175
Nosler Partition bullet, 66

Oehler Research Model 33 chronograph, 43
150-grain .308″ spitzer-bullet performance, 5, 6–7
150-grain 30-06 Springfield, 9, 10
Optimum Game Weight (OGW), 14
  calculation of, 139–140
  centerfire handgun ballistics, 190, 194–195
  centerfire rifle-cartridge ballistics, 115, 122–126, 140–142
  See also Game considerations

Palmisano, Lou, 78
Pattern density
  determination of, 225
  pellet size and, 218, 221
  steel shot, 246–247
Pellet size, 227
Pindell, Ferris, 78
Pinfire cartridges, 18
Plated lead shot, 224
Plinking, 149–150
Powder
  handgun cartridge reloading, 203, 205
  rifle-cartridge reloading, 160–161, 165
  shotshell reloading, 258
Pressure, 16
Primer
  centerfire rifle cartridge, 64–66
  handgun cartridge reloading, 203, 204–205
  rifle-cartridge reloading, 161–162, 165
  rimfire cartridge, 16
  safety precautions, 275
  shotshell reloading, 257

storage and handling, 271
Pump-action rifle, 27

Range
  accuracy and, 29, 30
  cartridge selection and, 5
  centerfire rifle-cartridge ballistics, 130–133
  lead shot, 221–222
  shotshell ballistics, 231
  shotshell/load selection, 244
  steel shot, 251
  22 Long Rifle cartridge, 24
Recoil, 51–62
  calculations for, 53–57
  firearm design and, 51–52
  firearm selection and, 51
  gun weight and, 60, 61
  semiautomatics, 52–53
  tables of, 58–60
Recoil pad, 52
Reloading
  handgun cartridges, 202–207
  rifle cartridges, 159–167
  shotshells, 255–261
Remington Core-Lokt bullet, 66
Remington 5mm cartridge, 18–19
Revolver
  centerfire handgun ballistics, 187
  rimfire ballistics, 43, 45–46
  See also entries under Handgun
Rifle
  accuracy and, 27
  recoil and, 61
Rifle cartridge. *See* Centerfire rifle cartridge(s); Rimfire ammunition (rifle)
Rifle cartridge reloading, 159–167
  advantages of, 159
  bullets, 160, 165–166
  cases, 162, 163–164
  operations in, 162–166
  powder, 160–161, 165
  primers, 161–162, 165
  safety precautions, 167
  See also Handgun cartridge reloading; Shotshell reloading
Rifled slugs, 235
Rimfire ammunition (rifle), 15–35
  accuracy, 26–30
  construction of, 16
  diagram illustrating, 16
  history of, 15–19
  interchangeability of, 267, 269

obsolete cartridges, 25–26
problems with, 31–35
22 Long, 21–22
22 Long Rifle, 22–24
22 Short, 19–21
22 Winchester Magnum, 24–25
Rimfire ballistics, 36–50
abbreviations used in, 37
barrel length and, 48–50
common sense precautions, 36
handgun ballistics, 39, 43, 45–46, 49–50
hold-under calculations, 40–42
revolver, 43, 45–46
rifle ballistics, 38, 39
trajectory, 47
up/downhill angle, 37, 40
variability in, 36–37, 42–43, 50
wind-drift and, 37
Round-nose bullet
centerfire handgun cartridges, 172
spitzer bullet compared, 3–4, 6–8, 117

Safety glasses, 275
Safety precautions, 274–276
shotshell interchangeability, 266, 268–269
storage and handling, 270–273
Semiautomatic rifle, 27
Semiautomatic shotgun, 52–53
Semi-wadcutter lead bullet, 172–173
7x30 Waters, 87
7mm BR
described, 86, 176
selection of, 197
7mm Mauser, 86–87
7mm Remington Express, 4
7mm Remington Magnum, 12
described, 88–89
medium game selection, 154
7mm Weatherby Magnum, 89
7mm-08 Remington
deer-sized game, 152–153
described, 87
target shooting, 148
17 caliber centerfire rifle cartridges, 70
Shotshell(s)
dram equivalent rating system, 211–217
interchangeability, 266, 269
lead shot, 218–225 (*See also* Lead shot)
nomenclature confusion, 13
Shotshell ballistics, 226–237
barrel length, 226
buckshot, 235

lead shot, 230
range, 231
rifled slugs, 235
shotgun and, 236–237
slugs, 231, 236
tables of, 228–229
time of flight/trajectory, 233–234
trajectory, 230–231
variability in, 226
velocity/barrel length table, 232
Shotshell gauge/load selection, 238–244
claims in, 238–239
load selection, 243–244
range and, 244
10-gauge 3½" magnum, 239
12 gauge 2¾", 240
12-gauge 3" magnum, 239–240
16-gauge 2¾", 240–241
20-gauge 2¾", 241
20-gauge 3" magnum, 241
28-gauge 2¾", 242
410 bore 2½", 242
410 bore 3", 242
Shotshell reloading, 255–261
advantages of, 255
cost savings, 255, 256
equipment requirements, 255–257
steps in, 257–261
See also Handgun cartridge reloading; Rifle cartridge reloading
Shot size, 227
Sighting-in
ammunition lot performance, 143
recoil and, 62
6mm PPC
benchrest shooting selection, 149
described, 78–79
6mm Remington, 80
6.5 Remington Magnum, 83
16-gauge 2¾", 240–241
Slugs
actual performance table for, 236
shotshell ballistics, 231
Smith & Wesson revolver, 19
Soft shot, 222–223
Spencer rifle, 15
Spitzer bullet, 3–4, 6–8, 117
Steel shot, 245–254
ballistics, 229, 251–254
characteristics of, 245–246
law and, 219, 245
lead shooting requirements, 247–249

lead shot compared, 246, 251
muzzle velocity, 248–249
pattern density, 246–247
range, 251
selector guide for, 251
shotgun considerations, 246
temperature and, 250–251
Storage and handling, 270–273

Target shooting
centerfire rifle cartridge selection, 148
recoil, 62
22 short ammunition, 21
T. B. Davies Arms Company, 17
Temperature, 271–272
10-gauge 3½" magnum, 239
30 caliber centerfire handgun cartridges, 176–177
30 caliber centerfire rifle cartridges, 89–95
30 Carbine, 89, 176–177
30 Luger, 176
30 Remington, 90
30-06 Springfield
deer-sized game and, 154
described, 93
300 Savage compared, 3–4
308 Winchester compared, 7, 8
velocity test of, 9, 10
30-06 Winchester, 148
30-30 Winchester
cartridge case, 64
described, 90–91
handgun use, 187
30-40 Krag
ballistics of, 13
described, 91
30-40 Winchester, 104
31 caliber centerfire rifle cartridges, 95–96
32 Automatic, 178–179
32 caliber centerfire handgun cartridges, 177–179
32 caliber centerfire rifle cartridges, 96–97
32 H&R Magnum
described, 177
selection of, 197
32, Long Colt, 178
32 S&W Long, 177
32 Short Colt, 178
32 Winchester Special, 96
32-50 Winchester, 95
33 caliber centerfire rifle cartridges, 97–98
35 caliber centerfire rifle cartridges, 99–101
35 Remington
described, 100

handgun use, 187–188
35 Whelen
cartridge case, 64
described, 101
36 caliber centerfire rifle cartridges, 102
37 caliber centerfire rifle cartridges, 102–104
38 Automatic, 180
38 caliber centerfire handgun cartridges, 179–183
38 Short Colt, 179
38 Smith & Wesson, 179
38 Special
recoil, 61–62
selection of, 199–200
38 Special (Standard Pressure), 181
38 Special +P
described, 181–182
selection of, 199–200
38 Super Automatic, 181
38-55 Winchester, 102
300 H&H Magnum
described, 94
target shooting selection, 148
300 Savage
described, 91
Springfield compared, 3–4
30-40 Krag compared, 13
300 Weatherby Magnum, 95
300 Winchester Magnum
described, 94
medium game and, 154–155
range of, 5
303 British
cartridge case, 64
described, 95–96
303 Savage, 89–90
307 Winchester, 92
308 Winchester
deer-sized game, 153–154
described, 92–93
range and, 5
target shooting selection, 148
30-06 Springfield compared, 7, 8
338 A-Square, 98
338 Winchester Magnum
big game and, 155
described, 97
medium game and, 155
30-06 compared, 14
340 Weatherby Magnum, 98
348 Winchester, 99
350 Remington Magnum, 101
351 Winchester Self-Loading, 99

356 Winchester, 100
357 Magnum
   described, 99–100, 182
   recoil, 62
   selection of, 200
357 Remington Maximum, 183
358 Winchester, 101
375 H&H Magnum
   big game and, 155–156
   described, 102–103
375 Weatherby Magnum, 103
375 Winchester, 102
378 Weatherby Magnum, 104
380 Automatic
   described, 179–180
   selection of, 198
Trajectory
   rimfire ballistics, 47
   spitzer/round-nose bullets compared, 7–8
up-/downhill angle, 37, 40–42, 133–134
velocity, 6
12-gauge 2¾", 240
12-gauge 3" magnum, 239–240
20-gauge 2¾", 241
20-gauge 3" magnum, 241
22 caliber centerfire handgun cartridges, 175
22 caliber centerfire rifle cartridges, 71–77
22 Hornet, 71–72
22 Long cartridge
   accuracy of, 27, 28
   ballistics of, 38, 39, 44, 46
   described, 21–22
22 Long Rifle cartridge
   accuracy of, 26–27, 28–29
   ballistics and, 36, 38, 39, 44–45, 46, 47
   barrel length/velocity, 12
   described, 22–24
   recoil, 61
   velocity, 43
22 PPC, 73–74
22 Remington Jet magnum, 175
22 rimfire ammunition
   advantages of, 35
   popularity of, 15
   See also Rimfire ammunition (rifle)
22 Short cartridge, 171
   accuracy of, 27, 28
   ballistics and, 36, 38, 39, 44, 45
   described, 19–21
22 Winchester Magnum
   accuracy of, 29
   ballistics of, 38, 39, 45, 46

   described, 24–25
22-250 Remington
   described, 77
   varmint hunting, 150
24 caliber centerfire rifle cartridges, 78–80
25 caliber centerfire handgun cartridges, 176
25 caliber centerfire rifle cartridges, 81–83
25-06 Remington
   deer-sized game, 151–152
   described, 82
25-20 Winchester, 81
25-35 Winchester, 81
26 caliber centerfire rifle cartridges, 83–84
27 caliber centerfire rifle cartridges, 84–86
28 caliber centerfire rifle cartridges, 86–89
28-gauge 2¾", 242
218 Bee, 72
220 Swift, 77
221 Fireball, 72
221 Remington Fireball
   described, 175
   selection of, 196–197
222 Remington
   cartridge case, 64
   described, 72–73
   handgun use, 188
222 Remington Magnum, 75–76
223 Remington
   described, 75
   plinking selection, 149–150
   varmint hunting, 150
224 Weatherby Magnum, 76–77
240 Weatherby Magnum, 80
243 Winchester
   deer-sized game, 151
   described, 79–80
   varmint hunting, 150
250 Savage, 81
257 Roberts, 82
257 Weatherby Magnum, 83
264 Winchester Magnum
   described, 83–84
   270 Winchester compared, 13
270 Weatherby Magnum, 85–86
270 Winchester
   cartridge case, 64
   deer-sized game, 152
   described, 84–85
   264 Winchester Magnum compared, 13
   velocity variation, 10
280 Remington
   described, 88

INDEX

7mm Express Remington and, 4
284 Winchester, 87–88

Up-/downhill angle
   centerfire rifle-cartridge ballistics, 133–134
   hold-under calculation, 40–42, 133–134
   rimfire ballistics, 37, 40

Varmint hunting, 150–151
Velocity
   ballistic effects, 5–6
   barrel length and, 48–50
   centerfire rifle-cartridge ballistics, 116–118, 144–145
   dram-equivalent rating system, 215–217
   rimfire ballistics and, 36, 43
   shotshell ballistics, 232
   steel shot, 248–249
   trajectory and, 6

22 Long Rifle cartridge, 23
   variations in, 8–12
   See also Ballistics

Wadcutter lead bullets, 172
Wad seating, 258–259
Winchester ammunition (historical), 277–287
Winchester pump rifles, 20
Winchester rifles, 22
Winchester Silvertip bullet, 66
Winchester Super Silhouette, 22
Wind drift
   centerfire rifle-cartridge ballistics, 126–130
   rimfire ballistics, 37
   spitzer/round-nose bullets compared, 8
   velocity and, 6
   See also Ballistics
WRF round, 25

Grolier also offers merchandise items.
Please write for information.